MY EDUCATION CONTINUES:
A Memoir
by
Fela Igielnik

Edited by Curtiss Short

"My Education Continues" ISBN 978-1-60264-941-5 (softcover); 978-1-60264-979-8 (hardcover) 978-1-60264-980-4 (electronic version).

Library of Congress Control Number: 2012903350

Published 2012 by Virtualbookworm.com Publishing Inc., P.O. Box 9949, College Station, TX , 77842, US. ©2012 Fela Igielnik. All rights reserved. No part of this publication may be reproduced, stored in a retrieval system, or transmitted in any form or by any means, electronic, mechanical, recording or otherwise, without the prior written permission of Fela Igielnik.

Manufactured in the United States of America.

Table of Contents

Editor's Note 1

Author's Note 5

Preface 7

Book One: Warsaw 15

    Chapter 1. The German Kids and Tante Trude 16

    Chapter 2. Summer, 1939 27

    Chapter 3. The Bombing of Warsaw 32

    Chapter 4. Surrender 48

    Chapter 5. The Unmasking 52

    Chapter 6. To the USSR 62

    Chapter 7. The First Year 67

    Chapter 8. Typhus 98

    Chapter 9. The Ghetto 102

Book Two: Labor-Camp 155

    Chapter 1. The Boat 156

    Chapter 2. Sandomierz 169

    Chapter 3. Skarżysko 225

    Chapter 4. To Leipzig 305

    Chapter 5. Liberation 346

Book Three: The Aftermath 393

Chapter 1. Łódź and Jacob 394

Chapter 2. Berlin 476

Accounting Page 542

Timeline 545

Glossary 552

Notes 562

Editor's Note

The original manuscript of the untitled memoir by Fela Igielnik contains no dates of composition. Consequentially, we have had to consult older, often incomplete, versions and handwritten notes in order to determine the current estimation of late 1970s through mid-1990s. Within this roughly twenty year time span, the author created two principle versions of her life story: the present version—which we call the "legacy version"—and another, shorter version, which she intended to serve as a kind of educational text, to be used by high school students (whom the author, in her later life, taught as a guest lecturer throughout the greater St. Louis area). Focusing on providing a genealogical overview of her family during the pre-War and post-War years, this "legacy" version goes into greater detail than does the educational version, fulfilling her intention—as stated in the "Author's Preface"—to provide for "future generations who will eventually look for a 'family tree.'"

The biggest challenge in editing both versions—particularly the "legacy"—was incorporating into a final copy all of the numerous handwritten notes and loose sheets of lecture notes and miscellaneous inserts. These scattered texts (which focus on the author's general reflections on the Holocaust, politics,

Editor's Note

and remembrance) constitute both the "Author's Note" and the "Author's Preface." All the words are the author's; we have only condensed and reordered the paragraphs to give what we hope is an accurate portrayal of her thoughts.

More technical changes to the manuscript include:

Breaking the text into three distinct "books," each of which focuses on a particular theme, time period, or geographical location: Warsaw (before and during the Ghetto), the Labor Camp (which includes life in two camps and life immediately after the German surrender, while living in Liberated Territory), and "The Aftermath," during which time the author struggles first with the reconstruction of Europe, then with the decision to leave for the US.

-Replacing numerous pseudonyms that the author had initially used for privacy issues, which have been rendered moot as time has passed.

-Creating notes for historical, cultural or otherwise explanatory or translation references that the author had placed—usually parenthetically—within the body of the narrative. We have done this in order not to break the rhythm or pacing of certain passages. Also, a comprehensive glossary, taken from the shorter, educational version, has been incorporated within the notes of this version. (Unless otherwise indicated, all note material is by the author.)

-Including a timeline of the author's life, situated alongside historical events and personages for context and reference.

-Silently correcting verb tenses and syntax in places, as well as modifying word choice and English idioms.

-Retaining Polish orthography in relation to place names and dialogue or phrases. (In cases of transliterated words or phrases—Russian, Hebrew, and Yiddish—we have used the author's own words, standardizing as needed.)

Author's Note

After six dreadful years, the War that devastated a large part of the world and left in its path destruction, death, suffering, and sorrow, came to an end. With it also ended the period known as the Holocaust—the deliberate, premeditated murder of million of Jews, Gypsies, and other "undesirables."

For years, I kept a box full of notes containing my eyewitness accounts of this grievous period. All along I knew that those of us who had survived the horror had a moral obligation to inform the world of this tragedy; that it was our responsibility, not to scare, but to warn future generations to be vigilant. That they must learn how to separate facts from propaganda and be able to prevent a reoccurrence. Despite the survivor's motto, "Never Again," the world still settles disputes by the sword—ploughshares are nowhere to be seen. We still use stereotypes and scapegoats, racism and bigotry, ethnic cleansing, prejudice, hatred. The ingredients that laid the foundation for the Holocaust are still with us and, regretfully, doing quite well. This is my third attempt at writing an account, and, I hope, it will be the last. I am determined finally to put all my notes together—all those boxes full of records and stories that have been piling up throughout the years.

Author's Note

We survivors are now on the endangered species list. A few years from now, we'll belong to history. But our legacy must go on; our message must not die. Every survivor has his or her own story. I am glad that I survived and that I am able to convey the message, the plight, of the millions who were not so lucky. How else can one make people aware that such hideous crimes could be possible in a so-called civilized world?

I would like to express my heartfelt thanks to those who fought the Nazis on all fronts, who struggled in the forests, in underground movements, and those who resisted the Nazis by disobeying their orders. I feel indebted to all my liberators—governments and individuals—who fought to protect the world from the Nazi plague and who helped to bring this horror to an end before my death sentence was carried out. My deepest gratitude also goes to the relief organizations—the Red Cross, the Salvation Army, HIAS-Joint—which helped me during my recovery from this ordeal.

To my husband, children, and grandchildren, I would like to say: *Thanks for your love and support. Without your encouragement, my notes would still be in the box.*

Preface

I am not a historian, and this is not a history book. To examine causes of wars, to debate whether a war was just and necessary, or unjust and preventable, is a job for historians. I will let them "decide"—and then later "revise"—who was the aggressor and who the aggressed. These are solely their interpretations.

This is a story about which the historians do not write: it is an account of individual people. Of people I knew and whose lives I saw destroyed; of suffering, death, and of survival. It is a story of people who by pure luck managed to survive the period known as the *Holocaust* or *Churban Europa,* and of some who were not so lucky. Looking back at the War years much later, we who lived through them could hardly believe that we really had made it through. The trenches and ravines full of unnamed corpses and all the mass graves are slowly being identified by special markers. The ashes of the cremated bodies have, most likely, fertilized some barren soil. "From ashes we come, to ashes we go"; so says The Good Book. All those former human beings exist now only in the memories of us, the survivors, who now have an obligation to provide eyewitness accounts of what happened during that period when the mass media was censored and the people silenced. In our hearts and minds they will live

Preface

until we, too, die. And when we are gone, only a chapter in a book or a verse upon a monument will commemorate their memories and "The Holocaust." To those spared the direct suffering, and to those born afterwards, the Holocaust will be only another page in a history book. I fear that someday, after all the eyewitnesses are gone, someone, somewhere, will issue a "Revised Edition" of this story. The future of the Holocaust is unpredictable. For this reason, I feel that we owe the dead who can no longer speak, and to future generations who will eventually look for family "trees" and "roots." So, I have written this account for my children and for my children's children. It is about their ancestors: how they lived, how they died. It is the story of their "roots." It is their family "tree."

This is also a story about my continuing education, about the things that I learned after I was thrown out of school at the age of twelve. It is a personal story, about a life from the earliest time I can recall to the time when I arrived to the United States. The people mentioned in this story influenced my life, for better or for worse, by contributing greatly to my informal but nevertheless essential education. For you see, I have also written this story to account for myself. According to Polish authorities, I was never born. When I wrote to the archives in Warsaw, to the place where I was born, raised, and went to school, asking for my birth certificate and any other documents that were available, the reply came, "There is no evidence of such a person." This, although I was born in a large hospital, not at home, or in a log cabin.

For years I found excuses not to pursue my story: moving from place to place, family obligations, work, school, any other disruptions. The real reason was that I wasn't ready or willing to relive my past. I felt that just because I had been caught up in such a misfortunate turn of events, I must not destroy the rest of my life, too. There were years of catch-up work from the six years of war and four years of reconstruction. I had much work to do, and no time to play around. This book is probably the best answer that I can give to all those who kept asking me why I never spoke or wrote about my life during those years. *Make the most of what you have and the least of what is gone.*

After the War, whenever we survivors met, we would cling together. We tried to live near each other; it made us feel more secure. We felt safer with our own people than with those who had not been touched by the Holocaust. Whenever a survivor met other survivors, he would invite them to join "The Family." We shared food and accommodations.

Then things began to change. We started getting married and having families and financial obligations. While our children were young we had no difficulty with explanations. They took their lives for granted, thinking that their lives were normal. But as they grew older, they began to realize that their lives were anything but normal. We had a dilemma: *What, when, and how much should we tell our children about their families and about history?*

The more our children became aware, the less they asked. They seemed to know more than we thought they knew. They had learned in bits and pieces. They had absorbed information from hearing us talk to one another, from seeing us cry, from our reminiscing on holidays.

We discussed this among ourselves. In general survivors are divided into two groups: The Talkers and the Mute. Some wouldn't miss an opportunity to speak about their war experiences. You'd meet one of them on the street and say, "Oh, what a nice day!" and the Talker would reply, "Yes, just as nice as the day the Nazis burned our synagogue." You'd ask the name of

Preface

his or her child, and the Talker would say, "He is named after my father, who died in the Holocaust."

The Mute, on the other hand, hardly ever spoke about his or her experiences. Many even had their tattooed numbers removed so as not to be reminded of the past.

I was hesitant to discuss my past. I started putting down my memories thinking that by writing everything down, I wouldn't have to burden others. Those who might become interested in my life would be able to read it; otherwise, there would be no burden. I also didn't want to make people doubtful, maybe even scared. Why talk about things that would make people feel so uncomfortable? I assumed that enough had already been written about wars, destruction, and death. Why would anyone want to hear more horror stories? Besides, who would believe such twentieth-century nonsense if I myself could not?

Once, I was in a doctor's office, filling out my health history application. I couldn't answer many questions about my family and relatives. Finally, I just told the nurse that I was adopted. If I had told her my story she might have thought that I was some kind of heroine—or else felt sorry for me, and called me a martyr. Those are the usual reactions. I don't think that either of those labels applies. Heroes are worshipped and honored, martyrs are pitied; I don't like either. I have seen too many "heroes."

Compared to those who perished or who were crippled for life, I came out of the whole mess relatively well. The Nazis orphaned me, made me homeless, poor, and headachy, but they did not succeed in keeping me illiterate or teaching me to hate.

Years later, I started putting my collection of notes together. When I started, I began to realize that I had more questions than answers, more confusions than solutions. The story of my life was not much different

My Education Continues

from what I had heard from other survivors. As a matter of fact, mine were milder than those of many others. I wasn't in any of the famous camps like Auschwitz, Dachau, Majdanek, or Treblinka.

Once I had a talk with one of my pious Jewish friends, Regina. She believed that all that had happened was God's will, and so was our survival. I didn't argue with her; I couldn't prove otherwise. Maybe it was a divine power that had interceded on my behalf. (We both reviewed our sins, going over the Ten Commandments and the Six-Hundred-Thirteen *Mitzvot*, to see if either of us had been worthy of such a divine arbitration. I don't remember Regina's score, but I do remember that she scored much higher than I did.) Still, I wondered about Regina's interpretation of God's will. I remembered pious and righteous Jews who were murdered. I thought of Catholics who were baptized, went to mass seven days a week, never ate meat on Fridays, observed Lent, visited the holy shrines. For all that, they, too, went through so much punishment on earth, while some of those who disobeyed most Biblical laws got through the War without a scratch. Myself, I had, during the War, falsified my name, age, even religion; and there were many other things about which I lied as well. I failed to honor my father and my mother many times during my childhood. I *never* obeyed Sabbath. What of those Jews who must have been obeying 20 Commandments and 1226 *Mitzvot*—and still were murdered?

I am not familiar with procedure in Heaven, nor do I know anything of God's scale for evaluating souls in Purgatory. I am sure, however, that there must have been people among those who did not survive who were as deserving as I, and who not only died but suffered so much that for them death must have come as a blessing.

Preface

I didn't know until I arrived to the United States that, according to psychologists, there are survivors who have "guilt feelings" for making it through the War while their families did not. I wondered which school of psychology could have invented this concept. "Do you feel guilty that you didn't die in the Holocaust?" Such a ludicrous question, one which does not address whether the others could have been saved, but whether I, too, should have died. It seemed to me that the question shouldn't be, "Why did I survive?" but rather, "Why did all the others die?" Since the Nazis didn't have time to kill me, should I feel guilty?

I am glad that I survived. I am trying to make the best of the time I have left to live. I am sorry I wasn't able to save the lives of those who died. I am glad that I *can* at least rescue their memories. I feel obligated to tell their story, to put their names into books of memories, to engrave them on memorials. I am glad that I am able to express my thanks to those who fought the Nazis, and to all those who helped to free me, even if their actions were in some cases done out of self-interest.

My survival had nothing to do with wisdom. Neither did I commit any crimes nor commit any courageous acts. I got well before they came and transported my sick friends to the gas chambers. I was sixth in line when every fifth person was chosen to be shot.

Not all the Jews perished. Some were saved by work camps, where they were needed to produce materials for the war effort. Some survived in concentration camps because they were freed before their turn to be gassed came. Others survived in Russia working and fighting. Some were saved by the forests, where they had joined the guerrilla movements. Some made it through working on special assignments in the ghettos. There were even some who

My Education Continues

survived in China, in Shanghai. A few managed to survive by hiding in the Gentile sectors under assumed names, or by the aid of Aryan friends, by Righteous Gentiles.—*While others, who did exactly the same things as the survivors, and under the same circumstances, perished.*

We were murdered—or we survived, by pure luck.

Life must be lived forward, but it can only be understood backward.
— Kierkegaard

Book One: Warsaw

> "We had to learn to make the most of what we had and the least of what was gone."

Chapter 1. The German Kids and Tante Trude

When we returned to Warsaw from our country vacation in the late summer of 1939, we found people busy taping up windows, digging trenches, and preparing air-raid shelters. The newspapers and radio kept reporting that "encouraging" progress was being made during the negotiations between Poland and Germany. The assurances designed to prevent the population from panicking did not help much. People read between the lines; they saw the grim situation. Prices soared despite threats of severe fines and jail sentences for profiteering. The radio started preparing the population for possible air-attacks.

I was twelve years old. Walking home from school I saw some people gathered by the entrance to Krasińskich Park on Shviento-Yerska Street, across from where we lived. Curious, I pushed my way into the center of the gathering. A boy and girl, about eight and nine years old, were giving a concert: The boy, the younger of the two, played a violin and the girl sang, in German, *"Schlafe, mein Prinzchen."* The tin can in front of them was quickly filling up with coins, and the girl's voice was becoming louder. Both children were clean and wore nicely pressed clothes, which seemed to be the wrong size. Probably hand-me-downs. Two buttons

My Education Continues

were missing from the girl's skirt, and from the ripped seam of her blouse rosy flesh peeked out. The sleeves of the boy's jacket were rolled up past his elbows to reveal small bony arms. The lapels reached below his waist and the pockets reached his knees.

I heard a woman in the audience say that they must be refugee children; I figured they must be foreigners because, after each jingle, the boy would say, *"Danke schön, danke sehr."* I recognized the language as German because the previous summer I had had a "German experience."

It was customary for middle- and upper-class families in big Polish cities to spend summers in the country. Those who could afford it went to expensive health resorts, but the majority rented small cottages in nearby villages, where mothers and children stayed for a month or two, while the fathers who worked in the city came out for weekends. It was in one of those summer villages, between the towns of Falenica and Michalin, that I met Fräulein Hilde. She was a German governess to the children of a well-to-do Polish family. That summer, we rented a cottage next to their villa, and became acquainted with Basia, Hanka and Rysiek, the three children, ages twelve, ten and eight. My sister was about nine and I was a year older. The children's parents were quite wealthy, the owners of a large cafe. They even had a private car, a small Chevrolet. The parents visited their children only on the weekends; during the week Fräulein was with them.

Sis and I spent a lot of time with Fräulein and the kids. We became good friends. I learned about a way of life I never knew before. They talked about the green mountains of Austria, long train rides, large forests in Germany, and about the sunny beaches of Italy. Fräulein taught them German and gave them piano lessons. Sis and I used to listen whenever Fräulein talked about Germany, about the places and people in

The German Kids and Tante Trude

that foreign land; and we listened to her German fairytales whenever she translated them into Polish. I memorized two German songs and played two tunes on the piano.

So when I saw the two kids playing the violin and singing in the street, I couldn't stop thinking about that summer in the country, and about our Fräulein.

When I got home that day I told Mom about those kids in the street. She said that they must have been German Jews, children of refugees who had come to Poland recently. She explained that a German ruler named Hitler had expelled all foreign-born Jews from Germany. The kids probably came to Poland because their parents, or maybe grandparents, were born in this country. I wondered if Fräulein would know anything about such a ruler.

Soon I began to see and meet more and more of these German Jews. There was a girl in my sister's class who did not speak Polish, and the children were trying to help her with her language. But this was only the beginning. It was when Tante Trude came to Warsaw that I really found out about the German Jewish problem.

Tante Gertrude—Tante Trude, we called her—came to Warsaw from Berlin. She was a German Gentile woman who was married to mother's relative, Uncle Harry. Uncle Harry was born in Poland, but had lived in Berlin for many years. He had a business there and, supposedly, was quite well off. At first, some relatives used to correspond with him, but after he married a non-Jewish woman, family relationships deteriorated. Uncle Harry came from a rather Orthodox family.

I didn't hear much talk about Uncle Harry until he and Tante Trude came to Warsaw as refugees. It could have been at the end of 1937 or the beginning of 1938 when I met her and Uncle Harry at his sister Rachel's home. I used to visit there quite often because Aunt

My Education Continues

Rachel's two younger daughters, Freda and Rena, besides being relatives, were our best friends. Rena was two years older than I and Freda one year older. We had known each other all of our lives, but we became very close when our two families lived in the same apartment for over a year—it was on Gęsia Street 33. My family was renting a room from them. That was a few years before Tante Trude came to Warsaw with Uncle Harry.

They were a middle-aged couple with no children. Tante Trude was of average height and weight; she had short, light-brown hair, and wore nice clothes. Even though I had little interest in clothes, I do remember the one blouse she wore because it was laced around the collar and had specially designed buttons; it looked like the kind that was sold in stores that carried only expensive, imported goods.

We kids really liked Tante Trude, even though she spoke very little—and only in German, at that. She was always very polite, nice, and friendly to us: She liked us! She told us some interesting stories, translated by Uncle Harry, and she taught us a few children's songs in German. Uncle Harry was tall, with nicely groomed grayish blond hair; he wore glasses. He wasn't as patient with us as Tante Trude was, but we had a lot of fun with him, especially whenever he mixed some German words into Polish or made mistakes in grammar and pronunciation. We giggled.

But adult conversations were not very funny. As refugees started coming to Poland, the Jewish people tried to find means of supporting them. By being all in the same room, we kids overheard many of the conversations. Some of them didn't make much sense; others sounded like adventures to me. And I remember the ones about German Jews being made to leave their homes and country, and how the old, the sick, and the women and children were now in the "neutral zone," and how no country was wanting to accept them.¹ And I began thinking about the kids I saw singing in the street, about Tante Trude and Uncle Harry, and about the little girl in my sister's class.

The refugees who were finally accepted into Poland were of Polish origin. Once the government let them in, they were distributed in many cities; the problem of supporting them fell solely on the Jewish population. Many came to Warsaw. Warsaw was a metropolis, with many modern cinemas, theaters, cultural centers, sports stadiums, schools, and universities. It was full of tall buildings with wide gates, stores with brightly illuminated windows, wide boulevards, parks, and fountains. After all, it was the capital city, the pride of Poland.

But even before the refugee problem arose, living space in Warsaw was very limited, and rent was very expensive. Other than the well-to-do people who lived very comfortably in multi-room apartments, and some even in private houses in the suburbs, the majority in Warsaw did not enjoy such luxuries. Though most apartments were quite spacious, they were often occupied by large, extended families, or by a few unrelated families. All had to share one kitchen and one toilet—if they were lucky enough to have one. Especially in the old and poor section, the only plumbing facilities many apartments had were a sink and a faucet with cold water. People used public toilets located in the courtyards, to which every family had a key. In some cases as many as two hundred people were assigned to a latrine, with only ten or twelve stools, as we liked to call them.

The refugees from Germany had to be accommodated in Warsaw's Jewish community. Those who managed, by some illegal means, to bring some money with them, rented rooms, but those who came

My Education Continues

with nothing (and they were in the majority) were put up in club houses, synagogues, or other places.

Besides conversations about the refugee problem, adults discussed politics. They talked about the headlines in the papers, and radio broadcasts and local news. They talked of uncertain times, about a war that could or could not be prevented, and about the German dictator Hitler, the head of the Nazi Party, who was very wicked and who hated the Jews. According to him, Jews ruled all the world's money and were responsible for all evil on the face of the earth; they had caused Germany to lose World War I and, in addition, they were all communists.

The adults talked about many other things that we kids had no interest in, about ongoing negotiations and names like Beck, Chamberlain, and Stalin. We enjoyed listening to Uncle Harry talk about life in Germany, its cleanliness and order; he kept telling us how much nicer it was there than in "backward" Poland. He loved Germany and the beautiful things that he had seen there, and the wonderful life he had had there. We would see Tante Trude and Uncle Harry occasionally, then for a while not at all. I only remember some relatives talking about the difficulties of finding living quarters for them. Aunt Rachel couldn't take them in; she already lived with her husband, Uncle Yakov, and four daughters, in a three-room apartment, one room of which was always rented out to help with the costs. Part of the spacious kitchen was taken up as Uncle Yakov's workshop for his luggage business.

The talk was about Uncle Harry's "rich" sister, Aunt Hanna, and her husband, Uncle Sruel, who had a lot of room in their large apartment—both of their children were grown and gone from home. Their son, Mordekhei, had left for Palestine against his father's wishes; the daughter, Regina, was married, and living in her own apartment with her husband and a baby boy.² Now Aunt Hanna and her husband were alone in their three-room apartment except for a live-in Gentile maid. There was another sister who lived far away, but there wasn't much talk about her.

Aunt Hanna was the one who might have found room for her brother and sister-in-law, but she couldn't take them in for a different reason: Tante Trude was not a Jew. And Uncle Harry, who was, didn't act like one. His marriage to Tante Trude was, supposedly, a family scandal. Such a marriage, according to Orthodox Jewish law, was not only a disgrace to the family but also to most decent Jews who believed in God and cherished their cultural heritage. According to this Orthodox view, the reason for German Jews being in trouble was their disobedience to God. They were punished for disobeying God's laws and for getting off the "right path" of life. Had the Jews only eaten kosher food, kept the Sabbath holy, and put on phylacteries daily, God would not have allowed them to be expelled from their cities. Even the Gentile population would have had respect for them.³

Marrying Tante Trude wasn't the only sin Uncle Harry had committed. He had many more to answer for. After moving to Berlin he shaved off his beard, stopped going to synagogue, ate *treif*—non-kosher—food, didn't cover his head, not even while eating, and, worst of all (it was said), his business had been open on the Sabbath. Anyway, it was the opinion of Aunt Hanna and Uncle Sruel, like most other Orthodox Jews who were proud that their customs had changed very little through the years, that such sins were unforgivable. Worse yet was the fear that such Godlessness was spreading fast and influencing the younger generation, who were already going in the "wrong direction"—away from tradition.

My Education Continues

Even though assimilation in Poland's large cities was moving quite fast, it was going much more slowly than in other Western countries. And in small towns it was crawling at a snail's pace. Yet the Orthodox movement was trying hard to slow it even more—if possible—in order to prevent even the slightest change in the rooted traditions. Criticizing everyone who tried to deviate from their norms, the Orthodox movement claimed that once changes start, no one knows where and when they will end. The surest way was, therefore, to keep everything "as is."

During the Thirties, the Orthodox had a lot to criticize: More Jews, especially the young, were gradually departing from old traditions, even going to such disgracefulness as founding their own secular organizations. The Orthodox also criticized foreigners, the young, and the big cities that provided atheistic education, and the press, which printed for it. They criticized the German Jews for abandoning God and tradition; they criticized young Hasidic boys who cast off their gabardines, shaved their faces, and mixed in political affairs.[4] And they reproached girls who fell in love with boys, and women who were discarding their matron's wigs and were wearing short, cut-out dresses that displayed their bare legs and arms. They criticized young people who were leaving their family homes and running off to faraway places like New York, Buenos Aires, or Palestine. They criticized parents who sent their children to integrated public schools, in which the "pagans" were teaching Godlessness and immorality. They even criticized parents for speaking Polish to their children instead of Yiddish, which should be spoken in all respectable Jewish homes.[5]

Mixed marriages, however, were a different matter entirely. Even though they were rare in Poland, they did occur. According to Orthodox beliefs, marrying someone of a different religion gave the parents of the bride or groom a legitimate right to disown the child who had committed such a sin. There was even a prescribed ritual: The family had to sit *shiva*, the same ritual following the death of a family member. Of course, the Catholic spouse—since Poland was almost entirely Catholic, it was most likely that the spouse would be—was not dealt with any better that his or her Jewish counterpart: He or she was automatically excommunicated from the Church, and usually treated as an outcast by the family and the community.

In such an environment it was difficult to tolerate "sinners." Yet a solution was found to help Tante Trude and Uncle Harry. Cousin Laib rented a room for them in his friend's apartment, and Harry's relatives got together and paid the rent. Such an arrangement looked more "dignified" than having a bareheaded sinner with an non-Jewish wife living with an Orthodox family.

The story of Tante Trude and Uncle Harry's living arrangement I learned from relatives by eavesdropping. I was quite aware of what was going on, even though the adults tried to keep this situation from being discussed in public or in front of us children. Anyway, many relatives helped Tante and Uncle get settled; previous problems were resolved and almost forgotten as time went on.

After a while, Uncle Harry found a part-time job translating to and from German, Polish and Yiddish; Tante Trude did some sewing at home on a donated sewing machine. Their daily life, like that of other German Jews who were helped with jobs and housing by the local Jewish population, seemed to have stabilized. But the economic conditions to which many German Jews were accustomed could not be duplicated by any Polish living standards, and coming from such an assimilated, integrated life style, the German Jews had a difficult time adjusting. Finding themselves in this new environment, many of them suffered from depression and nervous breakdowns; some even committed suicide.

We listened curiously to Tante's and Uncle's fascinating stories. They talked of the wonderful German countryside, about the good times there, how well they had lived in Berlin, and about the places that they had visited. But the stories they told their adult listeners were not exactly the same. There were additional chapters to these romantic tales that we kids weren't told. We overheard Tante and Uncle talk about the time Hitler and his Nazi party took total power, when getting uncensored reporting in and out of Germany became almost impossible. We also heard Uncle ask many questions: How much did the Polish Jews know about the Nuremberg Laws, since these 1933 laws were mostly decrees against Jews?[6] He wanted to know if the outside world had heard of the concentration camps, being built all over Germany, to which most of Hitler's opponents and many Jews were being shipped? He was curious if anyone had heard of the people who were being arrested at random, or of the dissidents who were being thrown into the camps without trials? Or of the Jews who were stripped of their citizenship, and whose property was confiscated? He kept asking many other questions concerning the Third German Reich—the Third Union of the German Empire. He wanted to know what was reported about the *Kristallnacht*, the so-called "Crystal Night," when Jewish properties were destroyed and many Jews were arrested and many killed?

Of course, most of these stories were heard even though many were not reported by the official media. There was uncensored news from Germany that was coming via run-away dissidents through underground sources, or through spy networks; anyway, people knew that something was wrong. Some of these tales were so bizarre that most of those who heard them either didn't believe them or thought that they were highly exaggerated. When rumors of a war started spreading, more refugee stories began circulating and more firsthand accounts were heard. Uncle Harry talked more often, and in more detail, about his trip from Germany, how he was pushed out of his apartment by youngsters wearing Nazi armbands—red bands with a white circle and swastika in the center—and how many other Jews were not only thrown out of their homes but were kicked and beaten; how he and thousands of other Jews had been expelled from Germany, pushed into trains and thrown into the Neutral Zone. He talked about the month he had spent on that strip of land between Poland and Germany, with no place to go. He said that people who had relatives with money or some connections had at least a chance to be helped, while others had no hope. Being cold, hungry, and humiliated, they forgot about the businesses, money, and belongings that had been taken from them.

Tante Trude was silent during these discussions. When Uncle Harry was asked the reason for her constant silence, he said, please, to leave her alone; that she had been through enough just thinking about the family she had left behind, about the harassment she had suffered for leaving her country.

I only heard Uncle mention one of the incidents that happened to her. He told of an evacuation supervisor, an older Nazi guard, who took Tante aside before she entered the train and had a talk with her. He gently asked her to reconsider the stupid decision that she was making, because nothing good would come of her hanging around a damn dirty Jew, and she would regret her foolish move.

Chapter 2. Summer, 1939

It was in the summer of 1939 that I became aware that most adult conversations concentrated totally on the subject of a possible war. The talks were about names like Hitler, Stalin, Churchill, Roosevelt. The questions were, What is in the news, on the radio, in the magazines and the newspapers?

For us kids, life was going on as usual. As in the summers before, we spent our vacation in the country with Mom; Dad was working in Warsaw, but he would come out for the weekends. Usually those small cottages we rented had no utilities—no electricity, gas, or telephone; many didn't even have water. They were equipped with kerosene lamps, a wood-burning stove, or oil burners, iron beds, and a table with chairs. The only news coming into the village was from the newspaper, which was usually a day or two late, and a daily dose of rumors from drivers passing through on the highway, and an occasional letter from the city.

Every morning it was my job to go to the general store on Main Street and buy food for the day. I remember one morning in August quite well, because something unusual happened.

Wearing an off-white flower-print summer dress, my hair in long braids, and shoes in my hands (Mom never let me go to town without shoes)—my money in

Summer, 1939

one shoe—I ran, as always, to the store. As I approached Main Street I saw a crowd of people gathered in front of the store. They were speaking loudly and nervously. I stood for a while and listened. No one paid attention to my presence. A young woman with a small child in her arm and a two- or three-year-old boy by her side was crying frantically. Waving a white paper in her free hand, she stuttered something unintelligibly. After a little snooping, I found out what had happened: Her husband, who was in the army reserves, had just received a draft notice; he was to report to the induction center that morning.

I ran home as fast as I could, bringing only a part of the food that I had been sent for. The saleslady, who was also the owner of the store, had explained that the money I had brought with me was not enough to pay for more groceries because the prices just went up. When I enthusiastically reported my adventure to Mom, my sister got very upset; she was sorry that she hadn't gone with me to the store, that she had missed out on all that excitement (even though she never had been the adventurous type I was). Mom turned pale. She sat down on the bed, and in a shaking voice said, "Children, we are heading for another war." She still had many unfaded memories from the War that had ended barely twenty years before. We kept hearing about that War, but to us it seemed ancient history. Besides, it was something heroic and fun. Seeing Mom that upset, I realized for the first time that something had changed; something was wrong.

For the rest of the day, Mom was nervous. She hardly spoke to us. She knew very few people in that village—she never liked mixing with neighbors or listening to gossip. She sat on that iron bed and looked lost. She told sister and me not to venture too far from the house, to stay where she could keep an eye on us. There might be some news before the day was over.

My Education Continues

Mom went to the post office to call Warsaw, but to no avail. Most private phone calls were made from post office to post office, where the receiving party was either dispatched or informed to return the call. Private phones were quite scarce among the general population. Mom tried to call Dad's store—many businesses were equipped with phones. But this, too, was to no avail. That morning all phone lines were jammed.

The most immediate problems facing us were how to get a hold of Dad and how to get home to Warsaw. The highway through the village led from Warsaw to the city of Lublin, a large city east of the capital. There were frequent buses, cars, and horse-drawn wagons going between the two cities. Mom tried to get bus tickets to Warsaw, but all the buses were packed full. As we later found out, many had been taken off the road to transport soldiers and new recruits. Mom tried the train station, which was a few kilometers away, but it was the same story. We knew why Dad wasn't coming or calling.

Mom contacted a drayman, the farmer who had hauled our belongings when we came to the village two months before. He informed her with tears in his eyes that one of his horses had been mobilized. "They notified me last night. They'll be picking him up tomorrow." With an ironic smile, he added, "They promised to return him as soon as they can." Then he wiped his forehead and said, "Sorry I can't help you, young lady." He told Mom to try another wagoner whose horse had not yet been taken.

A couple of days later, Dad showed up. He was very nervous. Mom and Dad had a long conversation. The following morning we all went to the bus station, where we waited until late into the night before we caught a bus (which had only standing spaces available). Our luggage came to Warsaw by a horse-drawn wagon two days later.

Summer, 1939

In Warsaw newspapers were being grabbed up as soon as they could be printed. Crowds gathered around all bulletin boards and under the loudspeakers which had been installed at all major intersections. Everyone was interested in the news, which was changing frequently, though none of it encouragingly.

Besides the official newscasts many rumors were circulating in the crowds. Some people were saying that Hitler was simply making idle threats so that Poland would hand over the "Corridor" to Germany.[7] Others heard that France and England had promised to help Poland in case the Germans attacked, that the two countries had guaranteed Poland's borders. There were people who were even more assured that war could be avoided: "The insane painter can bark as much as he wants," they were saying, "but he'll never get an inch of our land."[8]

Then there were groups who received their news from God. They heard that God will help; if only people will pray and obey, then everything will turn out fine.

Most rumors, however, were about a sure war. According to news slipping in through "underground channels" (traveling people, refugees, the military), negotiations were failing. Hitler was mobilizing his troops; there were more chances for war than for peace. "War is imminent." More affluent folk began stocking up on essential goods, such as fuel, imperishable foods, and over-the-counter medical supplies. Those without money stood by, helplessly watching as all available items kept disappearing from store shelves—an indication that something was wrong.

The seriousness of the situation became even more apparent when siren systems began being tested. "Testing! Testing all systems! Attention! Keep tuned! In case of an air-raid, you'll be informed where to go," the radio kept repeating. Another indication was an order

My Education Continues

issued to all men, ages sixteen to twenty and not yet in military service, to report to induction centers for duty in the OPL, which was to help with the civilian population in case of an attack.[9]

As for me, I found all of this change very exciting. I lived with my mother, father, sister, and Aunt Naomi, Mom's younger, unmarried sister, in a nice, comfortable apartment. I was happy with the things I had, and unconcerned about the ones I didn't have.

September was quickly approaching. School was about to start. But instead of school, a war started. On September first, at five in the morning, German troops, tanks, and artillery crossed the Polish border, and German planes roared through the skies. On that day a great period of education began for me. And, for the next few years, I got better educated than I could have in any school or university.

Chapter 3. The Bombing of Warsaw

A few days after the invasion, on a sunny September day, the sirens sounded in the streets and the radio music was interrupted by a special announcement. But this time, the "Testing! Testing!" part was omitted. The announcer started, "Attention! Attention! Air-raid!" It was followed by special instructions: "Go to your nearest underground shelter!" More sirens were sounded, then the announcer continued: "If there is no shelter close by, go to an enclosed room! Stay away from windows!" Then we heard OPL attendants yelling from the courtyard on bullhorns urging people to run for cover. They said not to worry, only to follow instructions.

Mom, Sis, and I went into our entrance hall; it was the only room without windows. We turned up the radio in the room so that we could hear the announcements through the closed door; we waited for further instructions. We believed it was still part of the preparations—just another test. We sat in that hall for about half an hour with nothing to do and nothing to see. It got very boring. Soon, my patience ran out, and before the "All Clear" was sounded on the radio, I opened the door to the room and ran to the window to see what was going on in the courtyard. "Close the door and come here!" shouted Mother. "If a window breaks, you may get hurt from the falling glass!"

"But we have them taped, Mom!" I replied, "That's what this tape is for. Besides, this is only another test." I was trying to reason.

Through the window I saw a few OPL attendants encircled by a group of men. They were standing in the yard, looking into the sky. They were pointing at something and talking excitedly. I heard a roar of planes. When the planes passed, I opened the window and heard the people screaming, "They are ours! Our Polish planes on maneuvers!" Then I heard the "All Clear" sirens. The air-raid was over.

Like chased deer, Sis and I ran down all four flights of stairs into the courtyard. After about half an hour of searching the three adjacent courtyards, and listening to the talk of the constantly swelling crowd, we returned to Mom with the news that we had heard: This was not a test. German planes had crossed Polish defense lines, had actually flown over Warsaw. There were even rumors that a bomb was dropped somewhere—on Sienna or Żelazna Streets—damaging a building. But this was quite a distance from us, and no one knew for sure.

The official radio station, *Warszawa II Druga,* informed us that everything was okay; it asked people not to listen to rumors, not to panic; that there were many stories circulating, but they were all false. "Polish defenses," said the announcer, "are strong and intact." He then added, "News accounts will be temporarily halted. As soon as we have confirmed reports, we will resume news broadcasting. People will know the truth." This announcement was followed by a nice, long pep talk about Polish heroes who had spilled blood during previous invasions, talking about Turks and Tartars and Mongolians and Russians and Germans; how great the Polish soldiers were and how great were their victories over many enemies. Finally, instructions were given for where to donate blood and how to administer first aid; and a plea was made to the people to stay close to shelters and to remain calm. The pep talk was followed by music.

After this first air-raid, civil defense rules became strictly enforced: All windows had to be taped and, during evening and night hours, hung with black sheets of paper, blankets, or other opaque materials. If someone forgot to draw his curtains, the OPL attendants roared reminders: "Darken your windows!" Even a cigarette in the open had to be extinguished after dark. A bomb-shelter, not a room, became the recommended place to go during air-raids. Our so-called "bomb-shelter" was actually a cold, damp, dark cellar with sewer and water pipes running along the walls and a dirt floor below. Here and there an electric bulb was suspended from a wooden ceiling beam. Mr. Gastman, who lived on the ground floor right above the cellar, installed an electric socket into which he plugged the radio donated to the shelter by Mrs. Berman, one of our neighbors. The OPL workers, helped by a few older kids, got some chairs and benches so that the few older people had a place to sit. The younger folks and the kids sat on blankets that were spread out on the dirt.

During my time in the shelter, I learned a lot. I got to know many of our neighbor kids who did not go to my school. We talked about our teachers and lessons, and about returning to school as soon as these bomb scares were over. I told them the stories that I was going to tell my classmates once school resumed. I knew that on returning to class there would be assignments, and some would be about what we had done during the summer—perhaps a description of an air-raid, a bomb-shelter, or other unusual events.

My Education Continues

The following day surely provided me with a lot of good topics. I started to keep a diary in which I would enter all of my new experiences. There was very little one could do sitting in that underground place, so the writing and talking kept me occupied.

One late afternoon, during an air-raid, we could feel the ground shake, and soon afterwards, a young man, about seventeen or eighteen, with a white OPL armband over his left upper arm, came running into our cellar announcing that a bomb had fallen on the house numbered 36, only four houses from ours, and that the whole west wall of the building had collapsed. In a scared, shaky voice, he said, "Some people managed to crawl to safety through a hole in the cracked door before it caved in, but many are still buried in the basement of the building. The exit is blocked by rubble."

The young man was looking for volunteers to help with moving the debris. He was especially looking for Dr. Flanzman, who lived in our building, and who was supposedly somewhere in our cellar. "Police, fire trucks, and ambulances are just arriving," he continued, "but we need more help to get the victims out of there."

I put away my diary and jumped up to volunteer my services, thinking that it would be a good way to break the boredom. Dad, as though reading my mind, turned to Mom and said, "You better keep an eye on that girl; she's getting a little out of hand."

After the young man left our shelter, taking with him a few volunteers, a long discussion started among the adults. They were speculating on what could have really happened on Świętojerska Street 36. Although everyone in our shelter had heard a few minutes before the thundering noise of the falling bomb, and had experienced the shaking of the building, most people thought that the young man had grossly exaggerated what really had happened. They thought that it was impossible for one bomb to demolish a whole, strong, brick-and-iron building. The talk turned into arguments about the 1936 Spanish Civil War, about which much had been written in the papers and shown in newsreels at the movie theaters.[10] One older gentleman mentioned that Hitler was supplying such bombs to General Franco just to try them out in Spain, and that these bombs were actually capable of demolishing buildings.

(The discussion reminded me of conversations I had overheard in 1936, the year my maternal grandfather died. I remembered how, during the *shiva* period, visiting relatives and friends talked about the terrible things happening in Spain's civil war.)

Meantime, the radio in our shelter was broadcasting patriotic speeches. It praised the civil defense organization and the great job it was doing; it was saving lives. The announcer kept commending the Polish armed forces for their brave fighting. Reports of defeats were very brief and vague. "The Polish Air Force lost only two planes. The pilots survived. We shot down six enemy bombers. The Army had to retreat somewhat, but it will regroup, and regain the territory. We'll keep fighting 'Till Final Victory!' 'To the Last Soldier!' 'To the Last Drop of Blood!'"

Many older people said that such talk meant defeat, that we were losing. I couldn't understand how they had come to that conclusion.

While the adults were discussing politics, some neighbor kids and my sister and I talked about our own problems—how to get out of this underground confinement as soon as possible. When the "All Clear" signal sounded, I turned to my sister and said, "Tell Mom I'll be back shortly," and with three neighbor girls, I ran outside.

My Education Continues

In the first courtyard garden where the water fountain had been turned off, we saw *Pani* Wilanowska watering flowers. We said *"Dzień dobry!"*—"Good day!"—and ran past her, into the street, headed for the bombed-out building.

By the time we got to Świętojerska 36, many people were gathered around the collapsed wall digging in the rubble, trying to find survivors. Young OPL attendants were carrying people on stretchers. Ambulances were picking up the wounded. Amid the rubble, we could see arms, legs, and other body parts separated from still-buried torsos. Screams were coming from beneath the wreckage. A woman who didn't know what had become of her child was pulling at her hair and screaming pathetically. Another woman in a half-torn dress and one shoe was holding this crying mother at the waist, saying something, trying to calm her down. Police blocked off the street around the ruined building, dispersing curious onlookers.

We ran home to tell everyone about our new experience, our first encounter with a real war. We were sure that everyone would be excited. But instead of listening to our adventure, the adults got really angry; each of us girls got her share of the scolding, and had to promise never again to venture outside the courtyard gates. I assured Mom and Dad, but my promise was short-lived.

Bombing raids became more frequent and more frantic. We were spending a lot more time in the shelter. We only left the cellar to change clothes, to bring some of the food we had stored at home, or to use the public latrine located in the second courtyard. Friday night, Jewish women lit their Sabbath candles in the cellar, praying and crying. They asked God for the bombing to stop, for their families to be spared, for life to return to normal. Spending that much time in that shelter, we got to know many of our neighbors who lived in the three adjacent buildings. There were over three hundred apartments in this complex, and I don't know how many tenants. The only person who knew them all was Jósef Kowalski, the building-keeper.

Many stories were told in this shelter during the long hours we spent there. Old men told stories of the War that they had fought barely twenty years before. Women would usually talk about their children and their personal problems. One story, repeated almost daily, was that of Mr. Greenfarb, the old man who refused to come to the cellar. No one, not the OPL attendant, not his friends, not even his family, could persuade him to leave his room. He insisted that God would protect him from the bombs, just as He had during World War I. Mr. Greenfarb had fought against the Russians. He had been saved by a miracle, and he strongly believed that "those predestined to be hanged won't drown"—he believed that those who are foreordained to die cannot hide from death. People finally gave up trying to get him to the shelter and left him in his room.

A specially memorable day was the Eve of Rosh Hashanah, the Jewish New Year. It was one of those days that almost everyone who lived through them will forever remember; where he was, what he was doing at the time. That day the Jewish section of Warsaw was the target of an air attack. Almost one third of the Jewish-owned buildings and businesses were demolished. This deliberate bombing on the High Holidays, especially in the Jewish quarter of town, was made to look accidental; but people thought that such an "accident" was very unlikely. Huge squadrons of Luftwaffe bombers flew in low over the Warsaw buildings.[11] They came in fives, tens, maybe more. They flew so low that we could almost see the pilots. The raid started in the early afternoon. Most women were busy gathering food for the holiday supper when the sirens began to blow, informing everyone of an incoming raid. Soon the roar of falling bombs drowned out the noise of the still-blowing sirens. Combined with the roar of the planes was the angry barking of the anti-aircraft cannons. The noise blasted our eardrums. Under our feet, the ground trembled. The bombing lasted, it seemed, forever.

People in the shelter were screaming, crying, cracking their knuckles. Women beat at their breasts, praying, "Dear God, God of Abraham, Isaac, and Jacob: Have mercy on us, forgive us our sins. In honor of this Holiday Season, please, Dear God, let us survive this terrible ordeal. Save our children...." Men kept quietly reciting the "*Tehillim.*"[12]

The radio announcer warned people to stay in shelters, and asked them to keep calm. He said there was good news from the international dispatch. "England and France are coming to help; they've promised to help; they've declared war on Germany. We'll win this war. The German aggressors will pay for their belligerence.... Long Live Poland! Long Live Our Fatherland!"

Meanwhile, the bombs kept falling. It seemed as though some must have fallen on our building. We just sat and waited for the walls to crumble down: No, not this time.... It wasn't our turn yet.... Then the earth shook again. All lights in the cellar went out; the radio voice died.

When finally the "All Clear" siren was heard, people hugged and kissed those sitting next to them. The OPL attendants opened the cellar doors. Daylight crept into the dark, muggy shelter. People thanked God Almighty that the raid was finally over, that the bombs had missed us.

The Bombing of Warsaw

My first thought was to get out of that cellar and see what was going on outside. As my eyes were still adjusting to the brightness of the exterior light, the courtyard was filling up with people who, like me, were crawling out of their burrows.

Despite the heavy bombing, our building survived intact. I saw my sister walking with Dad in the yard, and a great idea flashed through my mind: Why not go visit Grandmother Esther? In a loud voice, I said to Sis, "Let's go and see how Grandma is doing!" Our paternal seventy-five-year-old widowed grandmother lived on Pavia Street, across the street from Paviak Prison. It was not very far from us, maybe three or four kilometers.

Sis agreed. "Let's go together." She was still envious of my adventure at the bombed-out building. But Dad thought that neither of us should go. We tried bargaining with him. He wouldn't budge. A couple of neighbors started talking to Dad. I said loudly, "Daddy, we'll be back shortly...." I grabbed Sis by the hand and pulled her through the large entrance gate and into the street.

Narrow Świętojerska Street was filled with a continuous crowd of running people. Past Krasińskich Park, emergency vehicles were blocking the way to Nalewki Street. We decided to go around the block and take Franciszkańska Street instead. At the corner of Wołowa, a mob of young people had gathered around a burning pawnshop. Bricks were still falling from under the partly collapsed roof, and streams of water were pouring from fire hoses, when a group of young men and a few women started running in and out of the flaming building, dragging singed boxes and bags of goods. Some had just loaded their pockets or arms with soaked loot. Envious onlookers cowardly watched the "courageous" looters getting rich quickly.

My Education Continues

First aid workers helped by volunteers were carrying in their bare arms wounded men, women, and children; others had lifeless bodies thrown over their shoulders. A group of OPL attendants was trying to reach some people still buried under piles of smoldering rubble.

Closer to Nalewki Street, another building was on fire. Flames blazing through the boarded-up windows were meeting tongues of fire coming from the opposite wall. Curling smoke thrust forward, blinding those who were trying to escape the flames. Frightened people and small children, with wet blankets over their heads to protect them from the choking smoke, were running frantically, screaming, trying to cough out the smoke that they had swallowed, rubbing their burning eyes; all running, running aimlessly.

From the people hurrying down Gęsia Street, we couldn't make out a clear story. What they were saying seemed to be incoherent bits of horror. At first there was no way to find the house numbers; later, it was impossible even to find the street. Dad's business was Gęsia 3; his brother, Uncle Louis, lived at number 18. Sis and I got scared.

Loudspeakers on the street corner warned people of the potential risks, and warned them to keep away from the danger zone. They pleaded with the crowds to disperse, but people stood nailed to the ground, hopelessly watching their homes burn—and waiting to find out the fate of loved ones still trapped in the fires.

In a frightened voice, my sister said, "Let's get out of here," and she pleaded to go home. I looked at her face. It was blackened from smoke. Her eyes filled with tears and she sobbed. I pulled her across the street. For another few moments we watched firefighters, half-engulfed in flames, jerking their heavy fire hoses and climbing their ladders amid the swaying clouds of smoke.

The Bombing of Warsaw

Suddenly, I felt a strong hand from behind grabbing at my shoulder. Someone tugged at my braids. My whole body rocked. The hand spun me around. My braids flew in my face. A frantic man's voice was yelling at me: "What are you crazy little bastards doing here? Don't you have anyone watching you? Get the hell out of this godforsaken street! Go home! If you don't have one, follow me!"

I saw a man holding a little girl in his arms. His jacket was hanging over the girl's head. The front of his hair was scorched by fire.

I decided to follow the man's advice. Holding Sis with one hand, protecting my eyes with the other, we both ran as fast as we could, elbowing, pushing and shoving our way through the swelling crowds. As we finally approached our street, I thought, "Another great story for my diary," but I didn't dare say a word. When we at last reached our building, Mom, Dad, and Aunt Naomi, accompanied by a few neighbors (all of whom had by then assessed the extent of the damage done by the latest raid), were waiting for us at the entrance. We were sure that we'd be scolded—we were scared to death, both from our adventure and from what was to come from Mom and Dad. But it seemed as though they were so glad to see us back alive, that no one yelled at us; no one even said an unkind word.

I ran up to the apartment and changed my wet, smoke-stained dress, and then brought down to the cellar some clean clothes for my sister. On the second floor of the stairway, Moshe, the Hasidic son of Cantor Goldberg, was busy inspecting mezuzahs on Jewish doorposts.[13] He was checking to see if they had been disturbed by the raid. Old Mrs. Gurfinkel, our next-door neighbor, was walking down the stairs carrying a towel-covered basket. "Where in the world have you kids been?" she asked, handing me a potato pancake from the basket. But before I could start telling her my story, she said, "Eat, my child; that's all I can offer you." Then with a deep sigh, she said, "Thank God, you're okay," and continued walking down the steps. "*Baruch Hasham.* Praised be the Almighty...." mumbled Moshe, drawing out his words in a chant.

That evening, while lighting the holiday candles—and they were lit in the cellar because of another air-raid scare—there was hardly a dry eye. These candles were the only reminder of the Holiday, and they provided light for the dark cellar. Our holiday meal consisted of lukewarm potato soup that Mom had cooked between air-raids, and a few slices of old bread. Other families didn't eat any better.

Most of the following days and nights were spent in the shelter. Being scared, hungry, and worn, many people's behavior began changing. Some started acting strange: Any smallest of disturbances would provoke high tensions; any slightest of irritations would incite uncontrollable tears. Mrs. Ziegler, a widow whose husband was killed fighting in World War I, became a complete nuisance. When she first got to the shelter, she used to sit under a light for hours, quietly reading books. After a while she stopped reading and just sat in a corner without saying a word. Following the Rosh Hashanah bombing, she started acting strange. Every time she heard the sound of a siren, she went into a rage:

"Shelter mates!" (That's the way she referred to people in the shelter.) "Shelter mates! Listen to me, all of you! There is a fire!" Her frantic voice often broke into sobs. "I see a fire! Don't you see the flames coming?" She screamed breathlessly for fifteen to twenty minutes without stopping. "There are flames! Huge flames! Marion, help!" Marion was her deceased husband.

"She is mad, poor soul," a woman said. Some men put a damp cloth on her forehead to calm her down;

still her screams didn't stop. There wasn't much anyone in the cellar could do without outside help.

But now we had almost no connection with the outside world. With electricity cut off, and no radio, the only external news to the cellar was coming through OPL attendants, or from some individuals who were secretly slipping out of the shelter. After each raid, the same stories repeated themselves. But each time they were worse; and there were more of them in and out of the shelter. There were more irritated people, and people were becoming more irritated. Mrs. Ziegler's screams worsened. Besides her, we also had another woman, known only as "Mrs. *Oy Veh,*" a woman who had two sons on the frontline, and who cried day and night, not knowing anything about their fate.[14]

There was more massive destruction: exploding shells, collapsed buildings, rubble. There were more corpses of burned, smoke-choked children; more orphans whose parents' bodies were still under the rubble; widows whose husbands had died in the defense of the country; widowers of whom many were still on the front fighting, not yet knowing that their wives had been killed trying to save their children; and more mothers of missing sons and daughters. There was more chaos, more running, more fleeing, and there were more looters getting rich quickly, or dying in the process.

Buildings were being transformed. Świętego Jana Bożego, the St. John Church on Bonifraterska Street and the adjacent mental hospital, had now been converted to a field hospital. Nuns tended to the wounded. All mentally ill patients had been transferred to a state mental facility in Pruszków, from which no one was ever known to come back alive. School buildings were used as infirmaries; churches, synagogues, and other public buildings were filling up with those who were being left homeless by the bombings.

My Education Continues

Krasińskich Park was also transformed. Until the bombings, it had been a French-style park with a small lake ornamented with dignified swimming swans, carefully manicured flower beds, and long, wooden benches under the shade of old trees. The park was surrounded on three sides by a twelve-foot-high old iron fence-railing mounted on a five foot cement foundation, and on the fourth side by the federal court house. Now it had become a stop-over for hungry, wounded, and exhausted soldiers. Their dismounted nags, tied to fences, chewed on tree bark after all the grass had been consumed.

About two weeks had passed since the first German troops crossed the Polish border. Most of Poland was now occupied. The western part was taken by the Germans, the eastern part by our other neighbor, the USSR, which we still called "The Russians." These two, Germany and Russia, had signed a "Peace Treaty," dividing Poland between themselves. Only the city of Warsaw was still fighting, hoping, against all odds, for a miracle, or, as they put it, "to save our honor." "We will never surrender! Never give up our beloved capital!" the radios broadcasted through speakers on every street corner. "We will fight to the last soldier! Long Live Poland! Long Live Warsaw, the Heart of Our Country!"

The German army surrounded the city. The Polish anti-aircraft guns were silenced by German cannons, which thundered day and night. From the Żoliborz suburbs, over the viaduct, artillery fire lit the sky. With the thunder and lightning came the rain of shells and bullets. Air-raid sirens combined with the dull thunder of distant explosions to create the atmosphere of a storm.

Polish military men were fleeing the defense lines. Soldiers were running all over the city. Every park, every street, every courtyard was filled with retreating

The Bombing of Warsaw

Polish troops. Weary, wounded soldiers were dragging themselves through debris-filled roads. Some were shedding their uniforms and putting on civilian clothes given to them by kindhearted residents.

Abandoned military vehicles and dead or wounded horses were lying in the streets. Our courtyards, all three of them, those nicely groomed gardens, were filled with fleeing soldiers. Chained to garden posts, limping horses were eating Mrs. Wilanowsky's flowers.

During the night, our street was bombarded by artillery grenades. Though our apartment complex was spared severe destruction, we did not escape the attack. One building was hit by a shell that entered the top floor apartments through a side wall. A few apartments were stricken by splinter shells. We knew right away that ours had been one of them. But because of the constant, heavy bombing, we were unable to go up to find out the precise extent of the damage.

Looking from the courtyard, we could see that the roof seemed to be intact. The balcony was hanging on to the falling plaster. Like devils' horns, shards of glass were pointing from smashed window panes. The outside walls, though pockmarked by jabbing grenade splinters, remained standing upright.

A few days later, while taking advantage of a short interruption in the shelling, Dad decided to take a look at our apartment, assess the damage, and see what, if anything, could be salvaged. I couldn't resist such an opportunity, and asked Dad if I could go with him. To my great surprise he said, "Yes."

After pushing through the crowded courtyard, we started up the four flights of steps. On the third floor, Mr. Greenfarb's apartment was standing in ruins. A shell had entered through an outside wall. There was an intense odor of gas, sewage, and smoking cinders. The old man, who had believed in predestination, was dead.

My Education Continues

In our apartment, the parquet floor was covered with a heap of bricks from fallen interior walls. A pile of broken boards and smashed furniture was ornamented with shattered glass. All windows in the apartment were blown out. Most interior walls dividing the rooms were crumbled; but the outside walls remained intact. What used to be a six-room flat—three rooms, two halls, and a kitchen—had been reduced to an entrance hall, one room, and a large space filled with debris. The only unbroken thing in this place was a large, old mahogany wardrobe that we inherited from Grandpa, who had once been the owner of this apartment. The place where the wardrobe stood indicated the location where the wall used to be. On top of it, untouched, lingered a large carboy full of cherry wine, which Mom had made during the cherry season to be used during the next Passover holidays.[15]

Before Dad and I had time to look any further, we heard the sound of sirens: Another bombing. After a few days, the bombing stopped; but the shelling continued for two more days. During the second night, the central waterworks of Warsaw was destroyed. Other water supply systems, such as wells, were very scarce in the city; in many neighborhoods, they were nonexistent. The situation became catastrophic. All food provisions were exhausted. Medical supplies were almost gone. Water was cut off, and with fires raging in most parts of the city. Every available shelter was filled to capacity. On September 28, after four weeks of Blitzkrieg, Warsaw surrendered to the Germans.

Chapter 4. Surrender

The shelling stopped. A hush fell over the city. Poland had ceased to exist. All Polish military personnel, from high-ranking officers to privates who had not been taken prisoner, cast off their uniforms and put on civilian clothes. It was impossible to tell who was who. All of them tried to mix in with the civilians. OPL attendants removed their armbands and threw them into fires. Important leaders fled the country, or went into hiding. Those who didn't manage to escape were taken prisoner.

Inhabitants of Warsaw grieved for their city and their country; all Polish citizens grieved along with them. Yet, amid their profound sorrow, they found some slight comfort in knowing that the shelling and killing had finally stopped. Exhausted, weary, hungry, the civilian population started crawling out of their burrows to look for water, food, for whatever was left of their possessions. They had yet to face the clean-up job and an unknown future.

Dad and I walked out of our building to see what was going on. By the time we got out into the street, looters, many by now quite experienced in the profession, were hard at work. To avoid the danger of falling debris, Dad took me by the hand, and we crossed the street, to the side of Krasińskich Park. It was still full of abandoned military vehicles and dead horses, but the soldiers were gone. On the other side of the street, not far from our house, some youngsters were filling their bags with anything that they could grab from the still smoldering ruins. Unexpectedly, an older gentleman who had been standing next to us started yelling, "Loot, kids, loot!" Then he put both hands to his mouth, and through this megaphone, added, "Take everything you can! Don't leave anything for the German demons!" Turning to my father, he said, "Barely twenty years ago I finished fighting those sons-of-bitches, and here they are, coming again."

Dad and I continued on our way, our destination: Gęsia Street. We were trying to see what had happened to Dad's store. When we reached it, we found a heap of rubble. Dad took me home. Later that afternoon, he went with his partners to see what could be salvaged, if anything.

I think that it was the next day that German troops marched into the city. Sis and I, and three girls we knew from the shelter, took off into the streets to see the Germans. Bonifraterska Street was crowded. White surrender flags were hanging out of all the windows facing the street. Men, women, old and young, mothers with children in their arms, on their shoulders, by their sides—masses of people, all wearing white kerchiefs or waving pieces of white cloth—were coming from all directions. They were rushing to greet the people who had just finished bombing their city.

In order not to lose one another, we girls were holding on to one another's hands and dresses and braids. We kept pushing our way through the crowds. From the side of the Żoliborz suburbs, we heard some tunes—faint, distant voices singing in unison. They were coming louder, and closer: "Oh, la, reha, reha...."

As we pushed further through the swelling crowd, we saw a column of soldiers coming over the viaduct.

Surrender

They were moving closer, young handsome soldiers in spotless, tidily pressed *Feldgrau*, and shiny boots. They were marching in perfect formation and singing in German. Following the column of marching soldiers was a long line of military trucks. On each of the trucks, a few uniformed, young and good-looking soldiers were waving their hands. "What an enemy!" I thought. It was like being somewhere in a foreign country without ever having crossed a border. It was exciting. It was even more exciting because my sister, my friends, and I all had come here without our parents' permission. It was like being free for the first time.

From the crowds below, people were calling out a variety of messages. Some were yelling, "Welcome to Warsaw!" or "Hello, German Soldiers!" or "Glad you are here!" While others were trying to scream even more loudly: "Drop dead, you fucking bastards!" or "Get lost!" or "German aggressors, go home!" or "May God strike you with cholera!"[16]

Pointing to another little boy wearing a *kippah,* a little Polish boy, about ten or eleven, yelled at the top of his voice, "Mr. German! He is a *Jude!*"[17] The whole sentence the boy said in Polish, except the last word, in German: *"Yoode."* People were paying little attention to what others had to say. They were more interested in what was going on with the trucks. At a given signal, the victors started throwing bread from the trucks. Thousands of loaves went flying through the air and into the crowd of people. The soldiers, waving their arms, greeting everybody with friendly smiles, were yelling, *"Brot! Brot!"* They said something else in German, but I didn't understand. From the ends of the bread trucks, mounted movie cameras were rolling to capture this fantastic greeting, of the "Super Race" feeding the *Untermenschen*, the poor, starving, sub-people.

My Education Continues

It didn't take us long to figure out why so many people had been so eager to come out and "greet" the enemy. The bread give-away had been announced on the radio news that morning; those whose electricity was not bombed out and who could still listen to their radios, had alerted their friends and relatives. My friends and I came out of curiosity; most of the others knew about the bread beforehand.

Anyway, the five of us got home with three loaves of fresh bread, which we later divided. Such a precious commodity we hadn't had for quite some time.

Chapter 5. The Unmasking

As soon as the victors entered the city, they promised an end to the chaos and the beginning of good German Law and Order; they were to make the law, and we were to obey orders. To assure that no one dared to defy their authority, they took hostages and imposed a curfew. A few prominent citizens—professors, clergy, politicians—were arrested and kept in jail as "protection." Announcements were then made over all available media, newspapers, street bulletin boards, loudspeakers, radios: "If something should happen to any German person, military or civilian, there will be reprisals. For any non-compliance or civil disobedience, the hostages will be killed." A list of the hostages was posted for everyone to see. That kept the population under control, and the victors safe from harm. Many intellectuals, well-known professors, leaders, clergy, doctors, and lawyers, were rounded up and sent away to camps. "Without the thinkers," the Germans figured, "the population is easier to manage."

Collaborators were quickly found. A new government under German supervision was set up, and the new rulers were in business. Western Poland was annexed to the Third Reich; the east was governed by the Soviet Union and Central Poland was governed by the Germans. Poles lost all their rights; they now

My Education Continues

had only obligations. Jews didn't count; they needed temporary permission to live.[18]

Many new regulations were soon announced. Most of them started with *Verboten*: Not, Do Not, Do Not Go Here, Do Not Go There. Even more frequently, signs read JUDEN VERBOTEN. Hardly ever mentioned was anything that people *were* allowed, or what people *could* do, for water, food, housing, fuel, work, or medicine. Such trivial matters were left to the local authorities, who had very little to work with. The city was in a pathetic state. People carried water from the Wisła River, which was full of debris and within which floated human and animal corpses. Some people had to walk as far as ten kilometers to reach a source of water, which, in turn, had to be boiled to make it fit to drink. To boil the polluted water, fuel was needed. Gas and electric power were cut off in most places, and where they were not, they were rationed. People began to use broken boards and cracked up wooden furniture taken from destroyed buildings.

The problem of food wasn't any better. Stores not destroyed by the bombing and shelling were ordered to reopen, but the shelves in them were empty. Although transports with some food and fuel started rolling into the city, it was much too little to distribute among the large population. Shortages of the necessities were so great that people resorted to other means of getting what they needed for survival: Looting, stealing, illegal trading. People were willing, or rather forced, to pay whatever price was asked in order to appease their hungry stomachs and feed their children.

Ex-looters became entrepreneurs. The black market was booming.[19] Only perishable items could be bought for paper money, which had lost most of its value; it was not unusual to get a wallet of goods for a sackful of money. Ill-gotten gains and barter became the means of acquiring goods. Anything edible (outside of bricks, glass, and nails, everything was now considered edible) was traded for jewelry, clothing, luggage, or other non-essential commodities. Nothing was wasted.

To make sure that the horses did not die in vain, their dead bodies were pulled from streets, parks, and the river; they were then cut up and sold for meat. Horse meat, considered now a luxury item, was traded for winter clothes, coal, candles, or gold. Such was also the price for colored salt (blue, green, and red salt formerly used in industrial plants), now used as food.

We soon had to join the crowds and get into the act of bartering, or else face starvation. The pickles, flour, and rice that we had stored up were coming to an end. These precious items had come from burning warehouses. Aunt Naomi acquired them the day a bomb fell on the grain elevators and barges by the riverfront in Praga, an eastern suburb of Warsaw.[20] Aunt, along with thousands of other decent citizens, ran across the Kierbedzia Bridge to "save" the rice and flour from the burning grain elevators. Of course, they were saving the food from being burned in the fire, drowned in the water, or taken by the Germans.

Besides the problem of food, we also faced the problem of housing. Places had to be found for the thousands of homeless who were staying in temporary shelters. We stayed with Aunt Sara, Grandfather's widowed sister, who, along with her three grown children, lived in the same housing complex that we used to.

There were more problems than the local administration could handle. Most people were still hungry and exhausted, and many were getting sick. Only rats, flies, and the black market thrived. Insolent, fat rats paced the ruins. Large, greenish-black and obese flies soared over one another and banqueted on bodies. Days had passed before the city began the

My Education Continues

slow, hideous, clean-up process. The injured were taken to churches, club houses, school gymnasiums, warehouses, or wherever a field hospital had been set up. (All permanent hospitals had long since been filled.) The dead were buried. People who had lost many material goods were thankful to God Almighty that they had not lost their lives. The poor folk who had never had any material possessions were now boasting about the furs and jewelry that they lost in the fires.

There was a great deal of envy and misunderstanding among the people who were forced to live together. Those who had to rent out rooms were not very friendly to those who had to rent them, at least after the initial excitement of good will wore off. Those who had escaped from the flames with their lives had little respect for things such as dishes, clothing, or knickknacks, while these things were still cherished by those who had them. Sometimes unfriendly words would slip out and cause friction among the renters and the "rentees."

When our home was shelled, there was no fire. We found many usable items under the rubble. We cleaned up the one room and the adjacent hall, which were still intact; and we established residency for the five of us—Mom, Dad, Sis, Aunt Naomi, and myself. The windows that were broken—and there were only two that were not—Dad boarded up with plywood. With the help of Cousin Aron, he installed a wood-burning stove that we used for cooking and heating. Water we hauled from a faucet in the courtyard, and we used the public toilets nearby. After a while we made some home improvements. The first one came about accidentally. Sis was shoveling through the debris in the destroyed part of the apartment when she found an open drain pipe sticking out from under the smashed toilet stool. Mom poured some soiled water

The Unmasking

into the pipe to see what would happen. Lo and behold, it worked! The water went all the way down the drain. It was a great discovery. By practicing a few acrobatic maneuvers—climbing over debris and balancing over a fifteen centimeter drain pipe—we had a new indoor toilet.

Two other big improvements followed. One was a neighbor letting us get water from her restored home so that we didn't have to go down to the yard for it; the other was when Dad brought home some candles and matches, two precious commodities which he had received in trade for a jar of pickles. And there was light.

For three reasons, this small, crowded, pathetic living space turned out to be a great bargain for us. First of all, we didn't have to live with relatives or friends, or stay in public shelters the way many bombed-out people did. Second, we were not assigned to take in any refugees, who were then pouring into Warsaw from other cities and towns and being put up in many of the homes that hadn't been bombed. Third, since this place was so damaged, we didn't have to pay the full amount of rent, which was otherwise very expensive.

Beyond having a place to live, we had many problems to face. Ever since the German troops entered the city, there was not a day without new developments. The handsome, friendly, bread-giving, humanitarian occupiers had unmasked themselves and started showing their real identity. Almost every day, new laws or decrees were announced. The new regulations affected everybody in the general Polish population, but they were especially hard on the Jews. Some additional decrees applied to the Jews only. Two kinds of crimes were being committed against the people of Poland. One was by decree; the other came from the daily mood of the occupying forces. The

My Education Continues

troops had a free hand to do as they pleased. Nothing they chose to do against the general population was against the law.

I saw road blocks being set up on streets, people (especially men) being rounded up, loaded into trucks and shipped away. This was done without warning; people just disappeared off the streets. While most Jews seized in these roundups were taken to forced labor camps inside and out side the city, many Poles were being swept up by Gestapo raids and shipped off to Germany to work in the fields or in munitions factories.[21]

I saw thousands of refugees pouring into Warsaw looking for housing even as many bombed-out residents were still homeless. I saw Jewish refugees—the old and the sick, men, women and children, the rich and the poor, some with only a bundle on their backs—dragging along the streets. They were coming from small towns and larger cities, most of them from the territories newly annexed to the Third Reich. These territories were to be *"Judenrein"*—"free of Jews." All the refugees coming from these places were wearing yellow stars sewn to the front and back of their outer garments.[22]

Slowly, every available inch of space in Warsaw was full of refugees: Synagogues, basements, even burned-out buildings, were filled to capacity with the hungry, helpless, and hopeless people. They had no jobs, no income, and, most of them, no money.

Every day I saw new street posters announcing new ordinances. One read, "All men or women found guilty of crimes against the Third Reich will be hanged or shot on the spot." An offense against the Third Reich could be anything from smuggling a loaf of bread to such an abominable crime as crossing in front of a German guard.

Like most Jewish kids, I was instructed not to go to parks or public libraries or other such public

The Unmasking

places, like cinemas and theaters, because these were FÜR JUDEN VERBOTEN. Jews were also instructed to step off sidewalks whenever a German was walking there. Jewish men had to take off their hats when passing a German soldier, even though a head-covering for Jewish men was required at all times by Jewish law.

Anti-Semitism was not a new phenomenon to Polish Jews. Long before the Germans came—even before there was a Hitler in Germany—prejudice and injustice flourished in Poland. Jews were discriminated against, blamed for every misfortune, excluded from government jobs, barred from living in certain areas, and not allowed in many schools and universities. Jews were thus barred from employment in police and fire departments, or even in public transportation jobs. Only shortly before the War, after long protests and demonstrations, was one Jewish streetcar driver hired, and his picture was in all newspapers in the land. These practices were not part of official Polish constitutional law. It was simply a common understanding that Jews were not allowed to participate as equal citizens.

At some universities where Jews were admitted, Jewish students were not treated as equals. Often they were made to stand in the back of the class. In Warsaw, Jewish students had to enter and leave the university through a back door, accompanied by Jewish street groups who protected them from being beaten by the ENDEK, a group of militant anti-Semitic fanatics who identified Jews with international communism.[23]

In Poland the Gentile-Jewish relationship was best described as "mutual hate." As groups, Gentiles hated Jews, and Jews hated Gentiles. However, on an individual basis, many Jews and Gentiles were friends, some even close friends, some business partners. A

My Education Continues

few even intermarried. But in general, especially in large cities, the hatred was devastating.

Yet, amazingly, despite the prejudice, Jewish culture in Poland prospered. Even though the majority of Jews lived in poverty, they were rich culturally. Through the centuries, Jews somehow had managed to cope with discrimination and poverty. They had established their own way of life: They had their own schools, libraries, and theaters; they had their own self-supporting organizations: orphanages, hospitals, geriatric centers, synagogues.

Life between the Wars in Warsaw was a period of relative stability for cultural growth and technological advancements, even in the middle of an economic semi-depression. Times were hard, but people knew what to expect, and tried to adjust. But now, since the War started, no one quite knew how to cope with this new situation. To the Nazis, the word "Jew" was synonymous with "undesirable," meaning that Jews had no place among the Germans or, since the Germans now occupied Poland, the Poles,.

The Nazi plan was to get rid of the Jews first, then to take care of the Poles, whom they hated just a little less than they hated the Jews. Nazi propaganda against Jews was spreading like locusts. All troubles were blamed on Jews: problems with foreign governments, the economic crisis, bad weather—even dried up rivers—everything was the Jews' fault.

The propaganda campaign, along with the new decrees, led to unbearable conditions. My first personal encounter with the new laws came the day Dad was trapped in a street roundup. Along with about a hundred other Jewish men, he was caught in the street and taken away. He just disappeared. No one heard a word from any of the men, or a word about them. After five days, Dad showed up, exhausted, unshaven, dirty, his clothes torn, heartbroken. He said that when he was caught in the roundup, he wasn't really scared. He knew the Germans and he knew their language quite well. During World War I, Dad had worked in Germany, and according to his stories, he was treated fairly. He never complained about his treatment there even though he had been taken there by force. So when the Germans took him away this time, he was sure that he'd be all right. He only worried about how to let us know what had happened to him. His captors didn't give him any clue about his destination, or about how long he would be there. But all of the men put on the truck with him reasoned, logically, that such a large roundup would surely be announced over radio or in a bulletin; the men would be put to work for the day and then would be sent home as soon as the task was done.

What the men did not know was that with the Nazis, logical predictions did not work. Everybody turned out to be wrong. First of all, these were not the Germans many of the men remembered from World War I. No one had told these captured men what was going to happen to them or when, if at all, they would be released. Then, too, there was no information given out to their families.

What these men saw and lived through was in no one's imagination.

Dad was forty-three, of medium height, slim, fast-moving, and in very good physical condition. He could run up and down four flights of steps faster than I could (and I was fast). When Dad came home he was weak, his faculties were numbed; he looked sick. These captured men had been give three meals of bread, soup, and water during the five days they were away. They slept only three hours each night; the remaining time they worked cleaning up debris, scrubbing sidewalks, and unloading military trucks;

My Education Continues

they were preparing the King's palace at Plac Zamkowy for German occupancy.[24]

They worked hard and long hours. But it was not the work and hunger that made their experience so terrible; it was the treatment that they received that made it almost unbearable. Dad saw older men being beaten and dragged by their feet when they couldn't walk; he saw an Orthodox Jew having his beard forcibly cut off; he saw one man shot. Dad talked about his experience for many days. When he wanted to tell the more gruesome parts of it, he would tell Sis and me to go out to the yard and play.

After this first encounter with the "New Germans"—or rather with the Nazis—he was reluctant to leave the house. Yet he still insisted that the Germans were good, civilized people; that he had only encountered a bad bunch of them; that it had only been a freak incident. The guards responsible for holding him had been young drunken punks. "You cannot judge all Germans by the misbehavior of a few." But not everyone thought the way Dad did.

Chapter 6. To the USSR

The Nazi attitude toward Jews and Hitler's decrees against them were no secret. Now the Polish Jews had to face the dilemma that the German Jews had faced a few years before. They had to figure out how to deal with this new dangerous situation. The three major schools of thought were 1) run while there is still time; 2) this can't be true; it isn't as bad as it seems—deny the danger; and 3) stay put, flatter the enemy; things will turn out all right. All other suggestions fell somewhere among these.

For those who wished to get out of the danger zone, the decision to run was easy, but carrying it out was not. There was no legal way to get out of the country. For years, Jews had tried to get out of Poland, but had had no place to go. Some did manage to get to America, but they were only a small percentage of those who wanted to leave. Most countries had set immigration quotas. To get to the USA, to some South American countries, to Australia, or to Palestine, required a wait of years. And that was before the War; now the problem was even more difficult. In addition to having no place to go, there was no legal way to get out of the country. The only possible place for a refugee was a Russian-occupied territory. But going there was illegal.

My Education Continues

Many Jews and some Gentiles, especially the young and those whose political views leaned toward socialist ideas, solved their dilemma quite early on. With only small bundles of belongings strapped to their backs, they escaped the German-occupied zone as soon as the German troops entered Poland. These first groups of refugees were followed by Jews who took the plight and stories of the German Jews seriously. They weren't going to take unnecessary risks in the danger zone. Others who followed were young men and women who loved adventures, who wanted to try something new. All of these ran toward the Bug River, which had become the new border between Poland and Russia.

For those who responded to this obvious danger by denying and avoiding the existence of the serious situation, the execution of their idea was easy. They did it the same way many people react to an oncoming tornado: They know its bizarre and deadly nature, they see it approaching, but they would rather reject its truth, minimize its potential power, and make believe that it will disappear, or at least miss them.

Those who believed in peaceful coexistence with the enemy had their own mottos: "Don't anger the enemy. Don't oppose them. They have the guns and they are ready to use them, with pleasure, if you give them a chance. So don't give them reasons for retribution, and they will not bother you."

To figure out which of these choices would be best was a life-and-death matter. One could only be guided by instinct, or by a more logical approach: previous experience. But here again was a problem: None of these guidelines was very reliable. There were several precedents to choose from, but not one that could assure success.

Until about twenty years before, until after World War I, Poland had been occupied by three of its neighbors: the Austro-Hungarian Empire, Czarist Russia, and Germany. There was no problem now with the Austro-Hungarian Empire, since it no longer existed. (This empire was split into two separate countries—Austria and Hungary—both of which were now occupied by Germans.) Russia was another matter. In Czarist Russia, life for Jews had been hard, pogroms common, and prejudice appalling. After the 1917 Bolshevik Revolution, and at the end of World War I, things changed. Strict equality laws were passed by the now socialist USSR, and, at least theoretically, there was no more discrimination. In more "civilized" Germany, life for Jews was quite good before and during World War I. People were tolerant, society integrated. But in Germany, as in Russia, things changed. In 1933, when the fascist party came to power, discriminatory laws were passed, and Germany adopted a "Superior Race" and Untermensch policy.

Like my dad, there were many others who did not believe in such a German metamorphosis; they still couldn't picture Russia dropping its anti-Semitism and Germany picking it up. They just refused to believe it. They knew that things had changed, but they reasoned that the people could not have changed that much; and, because it was hard for them to accept the reality, they denied it.

Besides the Jewish problem, which, of course, was the major one for us, there were other factors that had to be considered when deciding whether to run or to stay. The Russian economy was stagnant. Lack of housing, food, medicine, and other necessities was very serious, and under the new Communist system, there was little hope that it would improve soon. In Germany, with the war machine in full swing, the labor market was booming; the standard of living was higher; there was hope for a better life.

My Education Continues

All of these problems were discussed by the adults. I was not too interested in the talk. My only worries were how to fill my stomach and how to have more adventures. School had not yet resumed. I was still keeping my diary, and I needed new materials for it.

One rainy afternoon, our neighbor, Mrs. Gurfinkel, asked me if I could, please, come next door, and watch their two-year-old girl since both she and her husband, who was a baker, had things to do. I liked to play with little Sarenka, so I gladly went.

In the living room of their apartment, a couple of packed suitcases stood against the wall. Mr. Gurfinkel was busy packing a knapsack. "Tell your father," he said, without looking up, "that we are leaving for Russia tomorrow morning." And in a sorrowful voice he added, "Only the three of us are going. The old folks and my sister Masha have decided to stay." Then turning to his wife he said in Yiddish (thinking that I wouldn't understand): "I don't know how to bake bread without flour; those German bastards haven't given me any since they entered the city. It is going to get worse, yet, just you wait and see. Thousands of others are leaving. I'm glad I decided to go."

That afternoon I had a nice talk with Dad. The reason I remember it so well was that it was the longest and deepest conversation I ever had with him. Dad was always busy working long hours or being too tired and impatient to listen to my stories. Now that he was home most of the time, we talked more often. I told him about young Mr. Gurfinkel, and asked him if we, too, could go to Russia.

He gave me a very funny look and a whole list of reasons why we couldn't go. He said that he knew a lot of other people who were going; but he didn't know if that was the right thing to do. From his answer it seemed that he had already thought about it before.

To the USSR

He told me that it was too dangerous to cross the border and that he had never done anything that was illegal. "Besides," he explained, "many people who left were turned back at the crossing; many others were swindled out of their money by the smugglers who take advantage of those who are running. Yes, they take away their money and never get them over the border." I was surprised by how much Dad knew about the exodus to the USSR. I thought that he had just heard it from me for the first time. "Besides being too dangerous, it is also late fall now, and it's getting colder. You kids might get sick on the way." All of these excuses sound funny. I just wanted to go. It was a great opportunity to see a foreign country; a new adventure. I had never been outside of Poland; as a matter of fact, I had been to few places in Poland, other than the suburban villages where we used to spend the summers. Once Dad took me on a business trip to Łódź, but that was when I was very little and could travel free.

So I kept reasoning with Dad to leave for Russia, but to no avail. Slowly, he walked over to the window. It was raining even harder now than it had been in the morning. He stood there staring for a while, watching the rain fall. The deep wrinkle in his forehead had become even deeper.

"What do you know about life?" he said, answering my question after. "Don't we have enough problems without looking for more? When will you grow up?"

Chapter 7. The First Year

Living conditions in Warsaw, as in all of Poland, were quickly deteriorating. Food supplies dwindled. There were shortages of everything but decrees, rubble, and misery. Endless bread lines had become a normal occurrence rather than an occasional phenomenon. It was not unusual for a family to take turns standing in line for twenty-four hours, often in rain and blowing wind, only to find out when they got to the bakery door that there was no bread left. Sometimes people stood in line all night not knowing if the bread would even arrive at that store. This happened a few time to us. We finally gave up standing in lines and resorted to trading on the black market. We bartered Dad's watch and Mom's necklace, and clothes and pillows, in order to get some food.

Dad had a few rolls of fabric which he had recovered from the debris of the destroyed store; these he had had to share with his partners, and they had yet to decide what to do with their "wealth." Thousands of people were in the same predicament. They had to decide whether to give up their cherished possessions or to go hungry. And while many were standing in lines worrying, complaining, and praying, those with access to food supplies, and those with connections to the new government officials, or with ties to the

The First Year

underworld, were doing a booming business on the black market, making more money than they had ever dreamed of. It was the first time I heard the saying, "Podczas wichury, śmieci dó góry"—"During a windstorm, trash flies to the top." Poland had always been a highly class-conscious society. Somehow, the mongrels taking over the market made no sense; everything was out of its natural order. People knew, certainly, that such chaos could not last very long, but in the meantime, those who had the means were stocking up on everything, thereby creating more shortages and running up prices.

Most of the established businesspeople, like legitimate merchants, bankers, and career people, could not function in such eccentric conditions. Many eventually just gave up trying. The black market took over the "new economy."

Legitimate jobs were scarce. Some people between the ages of sixteen and forty and with the right connections or money to bribe someone, found legal jobs in a few German-run shops, such as Toebens, Schultz, and Hallman, that were making military uniforms, brooms, brushes, and other textile items. It often took a lot of illegal money to get one of the legal jobs. With small home workshops almost gone, and factories bombed out or closed owing to the lack of raw materials, the "normal" way of sustaining life was all but eliminated. New means of supporting oneself had to be found.

People adjusted to the new "system." Many worked from their homes, legally or not. This would go on so long as there were no new ordinances. People did what they could to create work and trade with one another: The streets were slowly being cleaned up. Even some schools began to reopen.

If there is no way out, one either adjusts or dies. We learned that lesson quickly.

My Education Continues

It must have been in early or mid-November that it was announced that all primary school children would be returning to their schools. The 1939-40 school year was to be my last in elementary school. I had already applied for and passed the entrance exam for high school. Compulsory education was required only through seventh grade. Any schooling after that was voluntary and expensive. The kids who were going to continue their education past the seventh grade could transfer after completing the sixth grade. Because of the War, though, I was stuck. High school was out of the question, so I decided that if schools reopened, I would go back to the seventh grade. I was kind of glad to go back to any school, even if it was back to grade school. After such a prolonged vacation, I was looking forward to seeing my friends.

Besides, my diary was filling up with all kinds of exciting events.

My happiness, however, was short-lived. The second day of school, during math class, two Polish police officers walked into our classroom. They whispered something to the teacher and then walked out. The teacher, our beloved Dora Braff, turned pale. She was speechless. After regaining her composure, she told us that German gendarmes had surrounded the school; the building was to be vacated immediately. It was to be used as barracks for the military.

"Don't panic," she said calmly. "Don't run! Go straight home, all of you. We'll let you know when to come back and where we'll be meeting again."

This was the end of my formal schooling. But not of my education.

It seemed as if everything bad that was to happen had already happened. Rumors became more optimistic.

The First Year

"Be nice to your occupiers," said the dreamers. "Do things their way. Do as you are told, and nothing will happen to you." This was also the advice Uncle Shlomo gave during a heated discussion. He, like my father, still remembered the Germans of World War I. Others were not only giving advice; they were prophesying. "These odd conditions will not last very long; the world is watching. These are not the Dark Ages, you know. In these modern times, with telephone and electronic media—telegraph, radio—people must behave in a civilized manner."

People with more pessimistic views maintained that "This madness could last for months, maybe even as long as a year. So don't be surprised if it isn't over soon."

In daily life there were no indications that anything would change, and if it did, it wouldn't be any time soon, or for the better. To the contrary, there were more beggars in the streets asking for alms, and more singers walking from courtyard to courtyard, chanting songs of lamentation and begging for money or food.

But somehow—and I never figured out the reason—hope was running high. People had faith in the future. Maybe by believing in God, or by repeating their wishful thinking often enough, people gained the courage to proceed, or the hope to go on.

This type of thinking, of course, works both ways: when one hears often enough that he is an Untermensch, he begins to believe that, too. But with faith in God, Jews were always optimistic. And, for better or worse, life kept going on.

A Judenrat, or Jewish council, was appointed by the Germans. New, self-help organizations sprang up throughout the city. Supported by the still wealthy and the newly rich, they set up soup kitchens and shelters for the poor, the homeless, and the refugees who were still pouring in from other towns.

My Education Continues

Conditions in our house reflected the general situation. We had no income, very few items left to trade, and we were too proud to ask for help. And my sister and I were growing out of our clothes as nature followed its course.

With our school being closed, and no room in the house, we were looking for things to do. Before the War started, we used to play games, do our homework, read books, listen to the radio; or we visited friends, or went with them to the movies or to parks; there was ice-skating, hopscotch, social gatherings. We also had extracurricular activities—clubs organized around drama, reading, and sports. Then, too, there had always been theaters, shopping, or sleigh-riding. In summer, when we were not out of town, we'd go to the riverbank and visit the special recreation facilities for children; we could take short, one-day trips.

Now with most of these activities gone, we started exploring new territories in order to pursue excitement and adventure. Since neither Sis nor I was experienced in roaming aimlessly around town, we started our new ventures by visiting relatives. Almost all Mom's and Dad's relatives lived in Warsaw, so we had many people whom we could visit.

Our first venture was to visit Grandma Esther. She was not doing well. Ever since she returned from the bomb-shelter, she had been ill. I knew something was wrong with her when I went with Dad to see her after the bombing and she did not greet us at the door. Another indication was that she didn't give me candies or cookies, as was her custom with all the younger grandchildren.

Next time, when I went with Sis to visit her, she was in bed.

Gradually, Sis and I started venturing to visit other relatives. Aunt Sara, Dad's widowed sister, had been bombed out and had no place to live. She had a son,

The First Year

Sheye, about fourteen, a daughter, Golda, ten, two grown stepchildren, and a son, Marek, who was taken into service when the War started. The last we heard of him was that he was in a German POW camp.[25] Stepdaughter, Rosa, about twenty, went to stay with her "natural" aunt.

Aunt Sara was always poor, even before this war mess started, even before her husband died. Her job was stapling buttons onto cardboard cards, work that she did in her home workshop for a sewing supply company. She earned little from this and, compounding the problem, her husband had been sick and out of work for many years before his death.

Now, without home or job, her situation was even worse. After the bombing she was now staying with Grandma, who, as it were, was already living with two other daughters—Aunt Bella, who was married and had two daughters, and Aunt Polla, the youngest of Dad's five siblings, in her thirties and still looking for a proper man.

Each day, my sister and I ventured to other relatives. Uncle Louis, Dad's only brother, and the one who lived on partly bombed-out Gęsia Street, still had his apartment intact. His son, Cousin Shlomo, had run away to Russia with his quickly wedded wife. Cousin Abram, Shlomo's younger brother, was still in the hospital. He was wounded during the bombardment while on OPL duty, and had had to have his left leg amputated below the knee.

Cousin Yenta, or Jadzia, as we called her, was Uncle Louis' only daughter. She was fourteen, and when we came to visit her, she was very depressed. She was helping around the house, waiting on her mother, Aunt Tova, who was sick and heartbroken because of her son's problems.

We didn't visit Aunt Lea, Dad's oldest sister, or her married daughter, Sara. They all lived far from us, and

My Education Continues

we didn't have streetcar fare. We heard that they were doing fine. Sara's baby girl was growing, and her husband was back from the service.

My sister and I became the family messengers. As we visited relatives and friends, we would carry news from one to the other and then back to our home. We visited other aunts and uncles, most of whom were not any better off than we were. I heard of two of Mom's cousin's, Haim and Moniek, who had left for Russia. Another one, Laib, was supposedly getting rich on the black market; everyone was trying to borrow money from him. There were a few other cousins on Mom's side of the family who had not yet used up their wealth. But most of the other relatives were getting poorer by the day.

We liked to visit all these people. On Mom's side of the family there were just three children of our generation. Besides Sis and me, there was only Cousin Romka, about five years younger than my sister. In all fairness, I must say, we were somewhat spoiled by all the adults.

The person we liked to visit best was Grandma Ruth. We liked her a lot. Grandma Ruth was Mom's stepmother. Grandpa married her sometime during World War I after Grandpa's first wife, my mother's birth mother, died. I didn't know that I had another grandmother besides Grandma Ruth. It was only after Grandpa's death that I overheard some adult conversation and found out the whole story. But that didn't matter anyway—Grandma Ruth was always good to us, always patient and loving. (There was only one objection that Mom had: She spoiled us rotten.) After Grandpa's death, Grandma Ruth remained with us for about a year and a half—until she remarried. Neither Sis nor I liked the idea of her marriage. We did not want her to move out. We had another problem: What were we going to call the man she was marrying?

The First Year

We loved our grandfather more than we loved anyone else in the world. Calling another man "Grandpa" was unthinkable. Yet, how should one call a grandmother's husband? After some debating, Sis and I came up with a name, "Pan Dziadzius"—"Mr. Granddaddy."

Mr. Granddaddy and Grandma Ruth lived on Karmelicka Street 4, at the corner of Leszno Street. Their neighborhood did not suffer much damage during the bombing. They not only had their apartment undamaged but some food as well. One of Mr. Granddaddy's sons, Gersh, was a miller who lived in Sandomierz, a small town on the Wisła in southern Poland. Gersh was sending them food packages. Everyone who knew Grandma Ruth was happy that she didn't have to suffer the way many others did. Whenever Sis and I went on our daily ventures, Mom would tell us not to visit Grandma Ruth too often. "We don't want her to think that you kids need to be fed."

We dropped in on Uncle Harry and Tante Trude, who were now translating papers and documents for the newly founded Judenrat. They were managing well.

We visited a few schoolmates and even some teachers who lived not too far away. Mom didn't like for us to roam the streets, but there was little else for us to do. We didn't need to help around the house: there was nothing going on to make it dirty. Of course, we did our share of reading; that was something that both Mom and Dad insisted on. But from reading books I got no fresh stories for my diary. I needed real stories. Sometimes I got them; often I did not.

One day, while on a venture, we stopped to see our best friends, Freda and Rena. They told us that their school had closed a few days before. Most schools, especially in the Jewish neighborhood, were now closed. Many others had been taken over by soldiers and were now being used as hospitals or warehouses.

My Education Continues

Rena, who was the oldest of the four of us, told me about their new lifestyle and new plans. "It is actually a family plan," she said. "We've decided that the two of us are going to help our father with his luggage business. Suitcases," she explained, "are now in big demand, and if through some connections and bribes Dad manages to get some materials, we could start working again and reopen our workshop. Dad will make the luggage, as he always did, and we will take it to market."

The girls also told us that their oldest sister, Bluma, had fled with some newly married friends to Russia, and that their seventeen-year-old sister Ida had gotten a job in a German workshop that made brushes.

When I brought home this news, I told Mom that I, too, wanted to do something like Freda and Rena, or to help the girls in their new venture to sell luggage. I was even going to ask their father, Uncle Yakov, if he would let me do it. I kind of guessed what Mom's answer was going to be, but I asked anyway. Sis wasn't interested in the whole thing, but I was going to wait and see if the girls' plan would work out.

Well, it did work out: It worked better than even they expected. Not only were suitcases in great demand by the general public, but even German soldiers were buying them. As it turned out, the Germans were their best customers. Unfortunately, Aunt Rachel and Uncle Yakov didn't think that it was a good idea for me to go with the girls to deliver their wares. Of course, I was quite disappointed. Without telling anyone, I followed the girls to the market to see what it was all about. To my surprise, I found many teenage boys and girls, and even younger kids, selling and delivering goods to the market. Many kids were now turning to enterprising activity. I started nagging Dad to let me do something worthwhile, some kind of

The First Year

decent work, since I was getting bored with doing nothing. I told him that this would not be my first job. I reminded him that when I was about eight or nine I had a job putting on clasps and threading buckles on girdles and suspenders in our uncle's workshop. I was paid ten groszy a day. Dad laughed.

A few days later, Dad came up with an idea. Since he was afraid to go into the street after his experience with the work roundup, I could deliver some of his fabric to garment manufacturing customers who were now running small tailor shops out of their homes. The rolls of fabric which Dad had salvaged from the store would be cut into small sections, for one garment each. I would take two of them at a time: One I would wrap around me, under my coat; the other I could carry in my school sack. But I could only do this on one condition: I had to obey all the rules set by Mom and Dad. The first rule was that I had to take my sister with me, but not walk together with her, "just in case something should happen." Another rule was that we had to go always by streetcar, never on the streets, while carrying merchandise. We were not to stop on the way or to talk to strangers. If anything unusual were to happen, we were to separate, so that at least one of us would be able to give an account of the incident. I didn't like all of these rules, but I agreed to the deal.

Most of Dad's tailors lived all the way across town, in Mokatow, around the Plac Trzech Krzyży—which gave me a chance to get acquainted with new neighborhoods and to visit other parts of town. I was happy, and I obeyed almost all rules he set.

On Świętokrzyska Street, I stopped outside Aunt Bella's haberdashery store. I remembered visiting there many times before the War, especially during the Christmas season, when we used to help Aunt Bella decorate the display window. One time, about a year

My Education Continues

before the War, I went there with my mother. A picket line of Polish youths was standing in front of some Jewish stores, warning prospective customers that the owner was a Jew. They carried signs that said, "No beating Jews, please! Boycotting is okay" and "Don't buy from Jews!" These were the slogans of moderate Jew-haters. The radicals were calling for beating Jews and smashing windows. I never went back. Now the store was locked. The broken display window was boarded up. No one was in front of the store, nor inside it. It looked scary, abandoned. Now I was going back here because most of Dad's customers either lived or worked in this neighborhood. Since now they were working from their private homes, they were often hard to find, for they had taken their name plates off the doors. I learned never to knock on doors that had no mezuzahs on the posts.

I was doing quite well, and enjoyed my newly acquired freedom of movement, going to new places and riding streetcars and buses. Never before had Sis and I been allowed to roam the streets as we did now. My diary was doing well, too, filling up with new adventures. But this didn't last long. Once Dad's few rolls of fabric came to an end, my career in the delivery business was over.

I started looking for new things to do. For quite some time I had suspected that Aunt Naomi was doing something, but I wasn't sure what it was. I assumed that she was buying or selling things in the market—or on the black market. With her looting experience, and her Aryan looks, she could have been doing a number of things.[26] But she never talked about her ventures whenever Sis and I were at home. Still, I knew that the small amounts of food that had been lately trickling in were coming from her. Since I was looking for a job, I asked her if she would tell me where she was going, or if she would take me along. The answer to both

The First Year

questions was, "No!" In any case, Aunt Naomi was doing quite well. We, too, had a little more food in the house; at least, we weren't starving.

After a while, I found a new job. My new enterprise was selling candy. It brought me not only a little money but a lot of education, fun, and, of course, adventures with which to fill many pages of my diary. It all started on my thirteenth birthday. At that time, Jewish girls in Eastern Europe did not celebrate Bat-Mitzvah.[27] This happened only for boys. But Orthodox girls did have a special birthday at the age of twelve—or at thirteen, if they were not too Orthodox. My birthday was always special, for I was born on Hanukkah.[28] Like all the twelve years before, when the third Hanukkah candle was lit, we would celebrate my birthday. It became a kind of family tradition to celebrate Hanukkah, my birthday, and my sister's birthday at the same time (even though my sister's birthday was actually in January). Each year, uncles, aunts, and cousins would gather in our house for a Hanukkah party.

For this birthday, however, only those who lived very near to us showed up. They arrived before nightfall, which came very early in winter. I got a few useful gifts: a pair of woolen socks (wrapped in a newspaper), a skirt and a sweater that my cousin Zofia had grown out of, two books, and a game—all secondhand. Sis got some things, too. Then we both got some "Hanukkah Geld," a whole bunch of devaluated paper money.[29]

The menu always included dinner with cakes and latkes. Traditionally, they were served with "sugar and spice and everything nice," but now we were serving them with hot tea. Sugar was a luxury item that we had not seen for a long time. But the frozen potatoes were so sweet that no one missed the sugar. Everybody enjoyed the meal, and we all sang Hanukkah songs.

My Education Continues

Through the window, which was opened slightly to provide ventilation, an icy breeze was coming in and blowing the candles. We closed the window, and the room filled with choking smoke from the wet wood, the burning candles, and the frying oil. We continued singing songs, playing games, and telling stories. With occasional naps, we sat until dawn. When the curfew hours were over, the guests went home.

I found out about Gucia and her candy workshop. Gucia was a hunchbacked orphaned woman, who for many years lived with Aunt Dora (my dead grandmother's sister) and her family. Gucia might even have been related to them. A couple of years before the War, this poor, inconsequential woman, at the age of forty-five, married a well-to-do widower with five children, and moved into his apartment on Krochmalna Street, where "they all lived happily ever after."

We saw Gucia occasionally, in Aunt Dora's house whenever she was visiting there, but we never went to her Krochmalna Street home. I am not even sure if Gucia herself had ever been on that street before she married. Krochmalna Street was famous for its gangsters, who lived amid synagogues and pious Jews. Merchants of every imaginable kind traded there as children played in yards. Girls who wanted a fast buck were walking the street and guys looking for a lucky night or a use for their thirty-minute work break were walking there, too. Sis and I were never allowed on this street with its own language and culture.

I told Freda and Rena about Gucia and what I had heard about her candy workshop. I said that I would like to sell Gucia's candy, but I had no idea how to go about it. They offered their help. If Mom would let me, I could go with them when they delivered their suitcases, and they would show me where to go. "You'll see," said Rena with assurance. "There are many kids

The First Year

selling all kinds of things around the Plac Żelaznej Bramy. I don't think you have ever seen this place before. There are hundreds of merchants, all kinds of shops; the bazaar is gorgeous; it's covered by a huge glass roof. It's like a hall, like an enormous market in a glassed-in hall."

She sounded very convincing: The place must be interesting.

I persuaded Mom to go with me to Gucia's home and investigate the candy business. The kitchen of Gucia's second floor apartment had been converted into a factory. Gucia, her husband, all five children, who ranged in age from seven to eighteen, and three cousins, were all busy working. Even the youngest boy was helping. When Mom and I came in, he was licking sugar from his fingers and watching the cat. "During the summer," he told us proudly, "my job is swatting flies."

Gucia had a nice talk with Mom. She explained how, through connections and bribes, her husband was able to obtain sugar and other ingredients that were otherwise unavailable. Most of her candies were sold by kids.

After a lengthy discussion with Gucia, and then a debate with Dad, I was allowed to start my candy business. But again, as with my fabric delivery business, I had to obey some rules. First, Gucia was to show me how to do it and get me acquainted with the other kids who were in the business. also, I couldn't begin until spring, after the weather warmed up. Finally, I was to be home between one and two o'clock in the afternoon, no matter how much I sold—even if it was nothing.

The candy I was selling looked like peanut brittle without the nuts. It was actually rolled-out sugar dough flavored with artificial fruit juice and cut into

My Education Continues

squares. Once I began, I was selling the stuff as fast as I could get it to market. I used to be finished by eleven or twelve o'clock. Later, I started buying two trays of candy each day, and with the guidance and help from Freda and Rena, I had no trouble selling it all. As a matter of fact, I was going to have to find a partner.

My sister, in the meantime, found a babysitting job. She was to watch a three-year-old boy who lived in our complex. She wasn't getting much money for it, but she did get all the food she could eat. The people she worked for were very nice to her. Sis was very happy.

During the eight days of the Passover holiday, I stayed home. Already weeks before the holidays, I saw Dad meeting with his "Moes Khitting," an organization which made sure that every Jew in town had matzo, wine, and basic kosher food for Passover. Even though Dad was not too enthusiastic about doing such things to help out, he did it anyway. We were glad Dad was interested in doing something, since for weeks he had not gone beyond the courtyard gate.

Like every year, the organization members were planning the collection and distribution of the food for the needy. The ancient tradition was observed strictly during good times and bad. All who did not receive from the institution gave to it. I remember Grandpa giving special donations to this cause. (One time, I asked him if some people I knew were receiving the food or food coupons for the holidays. "Talking about people you help is not nice," he said. "To shame poor people and brag about yourself is not Jewish!")

We always had guests and family for Passover, at least for the first Seder Night.[30] For the first Seder of the War, Dad's sister Sara, with her two children, came over. Aunt Naomi was with us, and an older couple from Łódź who were living in the refugee shelter located in the third courtyard of our apartment complex, came, too. Usually Mom needed a lot of preparing for this holiday. It took time and effort to plan, clean, and cook. Guests had to be invited. The house had to be spotless. And the traditional meal of wine and matzo, fish, soup, and matzo-balls had to be prepared. A special tzimmes, a sweet vegetable dish, was usually served. Passover cake and cookies would be baked.

This year, the preparations were easy. We had only one room to clean, and not many choices of food to think about. We had matzo and potatoes, even fish and cake. We celebrated with the cherry wine that was miraculously saved from the bombs. Dad read from the Haggadah; Cousin Sheyele asked the "Four Questions," even though he was the oldest of the children, not the youngest. (Since all of us younger kids were girls, the honor had to go to the boy.) Sheyele asked, "Why is this night different from all other nights? Why do we eat matzo? Why do we eat bitter herbs? Why do we dip? Why do we lean?" After my dad answered the questions according to the Haggadah, everybody at the table talked about the parting of the Red Sea and the freeing of the Jewish slaves.[31] We all knew that God would soon perform such miracles again and free us from the Germans, the way He had freed our forefathers from the Egyptians. We wished each other "L'shana haba b'Yerushalaim."[32] The old couple went home; they didn't need to break the curfew. All others stayed until morning. Some slept on the beds, some on the floor.

After Passover, Sala, my classmate and friend, became my business partner. Every morning we went to pick up our candy at Gucia's home, then to the marketplace. Each of us took a tray of candy and suspended it over her neck; we looked like professional marketeers. Sometimes we met Freda and Rena while

My Education Continues

they were delivering suitcases. We'd have a chat or buy something; everything went fine.

Then one day, as Sala and I were selling our candy, a market guard walked over and asked politely if we had a permit to sell stuff at this bazaar. We really didn't know what he was asking for, but whatever it was, we didn't have it. It had really sacred both of us when we saw him approach. We thought that he was going to ask about the armbands—the white ID armbands embroidered with a blue star of David, which all Jews over twelve were required to wear. These armbands, like the yellow stars in the Third Reich, were to tell Jews apart from the Gentile population. It was hard to figure why Jews needed a special identity.[33] Long before the Nazi armbands issue came up, Jews, especially Jewish men, were already making sure that they'd never be mistaken for Gentiles, or for anyone else, for that matter, and their identification did not come on the thirteenth birthday but on the eighth day after birth.[34] Furthermore, Hasidim dressed in traditional satin robes, or gabardine coats; one could easily see the ritual garments with knotted fringes hanging from underneath their coats. They also wore special head coverings, beards, and earlocks. Still, the new law said they needed armbands to be identified.[35]

Nevertheless, after the license incident, Sala and I were careful not to linger too long around that market. We ventured into nearby streets, then into other neighborhoods. As we walked we told each other stories. Sometimes we'd pass some familiar places and we'd reminisce about our school days, friends, or teachers. Other times, we sang songs: school songs, folksongs, forbidden songs. While in the candy business, I not only enjoyed my freedom but learned from Sala, as well as from other sources, of many things that the teachers at school had never taught us.

The First Year

Sala turned out to be a great resource person. She was almost a year older than I. I was the youngest in our class and the oldest at home, while Sala was almost the oldest in our class and the youngest at home. She had an older sister and an older brother. I always envied kids who had older siblings. These kids had access to "special" information. They usually knew about adult movies, dance parties, special songs, and things I never heard of. In essence, I was not an envious kid. As a matter of fact, I never wanted anything that other people already had. I didn't need much to be happy; but I always dreamed about an older sister. I envied Gypsy kids who, barefoot and unrestricted, would run behind their covered wagons.[36]

Sala was telling me many stories about her life, and I was telling her about mine. I would tell her whatever came into my mind. I told her that my dad kept talking about how a long time ago, life was better. We had even had a nanny while Mom was still teaching.

I remembered visiting the old nanny in a retirement home. I also remembered a farm girl named Józia who lived with us and who helped Mom with the household. Józia got pregnant, and when she gave birth to a baby girl, she left us and went back to her folks on the farm. I remembered it well, because one day Aunt Naomi took me to visit Józia in the maternity clinic on Żelazna Street. The nurses did not let me in to see the baby. I remember sitting in the lobby crying.

These were the good times that I could recall. But as I grew older, at the age of about eight or nine, the economic conditions worsened. Dad was self-employed, and had to work long hours just to make ends meet. Mom didn't work at that time. Times were rough, but we kids didn't feel it. We always had enough food and clothing. No luxuries, but all the necessities.

I remembered the two dolls that we got from Mom's

My Education Continues

Uncle Heinoch. They were our Hanukkah and birthday presents combined. One of the ragged dolls was blond, the other brunette; both had braided hair. I let my sister play with both of them. I never cared about "playing house." When we did, with other girls, I was the father, and I went to work. Sis and the other girls did the cooking and cleaning, and tended to the babies. My favorite pastime, when I wasn't reading, was playing ball, usually with boys, or ice-skating, tree-climbing, or doing gymnastics. I also liked to play "Gypsy," preferring their lifestyle to ours because they didn't have to dress up or be bound by all the restrictions of our "civilization."

I remembered the summer that we spent, when I was five or six, in a village called Mrozy. I had a lot of fun there: I learned to pick cornflowers in the tall wheat, and to make wreaths for Grandpa.

Sala, too, shared many stories with me. She even told me stories about "the birds and the bees" in a way that wasn't explained to us in our biology books or in class. Actually, the first accounts of these secret tales I had already heard from Freda and Rena. But those that I heard from Sala were a continuation; more advanced, and more detailed. Anyway, I felt so grown up. I promised not to reveal the "source of these secrets" to anyone. Sala and I had a lot of fun together; almost every day I learned something new.

One day we went to the Piłsudski Square, one of the more prominent places in Warsaw. The square was named after Marshal Józef Piłsudski, a World War I Polish hero who fought for Polish independence. Piłsudski, who died in 1935, was especially respected by Jews for his liberal policies. After his death, though, anti-Semitism increased considerably. Now the square had been renamed "Hitlerplatz." The eternal flame that had once burned over the grave of the Unknown Soldier was now extinguished, and there was no one

The First Year

guarding it. German soldiers now occupied the buildings where government offices used to be.

Sala and I walked by a building where two gendarmes were standing guard. They looked at us and at the candy trays suspended from our necks; but said nothing. One gendarme who was on the other side of the gate came over. He said something to us in German. "I don't speak German," said Sala in Polish. She pulled the cover off her candy tray. "Bonbon," she said in German. Then she took out two zlotys from her pocket, showed the money to the gendarme, and added, "This much for candy."

Both gendarmes smiled. The one who had come from the other side of the gate switched his rifle to the other shoulder, took some change from his pocket, and asked, "Dobrze?"—"Good?" He showed us some German pfennigs. "This good Deutsch money," he said.

Sala looked at me. "Should we take it?"

"How do I know? I guess German pfennigs are as good as Polish groszy," I said.

"But how many of these pfennigs should we charge them?"

"Well, I really don't know. Let's take what they give us, and let's get out of here." There weren't too many people on the street that day. We hadn't sold too much. So we took the money.

Through a second floor window, soldiers were watching this extraordinary transaction, and one by one they started coming out of the building. They bought all our candy. "Come tomorrow," said one of the soldiers in broken Polish. "We want much candy." Sala and I thanked them, saying "dziękuję bardzo" and "danke schön," and then we left.

On the way home, we stopped at a gateway and counted our pfennigs. We still weren't sure whether taking the German money had been a good deal or not. (Later we found out it was more than we asked for.) We

My Education Continues

went back to the German quarters the next day, and the next, and were finally stopped by our parents when they found out. They didn't think that it was very safe.

It was not long after our soldier adventure that a new ordinance came into effect. It said that all Jews living in certain mixed sections of town had to move out, and that by a certain date they had to relocate to the Jewish section of town. No explanation was given. The sections mentioned in this decree were on our daily route. We started taking different streets each day to look for new customers; sometimes we took different routes, for safety or just for fun, or to break the monotony. On Bielanska Street we stopped once at the place called "Automaty," where there used to be an automatic confectionery shop that operated like a vending machine. I told Sala that I had always thought that there were people behind the wall who took the money and pushed out the merchandise. Sala said that she had never been there before; she didn't know. The store was now closed and boarded up.

"Do you remember the black man on stilts, the Negro man who advertised chocolate from the chocolate factory?" Sala asked me one day.

"You mean the one who used to give out chocolate samples?"

"Yes! Do you remember the day a bunch of us went there after school just to jump up and touch his hand to see if the blackness would come off? We got free chocolate samples."

"I'll never forget it! It was the first time I'd ever seen a real live Negro. All the other ones were in movies or pictures," I said.

Another day, we were walking home past Castle Square, right by the King's Palace. I told Sala about Dad's work at the Palace and about his encounter with the Germans and how afraid he still was to walk the

The First Year

street, even though the roundups had subsided quite a bit because of the new quota system.

(The Germans were still catching people off the streets to perform forced labor, but they were doing it to a lesser extent, and in many cases in a more "civilized" way. Providing the Germans with a free labor force was now the job of the Judenrat. The workforce gradually became more stable and better organized. In order to mitigate the terror that was aroused by the gangs that were seizing people at random in the streets, the Judenrat offered to provide labor battalions at specified times and in specified numbers for the use of the German authorities. Some German agencies continued their seizure of Jews in the streets; but many, however, were making their labor quotas known to the Judenrat, who would send notices to all Jews who were to report for work on a rotation basis. Rich and influential Jews could usually buy their way out. The Judenrat was using some of this money to pay the hired laborers. For many young, poor boys, subbing for the rich became a way to earn some money.)

When Sala heard about my dad's adventure with forced labor, she told me about her brother who was now making more money than he ever had before. His job was to work as one of these proxies for those who were assigned to do the free labor but who either couldn't do it or wouldn't do it. Hiring proxies and subbing for assigned labor had become a business, and Sala's brother was paid a small fortune by those individuals, who were glad to find somebody who dared to take the risk of working for the Germans. Sala and her siblings had always had a tough life. Her father died when she was only two. Until the War, her mother and sister were the breadwinners for the family. I did not know what her mother was doing, but I knew that her sister was a typist. She had a small office at home. I liked to watch her type three copies at

My Education Continues

a time, punching those keys through two carbons. Sometimes, after school, Sala and I played with the abacus or helped her sister fold papers and stuff envelopes. I was glad to hear that the sister, too, was doing well.

One summer morning, after we picked up our candy, we met Freda and Rena near the marketplace. The first question Freda asked me was, "Did you see Uncle Sruel lately?"

"Well," I said, "why would I want to see him?"

Freda didn't answer.

"But why would I want to see Uncle Sruel?" I repeated.

"Well," said Freda, "you should see the way he looks without his beard." She giggled. "He looks really funny. Two days ago, some German punks caught three traditional Jews and cut off their beards." Freda was getting more excited as she talked. "It was right there on Nalewki Street, you know, with all the people watching. The soldiers even took photographs! I'm surprised you didn't hear about it. You must go and see him. And while you're there, drop in to see us; Mom hasn't seen you for a while, and she always asks about you."

"I hope nothing like that ever happens to your dad!" I said, and I promised that I would go to see our uncle and visit Freda's family. They all lived in the same building.

Around the Plac Żelaznej Bramy, new announcements were posted. Sala and I stopped to read them. Names of the many streets from which Jews were required to move were on the bulletin boards. These streets were to be "Judenrein" by a given date.

Little by little, more streets in Gentile neighborhoods had to be free of Jews. Those who had to move, crowded into the Jewish section of town, to streets already overcrowded with the bombed out, the homeless, the refugees. These moves, it was explained, were necessary for the protection of the Jews due to some anti-Semitic outbreaks in the Gentile sections. Jews were given no choice in the matter, so they did as they were told. Jews in Eastern European countries were customarily very obedient to authorities. As long as Jews weren't bothered, they didn't bother anybody.

Here and there on streets bordering the Jewish section, eight-foot brick walls were being constructed so that " traffic can be rerouted because of congestion." The narrow wall that was built across the street from our house next to the thoroughfare was there, supposedly, to protect the German occupation forces stationed at the courthouses on Krasińskich Square and in adjacent Krasińskich Park. One time Sala and I took Chłodna Street while on our candy route. Just as we had the day before, we found that a wall had grown up there overnight.

Walking the streets every day, we kept seeing changes. Every day more refugees with babies in their arms and children at their sides were pushing belongings in handcarts and two-wheelers. And we kept seeing happy children jumping rope and playing ball in the streets, and restaurants filled with people sitting at window tables, eating good food; and we saw people lined up at the soup kitchens and those who couldn't stand up any longer lying on the sidewalks against buildings. And we saw beggars in the streets, along with vendors and singers.

One blind singer, led by a boy, had for many years earned his living playing his fiddle and singing songs for the people who would wait for him at their windows. He used to walk from one courtyard to another, performing. The neighborhood residents liked him because he usually composed songs about current events. Almost everybody would wrap some money—a few groszy—in a piece of paper and throw the small bundle into the yard. The boy who led him would pick up the money and put it into a small locked can that the blind man carried in his coat. Now the "Blind Man," as many called him, had a new hit song called "I Want to Go Home." In it, a man was describing the terrible conditions in refugee shelters—but these were not the shelters of deteriorating Warsaw but rather those in the Russian-occupied territories, to which most of the people who ran away from the Germans were taken. The lyrics talked about the inadequate food, the poor hygiene, the uncertain future.

I want to go back home
I'm a man from near Warsaw
I can't get used to your Russian life here
Thanks but no thanks for all your golden promises
I want to go back home
Hear me, brothers
I want to go back home

This song soon became very popular: It was very funny, but very sad, too. It was the kind of song that made people laugh to keep them from crying. It reflected the disappointment not only of the physical conditions in Russian refugee camps, but also of the whole new social system to which millions of disillusioned people had looked for new hope.[37] Many runaway Jews and Poles alike were actually returning from Russia to German-occupied Poland. Among the returnees were our two cousins, Haim and Moniek. Their families were glad to see their loved ones back.

Those who had no trust in the Communist system, especially the Hasidim, were even happier when they heard that the ventures of those running away were not working out. They had been warning the runaways all along about the "Godless Society."[38] Now they were

The First Year

saying, "I told you so."

The returnees, on the other hand, seeing the changes that had taken place while they were gone, were disappointed anew. They didn't know about the shortages of all necessities, the armband IDs, the unemployment, the Jews moving out of Gentile neighborhoods, the intersections being walled off. Often they found their rooms or even their beds rented out to people who were paying good money to the tenants who could make places for them.

After many streets in the Gentile sections became Judenrein, the Gentiles living in the Jewish part of town were ordered to move out. This order included the Gentile building-keepers who had for years lived and worked in the Jewish buildings. They were part of the establishment. Their multipurpose job was to keep the building complexes in order, safe, and clean. A good keeper usually knew who lived in the building, and who didn't. He questioned all suspicious persons entering the premises. Generally, all building gates were locked by eleven at night, and only those who lived in a particular building were allowed in. People returning home after the established time knew that they had to tip the keeper. In some buildings such as ours, the keeper, Józef, was instructed to keep out beggars, street singers, performers, Gypsy palm-readers, and other wandering performers and trespassers who, like the Blind Man, would venture from one courtyard to the next to show their skills; often performing acrobatic feats, playing instruments, or eating fire.

Now, with all the refugees pouring in, Józef lost track of the inhabitants. He wasn't even trying to identify the tenants, and he was no longer worried about keeping out the wandering entertainers.

Outside of his regular duties, a Gentile building-keeper in a Jewish tenement had one additional function, namely, to light fires and to turn on lights for

My Education Continues

the Orthodox Jewish tenants who would not do such chores on the Sabbath. For this he was paid by those who used such services.

Anyway, we were very sorry when Józef had to move out of our building. We were losing a friend. And even stranger than losing Józef was seeing a Jewish keeper take his place; taking care of buildings was hardly ever done by Jews.

Besides Józef, we also lost other neighbors. A few of them we were glad to see move out, but for most of them we felt very sorry, and we were heartbroken to see them go. As for our family, we missed our next-door neighbor, Pan Rys. He was a government official, but since the occupation he had been assigned odd jobs. His last words to us were, "We'll see each other as soon as this mess is over. This cannot last too long."

A few months before, while it was still winter, we had been hoping and praying for spring to come. "If we can only survive till spring," we thought, "we'll surely have it made." For a little while, it looked as if something better were actually going to come. After a few days of commotion, with walls going up, and people moving from district to district, life began to stabilize. Even the rumors had subsided.

But things didn't turn out the way that we expected. As spring came, then turned into summer, hardly a day would go by without new ordinances, new decrees, and, with these last, new rumors.

Sala and I were still running our candy business. We worked every day until noon. It felt good to get out into the streets after being cooped up in the building during curfew hours.

It had been a while since we last saw Freda and Rena in the market. One day, Sala asked me how the girls were getting along; she wanted to know if I ever went to see Uncle Sruel with his beard cut off.

"I'm sorry, Sala dear," I said, "I just forgot to tell you. I did see him a few days after Freda told me about him. Well, let me tell you the story from the beginning. On the Sabbath after we met Freda and Rena at the market, Mom, Sis and I went to visit Uncle Sruel. Mom had not seen him or Aunt Hanna for quite some time. She thought it would be nice to go. I didn't tell her about the beard. When we walked through the door, Uncle was sitting at the table reading a newspaper. My first impression of him was, 'Boy oh boy, does he look neat!' Believe it or not, Sala," I said, "it was the first time I had not thought of him as a very old man. He looked much better and much younger without that long reddish beard. 'Nice of you to come!' he said, looking at Mom.

"Mom glanced at his face. 'Well, you see what has happened to me?' he asked. He sounded like a broken man. 'Ah, Uncle,' Mom answered with a sigh. Tears filled his eyes. He was trying to hold them back, but they began dropping down his cheeks and into the rugged whiskers that were the leftovers of his beard.

"Mom said she was sorry for what happened. Sis and I didn't say a word; we weren't sure what to say. When he stood up, and we saw the long traditional gabardine coat he was wearing, and without his beard and earlocks, he looked funny."

"I hope you didn't laugh," Sala said, feeling sorry for the old man whom she didn't even know.

"No," I said, "We almost cracked up, but Mom pulled me by the hand. Sis and I just looked at Uncle Sruel."

Then I told Sala about how Mom had talked with Aunt Hanna, who gave her a detailed account of the whole "beard-cutting incident." She said that Uncle Sruel had been lucky, that one of the three men caught in the incident had protested, so he was

My Education Continues

beaten; the soldier who did the cutting hacked out a chunk of the protesting man's face along with his beard. Blood covered the man's coat and the ground below. "Can you imagine the pain that the guy felt, and the humiliation all of them had to endure? How could young punks do such a thing to older men?"

Aunt Hanna gave each of us a glass of tea and a piece of homemade cake. Then, as I expected, Aunt Hanna started talking about her son. Ever since Mordekhei had left for Palestine, she cried constantly, lamenting his absence. She was sure that he had done the wrong thing by leaving his family and venturing into the world. She wasn't sure if she'd ever see him again. But now, suddenly turning to Mom, she said loud and clear, "Do you know, my dear, I am really glad that Mordekhei is not here to see what is going on in this place."

From Uncle Sruel's home, we went to visit Freda and Rena and their parents. A refugee family was now living in the room where we once lived. Aunt Rachel showed Mom a postcard that she had received from her daughter, Bluma. It had come from some remote place in central Russia. It read, "I am fine. I am going to school learning to be a nurse. Please don't worry about me. Give my regards to all. Hope to see all of you soon." The way Aunt Rachel cried when she read that card, you'd think that her daughter had just died. Later, I heard Mom talking to Aunt Rachel about Tante Trude and Uncle Harry. The two were still translating papers, Aunt Rachel said. All the papers that they worked on for the Judenrat had bad news for the Jews.

Indeed, the news kept getting worse as the summer was coming to an end. Many more streets were being blocked off. Sala's brother was still working as a proxy in the "free labor force," and was now a part of the Jewish crews being forced to build the walls to blockade more intersections. Besides the general problems in the city and the country, we had a tragedy in the family. Cousin Balka, one of Dad's nieces, was run over by a truck. People said that it was an accident, but others insisted that it was a suicide, that she had purposely run into the path of the truck. Those who said that Balka had committed suicide would not say whether her deed had had any relation to the War and to the worsening conditions, or to some personal problem, such as a disappointing love affair. It really didn't matter to the family. The fact was that at the age of nineteen, she was dead, and it was a great tragedy for all of us.

Besides having to deal with her death and the difficulties with funeral arrangements (because of the many deaths and the crowded cemeteries), the family also had to worry about Jewish laws that interfered with burial procedures. The first problem was that of an autopsy. According to Polish civil law, all bodies related to accidents, or those of any unnatural cause of death, were to be taken by ambulance to the nearest hospital in order to have the cause of death determined. (There were dozens of suicides and accidental deaths in Warsaw every day, even before the War started. People from small towns would come to the big city to do what they would not dare do in their small hometowns. Lost love affairs, unwanted pregnancies, business bankruptcies—all used to bring many suicidal prospects to Warsaw. People used to jump out of the windows of tall buildings or off bridges. They ran under streetcars and buses; some poisoned themselves, or cut their own wrists. The newspapers were full of such incidents.) The Polish autopsy law was very strict. The Jewish law, however, forbade autopsies. Workers from an organization called "Jewish Watchers of Death" would cruise the streets of Warsaw day and night to make sure that they and not

My Education Continues

the Polish police claimed the corpse.

Besides the problem of autopsy, Balka's family had to deal with yet another problem, that of burial and mourning. Jewish people who did not die of natural causes had to be buried close to the fence, on the far side of the cemetery; also, the family was not allowed to sit shiva. (During the whole tumult, I found out something that really surprised me: Balka was not Aunt Bella's natural daughter. Balka and her older sister, Fronia, were Uncle Yitche's children. Aunt Bella married a widower with two children, just as her sister Sara did, but Aunt Bella had adopted the girls. To me it made no difference. Balka was my cousin, and I really liked her. She used to give me her outgrown ice skates, games, books, and other things that she no longer used.) I didn't realize how much additional trouble was created by Jewish laws. There was a big commotion with rabbis on all kinds of legalities—whether Aunt Bella was an official mourner or not, and so forth. In the end, Balka's body was returned to the family; it was not taken for an autopsy. I heard people say that the hospitals had no shortage of bodies, but they did have shortages of personnel. Because of some connections Uncle Yitche had, Balka was not buried at the fence. This spared the family some embarrassment. Uncle Yitche and Aunt Bella both observed the seven days of mourning. Balka's sister, who with her boyfriend had fled to Russia, was spared the pain of ever finding out.

Neither my sister nor I were at the funeral. Our family thought that we were too young. We did go to visit Aunt Bella during the mourning period. Both Uncle Yitche and Aunt Bella were sitting on low stools. The mirror was covered over with a white sheet. A candle was burning on the small table in the corner of the room.

Chapter 8. Typhus

With the summer and its warmer weather came the bedbugs, and with them, typhus. When the typhus epidemic started, it hit mostly the young. A large part of the population over the age of twenty had developed some immunity to this dreadful disease during the typhus epidemic of World War I. Trying to prevent further spread of the epidemic, authorities ordered special procedures that had to be followed: Disinfection brigades were instituted to check its spread. All cases of typhus had to be reported to the health department. All patients diagnosed with the disease had to be taken immediately to a hospital. All apartments in the building from which the diseased person had been taken had to undergo a thorough disinfection. All tenants had to be checked for lice and then be sprayed with disinfecting powder. The entrance gate to the apartment complex had to be closed during a quarantine period of ten to fourteen days. Thus the families of the sick and the unexposed alike were imprisoned in their homes.

The first typhus case in our building was Masha, the eighteen-year-old daughter of our neighbors, the Gurfinkels. Her parents did not report her illness for fear that she'd be taken to a hospital, and die there.

My Education Continues

The percentage of patients getting cured in the hospitals designated for Jews was known to be negligible. The hospitals were overcrowded, understaffed, under-equipped, short on food, and lacking in medicine. Most patients were taken there to die. Doctors and nurses worked under these trying conditions with rationed food, heat, and light.

After a week, Masha died, at home. When the burial agency came to pick up her body, there was no way that this case could be hidden from the authorities. The front gate of our building was locked. Guards were put on the outside of the gate to prevent anyone from leaving or entering the building. The inhabitants were stuck without food or other necessities. It became common practice that relatives or friends would bring by some food and pass it through the gate railing. Sometimes, black marketeers stopped by to visit the quarantined people and charge them even higher prices than they normally would have.

There was also an underground exit in the building that led from the third courtyard to Fraciszkanska Street. It was originally built as an escape route during the bombing period. If it were ever discovered, it would not only have been walled up, but many people would have been arrested and, most likely, executed. I was sure that the opening had been used during the quarantine period because some food was coming into the building during the night.

Aunt Polla, Dad's younger sister, brought us some bread and potatoes when she heard that our building was locked up. She passed it through the gate.

Besides the problems with food, there were also problems with disinfection. The disinfection process began as soon as the building was locked up, which was as soon as the sick person was reported to the authorities. A schedule was made so that by the end of the quarantine period, all apartments and all inhabitants would have been taken care of. The disinfecting powder that they used could kill not just the germs but those who were carrying them. Men, women, and children were taken into a designated room to be sprayed and checked for lice.

Sis, Mom, and I walked through the ladies' control and the spray stations. At the exit door, as we were getting our documents stamped, a young man from the sanitation department glanced at Mom's long, unbraided hair. He stopped her, touched the hair with his fingers, and told her to braid it up. Then, without saying a word, he took a pair of large scissors that were intended for cutting lice-infested hair, and cut off the thick, heavy braid hanging over Mom's back. He put it on the table and said, smiling: "Gorgeous hair, isn't it?"

We walked out heartbroken, not only because of the lost hair, which would eventually grow back, but because of the way he had cut it off. By now, anybody could do anything to a Jew without any retribution, without any concern for justice: It was "open season" on Jews.

I had never seen Mom with short hair. She had always worn hers in a Grecian knot. She looked somewhat strange in short hair. I carefully looked at her sad face. I had never before paid that close attention to her looks. She was my mother, and that's the way she looked. I knew she had lost weight since the War started. Now with short hair, she actually looked younger and better, I thought.

Anyway, our irritation with the hair incident did not last very long, for the next morning I woke up with a headache and fever. The first thought, of course, was "typhus."

Mom put her hand on my forehead, then the thermometer under my arm. The temperature showed

My Education Continues

39.5 Celsius. She gave me a pill that she had been keeping for an emergency, and said, "If the fever is not down by tomorrow morning, we'll have to hide you somewhere. Our apartment is scheduled for disinfection tomorrow." Then she sent Sis down to our Aunt Sara, Grandpa's sister, who lived in our building complex, so that Sis would stay away from me (even if she had very little hope that Sis had not already been infected).

Mom looked fearful. Two doctors lived in our building, and at least one of them would come if asked. But there was always the danger that he might be seen and followed. Besides, there was very little he could do with his bare hands.

Lying in bed with a wet towel over my aching head, I saw Mom blotting her tears with a cloth. Her voice broke, tears gushed from her eyes, and when she saw me looking, she quickly turned to hide them; but she had difficulty repressing her sobs. I saw her, turning her face away from me, walk out into the hall.

That night we went to see one of the doctors. Dr. Flanzman was an older gentleman who, like my dad, was afraid to go into the streets for fear of being caught in a roundup. He also had another fear of going out: When the Germans first came into Warsaw, they had shot a few doctors along with some professors, clergymen, and other intellectuals. His fears were well founded.

Anyway, Dr. Flanzman looked me over, shook his head, and said to Mom, "I am not sure what your daughter has, but it does not look to me like typhus. Watch her: If she develops a rash, it might be that she has scarlet fever."

By morning, I still had a fever, but I felt well enough to leave the room when the sanitation workers arrived. My illness continued for a few more days, and then it was gone.

Chapter 9. The Ghetto

It's assumed that "nothing lasts forever," neither the good nor the bad, but I'm not sure if it's also assumed that "neither the good nor the bad has limits." Every time we thought that we'd reached the abyss, there was still room deeper down.

More than a year now had passed since the Germans occupied Warsaw; a fearful, distressing year, in which many grievous decrees had been passed, most of them concerning Jews:

- A Jew had to be identified by a white armband or a yellow star.
- Jews could be assigned to or rounded up for forced labor.
- Jews had to tip their hats before Germans, and walk off the sidewalk when passing them.
- Jewish children were banned from schools.
- Jews had no right to assemble or to pray.
- Jews were moved out of Gentile neighborhoods and into a section of town designated "for Jews only."

My Education Continues

Luckily, we didn't have to move. Our building was the last one on the block at the Jewish side of the dividing line. On one side was Bonifraterska Street, also known as the new "East-West Thoroughfare"; across the street, as I've already mentioned, was Krasińskich Park. From the front windows of our building, we liked to observe German soldiers stationed in the park as they washed their topless bodies with freezing water or rubbed them with snow.

Every street beyond the park and thoroughfare belonged to the Gentile neighborhood.

Between the end of the park and the next building, which housed government offices and courts, was an alley leading to Krasińskich Square. This alley was now blocked off by an eight-foot brick wall topped with broken glass and an entanglement of barbed wire. The wall had been put up recently, built on the order of the German authorities with Jewish forced labor. It was constructed from bricks and glass found in the rubble of burned-out houses. The reason given for the wall was "to protect the German soldiers stationed in the park from the Jews who would infect them with typhus."

Adjacent to the wall, across from our house, was the block-long Appeals Court building, with an archway through which ran the "East-West Thoroughfare." Every day, thousands of people passed under that arch in order to go from the Żoliborz suburbs to the Castle Square, or over the Kierbedzia Bridge that crossed the Wisła River. When selling candy, I used to go through this archway almost every day, usually on the way home. But one day, something had changed at the archway.

It was on one of the Jewish High Holidays, I am not sure which. It could have been Sukkoth; but it is hard to remember for there had been no tabernacles built or decorations put up.[39] Everything in those days was

The Ghetto

very irregular, and untraditional. Because it was a holiday, I didn't sell my candies. And I remember that it was Dad's turn to have the prayer services in our house. Ever since the decrees had been announced that Jews had no right to assemble, all synagogues had been emptied of worshippers and filled with refugees. To conduct prayer meetings, Jewish men would get together a minyan and perform services in private homes.[40]

This one day, when the men started arriving to our house for services, Sis and I went for a walk. Across from our building, next to the archway, was an unusually large gathering of people. They were talking emotionally, flapping their arms; some were nervously walking back and forth, cracking their knuckles.

"Let's go over there," I said to my sister, and pulled her toward the archway. As we got closer we saw two Jewish men standing near the arch.

"Where do you girls think you are going?" one of them asked.

Before we had time to answer we saw, on the their side of the arch, two Polish police officers, two German gendarmes, and a huge German shepherd.

A woman pulled me by the arm. "You can't go through here. The gate is closed today." And she walked off.

Sis and I started paying more attention to what the people in the crowd were saying. No one really seemed to know what had happened, but they were all asking the guards the same question: "When will the road reopen?" There was no answer given. No one knew. The officers would only give the names of a few streets that were open to traffic between the Jewish and Gentile sections.

Sis and I ran home. I told one of the praying men, the one standing closest to the door, that I had something important to tell Dad. The man didn't

My Education Continues

answer but kept on praying, pointing to the door: He was showing me the way out.

I was angry—angry not only because he wouldn't let me in, but because I felt that it was something new, something important, I had to tell my father. It wasn't something silly; I was going to tell Dad about Jewish policemen who were standing guard at the gate. They weren't wearing uniforms, but people said that the cops could be identified by a pin they wore under one of their lapels. They belonged to a group called "The Thirteen," or "Trzynastka," a newly formed Jewish police force. (The name came from their address, Leszno Street 13.) Some people were calling them "collaborators," even though some had not volunteered for the job. But no one in this crowded prayer room wanted to listen to what I had to say; no one was interested.

Finally, Dad came out of the room; he put his forefinger over his mouth: "Sssh...be quiet," he whispered. "The service will be over in ten minutes. Go get your mother. She is downstairs at Aunt Sara's house." Sis and I walked down to Aunt Sara's.

Mom seemed to have already heard about what was happening at the arch. She said to us not to worry, that there were many other streets open, and we could use those if we needed to go somewhere. People were already talking about it. "There's too much traffic going to the Royal Square. Some dignitaries are coming from Berlin."

Actually, all kinds of rumors had been going around since Rosh Hashanah. For it was on Rosh Hashanah, on the anniversary of the terrible bombing, that the Nazis officially proclaimed the establishment of a ghetto—a section set aside just for Jews. A date was given by which all Jews were supposed to have moved to the designated one-hundred square block area and all non-Jews to have left it. The road across

The Ghetto

from our house never reopened. To the contrary, more roads were closed. And one drizzling November day, without warning, all entrances to the Jewish section were closed: The ghetto was sealed off.

At first, the Nazis tried to disguise the ghetto as a quarantine to prevent the spread of the typhus epidemic that was getting worse day by day. Then, once all Jews were in the ghetto, there were no more excuses necessary.

Gradually, the walled-off city became a separate world, self-administered by the Judenrat, with no German troops or Polish police inside it. (They were placed outside the walls and at each entrance point.) The ghetto had its own Jewish police force, sanitation department, even bus service. It seemed odd to see Jews in positions that they had never held before.

To cope with the new situation, Jews developed their own way of life, their own economy and welfare system. Ignoring German orders, the Judenrat set up more soup kitchens, more medical facilities, more mortuaries, and many clandestine underground education centers free to those who could not pay.

Again, as with all previous decrees, people were trying to adjust to new circumstances that they could in no way change.

What happened in the Warsaw Ghetto after that, I am not about to describe. I won't even try. It is beyond description, surely beyond my writing abilities. I only want to give a general view of that ghetto, and concentrate on the events that were directly connected with my own experiences and those of the people who were important to me.

If I should give a summary of life in the ghetto, I would simply say, "It was a sample of the inferno, an abyss of the Gehenna. Nothing that I have ever read or heard compares with it. It was the pit of human

My Education Continues

suffering. There was isolation, depression, epidemic; a feeling of world rejection and indifference; a feeling of complete hopelessness. Everything other than dying was prohibited. Going from the ghetto to hell would probably have been a welcome vacation."

And yet, most people held on to life. Of course, there were some who lost hope, and some who committed suicide; but they were rather the exception. The majority, surprisingly, chose life. They didn't want to give the enemy the satisfaction of dying on command, or on Nazi terms. Besides, suicide was against Jewish law.

Part of the scant food that was allowed legally into the ghetto was usually stolen and then sold on the black market for enormous prices. The small amount of food that finally crept into the stores was distributed on ration cards. The lines were endless, and there wasn't food for half of the people in the lines.

But food was only one of the problems. There were extreme shortages of heating fuel, lighting supplies, clothing, and hygiene accessories. The typhus epidemic was also spreading, and there were few medical supplies.

During the autumn months, right after the ghetto had been sealed off, a dying person in the street would attract a lot of attention. Passersby would gather around the motionless but still breathing body, trying to help. Sometimes an onlooker would give a piece of bread or a glass of water, or would offer to take the dying person to a shelter.

By the time winter set in, people were not only starving but freezing to death. It was no longer unusual to see men, women, or children dead or dying in the streets.

Hunger drove some people to madness, and many to death. Those who died in their homes were no better off than those who died in the streets. Often the bodies of

The Ghetto

the deceased who had died at home were hidden for long periods of time so that the families could collect the precious food cards allotted to their loved ones. Those who died in the streets had their ID cards stolen for the same reason. So many bodies soon to be corpses lined the streets that, after a while, those who were still able to walk didn't even bother to stop. Besides, there was hardly anything anyone could do but stare.

Many faces of the deceased were distorted beyond recognition. Even if someone did recognize a friend or relative among the rows of corpses, he would not acknowledge it, in order to spare himself, and the family, the high cost and complicated procedures of the burial.

Occasionally, an observant Jew—if he was not a Kohen[41]—would stop and cover the corpse with its outer garment, or with a newspaper, if he could find one; he would then weigh down the cover with a brick, so that the wind wouldn't blow it off; and with a few passersby, he would form a minyan and recite the Kaddish, a three-minute prayer for the dead, which sanctified God and asked that "the blessing of peace, and the promise of life, come true, and that the One who causes peace to reign in High Heaven let the peace descend to us."

With the mourners' Kaddish now finished, all assembled would say "Amen," and, with a sigh or a tear in their eyes, continue to their destinations. Sometimes one could hear a worshipper say to himself, "Dear God, when, O when, will all this end?"

Once I stood with Sala and watched the Kaddish being recited over a little boy's body. I whispered to Sala, "You know, we all prayed a lot in the bomb-shelter, and it did not help one bit. Our home was hit by a shell anyway. And the one Orthodox, Mr. Greenfarb, who never came down to the bomb-shelter because God would help him, well, he got killed."

My Education Continues

One of the men in the minyan, a traditionally dressed, bearded Jew, must have overheard what I said, because right after he said "Amen," he turned to me and very politely said, "Let me tell you something, young lady." He was focusing his eyes on the ground during the whole time he talked so as to avoid looking directly at me (for by now I was developing feminine features).[42] "The rabbis tell us that it is man's duty to bless God for the evil that befalls us, as well as for the good."

I was not very impressed with what he had to say. The only reason I remember the incident at all is that for the first time somebody had called me "young lady."

He said a quotation from the Bible. Then he said, before leaving, "I hope that you remember that God tests all of us. I assume you remember the story of Job."[43]

I didn't know the story, but I said nothing.

Besides the Kaddish reciters, two other kinds of people would stop at a dead body: those who would undress it so that they could either wear or trade the clothes, and those employed by the Pinkert Burial Organization. Both of them had to work fast. The first had to make sure that the boots came off before the legs became swollen; the second had to load the corpses onto their jinrikishas (trailered bikes and three-wheelers) and get to the cemetery before curfew hours.

A large number of those fading away and dying in the streets were refugees who had no place to live, nothing to sell or trade, and no connections. Everything in the ghetto went by connections, by knowing the right people in the right places. Also, being knowledgeable about bribing procedures could assure more ration cards, a job in a German workshop, a pass to the outside world, and other miscellaneous privileges. In many cases, local people had the advantage over newcomers, but not always. There were many local people who didn't know how to go about doing anything that was not legal; and there were many newcomers who did. Those who did everything by the law, by God's commandments, and by German rules, had barely a chance of surviving. They were starving and freezing, condemned to die. To defy the legal system was to become a sinner or a criminal. But abnormal conditions put people into a difficult situation; given the predicament that they were in, one decision was as bad and dangerous as any other. It was either waiting for a slow, drawn-out death by starvation, or getting into smuggling and black-marketeering, for which the penalty was also death (but usually a quick one: execution on the spot, even for children). Such executions were carried out without trials: a bullet in the head—quick and easy, and often painless. (Severity of punishments would depend on individual guards and their discretion, and mood. They didn't have to answer for their actions to anyone if their victim had been a Jew.) Many people had to make the crucial decision regarding which death to choose: the quick and easy death, or the long, drawn-out starvation and sickness. For the ultra-Orthodox Jews, there was no decision; the answer was easy. They were sure that God would intervene, because in His Divine Wisdom, He always knew what was right for His people; "If it is God's will that we suffer," they reasoned, "we should not defy His judgment."

For others, making such decisions was not easy. Aunt Naomi made hers early on: She decided to fight the system. Before the War, she had been a hard-working seamstress, sewing ladies' corsets and bras in a small workshop that she shared with two of her cousins, Mina and her sister, also named Naomi. The three of them were not rich, but they had been making enough to make a nice living for themselves. Now their workshop, like the rest of the economy, was legally dead, and Aunt Naomi had to find a way to support herself. Our aunt was tall, fairly slim, like Grandpa, and like most relatives on Mom's side of the family, she had blue eyes and light brown hair. During these unnatural times, she decided to take advantage of her Aryan looks, her looting experience, and her familiarity with the black market, and began traveling in and out of the ghetto, trading with farmers and Gentile smugglers.

Like many other established and new black-marketeers, Aunt Naomi was now doing quite well financially. The black-marketeers did not see their jobs as wrong; they saw them as legitimate business. According to their view, the only crime that they were committing was refusing to die of starvation. These black-marketeers were the only connection with the outside world. They were bringing into the ghetto food, fuel, soap, medicine, and other necessities; and, of course news. They were also providing raw materials for artisans, who were keeping busy making shoes, clothes, luggage, and other items in demand outside the ghetto. Without this trade, the ghetto population would have been condemned to death.

Black-marketeering took a lot of knowledge and skill; Aunt learned many tricks of the trade. Our cousin-friends Freda and Rena were still trading luggage; Sala and I were still selling candy. We had even added a new department to our business: We were now bringing sugar and candles into the ghetto. We were just small entrepreneurs who were crossing the border through gates that, at this time, were not well guarded; or we were slipping through friendly crossing points, where the guards were not doing their jobs properly; or we were going though places where the guards were paid off. Usually, whenever we made it

The Ghetto

through the crossing to the other side, we felt quite safe. Without the armbands, no one could tell us apart from the general population—unless, of course, we were stopped for questioning, as often happened to Jews as well as Polish black-marketeers.

Again, like all times before: as long as there were no new decrees, people adjusted to their troubles, constantly repeating the old Jewish saying, "Please, dear God, protect us from the conditions to which we human beings are able to adjust." Those who wouldn't or couldn't adjust were dying like flies (which were not dying; they were actually thriving, so long as they could keep close to the ground and feed on the dead). But as soon as people began adjusting and finding ways to live under prevailing conditions, new rules would go into effect. "Better," more reliable, guards were put on crossing points, and many underground passages were boarded up. Each passing day, it became riskier for us to get out of the ghetto.

Sala and I had to give up our entrepreneurship. Freda and Rena stopped theirs, too. Smuggling and black-marketeering were no longer for kids and amateurs; they had become the job for professionals. Only the big operators could stay in business. Prices soared. The smugglers justified their high prices by citing the high operating costs and the risks involved. They needed a lot of bribe money. Everyone down the line, from people who sold them goods, to those who helped transport them, and even guards—Germans, Polish police, the Jewish patrol—everyone from the bottom distributor to the highest-ranking officer, all had to be paid off. All wanted to get in on the game. Often, even people who just happened to see or know of the transactions, wanted a piece of the action: They extracted money for not informing the authorities. Those who did stay in business, if caught, paid with their lives; if not, they got rich. With the money they

My Education Continues

made, they would buy for themselves and their families places in the German workshops. As workers they were not only legally paid, but they also received special ID cards that enabled them to have privileges, such as not being sent away to forced labor or being shipped to one of the concentration camps that were being established all over the country.

But for us four girls, who had to give up our businesses, life was not so good. Eventually, each of us found something to do. My job was in our building: a combination of babysitting and instruction. I had to watch four six-year-olds, three girls and one boy, and teach them some elementary reading, numbers, and songs. The curriculum was given to me by their parents. I worked four hours a day, six days per week. Each day we would assemble in a different kid's apartment. In addition to a bit of money, I also got some lunch from one of the host families (and occasionally some of the food that the kids didn't eat). Yes, even during this period of starvation, there were people who still had plenty of food in storage, plenty to eat, even leftovers. I especially liked the days when we would assemble in Hadasah's home. This little girl in my group, whose father was in the fish business, was a fastidious eater. There were almost always some leftovers from her plate to help my hunger pangs.

In our house, we kept going through different stages of need, depending a lot on Aunt Naomi's luck and on the trading prices on the black market, where we were now trading our possessions for food. At times we had some in the house, at times we had nothing. Like that one day when the only thing in our house was a raw onion. I remember how we feasted on it, and how we kept washing it down with cold pre-boiled water. Looking at each other we could see tears rolling down our faces, or an occasional mouth bend that could be considered a cry or smile as the chewed-up nourishment glided down the esophagus. I remember this onion meal especially well: It was among those recorded in my diary. There were more such days, especially after I stopped venturing outside the ghetto and Aunt Naomi couldn't make it home. Sometimes, for days, there was nothing in the house but a bucket of cold water and a jar of boiled drinking water, which we kept in reserve. Even boiling the drinking water was not a simple matter. The damp, green wood was either not available on the black market, or not affordable. We had to use boards from the bombed-out rooms, or pieces of broken-up furniture for firewood. And even these were slowly coming to an end. Boiled water was almost a luxury item.

Another luxury item was soap. We kept in reserve a multipurpose washbowl of soapy water. We used it to wash ourselves, then to wash our clothes, then to wash the floor. There was hardly any water to dispose of by the time we were finished washing things. We didn't need too much of this luxury item anyway. By now, our house was clean most of the time; there was nothing to make it dirty: no garbage, no trash, no dirty dishes, no flies, no bugs. We could open the windows and enjoy the fresh air and not have to worry about flies or bees coming in. Even the usual smoke from the factories had ceased to exist. After a while, even the mice and rats that used to visit frequently after the bombing, disappeared.

Even the days when there was some food in the house, I was hungry. I was constantly hungry. My body, just emerging into adolescence, demanded nourishment. My knobs had turned into small boobs, and more people were now calling me "panienka"—"young lady."

Mom sewed, by hand, two of my dresses into one, making a lot of room at the top. Like many other women in the same predicament, Mom had become

My Education Continues

not only a very inventive seamstress but a scrupulous washerwoman, and a proficient cook. As the saying goes, "If you don't have what you like, you learn to like what you have." Not being able to buy what they needed to prepare a meal, those former housewives were now learning how to prepare meals out of the available food items. So-called "hot foods" had nothing to do with spices but were perishable foods occasionally available on the market for fair prices in moderate quantities. One time such an item was rotting cabbage. We ate cabbage for a week. When it was gone, there were weeks of absolutely nothing; then, frozen potatoes. These we had for my birthday latkes.

"Stinkies" was probably the hottest, most memorable, item to hit the city markets. It was supposed to be fish, but it actually was a component of the fish species that looked something like the waste from a fish processing plant. The largest piece in the mess was the size of a broken sardine. This mess, too solid to pour and too mushy to pick up by hand, was doled out with a ladle. It was first put into a bowl-like dish in which it was first weighed, then transferred into a customer's container. One kilogram, including the water, was allotted per customer. Whenever a shipment of this delicacy arrived in the stores and the "aroma" spread throughout the neighborhood, it would lure thousands of people out of their homes and into long lines. "Stinkies" was the only source of protein available to the masses. And here again, only the lucky ones, or those with strong elbows, were privileged to get some of this "fish"—even though this mess came in adequate amounts. (Through Hadasah's father, who, as I have already mentioned, was a fish merchant, we had good connections to the "stinkies." Through his intercession, we used to get extra doses of this delicacy.) Preparation of this delicacy depended again

The Ghetto

on luck—on the availability of water for washing it, of wood or coal for cooking it. Gas and electricity were rationed, available only two hours a day (in the Jewish section, usually after midnight hours). Again, into play came the ingenuity of the ghetto housewife. In many cases, the women would make joint "stinkies" projects. One woman would supply the "stinkies," one the fuel, another the flour or bread crumbs, salt or spices, whatever could be organized. Out of this mess they would make little patties and call them "gefilte fish." Whenever this gourmet food was served, we would have a party.

Hadasah's mother had no problem with food. She only worried about her looks. I liked to watch her put on her makeup. She beautified her eyes by lighting a match and then darkening her eyebrows with the burned-off tip. For lipstick, she used specially prepared red beets.

When it was her turn to host the kids, she would feed me well. I especially remember a Sunday when she gave me two bowls of soup and some bread to share with her daughter. It was the first food I had had since Friday. (Saturday was my day off.) I swallowed both bowls, offering the girl only a small piece of bread. I couldn't believe my luck when Hadasah said, "I don't like that lousy bread; you can have it."

On the days when we did have a bite of food in our house, it was my job to take some of it to Grandma Esther. For years, Dad and his brother and two of his sisters had contributed to Grandma's support. Sister Sara, who was the poorest, and Sister Polla, who was single, were excluded.

Grandma was now bedridden; only her mind was still intact. She appreciated the food that I would bring. She would ask about our family, and she would never forgot to tell me before I left, "Be careful going home, my child. You must survive this madness." On

My Education Continues

the way from Grandma's house, I could stop to visit with Freda and Rena. They lived not far from Grandma Esther.

Lately, the girls' parents' health was declining. Their father's luggage business had shriveled, but he was still making a living, which, in the ghetto, was no small matter. Doing any business now was so much more difficult. The girls were no longer venturing outside the wall. A professional smuggler was now taking out the luggage and bringing in raw materials, a procedure which was substantially diminishing their income. Yet Aunt Rachel would always give me some food whenever I visited. Sharing food was something very few people were willing or able to do in the ghetto.

On the way home from Grandma's I also would stop to hear news from and about other relatives. Usually there was nothing good to report. At the beginning, when coming home from these visits, I used to give Mom and Dad detailed accounts of what I had seen and heard. (Later, when the news got gradually worse, I would only answer questions. Mom and Dad could read my face before I said a word. They often wouldn't even ask. They knew if I was bringing good news or bad.) Uncle Louis had had to move from his Gęsia Street apartment. I don't remember where he moved to, but I can still see the one small room and the iron bed in which Aunt Tova lay sick. Before the bombing Aunt Tova had been a vigorous woman in her mid- or late-forties. But since her son Abram died of the infection that set in the thigh of the amputated leg, she had become a listless old woman without any interest in life. To her, life was no longer worth living, with one son dead and the other somewhere in Russia. She lingered a few months. By the time Shlomo decided that he didn't like the Russian adventure and chose to return home, she was dead.

The Ghetto

From Aunt Sara we never expected any good news; but one time we did get it. While visiting Grandma, I learned that Sara's stepson, Marek, had come home from the German POW camp, along with many other Jewish prisoners. Neither he nor anyone else I talked to knew why they had picked only Jews to send back. I went to see him. He looked worn out, but seemed to be in good health. It was the only time since her husband's death that I ever saw Aunt Sara smiling. She had visited us only a few days before Marek's unexpected appearance. She had been depressed and resigned, crying. With her two children she had spent the night in the hall on the floor: She had missed the curfew. Now I was glad to report that Aunt Sara was well and happy.

On Mom's side of the family, things looked a little better. Grandma Ruth and Mr. Granddaddy were doing fine. They were still getting food parcels from Mr. Granddaddy's son, Gersh, the Sandomierz miller. Often the packages would arrive opened, and part of the food missing from them. Grandma Ruth would share some of the food that was delivered with the mailman. (It was always advisable to tip the deliverer if one wanted to get the next package: It was a "live and let live" proposition.) I always got something to eat and something to take home whenever I visited Grandma Ruth.

Aunt Devora, my deceased Grandpa's sister who lived on Muranovska Square, was doing well, too. The day I visited her, she was standing beside the stove rendering goose fat. She wiped her hands on her apron and said with a smile, "Come in my little girl. Oh, my! How you've grown!" She told me to sit down, then asked about our family and about Aunt Naomi.

As she started to pour the rendered fat from the pan into containers, she offered me a few cracklings and a slice of bread. I hadn't seen cracklings for almost

My Education Continues

two years. Hard to tell where she was getting such luxury items in these trying times; but to think of it, all three of her husbands were well off. The one who had died, Uncle Motel, had left her with a lot of money. The one whom she had divorced gave her his first wife's fur coat and some jewelry—things which she was constantly showing off. The husband to whom she was now married was also well off, but he was also a sick man who, along with the money, was giving her a lot of trouble. Aunt Devora had only one child, a daughter who was married and had a little girl.

My sister was getting along well, too. She really liked the little boy whom she was babysitting. His parents were treating her nicely.

My sister was the exact opposite of me not only in appearance and in character but in behavior as well. She liked nice clothes, and she played girls' games and with girls' toys. She liked to stay close to home, in a secure place, near Mom and Dad. There were, of course, certain things that we liked to do together. We played games, picked flowers, collected books, and visited relatives. The only common friends we had were Freda and Rena. Each of us had her own as well.

Halinka was one of Sis's school friends. She used to visit us quite often. One day Halinka came over and asked if my sister would like to join a class that was now forming. Miss Alla, Halinka's older sister, who was a third year university student (and like all Jewish scholars, had been thrown out of school), had decided to give private lessons in her home to elementary and high school students. Halinka said that she had already spoken to Alla, who had agreed to take my sister into one of her classes free of charge.

Ever since our school closed down, Mom had tried to teach Sis and me at home, but it hadn't worked out too well. Mom was always worried about something.

The Ghetto

There was no food in the house, no heat, no light. Many friends and relatives were sick, many dying. Sis and I wouldn't listen or do our homework; we would fight about "unfair" grades. Mom was still giving us lessons, but we weren't really learning the way we should have been. It had been a long time since we'd been in school; worse yet, no one could predict when we'd return.

Of course, sister accepted Halinka's offer, and she joined Miss Alla's class. Everybody was happy for my little sister, and so was I. Mom wrote a nice appreciation letter to Miss Alla thanking her for her consideration and offering to help if the need came up.

Before starting her class, my sister asked me for my last year's textbooks. It was then that I realized that my sister, thirteen months younger than I, would soon catch up with me in school: Such a disgrace must never come to pass!

I organized six of my peers and formed a class. We went to Miss Alla for lessons. Miss Alla was giving "discounts" to those who could not afford to pay the full price.

The first sentence that I learned in my French class was: "Donnez-moi un morceau de pain"—"Give me a piece of bread." The sentence was not even in my French book, but it was the most appropriate at the time. Working half days, going to class, and doing homework in the afternoons, took away a lot of my freedom. There was little time to roam the streets or to visit relatives. All of my reading and writing had to be done during daylight hours. Kerosene was scarce and candles very expensive.

In history class we studied the First Crusade, Genghis Khan, the Tartar Invasion, and the plague during the Middle Ages. "Is this war, too, going to be history?" asked Riva, the smallest girl in our group. All of a sudden our eyes lit up. We were all happy. "Hey,

My Education Continues

we are living through real history! Our stories will be in history books!" we screamed almost simultaneously.

"What is our period going to be called, Miss Alla?" asked Malka, with a smile.

The discussion made us feel, well, important. It made us feel as though all our troubles were worthwhile. Not in vain.

The situation became even more difficult as winter approached and the days got shorter and the curfew hours longer.

Paying no attention to the walls or to the guards at the gates, cold winter winds kept entering the ghetto streets and the homes. They blew the coverings that were spread over the corpses, often exposing the naked bodies that had been stripped of their clothes. Then came the rains and snow; and added misery.

On the way to class, which was on Nalewki Street, the view was shocking. Every day an increasing number of dead bodies would be lining the streets. Occasionally I'd pass a small child sitting by the fading body of a mother or father. These children didn't cry. They didn't talk. Often their eyes were closed. When they were open, one could read in them what the child was unable to say. Once in a while a stranger would stop, maybe cover the parent's body. No fuss. A policeman sometimes would come over and take the child—probably to the already overcrowded orphanage on Grzybowska Street. The policeman would write something in his notebook.

I come home and record this in my diary.

As I keep walking down the streets, the picture is dismal. I observe and absorb.

People just keep on walking. By now dead bodies in the streets are being disregarded. Just another dead Jew. A vehicle from the Pinkert Burial Organization comes by. The man picks up the body, piles it on top of the other corpses. The cart rocks slightly. The body shakes as though it were still alive. I think that I will get immune to the sight of corpses. But I never really do. Not to the sight of dead and dying children, to those skinny, toothpick legs and distended stomachs. I ignore them for my own protection.

Pinkert's carts circle the streets from curfew to curfew, picking up as many corpses as they can handle. They can hardly keep up with the accumulation of the dead. Jewish law requiring that a body be buried within twenty-four hours of death is completely ignored. The bodies picked off the streets are buried in common mass graves at the Brudno Cemetery in Praga, located on the east bank of the Wisła River—a place outside the ghetto walls.

The Jewish cemetery on Okopowa Street—inside the ghetto—is filling up quickly. Without large sums of money and special connections, no one is being buried there any longer.

The Praga cemetery, being outside the ghetto, has many drawbacks. Families are prevented from attending burials and they are barred from visiting the gravesites. On the other hand, burying people outside the ghetto has one advantage: It provides a new smuggling route. Horse-drawn hearses never drive empty. One way, they deliver a load of corpses; on the return trip, they are loaded with food, fuel, soap, and medicine, for those whose turn has not yet come, or for those who simply refuse to die. The hearses go through the gates often unchecked. With good bribes, they just show their papers and get them stamped.

As I walk to my classes, I walk past the corpses. The carts are passing me by. I go to my lesson. I meet my friends. Miss Alla is waiting, her books and lesson plan on the table. We are taking one subject each day. Language arts in Polish, of course; math, which includes an introduction to algebra and geometry;

My Education Continues

science, geography, history; and a foreign language: Latin (of which Miss Alla admits to knowing little) or French (the only foreign language that she knows quite well).

Learning serves more than one purpose: it does more than just fill our brains with knowledge. It keeps us off the streets, and our minds off our constantly growling stomachs. For the two hours of the lessons, and the time during homework, we don't think about the winter, the dead, the dying; for a little while, we believe that we are still human.

In Poland, snow comes early. It is not unusual to have snow lying on the ground from October to March. Everyone in the ghetto, even the rich and influential, dreads the thought of winter. Snowed-in highways, impassable roads, frozen pipes, illnesses, all of these affect everyone. Even the rich find no escape.

Not only the Jews but the Gentiles, too, will be freezing and starving if the winter is long and severe. Yet, somehow, people believe that "Things must get better, because they just cannot get worse. If we could only make it through the winter."

We live on a diet of hope and new rumors. "Shipments of food are on the way." No one knows on the way from where or to where, but people are talking to keep up the morale. "The Germans are still settling down; they have problems of their own. Once they're established and settled, things will change."

Of course, things have been changing all along. Nothing ever stays the same. Ever since the occupation started, things have been changing—changing for the worst. But people believe what they want to believe, what makes them feel better, what makes their hopes rise, what they must believe in order to survive.

The House Tenant Committee that was organized during the quarantine period to help with common

The Ghetto

problems, starts meeting again. They discuss what can be done in case of frozen water pipes and broken latrines. These problems came up last winter when there was more fuel than there is now. The committee also discusses the problem of beggars who come from the street into the courtyards. Luckily, this year the committee does not have to worry abut rats, mice, bedbugs, or lice spreading over the buildings. If these creatures want to survive the winter, they must move outside the ghetto or else feed on frozen corpses.

The Committee decides to throw a potluck Hanukkah party for all the teenagers in the complex. Everybody contributes something—candles, food, or decorations. One of the apartments is designated and prepared for the party. The tenants of the designated apartment squeeze in with neighbors for the evening. All arrangements have been made by the tenants and the committee.

I remember that party quite well. It was the first time that I had ever gone to a party without my parents or my sister. I was a little scared, and at the same time very excited. The party started with the lighting of the Hanukkah candles. Then we ate some food: bread slices, boiled potatoes, some cabbage. We danced to accordion tunes and to recorded music. We sang songs and told jokes. We sang about Pinkert's burial company's booming business, about the rats and lice and mice that had moved out of the ghetto for the winter; we joked about the problems and advantages that people encounter while living in crowded conditions, where there is no place to undress but always a warm body next to yours. We talked about Hitler's funeral, and what the world would look like after this mess was over. One guy said that peace would come to the world only after "the widow of General Franco came to a dying Stalin to announce that Mussolini had suffered a fatal heart attack at

My Education Continues

Hitler's funeral."[44] Despite all of our war experiences, and no prospects for the future, people still had very naive ideas: They hoped and actually believed that there would be a time when the world would achieve a just and lasting peace, if only these four dictators would disappear from the scene.

This was my fourteenth birthday, and my first dance party ever. On an old cranked cylindrical gramophone, we scratched out many hit songs from collected records. Some of those songs I had already learned from girls in my class who had older siblings; others I knew from radio and from my aunts and cousins. I met many new teenagers, kids from other buildings in our complex whom I hadn't seen either in our bomb-shelter or in my school. Many were older, some even as old as nineteen, who had no place to go. They were locked in their houses because of the curfew. That night I had my first dance with a boy. His name was Jerzyk. He had been attending his first year of tarbut when the War broke out. He, like most Jewish boys, had had to study Yiddish and Hebrew, know his prayers, and learn the secular curriculum prescribed nationally.

We talked about school. He said that he, too, was taking private classes, but his were taught by a rabbi. I didn't know what else to talk about with a boy, so we just stayed with the subject of school: educational trips, teachers, secular education versus religious education. Then we talked about books that we were reading in our respective schools.

We had our "Dutch treat": a cookie and a glass of lemonade. For a while at least, I forgot about the freezing outside, and about the hunger pangs in my belly. The apartment where the party took place was hot. The source of heat was the crowd gathered there. It was the first time that winter that I ever warmed up. (We even opened a window to get some fresh air.) We

The Ghetto

danced and talked till the lights burned out. It had been agreed beforehand that the party would last only as long as there was kerosene in the lamp and the candle lights burned.

When it was time to disperse, Jerzyk, shyly, and in an unskilled manner, moved my hand to his lips and, imitating a gentleman, kissed the top of it. I thought that I'd die of embarrassment.

It was almost midnight when I walked into our dark, cold room. I knew then that the party was over.

At about eight in the morning a few days later, Cousin Khava showed up at our door. "Grandma Esther died during the night," said the fifteen-year-old girl in a voice mixed with yawning. Holding her hand over her mouth, she added, "Sorry; we didn't get much sleep. I had to wait until the curfew was over so that I could come here." Khava and her mother, Dad's oldest sister Leah, had stayed the night with Grandma. Living with Aunt Leah were also two other sisters, Aunt Bella and Aunt Polla.

Dad knew that his mother hadn't been doing well. He had visited her only a few days before and taken it on himself to bring her some food. She was feeling badly, but her mind was still intact. She was still worrying about her children, especially her sons. Their visits made her nervous: She didn't think that it was safe for her "boys" to be in the streets unnecessarily.

Dad, hearing the news, got up and prepared himself to go to Grandma's home and meet there with his brother and sisters. He knew that it was now his job, and that of his brother, to make the funeral arrangements. Before leaving the house, Dad wrote down a list of names and handed the paper to me. "Go, and tell all these people about Grandma," he said. "But first run over and tell the kids you work with that you

My Education Continues

will teach them in the afternoon." Dad then took his niece by the hand and they both left.

Later, when Dad came home, he talked about all the problems that he had encountered with the funeral arrangements. All funeral workers and vehicles were booked up already. They were picking up heaps of bodies from homes, hospitals, and in the streets. Even with money, it was almost impossible to get an individual gravesite. The Brudno cemetery in Praga was filling up. The one in the ghetto was out of the question.

Dad said that if it hadn't been for Uncle Louis (who within a year had buried his son and his wife, and therefore had developed some experience in these matters), Dad alone could not have made the preparations. After some bargaining, the price was agreed on, and paid up front. Grandma Esther was to be buried on the afternoon of the following day, in the Brudno cemetery. This meant that no one, not even her sons or daughters, would be allowed to attend the burial since it had to take place outside the ghetto. The funeral procession would be able to escort the hearse to the ghetto gate, from where the body would be taken by attendance to the cemetery. It was agreed that Grandma would be buried in an individual grave, and that a temporary marker would be put up.

I didn't work that day. In the afternoon we all went to Grandma's home. The neighbor next door opened her apartment and invited in some of the people who came to call on the family. Grandma's two sisters, her nieces and nephews, and friends came. It was cold outside, and some snow was on the ground. There were people in both apartments and some in the hall, blocking the stairway.

Grandma's body lay in the living room on the floor, covered with a black pall. She was resting on scattered straw, her feet toward the door. Only the two candles

The Ghetto

burning at her head gave some light to the otherwise dark room. The mirror was covered with a white sheet. An old, bearded man was sitting on a low stool, chanting prayers.

As the curfew hours approached, everyone left. Only the two sons, the people who lived in the building, and the old man reciting prayers, remained for the night.

Next morning, a few women came, washed the body, dressed it in a takhrikim, the traditional shroud, and prepared it for burial. The rabbi came. He said a prayer, then he "cut kinim," providing each mourner with a strip of black cloth.[45]

Late afternoon, and four hours behind schedule, a horse-drawn hearse arrived. Grandma's body was placed in a box for transportation to the cemetery. We walked behind the hearse only a few blocks, to Zamenhofa Street. There, some more bodies were picked up and put into the hearse. All four of Grandma's daughters wept when the hearse moved away; Aunt Polla cried the most. Some friends tried to quiet her down, explaining that no one lives forever, that her mother had lived a long, productive life, that "the two years she lived past seventy were, it's said, a gift from heaven, a favor from the Almighty."

The sons and daughters tried to obey as best they could the seven days' mourning period. According to custom, they should have stayed in Grandma's house for the duration; however, the rabbi ruled that in an emergency certain laws could be modified, and so the mourners were required to stay in Grandma's home only from curfew to curfew. During the day, all the mourners sat on low stools. The candle that was burning in a corner was watched constantly and carefully so that it wouldn't go out.

Aunt Leah, the most observant of all the siblings, sat in her stockinged feet. Dad had stopped shaving

My Education Continues

the day Grandma died. Uncle Louis always wore a small goatee, so his appearance did not change; Dad looked funny, though.

Every morning and evening, a quorum of men gathered for services. The sons recited the Kaddish.

During the day, friends and relatives dropped in, calling on the mourners and bringing tiny bits of whatever food was available, if only to make sure that tradition was not broken.

They talked about Grandma and her family. They said she had had a hard life, but that she had lived it in an honorable manner. She married at the age of sixteen, lost a couple of children in childbirth, and one of her sons was killed in battle during World War I. Grandma's husband, the father of all her children, died during that War, too. (I don't remember the cause of death, but I know that his name was Sheye, like Aunt Sara's son, who was named after him.)

I met a lot of Dad's relatives whom I hadn't know before. Besides Aunt Polla, Dad was the youngest of Grandma's children. Out of the fifteen cousins, there were only four who were around my age; all the others were much older. When Aunt Polla was born, her sister Leah was already a grandmother. I knew all of my aunts and uncles and all my first cousins, with the exception of two. They were Aunt Leah's very Orthodox sons, who didn't look at or talk to girls, not even cousins. (I saw them a few times, but they always turned their heads so as to avoid looking at me.) I never knew how many other relatives Dad had; I just remember that when Grandma died, they came in bunches. I had no idea who belonged to whom. I was being introduced to them as Dad's oldest daughter.

Almost all of them asked me the same questions: "How old are you? Where do you go to school? What grade were you in when the War started?" Some asked me what I wanted to be when I grew up.

The Ghetto

I was thinking about Grandma Esther, about how she hadn't liked for us to speak Polish; that we attended public school. According to her, good Jewish girls should have been taught Yiddish and know how to behave on the Sabbath; and how to pray. Grandma had seldom come to our house. Since she got old, it was hard for her to climb the steps. But that was not the only reason. She was skeptical of Mother's kashrut, even though we kept what I thought was a kosher home. The suspicion had started on one Sabbath day, a long time ago, when Grandma was visiting our house and caught my mother warming tea on a gas burner. Grandma had had a special kettle on the coal stove that would keep water warm all through the Sabbath; there had never been anything cooked or heated in Grandma's house on the Sabbath.

In the ghetto, Grandma did start eating Mother's food, but only after the rabbi had assured her that in an emergency it was okay, that kashrut restrictions had been somewhat relaxed because of the emergency. They called the rule "B'Kuah Nefesh," a law that applied in special situations whenever people's lives were in danger. The ghetto surely was such a situation.

Shortly before Grandma's death, we found out that Gucia (of the candy enterprise) had a new business. She wanted Mom to come and see it. The visit had been postponed because of the funeral and the mourning period. Besides, Mom had reservations about going to Krochmalna Street. In a very unexpected move, Dad offered to go with her. What they found out was that Gucia's candy business started declining when the connection with the Gentile customers was cut off. There were not enough Jews in the ghetto who could afford candy.

Now Gucia had switched to producing apple jam, a product that could be more useful and practical for

My Education Continues

ghetto consumption, and more affordable, too. She wanted to know if we would be interested in selling her product. Mom and Dad made one decision on the spot: "The kids are not going to do any more selling." But an idea flashed through Mom's head: She was going to try her own luck in the business world.

Mom had not worked for years. Before she married Dad she used to teach in a private school. Then two things happened to turn her career: One was the new requirements for teachers that would have sent her back to university classes, and the other was her new responsibilities to her husband and children. Her life shifted from being professional person to housewife and mother. From what I could gather, Mom had started by giving private lessons—tutoring students in preparation for college exams. But all this was many years ago. Now, Mom thought, was time to think about work again.

When Mom and Dad returned from Gucia's house, they were still discussing the offer. They talked until late into the night. Mom said that she was no longer willing to sit idly by and watch us all starving—or selling our possessions for nothing. She had cried over every item that she had to sell because the only things we still had were heirlooms given to her by her mother and father and her grandparents. And she was getting sick and tired of cleaning "stinkies" at home, or of spending all her days in food lines.

She was now recalling the humiliating experience that she had had a few weeks before while standing in a bread line. Her voice broke as she spoke:

"I was so glad that day," she almost sobbed, "to finally get a half loaf of bread, when this guy grabbed it out of my hands. I didn't know what to do. I think I screamed. Deep in my heart I felt sorry for the poor soul. He was dirty. His tattered clothes were full of snow, icicles hanging from his unshaven face, his feet wrapped in rags." She sighed. "Yes, I think I did scream, because I remember a Jewish policeman came over to ask me what had happened. (You know, there were always policemen on duty when bread was being distributed.) But before the cop had time to look around, that weak flimsy guy took the half loaf he'd grabbed from me and stuffed it into his mouth, and then, like a snake, he swallowed it while everyone was looking."

As if talking to herself, Mom added, "I will never forget that scene, but I am going to make sure that it will never happen to me again. I am going to do something about the situation, whether it be legal or not." Then in a really strong voice, she said, "If it's illegal to live, that's too bad! I'm not ready to die; at least, not yet!"

I'd never heard Mom talk that way before. Even Dad seemed shocked. "I can't believe it's you," he said. "Quiet down, please; you'll end up with another migraine."

They talked about the horrifying ghetto conditions, about the few months of winter that were still left before spring came; they talked about other depressing things, too. Mom said to Dad, "Aren't we fortunate that at least our kids are being fed at work?" Dad listened but said nothing. He must have been feeling guilty for not being able to do anything about the situation. He did not dispute what Mom was saying. He must have known that she was right.

Mom was always a quiet person. Not even the abhorrent conditions would make her take part in gossip or idle talk. She had a small circle of friends and relatives. She never even knew many of our neighbors before she met them in the bomb-shelter. Mom spent her free time in libraries, picking out books for herself and for us. She read a lot. Dad read, too, but mostly newspapers and magazines. Mom devoted a

My Education Continues

lot of time to my sister and me. She took us to movies, theaters, and shops, or just window browsing. During the Christmas season, when the display windows were artistically decorated, we really enjoyed looking at the decorations. In nice weather, we used to go to parks and on small trips.

Now Mom sounded like a strange person. Influenced by Gucia's talk, she decided to become a saleswoman, a business person. "I am not going to hope for miracles any longer," Mom said, in a reassuring, resolute voice. "I am going to do something constructive. I am, at least, going to try."

Mom now knew more people than she had ever known before. She got acquainted with many tenants in our building, at the shelter, and in the courtyards. There were no other places to go after curfew, and not much room or work at home, so people were spending more time in the courtyards, staircase halls, and gateways, in order to save on candles and kerosene. They met to talk and to discuss their problems. Even though Mom had not taken part in these meetings before, she now thought that it would be a good way to meet people. Besides, all these acquaintances might become customers. Mom had gotten to meet many relatives at Grandma's funeral and during the mourning period, many of them Dad's cousins, aunts and uncles, whom she had almost forgotten. Out of these friends, relatives, and acquaintances, she compiled a list of potential customers. In the ghetto one did not have to be a salesperson in order to sell. One only needed merchandise, and to know people who could afford to buy it.

Gucia gave Mom the first earthen pot of her jam on credit, on a "pay me after you sell it" account, something that she never did for any of her customers.

Slowly but surely, in snow and sleet and in below-freezing temperatures, Mom started going to Gucia's

The Ghetto

house to get her merchandise. She went by Jewish Public Transportation—a ghetto bus, one with a Star of David on it that circled only inside the ghetto. (Streetcars that carried Gentile passengers never stopped in the ghetto; they just zoomed through on a few designated streets. Aryan buses went around the ghetto.) It wasn't long before Mom had established a nice business. She even retained a few steady customers.

After a while, however, picking up the pots of jam from Gucia's home became a very difficult chore, and dangerous, too. Besides, Mom did not care for going across town, especially to Krochmalna Street. Sometimes Dad helped, but it was unsafe for him to be in the streets. He was pushing his luck too far as it was. After a long conference with Gucia and her husband, Mom and Dad decided that it would be better and safer if Mom learned the procedure for making jam and started making it in our house.

They agreed that Gucia was going to teach Mom the trade, but only on the condition that Mom buy the ingredients from Gucia and her husband. This was okay with Mom, especially since Mom had no connections and did not know how to go about buying the required ingredients. There was only one more issue before Gucia would give Mom the first lesson: The apples and sugar needed for the jam, Gucia said, had to be prepaid. Mom sold one more of her cherished heirlooms—and began her business, her first-ever enterprise. She finally was doing something constructive, something that made her feel useful and happy. (But it did not stop her from crying over the earrings that she had had to sell. Now, the only piece of gold that she still had was her wedding band.)

The night we cooked the first pot of jam, everyone helped. Sis, Mom, and I cleaned and washed the apples. It took a lot of willpower not to eat them. It was

My Education Continues

the first time Dad had put on an apron. He looked really funny. His job was to mix the jam in the heavy caldron that we had borrowed from a friend, and to tend to the fire.

It was past midnight before the apples were cooked for the prescribed amount of time and then poured into smaller containers. It was the first time that winter that our room was warm, and that we didn't have to blow out the candles and spend the evening sitting in the dark. Finally, Sis and I went to sleep. When we went to bed, we knew that the stuff that looked and tasted like applesauce would gel by morning.

Next morning, the stuff still looked like red applesauce; it didn't even resemble jam. Mom looked worried. Later in the afternoon, when I came home from work, Mom was sitting on a stool, looking into one of the "jam" containers. I looked into it, too. Nothing had changed from the night before. It was still applesauce. Mom looked pale. Red rings under her eyes suggested that she had not slept much that night. She might have been crying.

Something had gone wrong; she didn't know what. She was certain that she had followed all of Gucia's instructions, that she had written down everything that Gucia told her. Now all her heirlooms were gone, and so was the money. So were the apples, and surely her customers. But most of all, what was gone was her hope.

We ate some of that applesauce; we sold some for very low prices. Mom explained to her customers, who, for the most part, were friends and relatives, what had happened. They most likely bought "that stuff" more out of pity than because they liked the product. We lost, what was to us, a lot of money. On top of the money, we were now forever obliged to the customers who hadn't let us down, who had let us recover from the money losses and the disappointment.

The Ghetto

After the initial shock, Mom went to Gucia, taking with her a sample of that "sauce." The mystery was solved in no time at all. One of the ingredients was missing. Mom hadn't put in the gelatin. She had never heard of such an item. It was not on her list. Gucia told Mom that she used apples and sugar. Mom thought that the jam was made with saccharin because sugar was too expensive. Gucia insisted it was made with pure sugar, that she never cheated her customers. The discussion centered on the sugar versus saccharin. Gucia thought that she had told Mom about the gelatin, but Mom didn't write it down. Anyway, that was how Mom learned to make jam. She wrote off the losses as payment for education, or, as it is said in Yiddish, to pay "Rabbe Geld."[46]

The next batch of jam came out perfectly, and Mom was in the jam business. She was proud of her jam and of herself. And we were all happy and proud of her.

When things settled down, and people started adjusting to the conditions, new ordinances came up. After a while, the source of apples was cut off. The apples that did occasionally trickle into the ghetto were all frozen and could not be used. Besides, they were too expensive. We were out of business again.

This time, however, we had accumulated enough food and fuel in the house to last for a few weeks. Luckily, neither my sister nor I had quit our jobs. I lost two of my kids: One moved out of our building; the other kid's parents could no longer afford to pay. I tried to keep the little girl named Romka, but her parents didn't think that it was fair for me to work without pay. I did gain a seven-year-old girl named Lucia. Somehow, we all thought and hoped, "If we just make it to spring, things will improve."

My Education Continues

Spring finally did come. Our family had made it through winter. We were the lucky ones; thousands had not. The only thing that improved in spring was the weather. We didn't freeze, and the days got longer. In Krasińskich Park, we could see the trees budding and green blades of grass peeping out from underneath the melting snow. The warm rays of the sun warmed our frozen bodies and gave us new hope.

But conditions did not improve. To the contrary, there were more shortages and more deaths and more rumors. Yet the optimists had the ability never to lose hope, and so people believed either in the lies that were much nicer and more believable than the truth, or else in the propaganda being spread by the Ministry. Or they would make up rumors that "Mr. X said that he heard from Mrs. Y about Mr. Z, who knows...." People started believing in dreams, hopes, and imaginings. They had developed a special survival skill: "Push away, or wish away, or reason away, all unwanted or dangerous thoughts. Filter out all depressing notions. Believe in miracles, in fairytales, in God." In spring we lived on a diet of sunrays, rumors, and hope. With the warmth and the sun, the flies, lice, bedbugs, and rats resumed their visits to the Jewish neighborhood. We weren't sure whether the rats were Aryan or Jewish; we only knew that they were allowed into the ghetto without special permits. Wherever they had spent the winter, they could not have had such an abundance of food as awaited them in the streets of the ghetto. They came back to keep us company as they had the previous summers.

Passover holidays were approaching, and the Jews started preparing whatever they could find in order to make the holidays special. The rabbis—now even the Orthodox ones—were making many adjustments in order to acclimate to the prevailing conditions. Under the pretext of "B'Kuah Nefesh," they allowed many things to be eaten that otherwise were strictly forbidden on Passover. Bread was still considered treif, not pure for consumption; but beans, peas, and many other previously forbidden foods, if available, were allowed during the Seder, as well as for the duration of the eight-day holiday.

Aunt Naomi came. We also invited Aunt Sara, Grandpa's sister, the one who lived in our building, and her two grown daughters, Irenka and Natka. They didn't have to worry about the curfew. Mr. and Mrs. Gurfinkel, our next-door neighbors, were also asked to come. Their daughter now dead, and their son with his family in Russia, they were alone for the holidays. The refugee family that had settled into the Gurfinkel's apartment, spent Passover at a shelter house where a Seder was prepared for those who could not otherwise have it.

Charity organizations were no longer giving out matzo coupons to the poor. They invited those without food for Passover to join in a common Seder.

We still managed to put together our Seder. Our meal consisted of a few matzoth, some turnips, and a soup that was made of salted water and some parsley. We still had some cherry wine from that carboy that was saved from the bombing, even though we had used some of it the previous Passover. (We had tried to save some for good luck for the next year, hoping to celebrate the holiday in better times.)

Dad, like always, read from the Haggadah, and talked about the miracle of the Red Sea, about how Moses, with God's help, took the Jews out of Egypt. Mrs. Gurfinkel and Aunt Sara cried. Aunt Naomi and the two cousins talked about the miracle, but in their voices and smiles was some irony, a sense of skepticism. Sis and I talked about the times when we used to look forward to this special spring holiday; when we used to get new clothes; when the house was specially cleaned up and decorated; when we used our Passover dishes, the ones reserved for this special holiday alone. (These dishes were extra special. Mom's brother, Uncle Mendel, had given them to us when he returned from his trip to China and Palestine. Uncle Mendel and Aunt Helena had no children. They owned a textile workshop specializing in knitted sweaters and shawls. They used to travel halfway around the world, often for business, sometimes for pleasure. They settled in Palestine next to Cousin Mordekhei. The summer of 1939, a few months before the War broke out, they came back to Poland because Uncle had wanted to visit the grave of his father. He was overseas when Grandpa died, and he had missed the funeral. Now, he had come to put up a monument for his father and perform his obligation as a son. When the War broke out, he and his wife were stuck in Warsaw; they couldn't get out. That's the story of Uncle Mendel and Aunt Helena. They lived in the ghetto on Fraciszkanska Street.) Our Passover dishes, the ones which they had given us, were all shattered during the shelling. The only two cups that remained we had saved as reminders of the "good old days."

As at every Seder before, we sat until past midnight, chanting songs and telling stories. This time, Mom had a surprise for us: She had baked a potato cake for dessert. This Seder was a sad affair, but we still praised God for His wonders, and we admired His miracles and His wisdom. As the candles burned down, we sang praise-songs: "God is One, There is no other in the universe." The Seder ended with new hope and faith in miracles.

Next morning, we saw men walking to services that were taking place in neighborhood apartments. They were going to praise God for the miracle of taking the Jews out of Egypt. "The holidays must go on. Jews must pray," they were saying.

The Ghetto

Right after the German troops crossed the Russian frontier, in June, 1941, life in the ghetto took a turn for the worse. Hunger was so wide spread that even those who had survived the winter thinking that nothing worse could happen, were now not only starving but losing hope and their will to fight on. Corpses from the streets were being gathered like rubbish, thrown aboard hand-drawn cards, and buried in mass graves. People were no longer worried about where or how to bury the street dead. The perplexed Judenrat had been issued orders by the Nazi commander to clean the streets and bury the dead; and to take a census of the Jewish population by age, sex, and occupation, and provide the Germans with workers. In addition, the Judenrat had to account for the non-productive people—the old, the sick, children.

The Germans made sure that everything was done punctually and in exact order.

News from the Russian Front came in daily. It was suggesting that the German troops were penetrating deep into Russian territories. Newspapers were announcing the achievements of the "Super Race."[47] No one really knew which part was the propaganda and which was the truth; but many Poles coming from the East were confirming the German victories. The Nazis considered all of Russia a backward country, not even worthy of existence. The Poles were not much better: Their culture was not even worth preserving. Jews were not even regarded as human; and Gypsies were in the same category as the Jews. Such was the way in which the Germans stratified those not belonging to the "Master Race." To them, invading the Russians and ruling others was a god-given right. So the victories over Russia were taken by the Germans as a matter of fact.

As news of victory came in, news in the ghetto grew worse. Fewer Jews were willing or able to resist; more

My Education Continues

Jews were being shot, more were being sent away to various camps. Even the greatest of optimists wouldn't dare to predict when the craziness would pass. For almost two years they had been saying, "It cannot go on like this much longer." Most of the time they had been right: It hadn't continued to go on "like this"; it had kept changing for the worse. Jews were now being ordered to surrender all their tangible belongings: gold, silver, furs, small items like rings, earrings, fur collars; even fur cuffs and muffs. Germans needed money for the Eastern Front.[48] German soldiers needed warm clothes for the soon-approaching Russian winter. Some of the Jewish possessions were forwarded to Germany, to German wives, sisters, and mothers, whose men were fighting for the "honor" of their country. For the Jews there was a death penalty for non-compliance with the new ordinance.

Later, pianos, sewing machines, cameras, and valuable rugs also had to be turned in. All these items had to be taken to an assigned point. Trucks were waiting to haul them away. (In this situation, prices of these commodities kept falling. Those Jews and Poles who wanted to risk their lives and buy up these "forbidden" items were looking for bargains.) When the occupying forces first entered Poland, everybody had to surrender weapons, Poles and Jews alike. That was understood: It was for the protection of the occupiers. But what was happening now was outright robbery. People were astounded; they didn't know what to do. Many started burning their small items instead of giving them to the Germans; others hid their possessions under floors, in cracks, wherever they could think of. I heard of some people who threw their silver into the trash or gave it to a stranger who would smuggle it to the "Aryan side," just so it would not go to the Germans. But what was one to do with such things as appliances, musical instruments, rugs, or furs? Was it worth risking one's life over such things? Most people complied with the order; others broke up the items just so they wouldn't go to the enemy. Those who kept the forbidden items were risking their lives.

Before we had adjusted to this new ordinance, another was on the way: Jews had to report to the authorities and the police all non-Jews who were hiding inside the ghetto. This was not a new decree; the old one was simply being more strictly enforced. And there were greater penalties for non-compliance. The Germans were looking for communists, criminals, political opponents, and instigators who were supposedly hiding inside the ghetto. If the order was not followed as commanded, the whole ghetto would pay the consequences.

There was no end to the decrees and the torments. Mom walked around with an expressionless look on her face. It was strange that she had stopped having her migraine headaches. Under so much stress and with so many worries, by all logical means her headaches should have been getting worse. Instead, to everyone's astonishment, her condition improved; the headaches had become less frequent and milder in nature. Mom had changed. She did not read much. She didn't even care. She was constantly hungry; she was losing weight. The lack of food and hope was having its effect on Dad. I never remembered him being sick. Now he was walking slowly, helpless and depressed.

I was not doing well, either. I had lost one of my kids. Little Lucia had just stopped coming. She was sick. The little boy, Bolek, was still coming, but his mother could not afford to feed me lunch. I still had Hadasah. Her parents were still relatively well off; they had food every day. They were among the few who did. By now, most of the people I knew were starving.

We suffered not just from our own hunger and grief

My Education Continues

(even though they were devastating) but from seeing our relatives and friends going downhill, enduring so much pain. We had to stand by, helplessly, and watch people around us die. We didn't cry any more; most of us had long used up all our tears. Those who could still cry were lucky; a good cry could ease some of their mental torture.

Older people took it much harder than did the younger generation. Youth still thought of the future, of good times to come. Even on hungry stomachs, young people still talked of love, were falling in love, and, of course, making love. There were still gatherings and parties, songs and jokes. The worse the conditions became, the more jokes were made about them. Often a dangerous, unsuccessful smuggling trip, was turned into a joke, as whenever German gendarmes stuck their cold hands under the garments of women smugglers under the pretense of looking for hidden contraband.

One evening, while coming home from a teen gathering in our courtyard, I walked in on a discussion that Mom was having with Dad.

"What do you want me to do?" Dad was saying. "People are dying in the streets; I have no place to go.... I have borrowed money and food everywhere I can. I have no idea how to pay it back."

Dad stopped talking for a minute when he heard me walk in; then he continued; he just couldn't stop. He was finally saying what had been on his mind: "At forty-four I am too old to even apply for the workshops, even if I had the money. To do any business nowadays one has to be rough, strong, dishonest—either a right-out crook, or a soulless devil. One needs to rob and lie and push...." He stopped and took a deep breath and looked at me; he just sat there as if to say, "Why does this girl have to listen to all this." But after about a minute he started talking again as though he had to

The Ghetto

finish what he had started.

"You know what the rules of the ghetto are? Bribing, smuggling, price-gouging, manipulating, squealing; and I have none of these talents; I have not learned any of these skills. The people who can still make it the honest way are few and far between; they are very lucky or just happened to be at the right place at the right time." He talked nervously, but not angrily, as if to say, "If I want to survive, I'd better learn some of the new survival skills, or get out of the house and start looking for luck."

Mom sighed and started crying. I left the room.

It was about a week after this conversation that Mom and I went to visit Grandma Ruth. She was looking well. She showed Mom a letter that she had received from Sandomierz. It was from Mr. Granddaddy's son, Gersh the Miller. Grandma served us some tea and cookies. Then she brought out a bowl of groats and handed it to Mom, saying, "We just got it a few days ago. Take some of it home; you'll need it." Then, looking at me, Grandma explained, "If it weren't for him, God bless his soul, we'd both be starving in the streets." Grandma was referring to Mr. Granddaddy's son, whose picture hung on the wall.

A few days later, I heard Mom talking to Aunt Naomi in Yiddish, hoping I wouldn't understand. "We are making arrangements to leave the ghetto," Mom was saying. "We're taking a chance. Anything would be better than dying in this godforsaken place. If we are caught, it will all be over easier and faster."

"Who all is going? Where are you all going to? When?" Aunt Naomi asked, almost shocked about such a drastic decision. "Are you taking both girls with you?"

"No," Mom said. "The little one is staying here with her Dad. Polla and you can help. If things work out according to plan, all of you can join us later. I am going to take only the big one with me. She is tougher and more resistant. She always liked adventures. She can expect some on this trip." Mom probably hadn't mentioned names so that I wouldn't know that she was talking about me. Mom pulled over a chair and asked Naomi to sit next to her, face to face.

"Naomi," Mom then said, "we...I...will need your help. I know you have some experience with border crossings; maybe even some police connections?..."

"I understand," Aunt Naomi said. "But you will need more than connections. You will need money and instructions. You still didn't tell me where and when you are going."

"We are going to try Sandomierz. Mumma [as Mom and her siblings called Grandma Ruth] wrote to her stepson. He said he would help us get established if we could get there safely."

"Why did you pick a place that far away? It's almost at the end of Poland, almost in the mountains." Aunt Naomi was trying to understand.

"Well, we were trying to find a place closer, but we hardly know anyone outside of Warsaw. All of our relatives and friends live in this city. I know we have some relatives in London on our father's side. I am sure we are not going to travel there. Remember that some of the cousins we had in Germany escaped to England, too. We have quite a few relatives there. Here, in this country, we have no one outside of this forsaken city. I'll be glad to get to Sandomierz. If what I heard is right, they don't live in ghettos there. At least not yet. If we could make some connections through Otwock, that would be great. I know somebody there; maybe that would help."

Aunt Naomi breathed deeply. "When do you plan to leave?"

"We haven't decided yet. As soon as we can get the arrangements made, and get some bribe money together."

The Ghetto

"Don't call it bribe money!" Aunt Naomi said. "That is not an acceptable term."

"What in the world do you want me to call it?"

"Well, in the business, we call it 'live and let live.' You don't expect people to risk their lives for you and get nothing for it?"

"Okay, call it what you want. I am planning to sell my wedding band. I didn't give it up when the Germans asked us to surrender all valuables. I took a chance on the ring. For sentimental reasons, I couldn't give it up."

"But that won't get you enough money. You may need more just to cross the border."

"I know. I talked to my dentist; he is buying my teeth." Mom opened her mouth and showed Aunt Naomi a few gold-filled teeth in the back of her mouth. "I am selling everything, everything I can find, just to get out of this hell."

"And what does your dear husband have to say to all that?" Aunt Naomi asked.

"You will be surprised. He actually encouraged me. We have been talking about it for quite some time already. You must have heard some of the discussions. I know he is very scared inside, but he is trying not to show it."

"Well, since you are ready and set about going, let me tell you a few things you'll need to know, things that may come in handy—about the Jewish police, Polish guards, and German gendarmes. I'll also give you a few tips on how to behave on the Aryan side."

"That's exactly why I wanted to talk with you and said that I needed your help. Go ahead."

"Well, let me start with the Jewish police. Everybody talks about them, curses them, hates them; and, for the most part, people are right. They hate the cops for a good reason. There are many of them who take advantage of their positions and, like some Nazi

My Education Continues

Schweine, they torture their subjects just for the fun of it, or just to show their superiority. Many of them are such son-of-a-bitches that you'd be better off being caught by a German Nazi. These sonsa—" Aunt Naomi suddenly noticed me, put her hand over her mouth, and said, "Well, I mean, son-of-a-guns, took the job to build their invincibility, and are trying to retain an unblemished record on the job."

"Please, don't tell me about them," Mom interrupted. "I see some of them performing their work. I've been watching them working the food lines. I have seen them taking care of the quarantined buildings. I don't even want to talk about them being Jews."

"So, you already know this kind of cop. But how about the other kind, the policemen who joined the force to save their families from starvation? Those who daily go through conflicts within themselves trying to decide how to handle Jewish thieves who are stealing every item that enters the ghetto? Even the meager rations allowed by the Germans never reach you because the thieves steal them; some of the thieves are big operators. They are stealing by the truckload. I don't mean the poor souls who grab a loaf of bread to feed their starving children, but those who take whole shipments and sell the items on the black market, who do the stealing to get rich. And these Jewish thieves believe that a Jewish policeman should look the other way and let them steal. These bullies assault men, women, and even children; they even assault the cops—they'd kill anyone who gets in the way. They run a gangster-like operation, and they call the cops 'German collaborators.'"

Naomi paused; sighed. "I don't want to defend the cops, because many of them really deserve not only to be called collaborators but worse. I would even call them Nazis if they weren't Jews. They behave like Nazis. But don't put all of them into the same category.

The Ghetto

Many of the Jewish cops behave quite properly, doing their dirty duties the best way they can under very trying circumstances, sometimes even using their influence to help others."

"I think I have heard enough about the thieves and the good cops, and about the bad ones who wait for bribes, and—"

"I am not sure," Naomi interrupted. "I really don't know which of the cops are worse, the corrupt ones who look for bribes, or the honest ones who are doing their work according to German specifications. The honest cops are even worse than the Nazi gendarmes."

"I have never thought about it this way," Mom said. "To think about it, being a policeman, especially now, is not an easy job. In these inhumane conditions, to remain humane is hard. I still can't come to terms with the idea that Jewish policemen beat and abuse people. Every time I see such a scene I feel an ugly rage inside of me."

"I don't think I want to either praise or condemn them as a group. I am judging them on individual bases. I just want you to know what I have learned in my 'business.'"

"I am glad you told me. But you know this is a subject we could be discussing forever—why and how a Jewish man becomes a policeman, and what makes him behave the way he does. We can even ask the same question of the Nazi—why or how an otherwise decent person joins such an ugly organization. And why certain people behave differently, even in identical situations. But you know what, my dear sister, I have neither the time nor the patience to discuss psychology or philosophy. Just tell me about the border crossings. That is a more immediate issue."

Dad returned home from his walk through the courtyards. He said that he had been in the street. "There were some new rumors," he said. "People

My Education Continues

say that the Germans are asking the Jews to pay higher taxes. It's all about the war on the Eastern Front—"

Realizing that Mom and her sister were talking about the upcoming trip, he stopped his story and started listening to what Naomi had to say. She was telling Mom about a new crossing point with newly built underground tunnels. She was explaining that there were specially trained guides who did their job "professionally."

Dad was getting nervous and apprehensive about the whole trip. He asked Naomi how safe this journey was going to be, and what happened to people if they were caught on the "other side." "How are people identified, how are they caught? How can a German tell who is a Jew and who isn't if a person doesn't wear obvious clothes, or an armband, or if he doesn't behave differently?"

"Well," Naomi said, "they actually can't, unless, of course, somebody squeals. I'll tell you about it later, after you have made all your arrangements. Let me tell you first how this whole business is operated. You should know that everything you plan to do has to be prearranged and prepaid; and it all works through connections, and through people who do the preparations. Without the connections, you can't get anywhere. And, of course, the connectors must be paid off." Naomi smiled proudly. She was happy in her knowledge of the business and in being able to help. "So, let me tell you," she repeated, "these connectors have to be paid, and so do the guides, the tunnel makers, and all those involved. The venture won't be cheap. These people have large expenses; and they split their earnings with the guards on both sides of the gates."

Thus far, we had not told anybody about our plan. We were keeping it secret even from close friends and

The Ghetto

relatives. Only Grandma Ruth and Mr. Granddaddy knew about it.

Mr. Granddaddy gave us an address for a friend of his son's—a friend who, like his son Gersh, also lived in Sandomierz. The friend's name was Isaak the Tailor.

We did not write down the address so that we wouldn't be carrying any incriminating papers with us. We just memorized the name, "Isaak Schneider"—"Isaak the Tailor"—Żydowska Street. When we found him, Isaak the Tailor would put us in touch with Gersh, who had a house on the outskirts of town. "It is easier and safer," Mr. Granddaddy explained, "to get to Isaak Schneider, who lives in town, than to find Gersh the Miller."

It took some weeks before all "legal" preparations were made. During that time, we didn't talk about our plans to anyone. At the beginning, Mom, Dad, and Aunt kept as much information as they could away from even Sis and me. They figured that the less we knew, the fewer chances we would have to say something to an outsider. We could have accidentally said to someone, "There are people in our family who have decided not to die here in the ghetto." It was also possible that the adults didn't want to burden us with all the problems. Anyway, Sis and I pretended we didn't hear what was talked about in the house, while the grownups pretended not to have secrets from us. There wasn't much conversation between the adults and us kids concerning politics or social or family problems. Suffering was the only thing to share; silence was the best prevention against spreading it.

Soon before departure day, Sis and I were informed about the plan. We were told that Mom and I were leaving the ghetto soon. Dad and Sis, maybe even Aunt Naomi and other relatives, would join us later. We were not told any details.

My Education Continues

After that day, our family slept very little. We talked until late into the night, reminiscing about the "good old times" when food was plentiful and when the only thing we kids were afraid of was the barking of a loose dog. Talking about the past made us feel good. The present, especially the upcoming trip, and the arrangements, were dangerous and scary. The future was unpredictable.

The night before the departure, none of us slept. We didn't even talk. We just listened to one another's sighs, and to the squeaks of the iron beds as we tossed and turned.

As soon as the first ray of the sun peeked through the window, all of us were up. Everything Mom and I were to take with us had been packed the night before. Mom stuffed a few things into a wicker basket and put a jacket over the top of it, and took a small bag in her other hand—kind of a common housewife look. The few pieces of clothing that she was taking she was wearing. It made her look bulky, but it was better than carrying extra bags.

I put on my whole wardrobe—both dresses; the one Mom sewed for me and the one that was too large that had come from Cousin Zosia. I took a handbag and put Mom's coat over my arm. It looked somewhat funny in the summer; the only consolation was that many people were looking "somewhat funny" these days.

I braided my hair and folded the braids around the back of my head: It made me look older and also gave me a more Aryan look. For a woman over forty, Mom looked great. She had ear-length hair, and she was slim and young looking. Maybe it was due to my getting older or to paying more attention to Mom's appearance; or maybe I was beginning to realize that from now on, she'd be the only person I knew, the only one I'd be able to rely on and talk to.

The Ghetto

I don't recall parting with my sister or with Aunt Naomi. I waited for Mom in the hall outside the door while she was bidding farewell to the two of them. When she came out of the room she was wiping her eyes. Dad was following her. He went with us to the ghetto gate. I walked in front of Mom and Dad, thinking about the upcoming "adventure." Mom and Dad talked with each other the whole way.

The underground crossing through which we were to pass was somewhere on Przejazd Place by Mylna Street, behind a movie theater called "Promień"—"The Ray." Two young men, one carrying a rolled-up newspaper in his right hand, the other wearing a knitted cap, were waiting for us a block from the theater. A young woman dressed in a brown skirt and white blouse was standing a few yards away. She asked Mom for the "password," then she winked at Dad to disappear. Dad turned around, waved his hand at shoulder height, and walked away without ever glancing back.

The woman scratched her upper left arm—a sign for us to take off our armbands. She led us into a large courtyard where a group of Jews and a few Gentile smugglers were already waiting. (There were, I think, ten of us altogether.) She then led us to a basement apartment, then through it to a door where the man with the knitted cap had appeared again. He led us into a long, dark tunnel. We held on to each other. In front of us were a young couple, with a little girl about five or six years old, and the guide; all others were behind us. Once the door was locked behind us, there was no light either at the beginning or at the end of this long tunnel.

Growing used to the darkness, I saw pipes on both sides of the narrow aisle. Soft drops of water dripping from the pipes onto the dirt floor sounded like marching boots stepping over hard asphalt. Our guide gave a quick flicker with his flashlight. It was a signal that we were nearing the end of the tunnel. A door opened, and we walked into an unoccupied basement apartment. A Polish guide took over. He led us through some courtyards to a large gate located somewhere near Bielańska and Leshno Streets. He then wished us "Szczęśliwej Podróży!"—"Bon voyage!"—and returned to the courtyard from which we had come. Most likely he was to pick up more escapees, or more smugglers.

Equipped with train tickets, a few zlotys, and the Sandomierz connection, Mom and I were venturing into the world. On the Gentile side of the tunnel, the sidewalk was lined with people. There were a few adults, but most of them were boys and girls ranging in age from twelve to late teens. They waited for us with outstretched hands and, like beggars at the cemetery gate, were asking for money. In a "trick-or-treat" manner, they were saying to everyone coming out of the tunnel, "Give us money, or we'll call the police." To the Jews, they yelled, "Hey, kikes, the Schwabs will kill you if you're caught!"[49]

Thanks to the arrangements, which had been properly done, we were already prepared for these squealers. Mom had some money ready for them. Each of the escapees put some cash into their hands—there was no set price—and proceeded to his destination. Those who refused to give money were followed and yelled at—"Jews! Smugglers!"—until they paid up.

We walked to the corner and took a streetcar to Dworzec Wschodni. Mom and I sat in the back of the car, separately, just in case something happened. Even when we transferred streetcars, we tried to stay apart but within sight of each other.

The Eastern Station was crowded with men and women. Groups of German soldiers loaded with their gear were waiting for the military trains. They were smoking cigarettes and singing songs. We walked past

The Ghetto

the long lines of people at the ticket windows. We already had our train tickets; they were part of the deal. We went right to the gate.

The steam engine train (electric trains hadn't run since the War started) was crowded with people carrying bags, boxes, sacks, baskets, and packages of every imaginable kind.

We were heading for Otwock, a small resort town about fifty kilometers southeast of Warsaw, where we would get a boat to Sandomierz. Otwock was the last stop on a line of ten small resort towns. We were so squeezed in the car that we couldn't even turn, which was just fine since fewer passengers would be able to look at us or start the usual trip conversations.

Book Two: Labor-Camp

"It is good to learn from your experiences, but it is better to learn from another person's."

Chapter 1. The Boat

The distant view of green fields and forests looked refreshing after the tall gray ghetto buildings, the crowded streets, and the barb-wired brick walls. When the train stopped in the village of Miedzeszyn, the conductor got onto our car. He was barely able to squeeze through the crowd. I handed him my ticket. He stamped it, then pushed himself forward. I glanced at Mom. Her ticket had also been stamped, no questions asked. "Great," I thought. "A few more stops, and we'll be in Otwock." I hoped that there would be no checks by the gendarmes who often boarded the train to look for smugglers.

As we passed by the villages, I thought of the summers that we used to spend there and about carefree times. I looked at Mom standing across the car. I was that sure her thoughts were the same. One of the places we passed was the village where, a few summers before, I had met Fräulein. A few of Dad's relatives, who had a whole lot of kids, lived in the next village down the road. I remembered when I first met them. They tried to be very nice to us, and I liked them. But they were very Orthodox, and looked at us as though we were not worthy to be Jews. They looked at Dad with his shaven face and at mother, who wasn't wear a wig, as strange people. They looked at Sis and

My Education Continues

me—wearing our sleeveless dresses and showing our bare legs and arms—as though we were committing some terrible sin. They thought of us as transgressors because, on the holy Sabbath, we washed ourselves with soap, combed our hair, and did other forbidden things. I only knew the girls. Boys and girls did not play together after the age of about four or five.

All these thoughts kept my mind occupied. I didn't think about the danger of this trip. I thought of the time, when I must have been seven or eight years old, when Cousin Mordekhei, just before leaving for Palestine, spent a summer in one of those villages with us and his parents. He had a new phonograph that he kept going all day and late into the night, grinding out theater music for opera lovers, cantorial arias for the older folks, and pop dance music for the younger generation. I liked to crank up that phonograph and watch the people dance. I fought with Sis over whose turn it was to crank it–

The train screeched to a halt. "Otwock!" the conductor announced. "Everybody out!" The memories disappeared; reality set in.

Mrs. Lonia was the person who was supposed to meet us in Otwock, but instead we were met by her mother, an older lady, maybe in her fifties. She was from Warsaw, but had moved to this small town right after her house was destroyed by a bomb. She lived with her daughter and some relatives who owned a villa in Otwock. Mrs. Lonia and her family had Aryan papers and, thus far, no one had bothered them, even though all Jews who lived in these villages had long before been sent off to the Warsaw Ghetto, or else evacuated into other towns.

After Mrs. Lonia's mother picked us up from the station, she led us through some side streets to a prearranged place. The streets that we walked through

The Boat

were almost deserted. Only here and there a peasant woman would walk by, carrying a basket of vegetables or a bucket of water. The shops were closed. The situation suited us just fine: We didn't need any people staring at us.

The old lady took us to an apartment which was empty, other than for a couple of wooden benches set against the wall. We stayed there until late into the evening. After dark, Mrs. Lonia came over with her kids. They brought us some soup and bread. While Mom talked with Mrs. Lonia, I played with the girls, who were about ten years old.

We had known Mrs. Lonia for quite some time. She used to be one of Mom's private students. When she, her husband, and their twin daughters lived in Warsaw, they were neighbors of our cousin. Now, Mom was telling Mrs. Lonia about her memories of Otwock. She talked about her mother, my grandmother, who was buried there. I found out that because Grandmother died during World War I, it had been impossible to take her to Warsaw for burial. Another fond memory of Otwock was of Dad's favorite rabbi, who used to live there. Dad loved the *Mozhitzer* Rabbi; for some time, Dad had sung in his choir. That rabbi was well known for his singing and composing for prayer services. Mom often used to go with Dad to Otwock so that she could visit her mother's grave. Now, we were in the village again. But the rabbi was gone, and so was the Jewish population. Mom asked about the cemetery, and was told that, if there were any Jews left in town, they weren't going there. They were not going to "look for any trouble." After a while, Mrs. Lonia and the kids bade us farewell and left.

We sat in total darkness, looking through the window into the sky, counting the stars. Off and on, we napped on those wooden benches, waiting for the next step of our journey.

My Education Continues

At dawn, an old Polish farmer in a horse-drawn cart came to pick us up. Mom talked to him for a few minutes; she put something into his hand; he then tipped his hat politely and told us to go out and lie face down on the floor of his cart. He covered us with some old coats and a few empty potato sacks, and then put some straw on top of everything. We could look out and breathe through holes in the sides of the cart.

We had no idea where we were, or which route he was taking to the river. He explained that he often had to change roads for reasons of safety. Looking through the holes, we could only see the cobblestones passing underneath the metal-covered wheels. The cart rocked and shook and tossed us about. I began to wonder if this adventure was really going to be that exciting.

I only knew that I was with my mother in Aryan territory, riding in an Aryan wagon driven by an Aryan coachman and being pulled by an Aryan horse. We were not even sure if the coachman knew who we were or why we were going to the river with him. He specialized in transporting professional smugglers from the village of Otwock to the Swiderek, a stream from where his business partner, a young Polish fisherman, paddled passengers in his rowboat to the passenger steamboat dock on the Wisła River, only a few kilometers away.

Everything worked out according to plan. Our coachman dropped us off at an old fishing cabin, where an old woman, maybe his wife, was waiting for us. We stayed in this cabin until nightfall; then, under the cover of darkness, we boarded the small fishing boat. There were already a few people in it. In the darkness it was hard to make out who these people were. Mom gave an agreed-upon amount of money to the young boatman; he told us to sit down on the floor.

As the boat pulled away from the bank we heard the people talking. The men and women were giving

The Boat

each other business instructions: They were saying what to do and what to say in case of a raid or inspection. One woman was telling about the time she had spent in jail for smuggling, and how she had gotten out by pretending that she was pregnant.

The conversation died down as we reached our destination. It was about midnight when the boat let us off near the riverboat stop. Even though the ticket office was not to open until morning, the place was already filled with travelers. Since the War started, the riverboats had become the best means of transportation between cities located on riverbanks.

When the fishing boat let us off, Mom and I sat down on a tree stump and began to listen to the stories of professional smugglers. We didn't talk to them; and only very little to each other.

On the riverboat that was to take us to Sandomierz, we could sleep, read a paper, or crochet. "If anything should happen to any of us," Mom whispered, "if we lose each other, try to get to Sandomierz or any other place on the river. Go to farmers; maybe you can work there for food. For God's sake, do not try to return to the ghetto."

I assured Mom that I would do as she said, that I would be okay; but in reality I was scared even to think about being alone. What I was sure of was that I wouldn't know what to do if Mom wasn't around.

At about six in the morning, the harbor employees started showing up: A cashier, an information clerk, and four Polish guards. The passengers lined up at the ticket window. We bought our tickets early, so we were allowed onto the pier. This location by no means guaranteed getting on the boat, but it did give us a better chance.

The waiting passengers became worried when the riverboat finally arrived: it was already packed with travelers. Their worries proved well justified, because

My Education Continues

the rule was that the number of passengers allowed to board the steamer had to be the same as the number of passengers disembarking.

Mom and I were lucky. We were the first ones to get on. Those who did not get on had to wait for the next boat, which could show up at any time within six to twelve hours.

The voyage to Sandomierz would take three or four days, with five scheduled stops; there were also usually a number of unscheduled ones (that is, if the boat was stopped by authorities for an inspection or search).

Some of the people we met on that steamer had been on board three or four days already. Some were coming from as far away as Włocławek. Many were asleep on benches or the floor. Some asked us if they could buy any food at this harbor, and were disappointed to learn that there wasn't any.

Mom and I got to the middle deck, where we found a couple of vacant places among the passengers seated on the floor. We had taken some bread, some jam, and a two-liter bottle of boiled cold drinking water. These food supplies were to last us until we could get to a stop where there might be more available.

Despite having decided not to do so, Mom and I sat next to each other; but we tried not to talk. We had decided, as soon as we left home, to leave all of our worries and burdens behind the ghetto walls. We had sorted out the things that were important from those that were trivial. We had thought of the things that were essential for immediate survival, and left alone all the problems that were past and that we had no power to change. We had put all of our troubles into the proper perspective. We had agreed never to talk about the things that would have been, or could have been done better, or should have been avoided. Here, on this trip, we were preparing for new unknown problems

The Boat

that we could expect. We recalled an old Yiddish song that went something like this:

Yesterday will never return,
And who knows what tomorrow can bring?
Today is the only day that belongs to us,
So be happy, and enjoy it.

In these uncertain times, making plans for the future was just as meaningless as thinking of the past. Nothing could be done about either. We learned to take things day-by-day and to make decisions on the spot. Everything sounded trivial, so unimportant. Only a filled stomach and a safe place to put down our head were worth worrying about.

The boat whistle, the signal for departure, for some reason did not go off. Only when we could see the gray smoke dissipating into the clear sky, did we know that the boat was soon to be on its way. The sun was rising on the horizon. The gangplank was hauled away. The black water widened between the boat and the shore. The boat began swaying. "God spare us," whispered a woman next to us, crossing herself. We stood up to look at the river and the slowly receding harbor. We smelled the fresh, warm air, and enjoyed the view of people working in the fields. It was the first time in about two years that we had experienced the luxury of such a free view.

As the steamboat sailed southward down the murky Wisła River, we passed orchards and forests; we watched huts with thatched roofs peeking from behind green trees. I looked at Mom. She had tears in her eyes. She sighed heavily. I wasn't sure if it was the view, or the fresh air, or some pleasant memory, or the sadness of leaving her home and family, that made her cry.

I lost track of time, forgot where I was and why I was there. Then, a feeling of panic, like a flash of

My Education Continues

lightning, ran through my body, and weird thoughts hit my brain: "What if Mom and I get separated?" I looked at her. She was listening to a conversation among the people next to us. They were talking about the searches that happened quite often on the boat. They were regular travelers, professional smugglers. We weren't smuggling anything, except, of course, ourselves and—in our minds—the names and addresses of the two men whom we were to meet in Sandomierz. We had no IDs of any kind. If caught, it was safer to have "lost" one's ID than to have one that said *"Jude."* Being Jewish was a worse offense than smuggling. Smuggling was only punishable by confiscation of the merchandise, a jail or *KZ*—concentration camp—sentence, or forced labor in Germany. Punishment for being Jewish was torture and death. If caught by Polish police, a bribe was most often the best response. We were prepared for that. But being captured by German gendarmes was altogether another matter. There was only one positive side about dealing with the Germans: They were not very good at distinguishing Jews from Gentiles; so Jews could often go undetected—unless, of course, someone squealed on them. The safest way to travel was to carry some kind of documentation. There were people who would make counterfeit documents for large sums of money; some of them were real artists. But we had neither the connections nor the money for such luxury items.

At twilight, the steamer halted at a boat stop. We bought some bread and a small paper bag of sunflower seeds, and we filled our bottle with boiled water.

Some passengers got off, others got on, and we were on our way again. We slept very little that night. Besides the excitement that didn't let us sleep, there was a middle-aged, unshaven man drinking some

The Boat

stinking alcoholic beverage from a bottle and telling some rambling stories of his smuggling adventures and of Jews being taken off boats and trains. He talked about Jews being kicked, beaten, shot. He seemed to be enjoying the stories that he was telling. He told a few anti-Semitic jokes, and some people laughed. Then he dropped to the floor and began to snore so loudly that he most likely woke the fish in the river.

A couple of days later, at dawn, we halted in Kazimierz, a gorgeous little town on rolling hills overlooking the riverbank. The landscape was altogether different here from the flat plateau of Mazowsze, where Warsaw is located. I had never before in my life seen homes on hills, outside of those in picture books or movies. It was so overwhelming that I wanted to scream and let everyone know how impressed I was with this incredible view. Then I remembered the rule: "Don't talk if you don't have to." Mom went out to get some food while I kept our place on the crowded deck. As in every harbor, people were departing and boarding.

When Mom returned, she brought with her a new supply of water, a paper funnel of cooked garbanzo beans, and some bad news: "People on the pier were saying that there is going to be an inspection onboard." Then, in a shaky voice: "I would have stayed in the harbor if I had not left you here."

As Mom was talking, we saw four good-looking German gendarmes block the door to the gangplank. They were letting people get on but not off. Followed by three Polish policemen and two young SS soldiers, they entered the boat. One of the officers announced an inspection and started explaining to the young soldiers, who seemed to be apprentices in this trade, some of the procedures in searching and reporting seizures. Then he showed them how such searches were conducted.

My Education Continues

As soon as the gangplank was pulled away, the German gendarmes, accompanied by a Polish police translator, walked up and down the aisle, picking out suspicious passengers—or anyone at random—and pushing them to one side of the deck.

One of the gendarmes glanced straight into my eyes, but passed me by. Another one stopped next to Mom. He looked at her for a few seconds, stepped back, looked at me, and then asked Mom, through an interpreter, "Is she with you?"

Mom looked him straight in the face and said, "No, sir. I am alone."

The bulky garments which Mom was wearing must have caught his eye. With a gesture, he showed her that she was to follow him. Then all the selected people—there must have been sixty or more—were told to take their belongings with them; they were then lead to the lowest deck of the boat, to the place where the galley used to be.

The Polish policemen kept order on board while the gendarmes did the searching.

From a couple of women who came out of the search, we heard that each person was taken downstairs and put into a small closed room to be questioned and searched. One of the women said that the Germans had undressed her, searched all of her bags, and confiscated all of her better things, and all of her money.

While she was talking, I thought of all the things that Mom had told me before we left home and at the stop near Otwock. "What if Mom gets arrested?" I thought. What was I going to do alone? I thought that I was very brave and courageous, but actually I felt as if I were falling apart.

After some time—what seemed like hours—Mom came back on deck. She looked pale and shaken. I noticed that she still had her wicker basket, the one

The Boat

that she had taken with her to the inspection. I was so confused when they took her away that I hadn't even noticed that she had left the small bag next to me on the floor. It didn't really matter; no one was going to take it. Everyone was trying to get rid of his own bags and belongings. No one would have taken the risk of stealing another's unknown baggage. No, not during a search.

I didn't know what the searchers had done to Mom because I couldn't ask. But I was relieved to know that she was still with me, unharmed.

The search patrol was on the boat for about six hours. No one was sure if the ordeal was over until the gendarmes and police left the boat at the next stop. It was then that Mom and I got to say a few words to each other. She told me that whenever the gendarmes asked her a question, she would reply, *"Nicht sprechen Deutsche"*—"I no speak German"—even though she still remembered quite a bit of what she had learned during World War I. She figured that ignorance, in this case, would be wiser than wisdom. So she had talked only through the Polish translator. When one of the "apprentice searchers" told Mom, "take your *verfluchte Korb und raus!* [damn basket and get out of here!]" she almost started running. But luckily she caught herself in time and pretended not to understand, and waited for the translation. In her heart, she knew that she was safe—at least for the time being.

She told me how confused she was, and how difficult it had been to make that decision at the spur of the moment, whether it was safer to speak German or to pretend not to know what was being said. After she made the decision, she thought that terror had caused her to make the wrong choice, that she had unwillingly said the wrong thing, for which she'd now be punished. But by then, she couldn't have changed her statement, so instead she concentrated on not

My Education Continues

answering some untranslated questions. In her confusion, she had almost forgotten why she was scared: although she was not smuggling anything, being with all the Gentiles made her think that she was one of them who *were* worrying about the search for smugglers. Now, as in all of our previous experiences, luck had been on our side. The gendarmes had been assigned to look for smugglers, not for Jews. "It seemed as though these guys were just doing their assigned jobs," Mom explained. "They were looking for smugglers. I saw them taking away cigarettes, ham, flour, grits, and money from the people they were searching. The people, fearing terrible punishments, were relieved when only their merchandise was confiscated. I watched the gendarmes stuffing their own pockets with the confiscated money. They took the money I had on me, too, but I was glad they were not hunting for Jews." Mom breathed a sigh of relief. "It looked as though they also were dividing the confiscated cigarettes among themselves. One of the young apprentices took a small chain with a cross off a woman's neck and stuck it in his pocket." She paused again, then asked, "Do you remember that drunk who was snoring all night? Well, they arrested him, and a woman who was carrying some saccharine under her coat. The police took them both away."

The rest of our voyage to Sandomierz went by uneventfully. Again, we were enjoying the scenery and the fresh air. We got into a conversation with a couple who had been traveling all the way from Włocławek. They were already on the boat when we boarded it. We told them that our house in Warsaw was bombed out, and that we were going to live with some relatives on a farm. They told us that they had made a few trips before and had never had an uneventful journey. The husband was arrested once, but after a few days, and

The Boat

through special connections, he was let out of the Polish jail. "We keep telling ourselves that each trip is the last one, but somehow we always seem to go again."

We arrived in Sandomierz during the night and waited at the harbor until morning. At dawn, we admired the breathtaking view of green hills, the rising sun from beyond the eastern horizon, the clear, calm waters of the Wisła river. We could have stayed at that riverboat harbor for hours, just inhaling the fresh air—for even fresh air was denied to the Jews; after all, the ghetto boundaries had been drawn to exclude all parks and playgrounds.

After a while, we started walking toward town.

There was still no end in sight to my education.

Chapter 2. Sandomierz

Mom and I walked down the unpaved path on the side of a hilly road, watching horse-drawn wagons loaded with goods going toward town. We kept looking around, still admiring the hilly view, and wondering what our new life would be like. Everything around us seemed very peaceful and calm during these morning hours. Closer to the city we watched some merchants opening their shops. We passed a few bearded Jews dressed in their traditional clothes: gabardine robes, white hose, low-cut black shoes; their fringed ritual garments showed from under the robes, and all of them were wearing white and blue-starred identification armbands.

As we approached the town, more people began appearing on the road. Some of them looked quite Jewish among the blond, blue-eyed population, but they were not dressed in the traditional clothing, and they weren't wearing armbands. Most of the people we saw seemed to be going about their daily business.

Mom stopped an old, traditionally dressed Jewish man and asked the way to the market. We knew that the marketplace wasn't far from the house of Isaak Schneider the Tailor.

Sandomierz

"Follow the people and the wagons," the old man said in Galician Yiddish. "They are all going to the market." Mom thanked him, and we did as he said.

Sandomierz was a completely new experience for me. That small southern town on the Wisła River, and at the foothills of the Carpathian Mountains, was geographically and culturally very different from Warsaw. The people seemed calmer. They moved at a slower pace, even stopping to chat or say "hello" to strangers. Mom told me that the way of life here was quite different from what I knew, and she explained why: "Poland was occupied for one hundred years, until it became independent in 1918, after World War I. As a matter of fact, for a hundred years, Poland didn't exist politically. Western Poland belonged to Germany, Eastern Poland was a part of Czarist Russia, and the southern part, called Galicia—where we are now—was occupied by the Austro-Hungarian Empire. People in those occupied territories adopted various ways of life, depending on whose occupation they lived under."

I had heard these stories before. Histories of the occupation and of the war of liberation were not new to me; only now did the division of Poland and the war of liberation begin to make more sense.

Mom also explained that people in small towns lived differently from people in large cities, that they were more trusting and friendlier to strangers. I had begun to see that difference even before I entered Sandomierz. I also began to understand why the customs and speech of the people we were meeting on the way were so different from ours.

By the time we got to the market, the place was already full of wagons, trucks, horses, and people. We really wanted to see what was going on in this place, but we didn't dare stop in a strange place where we didn't know what to expect. We were trying to get to

My Education Continues

our destination as fast as we could. Our objective was to find Isaak Schneider, who was supposed to get us in touch with Gersh Mlynarz, Mr. Granddaddy's son. Gersh lived somewhere on the outskirts of town.

As I already mentioned, we didn't carry any written addresses on us, so that in case of an inspection, we wouldn't get other people involved. We had been told that any person in the Jewish section of town would know where Isaak Schneider lived. Another very strange phenomenon that could never have happened in a large city: finding a person without a proper address.

In those small towns, or "shtetlekh," as they are called in Yiddish, people were known by their first names and by surnames, the latter of which were usually determined by profession or by a characteristic—Moshe Fryzjer (Mike the Barber), Malka Garbus (Mollie the Hunchback).[50]

Our information proved correct. The first person we asked about Isaak the Tailor was an elderly Jewish man, and he did know right away who Isaak was and where he lived. He also knew of Gersh Mlynarz, but did not know him personally, nor where he lived. Before the elderly man showed us the way to Isaak Schneider's house, he wanted to know who we were, where we came from, and why we had come to Sandomierz.

Before Mom had a chance to answer his questions, he started telling her how much the people of Sandomierz had suffered from the War, especially the Jews. He said that a synagogue had been burned down; he talked about the many people killed by the SS invaders, and other terrible things that had befallen the city. But when Mom told him that we came from Warsaw, he stopped talking about the problems of Sandomierz. He said that he had already heard about the troubles in the big cities. He assured us that life in his shtetl, although no picnic, would be better for us than the life we had left behind in Warsaw. He then changed the conversation to his personal problems. He told Mom that his wife died a year ago because he could not get the right medicine for her; also, Jews were not admitted to the hospital without special connections or payoffs. Two of his sons had left for Russia with a group of other young men. "You can't talk to those young people nowadays. I asked them to stay here, at home with us. They wouldn't listen," he said nervously. Thus far, he explained, he had not gotten any letters from them, but he had learned through others that one of his sons was in the Red Army.[51] Before he departed, the elderly man told us about an organization in town that had been set up to help refugees, and about a public kitchen which provided free soup for the hungry. Mom thanked him for the useful information and the directions to Isaak's house, and we went on our way.

Coming from the marketplace, we had to walk up a hill to reach Żydowska Street. Since I had never seen buildings built on hills, I was astounded to see buildings that were three stories high on one side become only two stories high farther up the hill. I remember writing about this amazing phenomenon in my first letter to Dad. I even mentioned it in my new diary, the one I started writing once we came to Sandomierz. The diary that I left in Warsaw I had wrapped carefully and put into a drawer. I told Dad to make sure that it didn't get lost. He promised to watch it, and even asked jokingly if he was allowed to read it.

We had no problem finding Isaak Schneider's apartment. A mezuzah on the doorpost, and the whirring of a sewing machine inside, indicated that we were in the right place.

Mom knocked shyly on the door. We waited. Nothing happened. She knocked again, more loudly.

My Education Continues

"Come on in!" a man's voice said in Galician Yiddish. We waited for someone to come to open the door, but instead we heard another call: "Why don't you come in, whoever you are behind the door!" I pressed down on the door handle and the door opened. Mom and I looked at each other, surprised by the unlocked door.

"Come on in! What's the matter with you!" the man's voice repeated. "Who is it?"

We walked in. In the room, which was both a kitchen and a workshop, were two men. One, maybe in his mid-twenties, was sitting on the edge of a long table, his feet on a chair, a dark garment hanging over his lap, a tape measure suspended from his neck; he was sewing the garment by hand. The other man was old. He was sewing something on a machine, peddling quickly with his feet. Neither one of them had bothered to turn his head when we crossed the threshold. We stood at the door looking at the two working. It seemed as though they didn't care who came in. The younger tailor finally looked up. "Oh! Peace be with you," he said in the same Galician Yiddish. "I see you made it. I am sorry I didn't open the door for you. I should have know it was a stranger; our people open the door without knocking. Good to have strangers in town. How is life in the big city? I assume you must be the ladies from Warsaw we were waiting for."

He knew that we were coming. His friend Gersh the Miller, who had made the arrangements, had told him, but he had had no idea when to expect us. "Come on in!" the young tailor said again. "Why are you standing at the door?"

The old man stopped his pedaling. He turned his head, and in a very friendly voice said, "Baruch HaShem." Then he switched to Galician Yiddish: "We're glad you made it in safety; we were worried about you."

Both men put their work aside. The young one brought out a couple of wooden chairs from the adjacent room. "Sit down and make yourself at home," he said, as though he had known us all his life. "You must be very tired."

As we were getting acquainted, an old woman walked through the door. The old man pointed at her: "This is my wife—"

The young man interrupted the introduction. "Mother! These are the Warsaw ladies, the ones Gersh Mlynarz told us about."

The old woman looked at us curiously. She smiled, showing her few scattered teeth. The large mole by the left corner of her mouth enhanced her smile. She pushed her flowered bandana away from her forehead. "Oh! So you are the ladies from the big city, come all the way from Warsaw!"

The old man interrupted her. "She always talks too much." Then to his wife: "Hanne-Laye, fix something for them to eat; they must be hungry. How about some tea?"

In no time the smell of herring and onions indicated that food was being prepared. While the old woman was fixing the food, the young man ran out of the apartment. He returned a few minutes later with a young lady. She looked about twenty, braided brown hair wrapped around her head; she wore a blue flowered dress and gold earrings. The young man looked proudly at the young lady, then introduced himself: "I am Isaak the Tailor, as you have probably guessed by now; and this is my wife, Sheyndle. We got married only a half year ago. We live down the street with her parents." Then, pointing to the old couple in the room, he added, "They are my parents. I work here with my father. My brother and his wife live here with Mother and Dad. They are out of town now. They went to see her folks who live in Ostrowiec, a town a few kilometers from here."

My Education Continues

Before Mom had a chance to say a word, the old woman announced in an uncertain voice that food was ready. Turning to Mom, she added decisively, "You are going to sleep here in our house. Put away your bags; you may as well just make yourself comfortable. Feel at home." Then, turning to her son, she said, "Isaak, go and bring a straw mattress from your brother's bed and put it here on the kitchen floor." She then took Mom aside and showed her a covered bucket in the corner behind the door. "If you need to pish during the night, you can do it here; for anything else, you must go over there." She walked over to the window and pointed across the street to a long gray wooden building that looked like ten outhouses stuck next to one another. "Over there! See?" She took away the clothes and the sewing equipment that cluttered the long table, stretched a sheet over it, and set down the prepared food. "Now, all of you, sit down and start eating." The way she talked to us sounded as though she had already accepted us as part of her family.

On the table was a plate with herring decorated with cut onions, an earthenware pot containing boiled potatoes, a cup with salt, and an almost whole loaf of bread. "Tea will be ready in a few minutes," the old woman said. "Just start eating before the potatoes get cold. You can eat right from the pot. Don't be bashful; we have enough potatoes."

I exchanged glances with Mom. We might have been thinking about the same thing: What hospitality for two strangers....

During the meal, we found out from Isaak that Gersh Mlynarz and his family had fled into hiding after the Germans rounded up some prominent businesspeople and hanged them in the city square. Gersh was hiding somewhere either in the forests with a guerilla group or, by using Aryan papers, on some

Polish farm. In any case, his whereabouts were unknown, or a secret.

We stayed with Isaak's parents for a few days. Then, in the same building, we found a permanent place to live. Our quarters consisted of an iron bed with a straw mattress, a feather bed, a goose down pillow, and part of a chest of drawers, located between our bed and the bed of our landlady. Both beds leaned against opposite walls, with the headboards and chest toward the wall that faced the street. Above the chest of drawers was a small window that looked onto the street. Since we were on the ground level, the window was almost always closed and covered so that passersby would not be able to look into the room. The apartment had two rooms. One was a combination living-room-bedroom where our landlady lived with her two sons, and where we were now renting a bed; the other room was a kitchen-bedroom combination: living quarters for the landlady's mother-in-law and father-in-law.

Our landlady was a woman in her early thirties. She was short, and as a result of a childhood accident in which she broke her hip, she was lame and walked with a cane. Her dark straight hair was cut short. She always walked around the house with a rag in her hand, wiping or washing something. She was obsessed with cleanliness (which, by the way, didn't prevent lice and bedbugs from entering her otherwise spotless home). Her pastime was looking through her children's clothes and cracking lice. I must say, she was quite skilled at that.

The apartment that we all lived in belonged to her father-in-law, a man in his fifties who looked seventy. The old man was renting it from a rich Jewish man who owned many other buildings and farms. The bed that we were renting was the one in which the young lady's husband had slept before he ran away to Russia

My Education Continues

shortly after the Germans entered Sandomierz. Hershel, the twelve-year-old son, used to sleep in this bed, but from now on he had to sleep with his mother. Baby Moshele, about two years old, who was born after his father left, slept in a cradle on the opposite side of the room, next to the table.

The first few days in Sandomierz, Mom and I explored the neighborhood, the town, and the possibilities of survival. We found the refugee center with its soup kitchen, an institution that proved to be of great moral and physical support to us. This place became our source of nourishment, information, and entertainment, as well as friendship. It also was our center for news and rumors. There, we made many new acquaintances in a very short time. Almost every day new people were arriving, some having escaped the horrifying conditions in the big city ghettos, others having come from nearby villages from which they had been expelled.

Our chief entertainment was a blind, middle-aged woman named Fräulein Else. She had come to Sandomierz in 1938 when the first Jews were deported from Germany. She had come with her parents and a married sister. Her parents were now dead. Every morning, her sister brought Else to the center, where she would spend the day. Every evening, one of the center members walked her home.

Most of the day, Fräulein Else told stories, played the piano, and sang songs. She could sing in German, Yiddish, and Polish. She could also read Braille, but there were no Braille books available in the bookstore or at the library. So, Fräulein Else kept rereading the few books that she had brought with her from Germany, as well as the ones she had gotten from some people when she first came to Poland.

The day I came into the refugee center, which we called "The Club," Fräulein Else was singing, "Schlafe,

Sandomierz

Mein Prinzchen." I thought of the two German refugee children who, in 1939, sang this song in front of the entrance to Krasińskich Park. I recalled the little boy who played the violin, and how people threw money into the tin can that stood in front of the little girl who sang the song. I remembered how Mom tried to explain to me what it meant to be a refugee.

"Schlafe, mein Prinzchen" was quite a popular song, but most popular by far were the few Yiddish songs Fräulein Else sang. One of them was "Ich Will Zurück auf Heim"—"I Want to Return Home"—the same song that I had heard the Blind Man in Warsaw sing. Another one was much older, though it was new to me, sung long before the War. It was a Yiddish song by the same name, but about another period. It came from a movie about emigrants wanting to return to Poland and Russia from a disappointing life in America, where they had found neither jobs nor friendship. The newest song Fräulein Else sang was called "Vo Ahin Zoll Ich Geh'n":

Whereto shall I go when there is no place for me?
Whereto shall I go when all doors are closed to me?
Wherever I go, I am told to stop....

I learned many of Fräulein Else's songs, and listened to her stories. Whenever she spoke in German, she reminded me a lot of Fräulein Hilde, the German governess whom I met in that summer village; and of Tante Trude, my Berliner aunt. I wondered whatever became of Fräulein Hilde, if she went back to Germany, what she thought of the War, if she knew about all of the brutalities being committed by the Nazis. I even thought that she might be happy that the Germans were winning the war in Russia. Sometimes I wondered how Tante Trude was doing, and how sorry she must be for having gone with Uncle Harry, and

My Education Continues

was now starving in the ghetto when she could have been free and enjoying life. I even wondered if Fräulein and Tante belonged not only to the same people but even to the same species as the German Nazis.

Often, poor, blind Fräulein Else would talk about her life in Germany; like Tante Trude, she recalled only the good times she had had in the Nazi homeland. Only once did I hear her say, "We should have known that nothing good would come for the Jews once the Nazis came to power." I watched Fräulein Else's eyes look aimlessly toward the ceiling. "No one wanted to believe it. After the 1936 Olympic Games in Berlin, we hoped that relations between the Jews and the Nazis would improve; after all, the whole world was watching. The Führer couldn't possibly do the things he had written about in Mein Kampf. Well, we were all wrong."

Before the Nazis came to power, poor Else didn't even know that her grandparents had been born in Poland. Her father, like his father before him, had served in the German military and fought for the country. They considered themselves devoted German citizens; first German, then Jewish.

But now, she was not only bitter about the Germans but about the Polish anti-Semites. "Now," she said, "I don't know whether I should fear the Nazis, who are our enemies, or the Poles, who supposedly are our friends. We at least know what the Nazis are capable of; we know what to expect of them."

Every Monday we received soup coupons for the week. To receive these, one had to "volunteer" for work in the kitchen and the dining-hall. I thought that this setup was fair. Still, there were those refugees who would complain; there were chronic complainers—about the terrible living conditions in Sandomierz, about the heat and the cold, about the poor food, which they were getting for free, about the garbage. Many didn't even realize that having garbage was a privilege that was being denied to most.

Mom and I were very happy with everything we had. We were thankful to those who organized "The Club" and provided food for the refugees and the hungry. We just didn't like standing in line for the free soup: It made us feel like beggars. It was depressing and degrading. We finally decided to do something about the situation. After a little while I found a job babysitting for a six-month-old baby girl of a well-to-do Jewish family who, in addition to myself, were also employing a housekeeper and a washerwoman. I was paid in meals and money. I did not complain about the pay—I didn't go there to get rich—but I hated the job. There was very little to do, and nothing to learn. It was a boring, dead-end job. The baby's mother fed and bathed the little girl; she supposedly did not trust anyone with such important chores. My job was to play with the baby whenever it was awake. But the little girl slept most of the time. I just sat there, or looked onto the street from the balcony, where I had to keep the crib so that the baby could have fresh air. I was to chase away the flies. On rainy days, I just sat inside, looking out the window. The baby was either sleeping, or it was crying. She was a very darling little girl, but I had no patience to sit around and do nothing, day after day. I wasn't allowed to read or write on the job, "so as not to be distracted."

Mom, too, found work. She heard that many refugees, as well as local people who had no jobs or businesses, were making a living by trading with farmers. Mom decided to try it. Peddling became Mom's new profession. She would buy sewing supplies, candles, candies, socks, and aprons; then she would walk to nearby farms and trade the goods

My Education Continues

for bread, potatoes, beets, grits, flour, or for whatever food items she could get.

I quit my job and began going with Mom; I helped her to carry the produce home. In town, we sold some of the food for money so that we could buy new merchandise and pay our rent. The leftover food, the profit, we ate.

From these trips, and from the refugee center, I learned a lot about life in a small town and on farms. I had never been to a real shtetl or on a real farm. The villages where we used to go during the summer did not qualify as shtetlekh—they were too close to the big city, to which the people traveled often. Their inhabitants never developed the small-town culture or mentality.

Sandomierz was a real shtetl. Here the people only heard stories about big cities; few had actually been to one. The young people who had left shtetlekh for big cities seldom returned to live in these small places again. Young people had been coming from small towns to Warsaw for many years, and for many different reasons. Some came to find work, or to learn a profession. Many came to seek knowledge, to find good schools. Some small-town youths ran away from broken love affairs, or to look for new ones. Many went to big cities only looking for adventures.

In Warsaw, I had met only a few people who came from provincial towns. I knew our neighbor's relatives, who came from time to time on business. I remember one fellow who used to keep his money inside his boots, and who would always bring buckets of freshly picked strawberries. Another shtetl person I knew was Motle, who, attracted by free rent and food, slept and ate in Aunt Bella's store as a kind of night watchman. During the day he attended some kind of school. Sis and I had fun listening to the young man tell us about his hometown. He said that he had never seen a streetcar or a movie theater before he came to Warsaw. He told us that he had seen a couple of places that had electric lights: One of them was the city hall, the other a hospital in a nearby town. He had never used a flush toilet or water that ran from a faucet in a wall.

Sandomierz did not resemble Warsaw, nor was it quite as underdeveloped as was Motle's small town. Sandomierz had a movie theater in the main square. In town there were many two- and three-story buildings. The new section of town had electricity, and a few places even had running water. In Sandomierz, as in most cities, towns, and villages, Jews and Gentiles lived in mixed as well as separate neighborhoods. They had lived that way for years. Sometimes such segregated arrangements came by law, sometimes by chance, but most often by choice. Jews preferred living within walking distance of their synagogues, and they liked to be among their own people, among whom they felt comfortable in their traditional clothes and with whom they could speak Yiddish.

When Mom and I came to Sandomierz, the people still lived as they had years ago. Those who lived in Gentile neighborhoods had remained in their homes; they lived just as they had before the War. Of course, there had been evacuations, deportations, hangings, shootings, and arrests, after the Germans first occupied the town; but unlike Warsaw, the city had not been bombed; there was no physical damage. Most of all, there was no wall around the Jewish quarter. The only wall still standing was part of the medieval ramparts. Yet, like all of Poland, Sandomierz had suffered from the War. Many intellectuals had been arrested, the people had to pay more—and higher—taxes; many public buildings were occupied by stormtroopers; many goods would be confiscated and shipped to Germany. But, again, there was nothing regarding either the Polish population or the Jews that

My Education Continues

resembled the plight of Warsaw's people, or those of the other large cities. The Jews, of course, had to wear armbands and carry special ID cards, but only those in traditional clothes (who were identifiable anyway) did so. Jews were barred by decree from certain streets and public places, but these laws were seldom enforced. As long as no one betrayed the situation, no one paid attention to which laws were violated. Businesses were open; signs in shop windows posted regular hours. Market days were every Tuesday and Thursday. We were getting used to the routine of Sandomierz life.

From Dad's letters—even though he never said so directly—we understood that not much had changed in the ghetto since we left. From Dad's coded postcards, we understood that Aunt Naomi was still doing her smuggling. Her business was quite profitable, but much more dangerous. In one he wrote, "She plans to visit her sister"—we knew then that Naomi was planning to see us. As far as his health went, Dad was okay, and so was Sis; but they both missed us a lot.

Mom became more proficient in her business. We had enough food to eat. We saved what we could to send small parcels of food to Warsaw. Some we sent to an address on the Aryan side from where Aunt Naomi could then sneak them into the ghetto; many others we sent directly to the ghetto. We knew that not all of them would reach Dad; some of the packages would be opened, part of the food stolen. Often a package would get "lost." But still a few potatoes, and some flour or grits, did reach Dad. With these few food items in his possession, he was a hero among his relatives, with whom he would share his fortune. He alternated among all our needy relatives. (There was no shortage of the needy.) Dad also had to share with Grandma Ruth and Mr. Granddaddy because, for a while, they

Sandomierz

had not been getting any help from their Sandomierz son, who had gone into hiding.

For all this sharing, we were sending only five to ten kilograms of food!

Our farm peddling was not an easy task. When we first started the trading business, we would go to farms that were close to the city—only about eight to twelve kilometers away. Soon, however, we had to travel to farms farther away because there was too much competition among the nearby farms. We started walking farther and farther each day.

Again, we were slowly getting used to the new conditions.

We were learning to enjoy the long walks. The scenery was beautiful, the air fresh, the people we encountered on the roads friendly. We met peasants working in the fields; we learned about their lives and goals.

Sometimes we split the area, Mom going one way, I another, so that we could cover more territory. After doing our day's work, we'd meet halfway down the road and go home together. For this, though, I'd walk down the road relishing the view of the rising sun and the moisture of the morning dew still on the grass. Sometimes I'd sing or talk to myself. Passing people working in the fields, I learned to greet with the customary "Szczęść Boże"—"God be with you"—salute. The working people would cross themselves and answer with the traditional response, "Bóg zapłać"—"May God give you good luck."

Most days went by uneventfully: One day we would sell more goods, on other days, fewer. As I'd walk with Mom she'd tell me stories about her life when she was a girl and later, when she was fourteen, the War breaking out. My favorite story was about an electric streetcar:

My Education Continues

Mom was about five or six when she went with her brother and two of his friends to play in front of their house. That one morning the street was crowded with people. The kids paid no attention to the people, until they heard yelling: "Look! Look! Here it comes!" Then they saw a streetcar coming down the street. The streetcar was moving, but there were no horses pulling it. Everyone looked with astonishment. Mom's brother (my Uncle Mendle) and the boys, who were about eight and nine, started betting one another. One said that there were horses somewhere underground pulling the streetcar. The other bet that someone was pushing the streetcar from the back. Mom didn't remember what her brother said, but she did remember that all of the boys lost their bets after a man standing next to them explained that the streetcar was being propelled by a special power, "Electricity." The man said that he had read about it in the paper, and that's why he had come to watch. He said that in the same paper was an article explaining how, some day, even the gas lights in the streets might be replaced by electric lights.

Not all of the things Mom and I talked about were amusing, though. One day, Mom asked me if I knew anything about the "facts of life," about how girls got pregnant. Now that I was a "grown lady," and the boys were starting to look at me, as she put it, I should have such information. I told her that I knew only a little, that I had heard about it from "an anonymous friend, whose name I could not reveal." (I remembered promising Rena and, later, Sala, never to reveal the source of this information.) Besides, I reminded Mom, she herself always told us girls the truth. She never told us "the stork story," or that babies were bought in a hospital or a store. (I remember that when I was about four or five, one of Mom's cousins was pregnant, and Mom told us that Roza had a baby in her tummy. Mom heard a lot of criticism about it from her friends and relatives.) I reminded Mom of an amusing story that would always put her in a good mood. Although it had happened when Sis was about five, we continued to repeat the story so often that I could still remember it well:

One day, while Mom and Sis and I were walking down the street, we saw a lady walking a cute puppy on a leash. We stopped to play with the dog and have a little chat with the lady. After we continued our walk, my little sister, looking at Mother with pleading eyes, said, "Mama, proszę, urodż pieska dla mnie?"—"Please, Mom, can you have a puppy for me?"

Other times, I talked with Mom about life in Sandomierz, about how different big city people were from small-town folks. In a way, I liked the small town better: The people were much friendlier, much closer to one another, much more compassionate. There were also fewer restrictions on where to go and what to wear.

Occasionally, a drayman, if his wagon wasn't overloaded, would stop and pick up people who were walking down the road, especially women or people carrying heavy loads. We always tried to give these kind carters an appreciation gift: some candy, a candle, whatever we could get in the town. We learned to carry some extra stuff with us specially for them.

On the days I walked alone, I learned a lot about life on a farm, about how much sweat and hard work would go into producing food before it got to market. Even though there were some large estates in this general area, these were now being taken over by the Germans. The farmers I saw and visited were southern peasants, mostly small, independent farmers who had worked in the same fields in the same way for many centuries. They seldom complained, and they never lost hope. I learned how to converse with these people, how to avoid being bitten by dogs, and what to do

My Education Continues

when stung by bees and wasps. These farmers and villagers were unbelievably pleasant, very trusting, and ready to help. They could become friends with total strangers in no time at all. In the villages and farm homes, the doors were never locked—not even during the night. Yet the people here told me that times had changed since the Germans had come, that people had to be more careful now. I couldn't figure out how they had behaved before the War. Even now, their behavior astounded me.

In Warsaw, we had been taught from early childhood never to associate with strangers, never to talk to people we didn't know, and always to keep the doors locked and never let anyone into the house, not even over the threshold. We girls were taught not to accept help from anyone in the street, especially from men. If we needed help while walking alone in the street, we had to ask a policeman. That's why the extraordinary hospitality of the villagers and farmers was so strange to me. Their sharing of food was even more amazing, considering that their farm machinery and many of their horses had been either mobilized by the Polish armies at the beginning of the War or, later, taken away by the Germans. These farmers and villagers now had to work harder and longer hours doing all their work by hand.

On the other hand, the small farmers never had it so well financially. Since the beginning of the War, their products had become in great demand, and food prices skyrocketed. Produce prices had increased in value more than any other commodity, and now their goods were constantly in short supply because many of their crops were being confiscated and shipped to the Eastern Front for the German armies.

One time, on a very hot harvest day, I stopped in front of a farmhouse and, as usual, greeted the farm people who were standing in the yard. I asked the farm woman if she needed any small items from the city. I told her that she need not pay with money, that I would trade for whatever food she could give me. Her response, however, was not the usual "yes" or "no." Instead of saying, "No, I don't need a thing," or "Yes, let the gracious lady show me what she has" (Polish people always approached others in a polite form, in third-person singular), the farm woman answered, "For Christ's sake, young lady! What I need is a helping hand, not more junk from the city!" Then wiping the sweat from her forehead with her apron, she said: "These German bastards took away my son. He was only eighteen. The Good Lord only knows if they didn't ship him to Germany. They took him from a tavern. May the Virgin Mary, Mother of God, punish those enemies of mankind...."

One of the men standing nearby interrupted, trying to keep her from talking, but she moved closer to me. "Young lady maybe thinks my son had done something wrong? No! He was a good kid. He only had a few drinks, and was singing with the other guys. They were singing patriotic songs. Well, it's been a month and a half, and we haven't heard a word, not from him or about him. May these bastards perish! May they go to hell! May the cholera strike them!"

I stood there for a couple of minutes listening to her. Then (I don't know why) I told her that I was from Sandomierz, and that I'd be back in a couple of days to see if I could help her on the farm or at home.

When I returned from that trip, I told Mom about my conversation with the farm lady. "I want to help her. I've never done any farm work before; I'd like to try it. I think it would be interesting, maybe even fun. If nothing else, it would be a great education."

I didn't think that Mom liked my weird idea since she shook her head in disbelief. "You haven't been to

My Education Continues

Mount Everest yet, either; wouldn't you like to go there first?" Then she explained: "Farm work is very hard. I am not sure you'd be able to do it. I am glad you like to walk barefooted, because that's what you will have to do there. I also hope you won't mind having calluses on your hands and mosquito bites on your body." After some more thought, Mom added, "Well, I think if you really want to do it, you can give it a try. If you don't like it, you can quit. At least I'll know where to find you."

I was very excited about the unexpected permission, but at the same time I was rethinking the whole thing. "Mom," I said, "what will happen to our trading business?"

After a while, Mom replied, "I'll ask our landlady, and see if she would let her son Hershel go with me. He can help me carry some of the produce home. If I pay him, I think he might want to do it. Anyway, I cannot do the walking forever. I will have to stop this 'business' as soon as the cold weather sets in."

Actually, as I later found out, Mom had thought of taking the boy with us to the farms even before I talked about the farm job. Hershel was twelve, and had never been to a secular school. The kheyder that he had been attending had been closed since the War started. Hershel had been spending all his time in the streets playing palant, fighting with other boys, or chasing dogs and running after horse-driven wagons.[52]

Besides, Hershel and his family could always use a little extra money and food. Even before the War, these people had been barely making a living. Our landlady, orphaned at an early age, was originally from a nearby town, Opatów. Some of her relatives still lived there. Here in Sandomierz, where she had moved right after her marriage, she hardly knew anyone. Since her husband had left for Russia, she had to rely entirely on her in-laws for support. The old man, her father-in-law, had by profession been a water-carrier. According to his own accounts, he was the best water-carrier in town, and delivered water to only the richest homes. Even before the War started, his business had been steadily declining, ever since many of the rich homes had installed "water in the walls." That's when the poor old man had started moonlighting, becoming a substitute shamash in the rundown, almost abandoned, synagogue not far from his home. Presently, he was supporting his family, his wife, daughter-in-law, and the children, by begging for alms at the city market and at the Jewish cemetery. He was also doing some odd jobs at the synagogue. In his spare time, he prayed.

His wife had been a cleaning woman in her younger years and, like her husband, had worked only in "very prominent homes in the center of the city"—something that she never failed to add in her conversations. Her only hobby had been listening to street singers and watching troupes of jugglers perform in the marketplace, something that she was able to do by looking out the windows of the "prominent homes in the center of town." The old woman still liked to listen to the singers in the streets, but now she was sick—probably from cancer. She was bleeding a lot. Yet she was still cleaning a few houses each week because, according to her, "The most gracious ladies in the center of town never learned how to do their cleaning right." She was quite sure that in time she would get well; her husband was praying for her health. She knew that God would help her.

We got along well with our landlady and her family. As Mom predicted, Hershel was allowed to accompany her on her peddling ventures. I went to see the people on the farm.

When I got there, I found the woman who had offered me the job cleaning out the barn, spreading it

My Education Continues

with new straw. "Oh my!" she yelled when she saw me coming, "I didn't believe you'd come. Town folk don't like farm work. Well, let's go inside the house."

The smell of cooking cabbage entered my nostrils and made me hungry. The room was simple but spotless. The walls were hung with knitted placards with old Polish proverbs knitted on them: "Bez pracy nie ma kołaczy" ("No pain, no gain") and "Kto rano wstaje, temu Pan Bóg aje" ("The early bird catches the worm"), among others.

On the sofa, amid beautifully knitted decorative pillows and bundles of woolen yarn, sat a young woman, maybe in her late teens or early twenties. What attracted my attention was that her legs were on the sofa. She was holding knitting needles between her toes as she knitted something.

It is hard to say how long I stood at the door, speechless, unwillingly staring at that phenomenon; I only remember what I thought: "This cannot be true! What is happening to me? I must be imagining things! Am I getting sick?" The knitting lady must have noticed the astounded look on my face, and may have even sensed my thoughts, for she broke the silence: "Young lady," she said in a polite but provincial Polish, "you are seeing correctly. Look!" she added in a matter-of-fact tone, placing with her left foot a knitting needle near her on the sofa, and pointing with her right foot up to her right armpit. "Look! No arms! You see right, lady. I was born like this." Her mother, the woman who had brought me into the house, interrupted the conversation, saying to me, "This is my daughter, the youngest of my five kids." Then pointing at me she announced to her daughter, "Janka! This is the city girl who promised to help me. Remember, I said she'd never come back. Well, here she is!" The old woman turned to me again and said, "My husband was killed on the front the second day of the War. My brothers and my oldest son are now running the farm. Their families help, too. There's a lot of work here, and everything is done by hand."

"Mother!" interrupted the armless lady, "stop your miserable stories. Things aren't really that bad." Then, with a smile, she turned to me and in a proud but shy voice, said, "Let me show you something." She put away the knitting and picked up a pencil and a piece of paper from the sofa. Pressing the paper down with her left foot, and holding the pencil between the toes of her right foot, she wrote "Janka Brzeszynska." "You see, young lady, I learned how to write." She put the pencil back on the sofa. "When Mother told me about you, I thought you'd never show up."

Before the old woman was ready to leave the room and show me what I was to do, she pointed at the walls and proudly said, "You see the placards hanging here? Well, Janka knitted them all by herself."

"Don't brag, Mother!" Janka said, but she seemed to enjoy the compliment.

The old farm woman took me into the yard. She walked me around the house and the barn and the pigsty. She showed me all of the farm's operations, then gave me my first assignment. I was to go over to the other side of the field and help her son, who was mowing down ripe grain with a hand scythe. I was to pick up the mown wheat, tie the stalks into bundles, and put them onto the rows already there. "But before you go," the old woman warned, "be careful not to get your hands under the scythe. They'll be cut off, one-two-three!" She showed how it would cut by moving the edge of her palm over her other arm.

The young man was occupied with his work. He didn't talk much after showing me how to do my job. With what looked to me like very professional skill, he continued cutting the straw that kept falling to the ground. I worked until noon, when it became too hot to

My Education Continues

work. All the workers ate lunch at a long wooden table under a large shady tree. When I got to that table, the armless lady was already sitting there, on a high stool, feeding herself. With her wide-bottom skirt folded between her legs, she was holding a fork in her toes and putting food into her mouth. The two other women at the table were the old woman's sister-in-law and her daughter-in-law. They were feeding their children and telling each other stories. After the meal, the men napped, stretching out on the grass under the tree. I helped with the dishes.

I quickly learned that farmers don't work by the clock; their workday is from sunrise to sunset. My hours, for the time being, were to be from early morning until early evening, so that I could leave home at dawn and return by sunset. I refused to stay overnight.

As Mom said, work on the farm was hard, and as she warned me, I was getting calluses on my hands and feet; my body was covered with insect bites and scratch marks. Despite all of this, I really liked my job. It was new, interesting, and adventurous, and I was learning new things every day. Some days, while walking down the roads, I would think of the small villages near Warsaw where I used to spend summers, and how much I used to envy the Gypsy children whenever I saw them passing in their wagons on the highways.

I also enjoyed the clean air and the view of the distant horizon; I liked to listen to the chirping field mice and the humming bees. Somehow, being on this farm reminded me of my worry-free times. It made me forget my troubles, the ongoing war, the closed-up ghetto, my refugee status, even my Jewishness. I didn't think about what could happen if I were ever caught without my armband. I forgot that I might starve if the stores ran out of food. After all, I was well fed; paid in farm produce that I carried home every night.

Even though I never learned how to harness a horse, or to control a plow behind an ox, I did learn many things that I previously didn't know. I never realized how much there was to learn about farming. When I wasn't helping with the harvest, I was helping with other chores: I fed the animals and milked the cows; I chased birds and small animals out of the apple and cherry trees—a sort of living scarecrow. I picked ripe fruit and got it ready for the market. I cleaned the barn and the outhouses, strewing both with clean straw. I mixed manure with straw, and this mixture I used to fertilize the fields.

Somehow, standing on an ox-drawn wagon of freshly prepared manure mix and throwing it with a pitchfork onto the fields, made me feel very useful and very important. I was doing something that I never knew I could. I felt like a genuine farmer—or, rather, an accomplished farmhand. I was surely not a farmer. I realized that there was too much to know about farming. I heard that my farm woman's husband, the one who was killed in the War, was a real farmer. Neighbor farmers talked about him very favorably. They said that this man could tell different kinds of soil just by touching them, that he knew how and when to fertilize, how much moisture each plant needed, what soil was best for different crops, and when to plow and when to harvest. He knew which fodder to feed each animal, and when each female was in heat and how to find her a mate and then help her to deliver her young. He knew how to raise fowl and how to kill pigs. He could not only predict rain but tell how long each rain would last—he was his own meteorologist. He knew skills that his sons had never learned.

Often I wondered why I'd never before bothered to think of all the knowledge and work it took to produce food, why I hadn't thought about it while buying and eating my bread. Now I had developed a new respect for farmers and for farming.

The summer months passed quickly; the days began to shorten. I stopped my daily commuting and started going home only twice a week. This schedule lasted until the harvest was over and the busiest work was done. Then came the Jewish High Holidays. For ten days I stayed home "sick." During that time I learned a few ancient Jewish customs that were quite new to me. I had never seen Hasidim knocking on people's windows to wake the male worshippers to tashlikh. For the first time I saw men and boys gathered in the street intoning a prayer for the new moon. The day before Yom Kippur, our old man engaged in a ritual called the "Beating of the Scapegoat": I watched him whirling an expiatory cockerel over his grandsons' heads as he uttered a prayer. I asked him what it was all about, but all he said was, "That's the way things are done." He was surprised that a Jewish girl didn't know about it. I later found out more about the mysterious ritual, about the significance of the window-knocking, about what the moon means in the Jewish calendar. I heard the famous Bible story about the poor goat that would become the "Scapegoat."

During the holidays, as always, all Jewish businesses were closed. This year, however, for fear of German raids and Polish vandalism, all synagogues were closed, too. All prayer services were done at home. Streets in Jewish neighborhoods were full of Hasidim in their traditional silk robes and fur hats walking to and from their makeshift temples. Many of them would gather at street corners to discuss the War and the new laws against Jews that were constantly coming into force.

Sandomierz

On Yom Kippur day, I saw our old man putting on his kittel; he looked like a rabbi. I remembered that the only other time I had ever seen someone wearing one was during a prayer meeting at one of my uncles' homes. I even recalled the answer Uncle Moshe had given me when I asked about this garment: "It is the only thing, my child, that a Jew takes with him from this world to the next one." The answer stuck with me for years because Uncle Moshe had died about a year later. I wondered whether he was buried in his kittel, or in the customary shroud, the tahkrikim.

During the holidays, Mom and I went to our "Club" to have our meals and to celebrate with other refugees. We hadn't been there for quite some time. We were glad to see the people we missed. A couple of men were conducting services. They were chanted the prayers, and our blind Fräulein Elsa was providing the singing. Most of the people who gathered there cried. Mom and I sat quietly. We wondered what Dad and Sis were doing. Who had invited them for the holidays? We were sure that they had been invited somewhere. We wondered how our aunts, uncles, cousins, and friends were spending the holidays. We wondered how many people had died of hunger, typhus, and in the killings since we left the Warsaw Ghetto. We shared experiences with other refugees who, like us, were separated from their families.

After Yom Kippur I returned to work. I worked on that farm until the potato and beet harvests ended. I was getting quite proficient in my farm work, and slowly was even getting used to the awful stench of manure, an odor which had almost knocked me out at the beginning. With the other farmhands, I hoed potatoes and threw them into ox-drawn wagons. Then we drove them across the field and rolled them into underground burrows, where they would be kept for the winter. We had separated them so that some were

My Education Continues

saved for eating, while others were cut up to be used in spring for planting.

All work on the farm was hard and exhausting, but nothing to me was worse than the backbreaking work of digging sugar beets with frozen bare hands out of the frost-covered fields. We, the diggers, had to keep warming our numb fingers under our armpits, and jumping in place to warm our feet. Only a few lucky farmhands had some kind of gloves or warm boots. Beet-pulling was the only work that I hated, and also the last one to be done before the winter set in.

After the beet harvest my farm work was finished. I bade the farm family farewell, telling them to expect me back in the spring. Mom, too, quit her job. It was getting too cold, and it rained often. But Mom was not staying home. She started her old jam business anew. It all came about when during the holidays she had told some people at the club about her business venture in Warsaw. One of the ladies had asked her, "Why not do it here?" At that time of year, apples were still plentiful and relatively inexpensive. Mom thought about it seriously, but she needed time to look into it and to make the proper arrangements. Mom had to find a source of apples, find a cellar to store them in, and do some research on customers.

Meanwhile, right after the Sukkoth holidays, the old woman we lived with fainted while doing laundry at her job. She was brought home on a stretcher and put into bed. From that day on she was bedridden. Her condition worsened daily, and daily her husband prayed for her health. I watched from the other room as he wrapped himself in a prayer shawl, then put on his tefillin, kissing them and winding the strap around his arm and his middle finger, and prayed very seriously for her health. But his wife would not get any better. One dreary afternoon a healer was brought to the house. He wasn't told about the suspected cancer. He diagnosed pneumonia. He decided to use cuppings. There was no improvement. A few days later he tried leeches. They didn't help, either. The rabbi was summoned. He suggested a trip to the cemetery. "Go to the grave of her parents," he told the sick woman's husband and daughter-in-law, both of whom were at the bedside. "Seek intercession with her dead ancestors."

The old man did as he was told, but his wife's health deteriorated further. Mom suggested calling a doctor, or taking her to the clinic (since the hospital did not admit Jews). But such a godless deed was debatable. It first had to be run by the rabbi. Before any decision was made, the old woman died. All rituals were done as prescribed by law, as they had been at Grandma Esther's funeral. While the corpse was being washed, I left the house. When I returned, the corpse was gone. Our young landlady had scrubbed the kitchen floor and cleaned and laundered the dead woman's bed, filling the paillasse with fresh straw. She would now let her son Hershel sleep in it.

Every night, for a week, the old man kept gathering ten men for a minyan. They prayed for his wife's soul.

Mom's jam business arrangements were in progress. She offered our landlady some extra money for the use of her wood-burning stove. A Polish woman agreed to bring us the gelatin from Radom, a larger city a few kilometers to the north. Isaak the Tailor let us use his cellar to store the apples in. The cellar was a strange place. The entrance to it was through an opening in the kitchen floor. A ladder was lowered into it, then a basket was dropped on a rope to lower and lift the stuff kept there. We called this device the "mechanical elevator." The damp smell and the darkness of the cellar reminded me of the bomb-shelter.

My Education Continues

After all the preparations were done, Mom was, once again, in the jam business. We were cooking the jam at home and selling it in the city. We only cooked one pot at a time, for we had no money to tie up and no room for storing the jam. The business was not very profitable since the expenses were high, but at least we didn't have to venture far from home, especially with winter around the corner. We were making a living, and it was better than wandering to the farms or standing in line for free soup.

Twice a week, weather permitting, we would go to market. We traded with the farmers. Mom was never a good salesperson: She didn't know how to bargain or take advantage of situations, and she never cheated. But her jam was good; people liked it and bought it and we were surviving.

I liked to go with Mom to the market square. Talking with farmers made me feel better now than ever before. I felt myself a semi-expert on farming. After having cleaned outhouses and spread manure, the sharp odor of cow droppings that covered the market floor no longer bothered me. I looked at the farmers with respect.

I observed with more attention the things around me, and understood better the things that I saw. Sometimes I just stood at the marketplace, looking and listening. I liked to watch the heavily loaded vehicles bringing produce to town, and I liked to listen to the sound of wagon-wheels and sleigh-runners squeaking and groaning over the snow. I watched the loose straw blown by the wind, and the yellow sheaves of straw strewn over the ground held down by wagon wheels covered with animal dung and cart grease. I listened to drivers yelling at their horses and oxen and snapping whips over their backs. I watched porters busily carrying baskets of coal, bunches of firewood, sacks of potatoes on their shoulders.

Sandomierz

I listened to groups of performers and singers chanting their doleful songs. Sometimes I found myself thinking of our dead old lady, and how much she had enjoyed listening to them; I thought of the Blind Man in Warsaw, who sang in the courtyards. These performers provided the only entertainment for me; outside of Fräulein Elsa's singing at the club, I had no other place to go. I listened to them sing sad songs, some popular, some not. They sang about people going from rags to riches, and about some from riches to rags because of unfaithful women. And they sang about homeless orphans who lived in poverty and who were forced to sell cigarettes in the streets of old Russia. They sang about gangs of pimps who sold "living goods" to Argentina. I didn't quite understand the meaning of some of the songs, especially the last ones. Once I heard an older man in the audience start laughing, then murmur, "Oh, I know one of those girls who was looking for adventures in Argentina. Wow! did she have fun over there! She got rich, too!" A woman standing nearby gave him a dirty look. "Shame on you!" she said, and spat into the air. Among the songs that the performers sang were songs about the plight of refugees; one was called "Mister, Can You Spare a Dime?"—an American song, but sung here in Yiddish. Some of the songs I had heard before; others were new to me. I watched people throwing money into the hats placed in front of the singers and musicians. Sometimes I, too, would drop in a few groszy.

During warm days, in the buildings around the square, merchants sat on the steps of their shops praising their wares. Some women were dozing off, others were plucking feathers. Most of them were talking: Tongues buzzed everywhere, spreading gossip throughout the market stalls, from the tailor's shops

My Education Continues

and cobblers' benches to the butcher stands and the places of other artisans.

One of the merchants was our neighbor, a young man named Hershel—like our landlady's son, but this one we called Henyek. He was about nineteen or twenty, and lived on the top floor of our building. He sold candles and petroleum lamps and wicks from his tiny market shop. I used to stop and talk to him. He called me "the young lady from the capital," always with some sarcasm in his voice. Once he invited me for ice cream, which we ate in his shop. He was the first guy—not a relative—ever to buy me something. He asked me to "drop in" at his apartment on Saturday afternoon. "I have two brothers and three sisters," he said, as though to reassure me that he would not be there alone. "Every Saturday afternoon all our friends gather to talk and sing. We take turns. The gatherings are in different places, but they are most often at our house." Then he told me which Saturday they were meeting in his home.

I wasn't very interested. The boys and girls I saw going into his apartment did not appeal to me. But just out of curiosity, I did want to see what was going on there. I said that I would ask my mother. A weird smile appeared on his face. Like the smile on the "Mona Lisa," it was hard to tell what was really on his mind. He shook his head in disbelief and gave me a funny look.

I was busy helping Mom with the jam business. I cleaned and cored the apples and put the cooked jam into reusable containers—cups, glasses, bowls. I also helped Mom deliver the jam to customers and to the marketplace.

Winter was setting in. Ice covered the streets. Snow soon followed, and it drifted into frozen heaps. We celebrated Hanukkah at the refugee center. My birthday went by without any fanfare. Mom got me a pair of used shoes which she had traded for jam. I also got a postcard from Warsaw, late. It was signed by Dad and my sister. They wished me well, and conveyed greetings from "all."

As winter continued, our apple supply dwindled. By mid-January, most of them were gone. With the roads snowed in, it was almost impossible to get apples; the few that we could find in town were either frozen or too expensive. Our jam business was dead. The trading farm business was dead, too, at least until spring.

Besides money problems and boredom, we had to deal with visits to the outhouse across the street. There, icicles hung from the roofs and walls, and there were potholes. People would slide across the hill and stumble over piles of frozen feces that had accumulated around the latrines. Everyone complained about the problem. We cried, screamed, cursed; but none of those tactics helped. Finally we started telling jokes about the degrading situation. The jokes didn't help much, but the laughter felt better than the tears.

Day began to turn to night quite early. The idle days and long winter nights were tiresome, and boring. I had hardly anything to do that would be interesting or keep me busy. Some days I spent writing entries in my diary; they were impressions of my farm work, and from my life in the shtetl. I wrote things that I had not had time for during the summer. Now, there was nothing going on—nothing new to write about.

Mom and I started going back to the refugee center, where we could always find someone to talk with, and something to do.

One day, while talking to Tola, a young woman who not long before had come from Warsaw, I found out some bad news. Tola told me that our twenty-

My Education Continues

eight-year-old cousin, Moniek, had died of typhus complications, and that his mother, our Aunt Dora, was very sick. The situation in Warsaw was getting unbearable. Tola was sure that I'd tell Mom about it, but I did not. According to my notion of things, there was no reason to. There was no one else in Sandomierz who knew us, and I didn't think it would hurt Mom to be spared such depressing news.

Other news we were getting from Warsaw was equally bad. Mom was constantly worried. Aunt Naomi's arrangements for getting out of Warsaw seemed to have stalled. Getting out of the ghetto was now almost impossible. The difficulties were not only with getting out but with traveling. Traveling for Jews was difficult, but so was travel in general. The only good news from Warsaw was that Grandma Ruth was again receiving packages from her son, Gersh. He was sending them from time to time under an assumed name, and with a changed address. That's about all we could make out from the coded postcards.

We were still sending some food to the ghetto, even though we ourselves had very little, even though we knew that much of what we were sending was being stolen. Often we had to change addresses; it wasn't safe to send parcels to the same address more than once. So we tried to send some parcels to an address outside of the ghetto, where Aunt Naomi was picking them up. Sometimes the bribes were higher than the contents of the package were worth.

Conditions in Sandomierz were worsening, too. More vehicles and produce were being confiscated from the Poles and sent to the Eastern Front.

Mom and I were spending more time at "The Club." There we could talk about all the new problems facing us as well as help out with some work that had to be done at the center. My daily chores, for which I volunteered, were twofold: preparing firewood, and cleaning snow from the front of the building. I was working with two refugee girls from Łódź. Our job was to haul frozen tree branches from a nearby forest, chop them up, dry them, and then stack them in front of the fireplace. Then we had to make sure that the entrance to our clubhouse, and the street in front of it, were cleared of ice and snow.

Mom spent her time helping out in the refugee kitchen. She was also volunteering doing paperwork for the city clinic, which was always short of help and money and doctors and nurses and medical equipment.

Besides going to "The Club," I started taking walks with Sheyndle, Isaak the Tailor's wife. Even though she was quite a few years older than I, and married, she was very nice to me. While we walked, she would tell me stories of her life, of how she once fell in love with a guy her parents didn't like and whom they wouldn't let her marry; of how much she had suffered because of that; and of how they had made her marry Isaak. She still wasn't sure if she really loved him, but now that she was pregnant, she thought he was okay. She also told me stories about the lives of other people in town—about people I knew and those I didn't. She told me who was in love with whom, who was pregnant, who had babies, and who couldn't have any. Really, I couldn't have cared less; but I didn't have anything better to do with my time, so I listened.

Reading, which was another way to pass time, was really not so easy. There was a public library in the city square, but Jews were not allowed in. Besides, we were in town illegally, that is, without any ID papers, and without proper registration. With the help of some townspeople we organized a book exchange program at the refugee center. We read what was available, not what we wanted. It was a kind of potluck reading. I found it quite interesting not knowing what the next

My Education Continues

book would be. We read technical books, and love stories, all kinds of textbooks, fact and fiction, novels, religious books, books about religion—anything that we could get our hands on, our eyes on, enough daylight on. To Mom, reading was as important as eating. "It's the only thing that keeps me half sane here," she would say. "Even reading at random is better than not reading at all." One cold snowy winter day, Mom met Mr. Sikorsky, a middle-aged Polish city official, at the clinic where she was volunteering and he was working. Mr. Sikorsky started supplying us with library books. He liked Mom because, as he put it, "She is nice. and a lady." He didn't care about Jews one way or another.

As the winter dragged on, I started attending the Saturday night gatherings to which Henyek would invite me. I only attended the ones that were held in Henyek's house. Most of the people there were older than I was. Out of about twenty boys and girls, there were two girls my age. This place, like all of Sandomierz, turned out to be a great educational center for me, and a terrific source for my diary, for it was in Henyek's apartment that I would hear stories of young flames and broken hearts. I heard songs about love and sex and crime. The one about cocaine was all new to me; I had never heard one like it before. I wasn't sure what cocaine was, and I wasn't going to ask any of the people there because they would have laughed. I finally asked Mom, and I even sang a few bars for her:

> *Once I only dreamed of you, my dear love, my flame,*
> *But nothing is now left for me but tears, pain and delusive cocaine.*
> *Even though I know the white powder will eventually kill me dead,*

Sandomierz

*In my elusive dreams I feel your lips sweet
and red.
I sense the end of my days drawing near,
In my heart will always remain the drug
poison and you, my dear.*

Mom explained that cocaine was a narcotic. She said that it affected people the way vodka and wine did. (That didn't help me much since I had never experienced the influence of alcohol.) Mom also said that she didn't like me going to Henyek's place. I was surprised, and wondered how Mom knew that the boys and girls there were "making out," that they were using to their advantage the Jewish Sabbath law against turning on the light—that they were hugging and kissing and petting before the first star appeared. All of this was very strange to me.

It was all part of my continuing education.

I remember one of the guys who tried some of his petting with me. Coming up from behind, he put his arms over my shoulders and, without saying a word, stuck his hands inside my bra. I felt scared and pleased at the same time. It made me feel grown up. But after realizing what he had done, I pushed him back and moved away. I wasn't sure what else to do. I remember that I would never let him touch me again; I never talked to him after that incident.

The only guy I liked in this group was Henyek. He was nice, and he respected people. But I had nothing to talk to him about. He tried to explain to me that girls didn't have to get pregnant if the guy was careful, and if he knew what he was doing; he assured me that he knew. I paid little attention to what he was saying. It was all he liked to talk or joke about. Much of what he was saying had little significance for me, which he must finally have sensed, for he started paying less attention to me and more to some of the other girls.

My Education Continues

But I liked Henyek anyway, and just wished that he could be interested in other subjects.

Another young man I liked in this group was a tall handsome Jewish policeman named Moniek, whose name reminded me of our cousin who had died in Warsaw. Moniek used to drop in occasionally. He was married to a refugee girl, and they had a baby boy. His wife never came with him. He didn't talk with the girls, but he did have nice conversations with the guys. Almost everyone in Sandomierz had known him since his birth. He dropped out of public school and refused to attend the Jewish school, to which most of his peers went. His shoemaker father had wanted him to learn a skill, but he had refused that, too. He was still in the process of finding his way in the world when the War broke out. The German occupation came to his rescue. He joined the Jewish police force, and became quite influential in the city. Obeying the orders of his superiors, he kept advancing his position. Most people liked him quite well; only those who had to deal with him had a different opinion: They talked about him as rude, heartless, an abuser of power. Even though I seldom talked to him, I knew him as nice and polite.

Finally the winter was coming to an end. The masses of snow began to thaw; the sun was coming out from behind the clouds. People started coming out of their burrows. The smell of spring was in the air. One Sunday morning, I walked with Mom and a few other people to the river just to welcome the spring. Our walk was leisurely, so that we could enjoy the sun and warmth. We stopped at the pier where the ships docked and watched the thick clusters of broken ice float down the river. We watched the steamboats moving again; their whistles brought both pleasant and horrifying memories. Mom mentioned something

Sandomierz

to me about Aunt Naomi and Sis, but stopped talking when she noticed the other people listening.

Slowly the puddles of melting ice began to dry up in the streets and roads, bowing to the strong winds and the spring sunshine.

We got a card from Dad saying that everything went according to plan, that "the surgery took place the third." Mom knew that it meant that Aunt Naomi and Sis had left the third month, which was sometime in March. Mom started worrying, but tried not to show it. She started her trading business again with the farmers at the market. She now expanded her trading, adding to her arsenal reconditioned clothing, umbrellas, and soap (if she could get it). During the winter Mom had gotten to know some people who owned a home workshop for restoring old garments and other used items. They had offered to give Mom a start. Actually Mom didn't like it, but without apples for the jam, she had had little choice.

I planned to go back to my farm, but for the time being, I helped Mom.

With the beginning of spring, Jews started talking about and preparing for the Passover holidays. Women talked about housecleaning and purifying the house to make it kosher. Preparations for Passover took a lot of time and hard work. According to the traditions of the townspeople of Sandomierz, everything had to be taken out of the house. The walls and furniture had to be rinsed with boiling water and scrubbed clean with a steel-wool brush or with a kind of sharp grass. The floor, too, had to be scrubbed, and it had to be spread with straw or white sand. The old straw in the paillasses had to be replaced with new. Dishes had to be purified: washed, scrubbed, immersed in boiling water.

In Warsaw, we, too, used to make a general spring cleaning before Passover, but I had never heard of scrubbing walls and pouring water over all over furniture. And we didn't have straw mattresses. I did know about purifying dishes, but in our house we didn't do that. We had an extra set of dishes and silverware that we used for this holiday. If we needed more dishes we only washed those that we already had.

In Sandomierz, as in Warsaw, the organization "Moes Khittin" was busy at work collecting money and kosher food for the needy. Now, the number of takers was constantly increasing, while the number of givers was declining.

The bakery designated for the baking of matzo was preparing for the traditional oven-cleaning, and was hiring extra help. Already early in March the bakery manager had put up announcements in Jewish neighborhoods: "Looking for temporary workers to help with matzo-baking. Night work. Long hours. Good pay. Free matzo. Apply Now!" After talking it over with Mom, I signed up. Our old man helped me to get the job. He himself had been called to do the traditional bakery cleaning. "Purifying" or "koshering" the oven, as it's called, was his annual job; he was known to do it diligently, to the very letter of the law.

Shortly before we started our jobs, all temporary workers were called in for an "orientation" meeting. The procedures for baking kosher matzo were explained to us in every detail. Matzo-baking was not a simple task. I watched our old man purifying the oven. The rabbi himself supervised the work so that it would be done as prescribed by law. The baker boys heaped burning coal into the oven, and when it glowed with redness, they covered it with sand. All dishes, pots, and pans were put into boiling water, which sizzled as the dishes were immersed.

The matzo baking itself required skill. Everything had to be properly arranged, for the process of making the matzo kosher relied on cleanliness and the speed with which it was made. The dough had to be mixed, rolled, and baked before it had time to rise. There were people who would measure the flour, and there were the kneaders, and there were special people to carry the water, since the kneaders were not to touch the water jugs; then there were the people who would roll out the dough, and the hole-makers, who would prick it; and a person who would continually watch the dough, which could never be left alone; and then came the bakers, who, finally, would shove the matzo into the hot oven with unbelievable speed.

I was one of the rollers. The first few nights, the job was quite interesting. Everything in this place was new to me. While rolling out the dough into round matzoth I observed the "dough watcher," who was constantly staring at the dough; and I watched the rabbi snooping around the room, murmuring some prayers; I heard the girls around me spreading gossip about the townspeople; and I watched the Hasidim, who had come to the bakery to make their own matzo—Matzo-Shmurah—because they didn't trust anyone with the kashrut.[53] I watched them hurrying from the assembly line to the oven carrying rolled-out matzo dough hung over wooden shovel sticks. Each of them wanted to make sure that his dough got to the oven before it leavened. The run resembled an Olympic race. These were great stories for my diary.

After the first few nights, however, the excitement wore off. The work had become routine and boring. I stayed with the job until the matzo-baking was finished. Shortly before the holidays we got our pay and complimentary matzo for Pessah.

Our old man prepared for a Pessah at home. He designated all of his time and energy to making sure that everything was done correctly, that there were no

My Education Continues

discrepancies in kashrut in his house. With Hershel, he was reviewing the "Four Questions." He even tried to teach a prayer to the baby, who had just barely started uttering his first words. According to the old man, a child's first words should be "Shema Yisrael Adonai Eloheinu Adonai Echod!"—"Hear, O Israel! The Lord is our God, the Lord is One!"

The old man seemed content so long as he could do something for God. So long as he was busy with the holiday preparations, or with teaching his grandsons, he was not worried about food or money. The time before Jewish holidays was good for beggars; the old man was getting a lot of alms. He was also provided with all necessities for Pessah; for the tradition to provide Jews with kosher food for the holidays was still being upheld.

But when he had nothing to do, or in the evenings, when he was just sitting around, he would become depressed, talking to himself. "The first Seder without my Haye-Brandle," I heard him murmur. "A good wife she was to me. Three children she bore me; it was not her fault that God, blessed be His Name, took two of them away from us at such an early age." Or he would talk about his son, who had left for Russia: "We didn't want him to go. I begged him; his mother, may she rest in peace, begged him, too; even his wife, who was with child, asked him to stay. Oh, his poor mother cried so much. I am sure she'd be still alive had he not left. But he listened to his friends, not to his mother, not to me, not to his wife."

During some nights, I would hear the old man's voice from behind the wall after we were all in our beds, trying to fall asleep. "My son in that godless country. I hope he won't forget the holidays. I told him before he left, 'Son, I want you to remain a Jew. Remember the Sabbath, don't forget to put on your tefillin every day.'" Some days the old man cried on

Mom's shoulder. Mom would listen to him compassionately. But often he would just talk to himself, as though he was talking to his son directly: "My dear Laibele, I hope you have a kosher Passover. Please, say the Kaddish for your mother. Don't forget...." And he kept repeating and repeating. Sometimes, he would just talk to God: "O Dear God, please make my Laibele write a letter." He would also talk to whoever was around: "A Passover without my wife, without my son." Sometimes he would talk like that until late into the night, until he fell asleep.

Mom and I celebrated the Seder at the refugee center, at "The Club." Everyone pitched in to help with the preparations. Most of the food came from "Moes Khittin," but other groups had donated, too. An older refugee man conducted the prayers. He came with his married daughter, her husband, and a little grandson, who was chosen to ask the "Four Questions." The Seder leader read the answers from the Haggadah.

After the traditional prayers were over, someone suggested that we say a special prayer for the crisis of our times: "Maybe we should ask God to repeat His miracles." A man suggested the Tehillim. It was not in the Haggadah, but the Seder leader, who read the Psalms, found it in his little prayer book: "Lord, God of Mercy, God of the Universe, God of Salvation: Hear us, spare us, have mercy on Your people." Some old women at our table cried. Then they stopped, and seemed to feel better. Somehow they knew that God had heard them and would not forsake them. They had new hope.

We talked to some people at our table. The news that they were receiving from their hometowns was bad. Fräulein Elsa sang a few songs. After she finished, the mood became gloomy. We all missed our relatives and friends. Mom was nervous. We hadn't heard from Dad. We knew that Aunt and Sis were somewhere on the way. We had heard nothing from them or about them. Their arrival was way overdue. We were glad when the Seder was over.

On Easter Sunday, Sheyndle took me for a walk around town. We watched Christian families going to and returning from their churches. All the parishes were full of worshippers. These, too, were praying for miracles—for the end of the War, and the occupation. They prayed for their relatives to be brought back from wherever they were scattered, and for the resurrection of their country and the Polish people. Many Jews would stay away from Gentile neighborhoods during Christian holidays because beating up Jews on Christian holidays, especially Easter, was almost a tradition for some anti-Semitic hoodlums. "Jews killed our Lord," was their pretense, "so now we'll make them suffer." But Sheyndele had insisted that we go anyway. She said, "I want to show you Easter in Sandomierz." I agreed to go. Not to draw attention, we dressed up in our good clothes, so that we looked like everyone else on the holiday. She put on a nice dress that her husband had made her for Passover; I put on the dress that Mom had bought me for Passover—it was a used dress that she had found in the market. To me it was new, the first dress that I'd had since my cousin gave me one before I left Warsaw.

There were horse-drawn carts in front of us and behind us loaded with farm families heading for and coming from church. We passed by the German headquarters. SS soldiers were walking in front of the main entrance, parading their "Gott mit Uns" ("God [is] with us") belt buckles.

Sheyndele told me that neither she nor her husband believed in God. "We even eat bread on Passover, but we don't do it at home. Our parents would die if they knew," she said. She told me that she had married very young, and that she had miscarried her first baby. But she hoped to carry this one to term. "The baby is due at Rosh Hashanah, or sometime around then—that is, if my count is right."

We walked by the small park adjacent to German headquarters. "We better go to the other side of the street," Sheyndele said. "No need to look for trouble."

I was looking at the passing wagons loaded with peasants coming down the road when Sheyndele pulled me by the hand and said, "Look! Over there, in the park!" I saw a slim blonde girl, with both of her feet about an inch off the ground and both of her hands laced around the neck of a uniformed SS soldier, her flowered dress swinging in the April breeze.

"Who is she?" I asked, thinking that Sheyndele knew her.

"Don't ask stupid questions," Sheyndele said, "just look!"

Next to them, a few yards away, was another couple. The soldier's body and head were partly covered by the girl, who was standing facing him. She was wearing spiked-heel shoes and a skirt that was almost bursting over her large behind. Further inside the park were quite a few other couples of uniformed Germans with young and, most likely, Polish girls. Sheyndele grinned.

I thought that it was kind of neat to be friends with guys in uniforms. These soldiers reminded me of the good-looking Germans who had come to Warsaw, and of those German gendarmes from whom I had learned songs while selling candy at Piłsudski Square. I started singing one of the songs that I still remembered. Sheyndele told me not to sing it. It was not a nice song, she said. "If you want to know dirty songs, I can teach you some in Polish." She then sang one for me, but I couldn't understand the meaning. I didn't ask.

My Education Continues

Right after Passover, Aunt Naomi and Sis arrived in Sandomierz. It had taken them much longer than expected, but they arrived safely. The waiting period had been very hard on Mom, and on me, too, yet we both had tried not to show our sadness to each other. (But it would often show anyway.) Now that they were safely with us, we were all happy.

I wasn't home when they arrived. When I came in, Aunt and Sis were sitting on our bed talking to Mother. I saw Mom's happy face. Mom was relieved to see them unharmed. We talked loud and fast and without stop. Aunt Naomi and Sis told us about their trip. In the town of Kazimierz, they said, they decided to leave the boat after they heard rumors of an inspection. They walked across town to the railroad station, then took the train to Sandomierz. They passed some Jews who were wearing armbands. Many stores were open, but for the most part, the shelves were empty. In front of the few stores that supposedly had some merchandise, stood long lines of people.

"The situation in Warsaw," Aunt Naomi told us, "is terrifying." There were constant deportations of Jews. The Judenrat was now being compelled to provide the Germans with certain quotas of Jewish workers to be deported to other towns. There was a panic. Those with money and influence were, for the time being, buying their way out of deportation. They bought places, or just special IDs, identifying them as employees of the German workshops. Other Jews, the hungry and the poor, were signing up for labor camps voluntarily, just to be eligible for bread and soup. The black market, counterfeit documents, and news from the outside world, were becoming more profitable, and also more dangerous. Yet were it not for the smugglers risking their lives, everyone in the ghetto would be dead of starvation by now.

"Pinkert's three-wheelers—the undertaker's carts—are not able to keep up with the dead. Corpses and the dying are lining the streets. It is much worse than it was before you left, if you can imagine such a thing. Starvation, typhus, and the freezing winter have taken thousands of lives." Aunt took a deep breath. She stood up and stretched, then looking straight at Mom, continued: "I assume you've already heard about Moniek's death. Well, Aunt Dora couldn't take it any more; she died, too."

"No! This can't be true!" Mom screamed in disbelief. "What in the world is going on? Moniek was so young, in good health..."

"Typhus," Aunt Naomi said, "typhus complications. They couldn't save him. I was sure you knew it from the mail, or that Tola already told you!"

Mom looked at me, waiting for my reaction. I just stood there, and said nothing. I saw a mixture of grief and hopelessness on Mom's face. Her happy look had disappeared. She sighed and tears began rolling from her eyes. She was shaking. Aunt Naomi tried to calm her down, changing the subject, but Mom insisted that she continue telling her about other friends and relatives.

"Well," she continued, "only those with money—and they are few and far between—and those working for the Germans and the Judenrat, only those are still safe from deportation. The police and collaborators are relatively not so bad off, either. Many of them live off bribes and payoffs, but they have a difficult job to do. They are stuck between the Jews and the Germans, and don't know which way to go. Some turned really mean against their own people; others risk their own lives to help the ghetto inhabitants who are slowly losing hope. I am still doing some business outside the ghetto. It is very risky now." With that, she had changed the subject.

My Education Continues

"We really appreciated your packages; they were life-savers. You don't know how many people envied us."

Aunt Naomi gave us a detailed account of Dad's health, and the situation of other friends and relatives: Aunt Polla, Dad's sister, had gotten married. A young widower with a two-year-old girl had become part of our extended family. Second cousin, Zalmen, had changed his name to Zbyszek and moved to the Aryan side. He supposedly was living with a Polish girl somewhere on Marindad. Uncle Hersh, his father, was worried that he may convert to Catholicism.

I looked at Aunt Naomi. She had changed: some gray hair, and her face looked older. Wrinkles were showing around her eyes.

I kept looking at my "little sister," too. How much she had grown! She had slimmed down a lot. I noticed her boobs—they, too, had grown quite a bit. I was sure that she was wearing a bra. I couldn't help thinking of the little girl we had left behind barely a year ago. My thoughts went even further back. "Mom, do you remember the story with the puppy?"

A faint smile appeared on Mom's face. "Of course. How can one forget it—"Mama, proszę, urodź pieska dla mnie?" Her face lit up a bit. She was looking proudly at her grownup baby daughter. "What a beautiful lady," Mom whispered, and gave her baby a big hug.

Our landlady, with her baby son in her arms, walked into the room. "This is our landlady," Mom said to Aunt and Sis. Then turning to the landlady and pointing to Aunt Naomi and Sis, she said, "And this is my sister and my daughter. They are the people I told you about." To Aunt Naomi, she said, "This bed, the one we are sitting on, is our bed. There are two beds in the kitchen—you must have seen them when you walked in; one of them I rented for the two of you."

Sandomierz

Aunt Naomi turned her head and looked into the kitchen. Mom said, "There's an old man sleeping in the other bed. I am sorry. That's the best I could find."

We continued talking. Aunt and sister were asking questions about our life in Sandomierz. We told them about the trading business, and the jam business, and my job on the farm; about the marketplace and the refugee center—"The Club"—and my Saturday night meetings and about Mr. Sikorsky, who brought us books from the library.

We talked about Passover. We found out that Aunt and Sis had spent the holidays while underway. They had been trying to make it to Sandomierz in time for the holidays, but the trip was taking much longer than they had expected. They had to leave the boat a couple of times, not just the one time that she initially told us about. The first time that they left the boat, they had to wait a few days for the next one. "I ate bread during Passover," Naomi said, "but that little pious daughter of yours wouldn't touch it. She didn't eat a thing for two days until she found some carrots and potatoes."

Yes, it seemed that Sis was still keeping to her religious beliefs. She had refused to eat anything that she wasn't sure was kosher, even if someone had offered it to her while she was starving. With kashrut, she trusted almost nobody, not even her own mother. The only person she did trust was Uncle Sruel, and another uncle, the one who lived in the village on the way to Otwock. She had even consulted with Uncle Sruel about the trip that she was about to take: "What if we have to travel on the Sabbath?" Dad had tried to assure her that it was okay, but she didn't believe him; she had to check with Uncle. He, too, had said that it was okay, because this trip wouldn't be a pleasure tour; it was considered "Pekhuakh Nefesh."

It was our maternal grandfather, Sholom Meyer, who taught us about God and religion. He was not a

My Education Continues

Hassid, and not a fanatic. The Orthodox part of her beliefs Sis had learned that one summer when we visited Dad's cousins and became friends with their daughters. I, too, had played with the girls, but I never took their fanatical behavior seriously. We were surprised when Sis got caught up in their religious frenzy, but we let her do what she wanted, even though it was, at times, a nuisance to do everything just for her, strictly by law. Even more surprising was that during the most difficult times of freezing and starvation, she had not changed.

We sat in the room until it got dark, reminiscing. Then we all went into the street, where we sat in front of the house, and talked some more. We talked long into the night.

After a few days of excitement, our lives normalized. I went back to my work on the farm. For a while, Sis helped Mother in the trading business; then she found a babysitting job. Aunt Naomi returned to Warsaw against Mom's pleading that she stay with us. It was her smuggling business and her boyfriend that made her want to go back. She had good ID papers and spent some of her time outside of the ghetto.

Mom was happy that both her daughters were now with her and, for the first time in a long while, had their stomachs filled. We had a place to sleep. These were all that mattered.

As long as there were no new decrees, we could survive. We knew that times would eventually change. One day the War would be over. "Nothing lasts forever." Newspaper headlines were full of German victories. The Germans were advancing deep into Russia. They needed more workers to replace the fighting soldiers and more food, medicine, and vehicles for the army. The occupied countries, which by now included most of Europe, were to provide all the

Sandomierz

workers and supplies. Poland was especially hard hit because it was the "Corridor," the route for moving troops and supplies between Germany and Russia. There were rumors about American help coming to the Russians, and about guerilla movements in the forests; but the facts were that the German armies were occupying and ruling most of the European countries and the European part of Russia. Every evening, people sitting outside their homes would discuss politics and news from the Front. Those who did not take part in these discussions would watch for collaborators, informers, or eavesdropping policemen, all of whom were often willing or eager to get people arrested for "illegal activities"—such as talking politics.

On one of these hot summer nights, I came home from my work on the farm and stopped to listen to a conversation going on outside our building.

Mom saw me outside. "Don't you want to go to bed?" she asked me. "You need to get up for work early in the morning."

I went in, washed my face and feet, lay down on the bed, and fell asleep. I always slept well, but especially well after a day's work on the farm. I was still in deep sleep—it was before dawn—when Mom woke me. I felt her hand on my shoulder and heard her soft voice: "Wake up."

"What's going on?" I said, half asleep, "It's not morning already?"

"Someone wants to see you," she said in a shaky, half-crying voice. I rubbed my eyes to see what was going on. "Didn't you hear the knocking at the door?" Mom asked, surprised.

I opened my eyes and saw Mom and Sis standing by my bed. Behind them stood a uniformed Jewish policeman. After rubbing my eyes clear, I recognized him—Moniek, the one I kept meeting in Henyek's house at the Saturday night parties. (I also saw him

My Education Continues

often keeping order in the streets.) Next to him stood a tall blond guy in civilian clothes. I had never seen him before. I looked at the two of them and couldn't figure out what in the world these guys were doing in our house so early in the morning; or what they would want from me.

I was told that Moniek and the other man were rounding up Jews for work. The Judenrat had gotten an order to supply a certain number of workers for the Germans. "We are only obeying their orders," the two men said, quite politely, trying to minimize the shock. They had a list of names with them. Only my first name appeared on their list. They didn't even know my last name. They were more concerned with the number of workers than with names. They were looking for people between sixteen and twenty-four. I wasn't sixteen yet, but it didn't matter; I had no documentation to prove it. It probably wouldn't have mattered much if I had; the Judenrat needed to fill its quota. The people with bribes and connections were not going to be taken; that was out of the question. So here I was, in a strange city, without influence, without money, without acquaintances in high places.

I had to dress and then go with the two men. While I was dressing, I heard Mom asking Moniek, "For how long are you taking her?"

I didn't hear what he answered, if anything. He was watching me put on my dress. "Hurry up!" he said to me, looking at his watch. "We don't have the whole day!"

The two men took me to the city square. We walked. Mom and sister followed us. The men didn't object.

We got to the city hall. Near the gate, like a statue, stood a handsome Polish officer, his eyes like transparent glass, staring into nowhere, looking both scary and funny. He said nothing.

Sandomierz

I turned around to see if Mom and Sis were still behind me. They were. I saw more young people being led into that government building. We entered a long corridor that took us into a large assembly hall. One Polish policeman and one uniformed German gendarme were guarding the door. Moniek said something to them; they motioned us to go ahead. At the entrance, inside the hall, stood a long registration table. Behind it sat three clerks holding ink pens and lined sheets of paper. Moniek and the other guy took me to the table and turned me over to one of the clerks. The two men left the hall. The guards locked the door behind them. One of the women at the table asked me for my name. I told her. She asked no more questions, just marked something on her papers, and told me to move along.

The hall was filling up with young women. There might have been about one hundred of us. The group of rounded-up men were being taken to a nearby building. We could see them walking through the gate.

The sun was now rising over the eastern horizon. Through the open windows, looking out into the square, we could see a crowd gathering outside the buildings. In the crowd were friends and relatives of those locked up inside. They were desperately trying to find out where we were being taken, and for how long.

Like my mom and sister, they, too, had followed their loved ones to the square. As the news about the roundup spread through the city, more people came to the square just out of curiosity.

I saw Mom and Sis standing not far from my window. I waved. They waved back.

Some folks in the crowd were weeping, some screaming hysterically. "Where are you bandits taking our kids?" yelled a heavyset woman, wiping her eyes with her sleeve.

My Education Continues

"Stop it! Stop it! It's not a funeral," yelled a woman standing next to her.

From inside the crowd, I heard a voice shout, "Hey, you! You're making all of them and all of us nervous!" But again, and again, I heard the same question: "Where are you taking our people?" I heard no answer.

There were rumors that we were being taken to Germany in order to work on farms; someone had heard that we were going to work in a munitions plant located somewhere in Poland; others in the crowd said that we were going to be cleaning German quarters and barracks.

The answer from the police and guards was, "Don't worry! They'll be okay. They'll be returned home after their assignment is done."

A police officer walked into our hall. He called two names. Two girls pushed their way to the front of the hall. The policeman nodded for them to follow him, which they did. Through the window we saw the two girls walking outside the building, trying to get through the crowd. "Connection money!" said a voice behind me.

Many of the friends and relatives tried to get their loved ones released. People claimed that their girls were in poor health, that they were the only breadwinners in the families, that they had small babies at home. Mom thought that she could get me out on account of my being under the minimum age.

The authorities assured the crowd outside that we would be well treated, that they had nothing to worry about, that all their pleas would be taken into consideration. They asked the people with special claims to line up at the table that was next to the front door, and fill out some papers.

While a line of relatives and friends of the rounded-up people was forming at the front door to fill out the "claims," we, who were inside the hall, were being lined up at the back door, to be loaded onto some open trucks.

My truck drove by the front of the building. I saw Mom and Sis standing in line where people were filling out claims.

Chapter 3. Skarżysko

As our truck pulled away, onto the open road, the square was still full of people. There were about twenty-five or thirty girls with me on the truck, which took us over a paved highway and some cobblestone roads. We passed through towns and villages, as well as unpaved side paths and fields. Many farmers working in their fields waved to us; we waved back. The heat of the day, the dust, the thirst, and the bumpy road wore us out. Many girls sat down on the dusty truck floor; some napped.

Late afternoon I heard one of the standing girls read out aloud, "Skarżysko-Kamienna." One of the girls sitting on the floor said, "I have an aunt who lives there. I wonder where they are taking us?" Other girls on our truck had also heard of this town before. It was more than one hundred kilometers northeast of Sandomierz. I had heard of Skarżysko in a geography class. It was known as a transit point, a crossing of railroad tracks from where trains would go into many different directions.

Hot, thirsty, hungry, exhausted, worried and curious, we arrived at our destination. The truck stopped in front of a large building that could have been a factory, a school, or a government office; in the semi-darkness, it was hard to tell what was really there. It was surrounded by a large field. Only the entrance to the building was lit from inside. In front of us was a truck unloading people. We waited our turn. In front of the large entrance gate stood what looked like two guards carrying rifles and flashlights. On a signal from one of them, the truck in front of us drove away, and our truck pulled up closer to the door.

"They must be Ukrainians," I heard a girl say. "There are many Ukrainian collaborators around here." I had never heard of them. But some of the girls were saying that since the Germans occupied Russia, many Ukrainians had started helping the Germans; they were known to be Jew-haters.

The two guards, whoever they were, ordered us to get off the truck. A few Polish uniformed women guards were waiting at the gate. We were searched, counted, and then taken inside the building. At the end of a long corridor was a large hall. Through the wide open double doors we could see long lines of wooden platforms stacked four high; they looked like planks or bunk beds that were stuck together. Some of the platforms were covered with loose straw; others were bare. There was a long table at the end of the corridor by the entrance to the large hall. Sitting behind that table were a few uniformed Polish police women. We lined up in the long corridor and then walked down to a table marked "Station #1," from where the induction procedures started. There were girls in front of me and behind me.

At "Station #1, Disinfection," every girl was sprayed with some kind of disinfectant, then was told to move on to the next.

At "Station #2, Registration," I stopped. "First and last name," the woman behind the table said. I told her. She wrote the information in a roster on a line next to a number, then said, "Nine-twenty-one." She then pointed to one of the two-by-five centimeter red

My Education Continues

cloth tags that were lined up on the table. "Take number 921 and pin it on your dress," she said in Polish, then added in German, "Macht schnell!"—"Be quick!"

At "Station #3, Marking," stood a man with a paint brush in his hand. Next to him, on the floor, was a large bucket filled with red paint. A couple of Ukrainian guards, and a couple of Jewish policemen, were keeping order. The man with the brush painted two red stripes across the full length of my dress; one over the front, the other over the back. "Macht schnell!" he said. I moved forward and joined the already "processed" girls.

At "Station #4, Food," each girl was given a slice of black bread and a half-liter tin can of beet soup.

At the last station, "Station #5," we were given gray army-type blankets, and were shown to our place on one of the planks.

I climbed to the third-floor bunk, as directed. I sat down in my space next to a girl with long blonde, braided hair. Her new name was "894"; her given name I didn't know. I sat there for a while, drinking my soup and nibbling on the bread. I watched the long line of girls still waiting at the processing stations. Everything was proceeding in a very orderly fashion.

It was very quiet in that large hall. Every processed girl was in her assigned place. Some of the girls were eating, others were lying down, exhausted, holding their soup cans by their sides. No one said a word; no one knew what to say or what to expect. I laid my head on the straw. There were still many girls lined up at the processing stations. I closed my eyes. I saw my mother standing at the square in Sandomierz, trying to get me released.

I heard a voice and opened my eyes. Two Ukrainian guards, accompanied by a civilian-dressed, tall, heavyset woman, were standing in the center of the hall. The woman was talking to us in a Polish that was mixed with German. "You are now part of a labor brigade," I heard her say. "You will work in the newly established addition of the HASSAG munitions plant. You'll be working for the Third Reich. If you work fleißig [diligently], you will be provided with food and a place to live."[54] She stopped, looked around the room. "This is not a Konzentrationslager, but it is not a Scout Camp or recreation center, either. My advice to you is this: Don't think about sabotage, or escape!"

She stopped and looked at the piece of paper on which she had written out her speech. "Don't get any funny ideas," she said, in a confident voice. "If anyone of you disobeys the orders, or if one of you is missing at Appell [roll call], all of you will pay the consequences. The price for such an offense is high!" She stopped again, glancing around the room in such a way that her rolling eyes met almost everyone in the room. "We'll hang one of you right on the spot for each one missing. Verstanden? [Understand?] We just pick one at random. That is how we operate!" She folded the paper in her hand. "Now you may all go to sleep. Someone will talk to you in the morning." She started walking to the door. She turned around and added in a no-nonsense voice: "All of you will have to watch the hanging, so think about it." Happy with her performance, proud of what she had said and of her superior position, she turned off the lights and left the room. Someone on the top bunk said, "I wonder how long they'll keep us here?" To which a voice answered, "I assume not more than a month or two."

In the morning, reveille was sounded. We were awakened by a tall, heavyset woman who looked almost like the one who had talked to us the night before. This one had a Ukrainian accent, and spoke in a broken Polish mixed with Ukrainian and German words. "Achtung! Attention!" she shouted through a

My Education Continues

bullhorn. "Everyone up and na dwór—into the yard! Machen schnell!" She kept yelling until everyone was out of the hall.

We assembled in the yard, in front of the large gray building. "Stay right where you are!" yelled a short stout woman in a Polish police uniform, who was standing in front of us with her hands on her hips. "You are new here, I know. From now on, I want all of you to learn these words: Achtung! Appell! Halt! Heraus! [Out!] Other words you'll learn later." She looked straight at us, as if to make sure that we were paying attention. "You will hear these words often."

We were told that from now on, Appells would take place twice daily, in the morning and in the evening. And we had better be sure never to come late or miss one of them. "Today each of you will be assigned a job, and you will be given the appropriate rules and regulations. You better listen closely and follow each one of them. And now," she said, in the voice of a military commander, "line up in rows of five!—I mean five abreast!" We followed the order. Two Ukrainian guards counted us and wrote their findings on a special form. They gave the paper to a German gendarme, who signed it and then drove away on his motorcycle.

One of the Ukrainian guards explained that we would be taken to work shortly. There must have been two hundred of us girls in the column that had formed in that yard. More Ukrainian guards arrived and formed a fence around our column. "Turn right!" one of them yelled. We followed the order. "Forward, march!" was the next command. We followed the order.

Surrounded by Ukrainian guards with pointed rifles, we walked though deserted side roads until we came to a large iron gate shielded by two high watchtowers. We stopped. There were German gendarmes in front of the gate, behind it, and more in

Skarżysko

the watchtowers. As far as the eye could see stretched a high brick wall topped with rows of barbed wire. One of our Ukrainian guards handed some documents to the German soldiers. The soldiers counted us. They stamped the papers and opened the gate. We marched in; the gate was locked behind us. The Ukrainian guards who had brought us to this place left.

Scattered about the large area inside the fence were large and small brick buildings. Our group of about two hundred was divided up into groups of twenty-five—five rows of five girls each. Each of the small groups was assigned a supervisor who then led it into one of the buildings.

My group was taken to a building that had a small sign over the main door that read malarnia—paint shop. A line of work stations mounted to the cement floor filled the long, brightly lit hall. Polish men and women, as well as a few Jewish workers in civilian clothes, were minding the stations. I recognized the Jews by their painted stripes and pinned-on numbers.

I saw one young Jewish man pushing a cart loaded with what looked like large, empty aluminum bottles with wide-open necks. He pushed the cart over to one of the work stations. I watched him unload the cargo, and I was just about to ask him something when I heard someone speak in German. It was our group supervisor, a German gendarme. He had to speak through an interpreter. We were told not to talk, not to ask questions, never to leave the workshop without supervision or a special permit, not even when going to the latrine. "Verstanden?" he said.

We were told that the Germans, by nature of their birth, were our supreme rulers. The Ukrainians who worked at our camp and the Poles who worked at the plant were friends of the Germans. "You Jewish Häftlinge [prisoners] are here to do what you are told, and to listen to your superiors. Verstanden? If your

My Education Continues

work is satisfactory, you'll be treated nicely. If not...." The interpreter stopped. "Verstanden?"

The shop foreman, a middle-aged Pole, assigned jobs to us. He called us by our numbers (even though our names were next to the numbers on his list). I was assigned to work with a good-looking and tall, young blond Polish man. "Here, Janek!" said the foreman. "She'll be working with you. You tell her what to do. Show her how, and make sure she does what you say." This man introduced himself politely: "Janek Kaczmarek," he said. I knew his name since the tag on his jacket stated it clearly, but I appreciated his saying it anyway. "You are new here, I see," he continued. "Consider yourself lucky. This is a fairly good place to work." He told me that he lived in the city, and had been working here for about a year. I said nothing; I just nodded my head in approval. I was playing a kind of "Whom do you trust?" game, with a wait-and-see strategy.

I found out that his job was to spray-paint the insides of the aluminum "bottles," which he did with a long-handled spray-gun. He was wearing a mouth-and-nose mask during the spraying. My job was to put protective covers over the screw-threads in the bottlenecks before he sprayed them. When the spraying was done, I would take out the protectors and make sure that the threads were clean. Janek—Jasiek, as he was called—politely explained this assignment to me in detail. He pointed out a large box of rags. "Always make sure to use clean rags, so that no oil or paint is ever left on the threads. I am responsible for the work." He took me over to the box and pulled out a few of the rags. Pointing to the "bottles," he said, "These are grenade shells. If they find anything wrong with them during the German inspection, my head will be chopped off." He moved his right hand over his throat. I asked Jasiek about the rules of talking on the

Skarżysko

job. He said, "It is okay, as long as there are no guards around, and no squealers to report on you. In a little bit, I will show you who to watch out for."

At noon the Häftlinge were given a soup made of beet greens, potatoes, and groats. It was poured into the tin cans that we had been given the night before, the ones that we were told to mark with our numbers and always to carry with us.

At the first opportunity, I walked over to a Jewish woman whom I had seen working at the paint station. I asked her where she was from, and how long she had been working here. "I am from Ostroviec," she said. "I have been here a little over three months." She was eating her soup and talking at the same time. "Looks like you just came. How many people arrived on your transport? Every few days now, we are getting new people. Where did they take you from?" I answered all of her questions, then I asked one of my own: "When are you and your group scheduled to return to Ostroviec? I heard that we were brought here to replace workers who were going back home."

The woman gave me a funny look and said nothing. Then, turning to the Jewish guy who was delivering and picking up her work, she said, pointing at me, "Did you hear, Archie? This naive chick thinks the new people were brought here to replace us. Ha!...Ha!...." Then, looking me straight in the eye, she said: "Don't be stupid, kid. Here, people only come; no one ever leaves this place."

A Polish woman who was working next to her was quietly listening to our conversation, saying nothing.

"Pani Grarzyno!" said the Jewish woman who was speaking with me. "Did you hear what that girl said? I hope not all of the new arrivals go around with the illusion of going home soon." Then the Jewish woman turned to me again and explained, "The only people who are being replaced here are the dead ones."

My Education Continues

The rest of the day, I concentrated on learning my job. I kept thinking about what the woman had told me. Before the work day was over, I found out that this plant was working in two ten-hour shifts. (I had been assigned to the dayshift.) I also learned that there were three separate branches of the plant: Branch A, where I worked, and Branches B and C, both of which were located within a fifteen to twenty kilometer distance. Each had its own labor camp.

In the days and months that followed, I learned enough new things to fill many diary books, and enough to get a doctorate in human behavior and durability. The curriculum consisted of physical education, mental conditioning, medical miracles, endurance, and survival skills. There were only two grades: Pass or Fail.

The first things I learned were survival skills: Forget everything you know. Don't complain. Follow the leader. Follow instructions. Don't make your own laws. Don't argue with your superiors. The sooner you learned these rules, the better were your chances of survival.

Every few days now, transports with new young Jewish men and women would arrive to the camp. One day after work, instead of going back to our by now overcrowded building, we were put into groups of fifty and taken to an army barracks located by the railroad tracks. We were told that these were only interim quarters, that new barracks were under construction. The large building was being used for processing new arrivals. Next day this information was confirmed by some Polish people at work who had seen brigades of male Häftlinge building new barracks not far from the plant. After a few hectic weeks of induction, work assignments, and moving, life for our group "normalized."

Skarżysko

Everyone had an assigned number, a job, and a bed. Food rations were allotted: Coffee in the morning, soup at noon, bread with margarine, jam, or cheese in the evening. We could save some of the bread for breakfast if we wanted, and if we had the willpower to do so. Appells were twice daily. We were working six days a week.

Postal service was established. The mail, of course, was censored; and only postcards were allowed. But the mail moved fairly well. We were encouraged to write. We were even given some postcards by the camp authorities to send home so that we could tell the people who were not yet here "how well we were being treated." (To be truthful, as long as we did our jobs, we were not beaten, or otherwise physically hurt.) After a while, even parcels were allowed into the camp. In my first package, Mom sent me some bread, a couple of cucumbers, a few carrots, and some other ready-to-eat items. I shared the food with a few girls in my room. A postcard arrived a few days later: "We got your card," Mom wrote. "Glad you are okay. We are fine. I sent your new address to Dad. Take care of yourself. Love, Mom. Regards from your 'little' sister. P.S. Write when you can."

Many girls would receive food from home. Nothing else was allowed into the camp. All parcels were opened and checked. Some packages would contain cookies or fruit. Whenever a package arrived, many girls would share in the feast.

One day, after our dayshift girls had come from work, we heard from the girls who worked on the camp premises, and from those who worked the nightshift and were in the barracks during the day, that something very unusual had happened in the camp during our absence:

The nightshift people were awakened at noon. They were called to an assembly. There was a commission of

My Education Continues

German officers, one of whom announced that a new ordinance had just been received stating that anyone who wanted to leave the camp and go home for any reason, medical or otherwise, might do so by registering at the office. Our plant now had enough people to work. The authorities wanted only those who were fit for work and who wanted to work hard. Those who wished to remain would move to a new camp. Many girls registered. Some were accepted and, for unknown reasons, others were rejected. The commission made their decisions on the spot. We were sure that the same chance to register would be given to our dayshift workers; so we waited.

But nothing happened. The commission had left the camp, we were told, and now no one knew if it would be returning. I remember sitting on my bed that night wondering what Mom would think when she saw other girls coming home and not find me among them. All the girls in my barracks felt sad and depressed. We thought that we should be given the same chance as the nightshift. This was not fair. I knew only a couple of girls who ever got to go home from the camp; they were from Skarżysko, and had been released the day after their arrival. The right connections, probably. For all the others, this was only an impossible dream.

In the morning, at Appell, we heard new rumors. People were saying that another commission would be visiting the camp shortly. We went to work filled with new hope. When we arrived at work, we heard from some Polish workers that the night before, they had seen a lot of Jewish girls with the red stripes on their clothes assembled at the railroad station, being loaded into a cargo train. Did we know anything about it? Of course, we knew that they were talking about the girls from our camp. We told them about the registration. I remember the skeptical smile on Pani Kristina's face. She was a Polish woman who worked not far from me.

Skarżysko

She just looked at the Jewish girl who had told her that and said nothing. Jasiek, who had been listening to the conversation, bent over and whispered in my ear, "I've never heard of any Jew who went home from here."

The nightshift people had already left for work when we arrived at the barracks that evening. Some of the people who worked in the camp told us that at about noontime, they had seen a long freight train passing behind the barracks. The boxcars had been carrying people; they had seen heads peeking though the small windows at the top of the cars and hands waving through the cracks in the walls. Some voices had been coming from the railroad tracks, but because of the roaring of the train, there had been no way to hear.

Whatever happened to the people during, or after, that train trip is still a mystery; we never heard from, or about, any of them again.

A couple of weeks passed. No commission came. Our lives went back to the daily routine. Autumn winds started blowing; days were getting shorter. Rains became more frequent. We moved to a new quarters.

The new place was much bigger than the interim army barracks. There must have been about forty barracks or more, set up on a large, bare, sandy field. It was surrounded by two rows of tangled barbed wire. At the entrance gate was a checkout booth where two Ukrainian watchmen with clubs and German shepherds kept guard. Outside the gate were two watchtowers from where other Ukrainian guards, with rifles, kept their eyes on the camp. We felt quite secure and well protected.

The camp yard was a bare, muddy field that was divided into three sections. One section was set up

My Education Continues

with a barracks for women; one, of equal size, had a barracks for men; a smaller one, but no less important, had a "miscellaneous" barracks. Each section had its own latrine and an outside row of water faucets nearby. The yard in front of each barracks served as an assembly point for Appells. The men's and women's sections were used as living quarters for the rank-and-file inmates. The barracks in the "miscellaneous" section was used for administrative offices. There were barracks for offices, kitchens, and for a so-called clinic. There were also living quarters for the Jewish police and the kapos—the so-called camp "executives."[55] Each "executive" barracks was divided into small rooms in which the specially privileged, high-class inmates could live alone, or with their wives, girlfriends, or their "cousins."

The men's and women's barracks (or "blocks," as they were called) housed the common inmates, and were divided into three large rooms, with each room holding about forty people. Each of these rooms was furnished with a long table that was located in the center of the room. The table was used for cutting bread and for distributing the rations.

Also in the center, and somewhat closer to the door, was a wood-burning space-heater with a large tin-plate tube leading to the roof. A large covered bucket stood next to the door. Double-decker bunk beds stood with their heads against the walls. There were six on one side of the room, and five on the door side. There were two-foot aisles among the bunks—just enough space for getting in and out of bed.

In this new camp, the use of loose straw for bunk spreads was discontinued. Each bed had been outfitted with a straw mattress and a gray, army blanket. Each bed would be used by two girls who were working opposite shifts. We could not choose our beds, but we could choose our bedmates. My bedmate was a native of Warsaw, a girl named Sala Frenks, who had been brought to the camp from the town of Ostrowiec, where she had lived with her grandmother for many years, ever since her parents divorced.

This new place was a great improvement over the large building and the army barracks where we lived before. Here, everything was skillfully organized. Most of the girls who lived in the same room also worked in the same place. Most of those in my room worked in the paint shop. Only six didn't work there—three in a nearby department where small bullets were made, one in the kitchen (a job that she got through special connections), and two on the camp premises. These latter belonged to a brigade that was assigned to keep the camp clean. Girls in this brigade had to take care that the women's latrine was clean, and to watch the heaters. Cleaning was not a big problem; there was hardly any dirt, trash, or garbage in the camp.

One girl in each room was assigned as a Stubenälteste, a "room leader." She worked at the plant, but after work she was the boss of the room. Her duties were to keep order in the room, and to take care of the rations, for which she was given extra bread rations and some special privileges, such as going outside the barracks after curfew hours or talking to the authorities. Our Stubenälteste was a thirty-year-old woman, originally from Warsaw, who had gotten out of the city just before the ghetto was closed up. She had lived in Tarnobierz with her husband and four-year-old son, in the house of her in-laws. Her name was Wanzia, or Wanda. We called her "Dziobata Wanda" because of her pock-marked face.

After being in this camp for a while, our lives became quite organized. We were constantly watched, but after some time this became normal to us. There were guards at the gates, at the doors, outside the barracks, at work, at camp, even watching the latrine.

My Education Continues

"Appell," "Forward, march," "Mach schnell," each of these became part of our daily vocabulary. We were counted coming and going, eating and sleeping; checked and rechecked so that, God forbid, none of us would get lost. On its way to work and on its way from work, our column was watched by Jewish camp police, Ukrainian guards, and German gendarmes. Everyone was protecting us. We felt secure, shielded, safe; after all, young girls must be chaperoned.

Daily we arrive at the plant; we stop at the gate. "Five, five..." The guards count each row. Someone signs the papers. Salute. Split into brigades. Each brigade goes to it assigned place. The work day begins. The daily routine in camp, as at work, varies little. At work it hardly varies at all. At camp it varies from time to time: If the count does not come out right we get additional time at the Appell. Occasionally there comes a visiting commission headed by the German Wehrmacht. They come to select the sick, the weak, and those unable to do the hard labor. All the "unfit," as they are called, are sent away to some unknown destination, never to be heard from again. Another variation at the camp is watching public beatings, which occur frequently now that our initial "honeymoon" of recruiting is over. Especially popular are beatings of men who are being punished for such offenses as getting an extra slice of bread or pulling a beet from a field on the way to or from work. Sometimes there are beatings and kickings of men who have crossed the path of an officer, or have disobeyed an order, perhaps for not fulfilling orders to exact specifications.

On a very lucky day, the variation might be extra soup, or a potato or turnip. It all depends on the mood and discretion of the superiors. We can only hope and pray that these "chiefs" are having a good day—or a good night—and that their mood is not gloomy whenever they are with us.

Skarżysko

For most of us, going to work was a blessing. The plant was an escape from camp. It was the only place where we could have contact with people from the outside world. It was at the plant that we could find, in the trash, or on the floor, a page of a newspaper and learn what was going on outside the barbed-wire fence. It was at the plant that, occasionally, a Polish worker, who was himself on rationed food, would share a slice of bread with us. It was at the plant that a foreman would let one of us scrape out some leftover soup from the bottom of the "general caldron." (There were never any leftovers in the "Jewish Caldron.") It was at the plant that we didn't feel completely isolated. The plant was the only place where we were safe from a "selection."[56] Even though the majority of Polish workers—and Poles in general—did not want to mix with the Jews, there were a few gentle souls, or "Righteous Gentiles" (as they were later called), who would occasionally help us by mailing letters to our families or by bringing us news from them. Life for the Poles wasn't easy, either. They had to deal with hard work, rationed food, killed or abducted relatives, and illnesses, among other troubles.

Our camp was not a resort: The woman who spoke to us in the "big building" had told us this loud and clear. She knew what she was talking about. Yet, as bad as this slave camp was, it was nothing compared to the ghetto as I remembered it. Here, at least, we were getting our soup and some bread every day. Even if the food was bad and insufficient, we could always count on a bite to eat. Here, we also had a place to sleep; no one had to sleep on the street. Often while eating my soup or munching on a piece of bread, I would think of the dead bodies in the streets of the Warsaw Ghetto; I could see the corpses of children being hauled away on Pinkert's three-wheelers.

My Education Continues

I wondered how Dad was getting along now; and I thought of other friends and relatives who were facing another winter without food or fuel; and I thought of Mom and Sis, who had to worry about their daily existence (for I had heard that conditions in smaller towns were worsening, that there were critical shortages of everything; medical supplies were things of the past). The Polish workers at the plant kept saying how lucky they were to have their jobs.

One day I received a card from Aunt Naomi, postmarked outside the ghetto. She said nothing about the conditions in Warsaw, nor of those in the ghetto. She just wrote, "Freda and Rena voluntarily signed up for work in a labor camp. The girls were given some food, and were promised good jobs. Stay well. Aunt Naomi."

I knew that the girls' father, Uncle Yakov, had died, right after we left the ghetto. Dad had written about it. While we were in Sandomierz, I had heard that their mother, Aunt Rachel, had also died in the ghetto. Now the girls were gone. I wondered if their sister, Ida, was still working in the German workshop, and if anyone knew what had happened to their oldest sister, the one who had left for Russia.

News from the Russian Front kept changing. The latest tales were suggesting that things were not going too well for the Germans. Heavy snows had started covering the Russian roads, preventing German advances. The papers didn't say this; they had just stopped reporting victories. People, reading between the lines, could figure out the rest. They knew that something must be wrong. Trains that crossed from Russia to Germany and vice-versa were full of soldiers and war equipment. More Polish people were being sent to Germany in order to replace the German reservists who were being called to active duty—sent to the Front to replace the huge numbers of dead and wounded.

Skarżysko

Our workplace was kept fairly warm, and very busy. We started working twelve-hour shifts.

At camp, the men who did not work at the plant hauled firewood from a nearby forest so that we could heat up our rooms in the mornings and evenings; during the day and night, while people slept, there was no heat in the barracks.

The wood-hauling men reported that some strange things were happening in the forest, things which they could not explain. They heard shooting in the distance. Some even thought that they could hear screaming. Others insisted that it was only their imaginations. The guards were nervous.

Trucks with used winter clothing arrived one day. Coats, jackets, and sweaters were distributed. I got a long beige coat. It was three sizes too big, but it was made of good woolen fabric, and it kept me warm.

The days were getting shorter, the curfew hours longer, the rations smaller, and the problems larger. Evenings we spent sitting on our beds, talking and telling each other stories. Our room was a conglomerate of girls from all parts of the country and all walks of life: There were girls from large cities and small villages; there were the rich and the poor, the very religious and the nonbelievers; we had two high-society girls and a few from the "dump" (even a couple from the red-light district). Their ages ranged from eighteen to early thirties. I was the youngest in our barracks.

The large majority spoke Yiddish, many with a Galician accent. Even though I understood some Yiddish, it was hard for me to understand everything that was being said; sometimes because of the accent, other times because of the unfamiliar subject matter, or the strange vocabulary. I heard some girls making fun of my Yiddish. Sometimes they reminded me of my Grandmother Esther. I thought of her a lot. She always

My Education Continues

complained about my poor knowledge of the Jewish language. I remembered how sad she used to be because neither Sis nor I could speak our "mother tongue." Now I was sorry that I hadn't listened to her. Quite often I sat on my bed just listening to the talk. I didn't speak, but I kept learning.

One evening, I had a conversation with Wanda. She knew that I was from Warsaw, and she wanted to know where in the city I used to live.

"Świętojerska Street 28," I told her.

"Oh! No wonder you don't speak your mother tongue!" She shook her head and put a funny grin on her face. "People over there were ashamed of Yiddish." Then, with an amused voice: "I bet you are still a virgin!" She had purposely spoken in Yiddish, and started laughing.

I didn't understand the question, and said nothing. She kept waiting for my answer. She repeated what she had said. "Well, I don't understand what you are saying," I told her, somewhat ashamed. Many girls started laughing.

"A virgin! Do you know what a virgin is?" she asked, smiling; then added in almost hysterical laughter, "I already forgot what it is. I forget when I was one!" She looked around the room to see what the other girls had to say. I didn't answer. There was more laughter in the room. Wanda was the most popular woman in our block, and quite well known around the camp. In our room she was not only in charge of food distribution; she was also our protector, judge, and source for entertainment. She was good-natured, witty, and always fair. In our room there were never disputes over food distributions, chore assignments, or unfair practices. She always cut the bread rations with skilled precision. No one in our barracks was ever abused by a Jewish policeman or a kapo, not if she could help it; and she usually could.

Skarżysko

From our evening talks we were finding out a lot about her, and about one another's lives. Even though we were all different, we learned to live together, and often tried to have fun. We even learned to like each other.

In December, around Christmas, we celebrated Hanukkah. My birthday was completely forgotten. We didn't light candles, but we did sing Hanukkah songs and talk about latkes, and about the miracle of the Holy Oil and the triumph of the Maccabees. We always liked to talk about the miracles. The religious and the Orthodox girls still believed that God would send us one of His miracles: "Just wait and see," they said. "He has never forsaken His people; and God, blessed be his Holy Name, will never let us down."

Another argument that the religious girls presented on this subject was that we, secular people, didn't understand how God operated. "Remember, He tried Job." By now, I knew the story of Job.

Meantime, instead of miracles, diarrhea, influenza, and typhus raged through the camp. The winter was cold, and snow and ice covered the ground. Freezing winds blew through the cracks in the barracks walls. To keep our feet dry and warm, we wrapped them in paper—if we could find any. Trashcans at work were a good source of old paper. I used some of the rags I worked with, but I just had to make sure that what I was doing wasn't obvious. It was stealing German property, and that was illegal.

Slowly, the so-called "hospital barracks" was filling up with the sick and dying. Selections became more frequent. After a while, even the word "selection" was enough to cause panic: We had not heard from, or about, any of the people who had been "selected" and sent away. Two girls from our block were among those who had disappeared. One of them was Sonya, a small, shy girl with long black hair, who was from

My Education Continues

Sandomierz; she had been taken away that one day when she stayed home from work with what could have been the flu, or perhaps pneumonia.

The next big selection was on a Sunday. Everybody was in the barracks. Just before lunch a general Appell was announced: "Assembly! Out of your barracks!"

A commission of German gendarmes, assisted by Jewish policemen, appeared on the scene. We were told to form a single line, then to round it into a circle. The commissioners, walking around the inside of the circle, scanned each girl. The gendarmes heading the commission stopped occasionally, pointed to a girl, and continued walking. It was the job of a Jewish policeman to pull the girl out of the line and turn her over to the Ukrainian guards, who would put her into the waiting trucks.

That Sunday quite a few girls were taken away from the camp. There was nothing special or different about the girls that would have attracted anyone's attention. They didn't look or act any differently from the other girls.

Of course, the selecting was all up to the "selectors," who acted according to their own mood and discretion. There were no rules or regulations for selecting, or even consequences for wrong decisions. We created our own ideas about which criteria these selectors were using, how they were picking their prey. Rumor had it that they were looking for pale faces; for smooth, delicate hands; for short people; for people with freckles—or those without them. Some rumors had it that they were looking for people who were distinguishable from the crowd, for those who wore glasses, or with some handicap; for those who would meet their eyes. No one really knew for sure.

Until the next one came around, we would stop worrying after a selection, worrying about what could have been, or what could be, and we concentrated on our day-to-day living: how to make it through the winter. In our hearts we were still hoping for the day when we'd be sent home. Maybe we just wanted to believe that this day would come sometime soon. Meanwhile, we were going and coming from work, filling the orders, obeying our superiors, getting to know the people around us, listening to rumors and tales.

Our camp, the place behind the barbed wire and watchtowers, was a separate world. Most law and order inside the camp was kept by Jewish police and the kapos, who were armed with sticks and clubs. Germans and Ukrainian guards were mostly on the outside, tending gates and watching towers. They would escort us to and from work. They were also in charge of taking care of the new arrivals, and sending away those considered unfit for hard labor. The Jewish police were picked from among the rank-and-file inmates. I am not sure by which process they got their "prestigious" positions, whether they were chosen, appointed, or volunteered, but I do know that, whenever possible, we tried to be on good terms with all of our superiors—the Jewish police, the kapos, the Stubenältesten.

Among our Jewish superiors—as among the Germans, Ukrainians, and the Poles; we had no shortage of "superiors"—we could find the humane and the malevolent. We knew of policemen who would hit us over the head with their clubs, often for no reason. Some would do it for sheer fun, out of a sadistic nature; some to show off their power. This is not to say that all beatings were unfounded. Often the police did have to take measures in order to prevent misbehavior and anarchy in the camp. There were many inmates who had to be disciplined for stealing and for getting into fights with others. Many inmates, just like people

My Education Continues

on the outside, didn't give a damn if others starved, so long as they could fill their stomachs and keep warm. Many, especially the male inmates, were beating up one another and breaking camp property. Surely, in such cases, police had to act. It was their job to enforce the law and keep order in the camp.

(But there were laws and rules that could have been overlooked: Under camp rules, only working like horses, staying on a starvation diet, and freezing to death, were allowed. Everything else was strictly forbidden.)

Still, we had many Jewish cops and kapos who made our lives miserable. They made sure that none of the camp rules was ever violated. Such hideous crimes as stepping out of the column during a head count, or taking an extra trip to the latrine—even in the case of diarrhea—would never be tolerated while they were on guard. Such a dereliction of duty might have tarnished their reputation, or prevented a promotion. In this respect, there was not much difference between the Jewish police, the Polish police, and the Ukrainian or German guards.

On the other hand, as Aunt Naomi once told my mother, "Remember, there are other kinds of cops." In camp, too, we had "the other kind of cops"—the kind who tried to use their superior positions to help others. Unfortunately, they were very few. These looked the other way whenever someone brought a turnip from work, or whenever a male inmate from the men's side of the camp crossed to the women's side—a deed on the list of strictly forbidden behaviors. (During the winter months, the guys used to come over to the women's side of the camp, though only on Sundays. They would come with the knowledge, but not the approval, of the Jewish police and kapos, who themselves had started the practice with the pretense of visiting a "sister" or a "cousin.")

Skarżysko

Weekdays during the winter, and after working hours, we had no visitors. We stayed in our rooms. To be more precise, we sat on our beds. We were allowed to go outside the barracks only in groups and only under supervision; and only on trips to the latrine. While there, we could wash ourselves, which usually meant rinsing our hands and faces on the days when the water in the outside faucets wasn't frozen. We were very lucky that the latrine was only a hut with holes in the ground, and not a flush toilet, or else it too, would have been frozen up.

Our evenings started with Appell. Then the rations were distributed. The days when we had jam I hardly took part in anything that was going on in our room. The jam always reminded me of my mother. I wondered how she was getting along. The postcards that I used to receive from her quite regularly were now coming very rarely; the messages were shorter and vaguer. The last message that I got was written on a small piece of squashed paper that I found inside a loaf of bread. The paper, in Mom's handwriting but not her style, simply said, "Dear child, got your card. Glad you're doing ok. Take care of yourself."

My name was not on it, neither were Mom's usual remarks, like "We are doing fine.... Write when you can.... Greetings from...."

I saved the note. I had developed the habit some time before of saving every written message until receiving the next one. Many girls did the same. The evening when I received this short note, my mind wandered off into the farm and the ghetto. I wondered if Sis had been reading any of my diaries, the ones which I left in Warsaw, or the newer one I left in Sandomierz. I thought of all the things that I could have written about, and could have been writing in a diary since I came to this camp. I thought of how relative the idea of hunger was by watching the girls

My Education Continues

who came from the small Galician towns complaining of the camp conditions, as compared to the girls who had been through the ghettos and through real hunger.

Wanda's voice echoed through the room: "Everybody line up for the latrine trip!" I knew that I wasn't in Warsaw or Sandomierz. I obeyed.

On the way back we stopped at the pile of firewood and picked up some for our space-heater. We were never afraid to do those forbidden things whenever Wanda was with us. With her as our Stubenälteste, we were always provided with firewood and protected from the Jewish police. Her light-brown, short hair and her pale blue eyes gave special character to her pockmarked face. Her witty tongue was quick enough to scare even the toughest guys. No Jewish policeman dared to stop her, or anyone under her protection.

After our rations were distributed and the trip to the latrine over, we spent the rest of the evening singing or talking or telling stories. In our room it was Wanda who usually led the discussions. She had the most interesting stories to tell. Surely, very few girls in our room had ever heard anything like what she had to say. These were firsthand accounts of Wanda's own colorful life. At first, she let us know that she felt sorry for all the guys behind the fence who were spending lonely nights, and for all the girls who were still virgins, who, according to her, "missed out on all the fun"; and now, with the guys locked up behind the wire, they didn't even have a chance. Wanda herself had a fascinating, rich background. She was married, divorced, and, a couple of lovers later, married again. She had a few lovers in between who had fought over her with knives. After the lovers left she started using her experience to make money. She told us about her boss: a good Jewish boy from Warsaw, the best-known pimp on Smocza Street (a street known to be on par with Krochmalna). Now I knew exactly why I was never allowed to visit these "famous" places or to sell my candy there.

Wanda also gave us detailed accounts of her more memorable clients, often even their names and dimensions. She used to describe various methods and positions. "After all," she said, "it wasn't for nothing that I was one of the most popular workers in the neighborhood: I always tried to do an honest job, especially for my steady customers." The direct language that she used seemed to shock the girls who understood it; but to the majority of us, it was new and not quite comprehensible. Some girls were laughing, some blushing. The older women tried to cover their ears, but their faces showed that they, too, were amused.

When Wanda spoke, we all listened. Maybe it was her special way of telling stories, or her ability to approach people, or her extraordinary life, which was so new to most of us. Maybe we listened because she was so honest about it all; or maybe because of her sense of humor. She could interrupt her tale and yell across the room, "Hey! All you virgins! You need some interpretation?" Often she provided them without being asked. I thought that I had learned a lot at Henyek's house on those Saturday nights in Sandomierz! There, I had felt so grown up, so knowledgeable. Wanda's class seemed a university education in comparison. A group of small-town girls gathered in one corner of the room, listening to Wanda's stories. They were more interested in the adventures of the big city, the red-light district, than in her personal life. Other girls listened for various reasons, and had various reactions. Some listened just for fun, some for information; some thought that it would make them grow up. Many really didn't know how to handle this whole situation: whether they should laugh, cry, or say something—or just remain quiet.

My Education Continues

Pani Milstein, a thirty-two-year-old woman who had been taken away from her husband and a small daughter, was one who would occasionally speak up. She thought that Wanda's stories were out of place, that they were filthy and disgusting, not only to young girls, but unfit even for the gutter. During these stories Pani would usually climb onto her second-story tier, cover her head with a blanket, and just lie there.

Fortunately, Wanda did not hold the concession on all storytelling. We had other girls with very interesting tales on completely different subjects. Regina, a small blonde girl from Łódź, told us stories that were on the other side of the spectrum. Brought up in a very Orthodox home, Regina had lived with her oldest brother, a rabbi, and his family near the city of Opatów. She was about nineteen years old when the War started. She had pale blue eyes and a very white skin, almost albino. She left Łódź when most of the Jews were expelled from the city. A few of her relatives, who were working in German shops that made army uniforms, were allowed to stay.

Regina loved to share with us religious stories. She recited passages from the Bible that she had learned while in her brother's house. She herself finished the Bais Yaakov girls' religious school where Yiddish and Hebrew, as well as secular subjects, were taught. Regina talked about religious laws and Jewish writers. She talked about some philosophical concepts that were way above the heads of many girls. Since most of us were young, and most of us were not well educated, her old stories, like Wanda's old jokes, turned out to be very new to most of us. And, like some of Wanda's stories, many of Regina's needed interpretation for those of us who were unfamiliar with the lives of the people whom she was describing, or with the Bible stories to which she was referring. Even the vocabulary often needed interpretation.

Skarżysko

Help with explanations usually came from Bella, a tall heavyset girl who lived in the adjacent room in our barracks—where Wanda's best friend and counterpart, "Rachu Sukka" ("Rachel the Bitch"), was Stubenälteste. Bella used to have nice discussions with Regina, and would explain to us many of Regina's Bible stories.

Between these two extreme types of stories, most of the things that we talked about were commonplace: Girls talked about their home lives. We found out about the various customs in different parts of the country and among different Jewish groups. My bedmate, Sala, talked about her father, who served in the Polish Legion during World War I. According to Sala, he received many medals. When the War was over he joined the illegal Communist part. Her mother divorced him.

Hanna kept talking about her boyfriend, her first and only love. Sometimes her longing became unbearable; she would sob herself to sleep. Once during an evening talk, she confessed quietly and with great pain that while hiding from the oncoming German troops, she and her boyfriend had gone "further than we wanted to." Her conscience was bothering her for having had sex before marriage, and she had no one to talk to about it. Maybe it was the longing that bothered her more than her conscience.

Wanda, trying to soothe poor, crying Hanna, spoke to her so that we all could hear. "Be glad you tried it; who knows if you'll ever get another chance." Then she looked around the room, making sure that we all could hear. "A little fucking never hurt anyone."

Personal stories were by no means the only topics we discussed; and neither were all stories related to the past. Food, for example, was another popular topic that kept our tongues and imaginations busy on those long, cold winter nights. We could fantasize a meal

My Education Continues

served on a plate, a loaf of bread in the center of the table, bread that could be sliced and eaten at will. Or we would imagine a holiday meal, with meat and challah and cake. Girls would talk about their favorite recipes, and give such detailed descriptions of food that we could actually see, smell, and taste it. They'd talk about the ways that their mothers and grandmothers used to cook chicken soup and matzo balls, and how they had baked cake and rendered goose fat. We could taste the food, our stomachs growling. When we could no longer stand smelling and tasting the food, one of us would change the subject.

We sometimes imagined the end of the War, and what we'd tell our friends and relatives about our lives in the camp. Often we wondered how our loved ones were doing, how worried they must be about our well-being.

We reported to one another news that we had heard at work. We didn't know what to believe. Public announcements? Special disinformation bulletins were often issued to mislead the public and the enemy. A lot of news was coming through different underground channels; and by the time it had reached us, it had traveled so much from mouth to mouth that it now sounded like the game "broken telephone": The message was confused beyond recognition. By the time a true story did reach us in its correct and original form, the situation had already changed.

Rumor had it that the Germans were advancing deeper into Russia, and had already taken Stalingrad. We also heard that the Germans were losing many battles, and retreating. Then we heard that the Jews from the camps and the ghettos would be exchanged for German POWs; then that all Jews would be sent deep into Russia as soon as the Germans occupied that land. And since no one knew what the truth really was, most people believed what they wanted to believe, and discarded the rest. However, everyone was concerned about the talk of Jews being massacred in forests, and of whole Jewish settlements being set on fire.

In our barracks, the most discussed subjects, by far, were the problems facing us daily. We talked abut the girls who were sick, dead, or dying, and of those going missing after each selection (and there were more of them each day). It was difficult to get over the pain of losing friends and not knowing anything of the fate of many others.

We talked about tragic and urgent situations, like what to do about Rivkale, a young, beautiful, black-haired and -eyed girl who was spitting up blood. We feared for her life, and we feared for our own health. But no one would report her to the authorities. For days we dragged her to work with us because there were rumors of an upcoming selection.

We wondered why no one was receiving mail from home any more, and from where the truckloads of used clothes were coming to the camp. I was still carrying around the note that I found in Mom's last package. I kept it hidden inside my shoe between the foot wrappings. The writing on it was faded, almost unreadable, but since no other package or card was coming from home, I didn't want to part with this note.

A few people in camp were getting some news from their respective homes, but not in the mail. These were usually people who lived in and around Skarżysko, and who had some connections with the Polish workers. Through them, the girls heard accounts of their families. The news was bad, and getting worse: shortages, sickness, evacuations to camps, deaths. Sometimes we began to think that we were better off behind the barbed wire than they were inside their homes.

Another subject of common interest among the girls in camp was the peculiarity of our menstrual periods. Almost from the time we came to this camp,

My Education Continues

most of us stopped menstruating. The few girls who were still having their periods said that they were having them irregularly and infrequently. To be honest, we really didn't miss having to bother with it. The few girls who still had to deal with this monthly nuisance used dirty rags, paper, even leaves that they had collected by the fence. So we were actually kind of glad. But we were still trying to figure out how such a phenomenon could have happened to so many girls in such a short time. Rumor had it that there was something in our food, or in the coffee, that had caused it; but no one knew for sure.

As the winter progressed, illness became our biggest problem. Things got so bad that no one ever dreamed of being spared, only of when and how severely it would hit.

One freezing winter morning, like always, we were called to Appell. During the night new snow had piled on that already on the ground from the days before. All night long we had heard the blowing of the wind and the whistling of it through the cracks in the barracks walls. Like all mornings before, I had heard in my sleep a voice yelling from the room behind the wall. I knew it was the voice of "Rachu Sukka," the next room supervisor. "All day whores, it's time to get up! Up! Up! Up! Your night colleagues are back. We need the beds!" Like Wanda, Rachu had a vocabulary all her own. This early morning greeting was an indication that it was time for the dayshift to prepare for Appell. By these morning calls, Rachu meant to show her sense of humor. She had named herself "Suka" for the same reason: She thought that it was funny, and gave her class. Rachu's morning signal was always echoed by Wanda's call: "Appell! Let's go! Let's get ready! Get out!"

Anyway, that one morning I was trying to open my eyes, but they kept falling shut. I heard Wanda's voice above my head: "Get ready! It's late!" I heard the girls

Skarżysko

jumping down from the upper bunks. I tired to raise my head, but it didn't move. I felt someone pulling on my leg and shaking me. I thought that it was my mother standing by my bed. I opened my eyes again: It was Sala. I recognized her face, but wasn't sure how she had gotten so close to my bed. I felt her hand on my shoulder. "Time to get up!" she said. I knew what she was saying, but my eyes were glued shut again. I tried to open them; I rubbed them with my fists. They were too heavy. Sala pushed me again. I heard her voice calling from a distance, "Get up quickly. Everyone is out on Appell!"

"I can't move my legs," I remember saying through a delirious doze. I also remember seeing Wanda's silhouette. She touched my head: "You are awfully hot," she said. "We don't need another sick one here." Then I heard her steps moving toward the door. "Appell!" I heard her shout, then the door closed.

I have no idea how much time had elapsed, but the next person I remember seeing was a cop who was doing his daily routine inspection of the barracks. He found me in bed. I knew that he was talking to me, but I didn't know what he was saying. The next thing I remember, I was on a stretcher. Two skeletons, one on either end, were carrying me away.

When I awoke again, I was sitting on the icy ground near a long wooden board that was supporting my body against a barracks wall. A few girls were sitting in front of me and some behind me on the long board. My eyes fell shut again. I was trembling inside, my teeth chattering. Cold sweat covered my body under the thin dress and long coat. I had on the same clothes I had had on when I came from work the night before.

I heard a door to the barracks open, and a voice yelling, "Get in, all of you, before you freeze to death!" Holding on to each other, a couple of us girls got off

My Education Continues

the ground and tumbled into the open door. The girl next to me was holding on to a tall skinny woman. The woman walked toward the door, the girl dragging behind her on the ground.

What happened after that I remember only in sketchy bits and pieces. A hand grabbed me from behind. My knees bent, and I felt someone dragging me over the icy ground. Then the ground under me changed into a relatively warm wooden floor. The hand let me go; my body fell to the floor. I don't know how long I was lying there; I just know that my eyes were opening and closing. I had no control over them or over any other parts of my body. Then there was an abominable stink, mixed with the warmth of the wood-burning heater, making me nauseous. I was trying to vomit, but only greenish yellow discharge was coming out of my mouth, falling on my coat. A bitter taste filled my mouth.

I fell asleep on the floor, and then woke feeling somewhat better. I looked around. A couple of male inmates were dragging something on the floor. "A former patient," I hear someone say. "Yes," said another. "A corpse."

Many rows of two- and three-decker planks filled the room. They reminded me of the big building in which we had been processed on arrival. The planks were strewn with heaps of loose straw and filled with people's bodies. It was hard to tell whether they were corpses or still breathing creatures.

I lifted my body off the floor and held on to a plank post. A woman's voice was saying, "There will be room for you in just a little bit." I didn't know to whom she was speaking; she was on the other side of the heater, and there were a few of us "newcomers" on the floor. Her voice said, "This is the Special Care Unit. It is our hospital. This is not a sanatorium; that I can tell you. I am your nurse for today."

Skarżysko

The two men kept pulling corpses off the planks and dragging them right by me. I could touch them with my frozen feet. Then I felt someone touch my shoulder. "Get up," a woman's voice said. "Climb to the top bunk."

"I can't," I remember saying.

"Then go down here." She pointed to a place between two still breathing bodies from where a corpse had just been pulled. Holding on to a post I pulled myself up and crawled onto a bunk. The nurse pulled a part of a shredded blanket from under one of the bodies and said, "This will be for both of you." The body didn't move. I put my head on the straw. Colored bubbles appeared in front of my eyes, circling and circling. Around and around they danced, around the bunk, touching the ceiling; then the ceiling tilted to the floor. My mother appeared out of nowhere: I was in the ghetto, in my bed. I had dysentery; Mom was crying....

A smell of soup and the clinking of cans woke me. Through a crack in the wall I could see that it was dark outside. The "nurse" was standing by a soup caldron and, with a long ladle, was dishing out soup to those who could walk over and get it. Then I saw her standing in front of me. "Hey, you!" she said. "Want some soup?"

I lifted my head. She handed me some liquid in a can. I tried to put it to my mouth. The can slipped. The contents spilled on the straw. The smell of the warm liquid, mixed now with the smell of urine and the other excrement that was already there, made my stomach turn inside-out. I pulled a handful of straw from under me and put it over the spilled soup; I put my head on it and fell asleep again.

As if in a haze or fog, I remember waking up sporadically. I think, one time, that I even drank some soup, or water or tea; or maybe I just dreamt that I did. Another time (and this I do remember), a woman

My Education Continues

trying to get off the top plank stepped on my head and nearly killed me. I also remember the time I tried to get up and my legs folded under me and I fell. I don't remember anyone picking me up. When I awoke I was on the plank. I think someone handed me a can of water.

I have no idea how long I slept between these half-conscious moments, but the next time I remember waking up was when two women were pulling at a corpse that was lying next to me. I tried to turn away, but my back was sore, my legs wouldn't move, my arms were dead, and my eyes fell shut. In the dream I saw the ghetto streets lined with dead bodies—bodies of children—and I saw my father walking over to me. Then he changed: his figure turned into my mother's...then more corpses, camp wires, and I was flying over the wires and the ghetto wall.... I don't know how long I was in and out of this delirious dream. Then I woke up with an excruciating headache. I think that this was the first time since getting sick that I felt any pain at all.

Next time I awoke with hunger pangs, and my body was itching. When I tried to scratch my leg it I saw that it must have been scratched before because my fingertips were bloody and there were scabs under my fingernails. My eyes were now opening wider; I knew where I was, and why I was there.

The straw on the plank was full of discharges that could been bloody diarrhea or revived periods. That terrible stink that had almost killed me when I first came into this place, no longer seemed to bother me. For the first time, I could hear the wails of the dying and those delirious with fever. I could hear voices asking for water, and people screaming for help. I knew that I was conscious.

Around me were lice, visible lice marching in the straw and passing over the still living and over the

Skarżysko

already dead. Lice, in themselves, were not a new phenomenon to me. I still remembered them from the ghetto; and there had been no shortage of them in Sandomierz. Here, they were thriving, multiplying, feasting. Here, we could pick them up by the handful. It was no use trying to kill them; killing each separate louse would have been a wearying and endless process. The little beasts were hard to crack; they slipped from the nails. I had no idea how long they had been my companions, nor did I know how long I had been in this "Special Care Unit." I only remember that I started feeling thirsty, very thirsty. My mouth was dry, my lips cracked, and all I wanted was water. I was still falling asleep and waking up, but I knew what I was doing. I heard people around me talking.

My mind kept wandering back to the time I came to this hall, and to the time I came to Skarżysko. I thought of my mother, and in a way I was glad that she wasn't here with me. I remembered how worried she was the time that I got sick in the ghetto. I thought of happy times, of my school days; sometimes I thought of my work in the paint shop, and wondered if Jasiek would still need me when I got back. I thought of the girls who lived in my barracks and those who worked with me. I remember asking for water. The "nurse" brought me some in a can. "Slowly, slowly, drink slowly," she warned, holding the can to my mouth. After two or three sips she pulled the can away. "Let's see if the water stays down in your stomach; then I will give you more," she said.

I looked in the direction of the daylight coming through the open door. I noticed the thin blades of green vegetation that had sprung up in the sandy soil outside the barracks. There was no trace of the snow that had lain thickly covering the ground the day I came into this "hospital."

My Education Continues

I feel better now, and can for the first time see clearly the room I am in. A woman across from me is reaching for a can. She pulls it over to her mouth. I see her choking, but no one pays any attention. She catches her breath. Suddenly, a half-dead body, lying not far from me, revives. I can see it moving. From a top bunk comes a voice: "Water!" No one answers. Beside the door, two men are carrying a skeleton. They throw it out the door. A scream. "Help! Help!" comes from the corner of the room. The voice stops. I watch the nurse dishing out soup. "Want some?" she asks, looking at me. I nod my head. She gives me some in a can. I sip, then wait to see what will happen. It stays down, down in my stomach. "Well," says the nurse. "Looks like you made it through the crisis." She walks over to another bed. I pull back the hair that has fallen into my eyes. A bunch of it stays in my hand. I touch my head; the hair starts falling on to the straw. I stop touching it.

Every day more girls were brought into this place and more dead ones were taken out. This "Special Care Unit" was constantly filled to capacity. The dead, the living, and all those in-between, which included the dead who are still breathing and the alive who are unable to move or act, were all squeezed together. Most of the people here died, but not all. A few did get out. Those who were sent back to their regular barracks were the lucky ones. Here everything depended on luck.

Rumors about an upcoming selection started circulating in the hospital. There hadn't been a selection in the camp since the cold weather set in. The people who were removing the corpses and delivering the food were also rumor-carriers, our news media. From them I learned that the word "selection" didn't apply to the people in the hospital. However, everyone caught in the "Special Care Unit" during the

Skarżysko

inspection was, along with "selection," loaded into waiting trucks to be taken to another place for "treatment and rest."

Knowing nothing about the fate of those previously "treated and rested," anyone who was able to breathe and move would rather thank the commission for its generous attentions and skip the offer. Hearing rumors that a commission was due any day, everyone who was not in a delirious state would try to get out of the "Special Care Unit" as soon as possible.

I knew that I had to leave this place, but there was no connection between my brain and my body. Every time I tried to stand up my body folded: It became limp; it kept collapsing. I was still sick and weak and my hair was falling out in clumps.

A few girls from my side of the room recovered from whatever illness they had had (which could have been diarrhea, typhoid, typhus, spotted fever; who knows what) and were sent to their regular barracks.

One morning, about three or four days after the rumors of a selection started circulating, I asked the "nurse" on duty if she'd let me go "home." She said, "Yes, you can try. Go after the morning body count." Yes, there was a body count, twice daily, even in this hospital. Every body had to be accounted for. Under German law and supervision, everything was done by the rule, and with precision.

I pulled myself up, and holding on to the bedpost with one hand, I brushed the straw off my coat with the other. I could hardly stand. My knees were buckling and shaking. The nurse, carrying a notebook in her hand, walked over to me and said, "Try to go. If you drop dead there will be one less to count in the evening. Besides, there are new people coming in daily." Then, tapping me on the shoulder she added, smiling, "Good luck! I hope you make it." She straightened out the number on my coat so that she

My Education Continues

could read it; she marked something in her notebook; and said goodbye.

I managed to drag myself to the door. A Jewish policeman who was guarding the door walked over to the nurse, checked her notes, looked at my number, then opened the door wide. I walked out.

The fresh air made me dizzy. I held on to the barracks wall and didn't move. But everything around me did; the ground, the barracks, the sand, the sky, were all in motion. I was sure that I was seeing the world turn on its axis. I wondered why I had never seen it before. I sat down by the wall and waited for something to happen.

It must have been around noontime that I saw two kitchen workers carrying a caldron of soup to the hospital. "What are you sitting here for?" asked one of them. I didn't answer. I felt so weak, sick, and tired, and on top if it all, motion sick: I just sat there and looked into nowhere. After delivering the soup, the two men stopped and asked if I needed some help. I thanked them, and said that I'd be very grateful if they would take me to my barracks. They lifted me under my arms and dragged me along. We were stopped at the crossing to the women's field. The cop on duty asked some questions, but he let us through. The two men dropped me off at my room and left.

The nightshift girls were sleeping. I sat on the floor and napped on and off. One of the girls woke up and noticed me. She cleared her bed and helped me get on it. She then crawled onto a top bunk and lay down next to another girl. I fell asleep, and didn't wake up until the dayshift girls returned from work.

I had no mirror, but from the expressions on the girls' faces, I could tell that they weren't quite pleased with my looks. They weren't sure if I brought them new hope or the pestilence.

Wanda was the first one to take action. She pulled off my lousy clothing and handed it to one of the girls who was to drop it into one of the latrine holes. (Had she put it on the floor it would have been carried off by the marching lice.) Then she collected some clothing from the girls and put it on me. Luckily most of the girls had some extra clothing—a new transport of used clothes had arrived only a week before.

My hair had kept falling out until there was hardly any left. Sala now made a bandana out of a blouse and wrapped it around my head. Other girls cleaned me, fed me, and the next morning, took me to work.

I stood at the Appell dizzy and shaking; I thought that I might faint. The ground under me was moving; the merry-go-round wouldn't stop. The tension was just more than I could bear. My knees bent. I fell. The girl standing next to me picked me up and held on to me until the count was over. Supported on both sides by my friends, I dragged myself along to the plant.

Jasiek looked at me, but didn't say a word. He asked the girls who I was, but before they could answer he recognized me. He tried not to look shocked, but it showed. He asked me calmly how I was feeling. I couldn't talk. Tears were rolling down my face. I don't think that I was crying; uncontrollable tears were just dropping from my cheeks down onto the jacket that I was wearing. I wasn't thinking of anything. Nothing bothered me. I just sat down staring into nowhere.

Jasiek went over to the foreman, talked with him, then told the boy who was working in my place to go back to his previous job. He told me to start helping him with the spray-painting. I couldn't even lift my hand, let alone work the equipment. My back was hurting. The cement floor under me was moving and the work station was turning: I felt seasick again. I began to doubt if it had been such a smart idea to get back to work before I was ready. I had no idea how

My Education Continues

long I had been in that hospital; I didn't count the months or the days; I forgot they had names. It was winter when I went in, and it looked like spring when I came out. Not only was I ignorant of the dates, and the length of time I was in the hospital; I didn't even know what disease I had. People at work and at the barracks told me that I was gone for at least a month, maybe longer. From the way I described my illness, people diagnosed typhus or typhoid fever. Both to me were the same.

I couldn't believe how nice people were to me when I returned. If any of the supervisors or workers in the paint-shop had done their jobs according to the German rules, they would have had to report me. I would have been sent back to the hospital barracks and not allowed to stay at work. Had it not been for the people at work and those in the camp, I could never have made it. There surely would not have been a story about me, only another number added to the six million. But Jasiek Kaczmarek did not report me, and neither did anyone else. A few girls who worked near my station pitched in and helped Jasiek with the work. Another person who helped in my recovery was a Polish worker, named Mr. B. He was an older gentleman, in his late forties. He was a foreman in a building located on the plant premises, not far from the paint-shop. There were no Häftlinge working in his department, so whenever there was soup left over at the bottom of his caldrons, he would let some of our camp people scrape them out. The Polish workers had a different kitchen, and were getting different food.

So when I got back to work still sick and weak, some people at the paint-shop suggested that I try my luck with Mr. B. But to get to Mr. B's building was not such a simple matter. Only prisoners with passes were allowed to walk between buildings on the plant premises. With Jasiek's intercession, I got a latrine pass. When I got to Mr. B's place, he looked me over and said, "Sorry, we don't have any soup today." Then, looking at this skeleton in a bandana, he said, "Try tomorrow." Mr. B afterwards saved some leftover soup for me every day for a month. Our station foreman, weird Mr. Wieczorkowsky, contributed, too: He gave me extra latrine passes.

Mr. Wieczorkowsky was the oldest man in our paint-shop. He was perhaps in his early fifties. He was of average height, slim, always clean-shaven, with a carefully trimmed Hitler moustache and hairstyle. He worked next to my station in the room where the grenades were prepared for painting, where they were boiled in a chemical solution. Old Wieczorkowsky was an unpredictable type. When drunk, he would kick and beat the Jewish boys who worked with him. Whenever he had a hangover, he was vicious: He hated everybody, especially the mongoose, the rats, the Schwabs (Germans), and the Jews. The boys who worked for him were always scared. He would call them "kikes." On more than one occasion, he "accidentally" sprayed them with the hot chemical that he prepared for the grenades. The Polish people who knew him said that he even beat his wife, and that he had beaten his sons when they were young.

Whenever he was sober he would undergo a metamorphosis: He'd bring bread, soup, and potatoes, often even newspapers, to the Jews whom he had beaten up the day before. He would tell them how much he hated the Schwabs, and how he was going to kill all of the "stinkin' invaders" the first chance he got. Who would believe that this man was giving me passes?

It took quite a while for me to regain some of my strength. The boils that had formed on my back were getting worse, and dizziness would keep me constant company. The road would turn whenever I walked, and

My Education Continues

the room would sway whenever I lay down; there was nothing that I could do about it. As for the boils, the suffering they caused was becoming unbearable. My clothing was soiled with pus and secretions that oozed. Two of them wouldn't open. There was no way that I could lie on my back, or bend, or even breathe, without excruciating pain. One day at work I asked Pani Grarzyna if she could bring me a razorblade. I had a dress that was way too long, I told her, and it needed cutting. She was very nice about it, and suggested scissors instead. I persuade her that scissors were too difficult to get through plant security (which was the truth). A day later, she did bring a razorblade. On Sunday morning, right after Appell, Teresa, a girl from the nightshift who had some nursing training, performed an operation on my back. She cut open the boils, squeezing out whatever she could, and then bandaged them with one of the old rags that I had brought from work. I was very grateful to Pani Grarzyna. I even told her how her razorblade had been used. She said that she would not have brought it had she known: The wounds could have gotten infected. I was really surprised by how she worried so about me. It was peculiar how the Polish people, who as a whole hated Jews with a passion, seemed to tolerate, even like, those individuals whom they knew.

Slowly, aside from the dizziness that persisted, my life started returning to "normal." I had learned quite some time before that if a situation couldn't be changed, the best thing was to adapt to it, kind of a "if you can't beat 'em, join 'em" attitude. That's exactly what happened to most of us; at least to those who were not yet ready to give up all their hopes for survival and commit suicide by either disobeying the authorities or fighting them.

Skarżysko

Time was passing. New rumors were reaching the camp. The Germans, we found out, were still deep in Russian territory, but their armies were suffering devastating defeats; they were running short on supplies and equipment. Many soldiers were being killed, many more were being wounded. Food, fuel, soap, and medicine—whatever was left of them in Poland—were being taken out and shipped to the now retreating Germans. "The Schwabs don't care if we Poles starve; they don't give a damn," said Pani Krystia when she arrived at work one morning. "All our important people are being arrested, many others are being sent to Germany for hard labor. They took my brother yesterday. Our people are tired, exhausted...."

Other news from the outside world was that a division of a Polish resistance movement was hiding in the nearby forest. The Polish fighters coming in and out had seen many Jews being shot in that forest. The few who would manage to escape were joining the guerilla movement.

The Germans, not being able to cope with the latest defeats, were, like always, blaming all of their troubles on the Jews. Of course, everything bad being blamed on the Jews was not in itself new; but now the Germans were seeking revenge on the Jews. Polish workers talked about seeing freight trains full of Jewish men, women, and children bound for deportation; no one knew where they were being taken. It was supposedly for resettlement.

We heard stories about Jews being shot in forests and their bodies thrown into ravines and ditches that were being dug by bearded, Orthodox Jews. Some of the stories were so bizarre that no one believed them, not even the people who were telling them. We knew, however, that something was happening. We had not been receiving any mail. Our food rations had been cut, and so had our soap allotments. We were

My Education Continues

spending less time eating and cleaning up, and more time checking for nits and cracking lice. There were more hygiene inspections and more hair-shavings. I no longer felt odd being hairless. Since there were frequent delousings and disinfections, I was glad to be bald; there was no way to wash and keep hair clean.

There were terrible shortages of everything but slave labor. No matter how many workers were sent away during the now more frequent selections, or how many had died, new supplies of slave laborers were constantly coming into the camp in order to keep the plant machinery going.

I was still being updated on the events that had gone on while I was in the hospital. I found out about all the new "cousins," and about new people arriving in the camp. Now that the days were longer and warmer, and the curfew hours extended, we had more time to walk between barracks and discuss things with other people.

One nice spring day, on returning home from work, we found on the camp premises a large group of new arrivals. The new women were standing in front of the barracks that had been previously vacated, being counted. It was hard to estimate their ages for they all looked tired, worn, and dirty. If one could guess, their ages could have been somewhere between twenty and thirty. Their outer garments were painted, on front and back, with large red letters: "KL."

After Appell and ration pickups, many of us oldtimers ran over to meet the new arrivals. Before any of us had a chance to ask them who they were and where they came from, the KL girls (as we started calling them) began asking us questions in Polish and Yiddish. They wanted to know what kind of camp this was; if it was a "real" labor camp; what kind of work we were doing; if there was a concentration camp located nearby. As we tried to answer all these mysterious questions, the KL girls stormed us with more inquiries: "How long have you girls been in this camp? Do you get any food?" Voices kept yelling from all directions.

Wanda, who came with us to investigate the newcomers, interrupted the squabble: "Shut up, all of you! Just wait a minute, all you novices! Let's start talking one at a time. I can't understand a word you're saying!" Then in a calmer voice: "I assume many of you must be from Warsaw; I can tell by the way you talk." Wanda was referring to a specific pronunciation of some vowels typical of Warsaw Yiddish.

"We are all from Warsaw," one of the girls answered. I looked into the group of women, hoping to find a familiar face. I found none. I stood, along with a few friends, listening to the conversation that Wanda was carrying on with a couple of the KL girls.

The letters KL, we found out, stood for "Konzentrationslager," and had been printed into the girls' garments at a camp named Majdanek, a place near Lublin, from which the girls had just arrived. The girls told us that before getting there, they had heard of the Majdanek camp and another one named Treblinka. Rumors circulating in Warsaw lately had it that many people were being deported to these places, which were called "labor camps" and "concentration camps." There was even some talk about certain camps where people were being exterminated; but no one paid attention to such nonsense.

Looking at the KL girls and hearing them talk brought many memories of Warsaw to my mind. I saw myself running happily with other kids though the streets and squares and parks and around the fountains. I thought of the Belweder Palace and Chopin's Monument in Łazienki Park; and of the relatively new sculptured "Syrena," the mermaid emblem of Warsaw, proudly holding a sword over her head.

My Education Continues

My thoughts were interrupted when I heard the KL girls say something about an Uprising, and about Passover. That's when I remembered that last Passover was not so long ago. We had celebrated it, as we did other holidays, at an approximate time and in a symbolic way. Since we got into this camp, timekeeping devices and traditional foods were only memories of a distant past. We knew that Passover was around Easter, and that flattened-out bread rations were make-believe matzoth.

Recalling the Passover story, we wondered if God had used up all His plagues on the pharaohs and therefore had none left for Hitler.

I was getting homesick. Surprisingly, I didn't think of the bombed-out Warsaw, nor of the ghetto, with its hunger and misery. I kept seeing Warsaw in its splendor. Only memories of carefree life in that beautiful city kept flowing through my mind.

When my thoughts returned to reality I heard Wanda prying for answers from the KL girls. She wanted some clues that would explain the fate of the Warsaw Ghetto in more detail. Up until now, the KL girls had spoken of it only in very general terms. They were sure that we knew the ghetto story. "After all," one of them said later, "how could anyone not know it?" As much as we could see, these girls seemed more interested in the conditions in the camp than in telling us what they knew. On the other hand, we were trying to find out what the outside world looked like, and how the KL girls got to the Majdanek camp, and how they finally came to us.

Most of the following evenings we spent in the KL barracks, trying to unravel the incoherent bits and pieces of the ghetto stories that the girls were telling us. From rumors that we had heard at work, we assumed that the situation there had been, at best, dreadful; yet we were not prepared for what the girls

Skarżysko

were about to tell us. They informed us that the Warsaw Ghetto no longer existed. What was left of it were ruins and ashes. They told us, little by little, about the conditions and events that had led to the ghetto uprising and to its destruction. The people who survived the shootings, shellings, and burnings had been taken, the girls said, in freight cars to Majdanek and to some other camps. One by one, the girls started telling us stories of their own experiences, and those of the ghetto in general. They talked about their "adventurous" trip that had taken them from Warsaw to Majdanek, and then to the Skarżysko Camp. They told us that they had been transported to Skarżysko in cattle cars, and that they were glad to be here in a "real" labor camp. They also let us know that they were worried about the men who had been with them on the train from Majdanek. The men had traveled in different cars, but they never showed up here.

Wanda, trying to calm them down, explained that there was a men's camp behind the barbed wires; it was possible that their men might show up there (a guess that turned out to be correct). She told the KL girls that she, too, was a native of Warsaw, and had lived there all her life. She explained how she had managed to get out of the ghetto just before it was closed up. "There are a few more girls from Warsaw in our group here," she said, "and we would like to know what happened over there."

The girls started telling us whatever came to their minds, without any kind of order or logic. One girl told us how her nine-year-old nephew was shot by a German guard. "He wasn't the only one," she explained. "Many kids were shot if caught bringing food into the ghetto, or just trying to grab some food. But you know, not even this punishment could deter other kids from trying; that's how unbearable the starvation was." The girl also told us about the "high-

My Education Continues

class" smuggling business, about German workshops, the Jewish police, the Judenrat; they talked about hunger, the arrests, the roundups; the Nazi brutalities.

What they were telling us thus far was not new to me. I remembered most of these things, and I remembered the epidemic, and the corpses that lined the streets of the Warsaw Ghetto. What I didn't remember seeing, I remembered hearing about. I could recall overhearing the horror stories that Aunt Naomi told Mother when she came to Sandomierz, even though Aunt had usually whispered them, as if they were military secrets. I remembered her talking about some deportations of the ghetto Jews; she mentioned that they were to be resettled in some "other places."

Then the girls talked about events that happened after I left Warsaw, and about those I didn't remember Aunt Naomi mentioning. They talked of a "Resettlement Program" that was taking Jews to labor camps, which I knew about only from sketchy talks that I had overheard and from a postcard I had received in Skarżysko camp from Aunt Naomi saying, "Freda and Rena volunteered for work outside Warsaw. They were promised good jobs and good food."

The KL girls also talked about deportations, transportations, and evacuations. They told us the story of Janush Korczak, a Jewish doctor who founded an orphanage; how he, as a physician, could have remained in Warsaw and been temporarily safe. But instead, he decided to go with his kids when the orphanage was scheduled for deportation.

Each day we were finding out more about the systematic, apparently deliberate, destruction of the Jewish people of Warsaw. Thus far, all the stories we heard were in bits and pieces, and out of context. They were difficult to fully comprehend. To many of us Skarżysko girls, especially those from small towns who had never been to a large city, or had experienced life in a ghetto, these stories sounded very strange. So, for the sake of those who knew nothing, and for those of us who knew only part of the Warsaw Ghetto tragedy, we asked our KL friends to give us a summary of the ghetto from its beginning to its liquidation. After a few weeks of nightly talks, we put together the following summary:

The plight of the Warsaw Jews started in September of 1939, with the bombardment of the city. Then, Jews had tried to deceive themselves by believing that the bombs that were falling on the Jewish section of town during Jewish High Holidays had been dropped there coincidentally, that they had not really been meant for the Jewish civilian population. Later, while thousands of Jewish people were being deported from other towns, and as refugees began to flow into the already overcrowded Jewish quarters of Warsaw, Jews made believe that it was only a temporary situation: Soon things would improve. As time passed, conditions grew worse. Eventually, a wall was built around the Jewish section; then the ghetto was sealed off.

Since the War began, Jews were living on a diet of faith, hope, and rumors. It seemed—and we talked about it quite often—that on the subject of rumors, many ghetto residents considered themselves experts. They were almost sure that they could recognize and interpret each kind. They could predict their outcome, and figure out different ways to deal with them. That, of course, took special skills, for there were fabricated rumors (those simply made up); rumors that consisted of exaggerated true reports; and rumors dispensed by the Germans to confuse the population, spread fear, or prevent panic. The problem for these rumor experts was to identify which of these rumors to take seriously and which to dismiss, and what to do with those that

My Education Continues

fell somewhere in-between. To differentiate which was which was not an easy task either. The KL girls who talked about ghetto events and the rumors supported this view.

One rumor circulating in the ghetto for quite some time, they told us, suggested that the Germans were talking about a "Final Solution" to "The Jewish Problem," a plan that called for the destruction of all Jews—men, women, and children.[57] It was quickly dismissed, too idiotic, too bizarre to be even taken under consideration. "Why would anyone be so dumb as to kill off cheap or free labor; or why kill people who could, eventually, be traded for something?" Besides, what would the world say of it?

Another rumor had it that the Germans were developing a plan for liquidating the ghetto. People didn't believe this one, either, but they could not completely dismiss it due to some new developments. For quite some time, the authorities had been asking ghetto residents to sign up for a resettlement program. The people were to be transported to other cities and to some labor camps where they, supposedly, would work for the German cause. For a while these registrations and transports went on quite orderly. Special tactics were used by the Resettlement Office to lure volunteers. The Jews, exhausted by years of ghetto life, were signing up freely and in large numbers. They were sure that no matter where they were taken, conditions could not be worse than those in the ghetto. To further lull suspicion, those who volunteered were allowed to take with them most of their possessions, including money. In addition to promises for a better life, each volunteer was given a bag of food for the trip. (I began to understand why Freda and Rena volunteered.)

After a while, though, when there was no news from or of the whereabouts of the deportees, people became suspicious. Voluntary registration slowed tremendously. No one knew for sure where these people were being taken. Rumor had it that the trains leaving Warsaw were seen in the vicinity of places named Treblinka and Majdanek, and that from these places, the trains were returning empty.

"Out of this information," one of our KL friends told us one day, "some people started making up all kinds of bizarre rumors. A guy I knew was telling a group of people that men, women, and children were being gassed in specially designed chambers, and their remains burned in ovens; or, that some of these deportation places were actually extermination camps. That guy even swore that he heard it from a 'reliable source.' I think people started going crazy in that ghetto."

Another of the girls added that there were stories reaching the ghetto which suggested that in the resettlement places, people were being shot, beaten, and tortured to death. None of these stories could be verified, of course, but the story of the beatings was taken quite seriously. Voluntary registration came to a halt.

As a result, the Germans resorted to new techniques. Instead of relying on voluntary registration, they ordered the Judenrat to come up with a certain number of Jews for the "resettlements" each day. They threatened to deport the Judenrat members and their families if the assigned number of Jews for daily deportation was not provided.

At first, Jewish police were appointed by the Judenrat to supply people. Police kept running frantically from house to house searching for "volunteers" and urging people to sign up. Those who refused were beaten, clubbed, kicked, and thrown into the streets.

Later, rounding up of Jews for resettlement was done by Ukrainian, Lithuanian, and Latvian guards,

My Education Continues

Nazi collaborators who were ruthless, brutal, and savage. No Germans were involved in the house-by-house searches. The job of the Germans was to patrol the roads and pick up those Jews who had been thrown from their homes into the streets.

Eventually, many of these roundups turned into massacres. Blockades were set up. Jews found hiding were shot on the spot; all others were pushed into the traps of the waiting SS guards, who forced them to march to a checkpoint named by the Germans "Der Umschlag Platz" or "Transfer Place."

(I knew this place well. It was located at Dzika and Stawki Streets, next to the railroad tracks. It was by a row of lumberyards, of which one belonged to two of my mother's uncles, Yitche and Heinoch. I remembered going to these lumberyards with my sister and watching the sawmills in operation. We liked to watch our cousins work the electric saws that transformed large logs into boards, two-by-fours, canes, and broomsticks. We were fascinated by the goggles that our cousins let us wear, and we liked to build castles, tunnels, and "sand" cakes out of the sawdust. We watched the freight trains arrive full of logs and leave filled with boards and other lumber products. I had so many pleasant memories of the location that had eventually become the gathering point for deportations.)

The KL girls, while telling us their ghetto stories, often argued among themselves about whether or not the Judenrat and the police had handled the roundups in a proper way. From these arguments we learned about dreadful ghetto politics and corruption; about Jews and Poles, even German guards, who, sometimes at the risk of their own freedom, would try to help others.

As the roundups continued, the KL girls explained, the Jews were running out of hiding places and ideas to avoid deportations. Even those in the German workshops were no longer safe. Some of the smaller shops were entirely evacuated when the guards couldn't meet their deportation quotas. Even members of the Jewish police, the Judenrat employees, cemetery workers, and others of the once specially privileged class, were no longer exempt from deportation. There seemed to be no rule, no pattern to these new raids. Everyone agreed that something more drastic than hiding had to be done. By now everyone knew that things would not improve, that there was nothing to wait for. But political and religious groups were sharply divided as to what to do and how to do it. Some groups suggested fighting. Others were opposed to any kind of violence, and did not waver in their views, still believing that the only way to change the situation was through faith in God and through prayers. Most people, however, had no idea at all about what could or should be done about this hopeless crisis.

After the latest atrocities, everyone realized that, divided, no one would be able to survive, even though they weren't sure if they could survive united. To fight or to wait for God was not an easy decision to make. People were caught between the frying pan and the fire—or, as the Polish version goes, "between the hammer and the anvil"—in trying to balance logic and moral values.

As the violence escalated, more people were willing to talk about armed resistance. The problem by then was not whether to die or not to die, but whether to die submitting or resisting. As one of the girls said, "We knew that the Germans would not hesitate to kill us all to avenge even one German life, but we also knew that there was no way to commute our death sentence." A fight with the Germans meant suicide; yet suicide was forbidden by Jewish Law. The people were in a dilemma. And so, little by little, the KL girls told us how the Ghetto Resistance Movement was started, how the weapons were organized, how they, the ghetto Jews, had finally taken it upon themselves to resist the mighty Germans.

"It was during the Passover Holidays, when the guards came to round us up, that we started shooting and throwing Molotov cocktails. As soon as some of the guards started falling to the pavement, reinforcements were brought in. For a few days there were constant shootings. The streets were full of dead bodies and burned vehicles. Then, the whole ghetto was set afire.

"To escape the flames people were jumping from roof tops and from windows, only to be rounded up by the Germans who were waiting in the streets. There, we were gathered and shipped off. From the railroad tracks we could see the ghetto engulfed in flames....

"We don't know how many people were left there; who was dead, who alive.... We were taken in freight cars to Majdanek."

About the camp itself, the girls could give us very little specific information; only that the camp was surrounded by a triple facing of tangled barbed wire, charged with electric current. From what the girls could see, the camp was divided into a few separate sections. There were many barracks, and a few brick buildings.

On arrival, people from many incoming trains were assembled for selection. First the Jews were separated from all non-Jews, who were then taken to another section of the camp. Then, the men were separated from the women and children, and then they, too, were taken away. Then the women were sorted into groups, with the old, the children, and the sick left in the field. All the young, strong, and healthy looking were taken into special barracks. "We were in this last group," explained one of them. "The processing went on smoothly, and in an orderly fashion. During the few days we spent in this camp, we heard many bizarre stories. One of them—almost unbelievable—was that the Majdanek camp was built for and by Russian POWs, and when the work was finished, all the prisoners who had worked on it were executed.

"Another story, just as outlandish, was gas chambers. People were saying that men, women, and children were led into 'bath houses' where, instead of water they encountered gas showers. We'd heard this weird story before, but now the people were saying that these 'gas chambers' were located somewhere in that camp. Most people, however, believed that Majdanek was a labor camp, even though none of our KL girls worked there.

"A few days later all girls from our barracks were called to a special assembly, which was not our regular Appell. We were counted; but after the count, instead of going back to our barracks, we were taken for another selection. This time, all able-bodied girls were taken aside, our clothes were painted with the red KL letters, and we were marched to the railroad tracks, loaded into boxcars, and shipped off. The weak and the sick were left in camp. Rumor was that the Skarżysko labor camp had sent in an order for workers. But it was anybody's guess where we were being taken."

Another time, during our evening discussions, a girl who looked to be the oldest of the group described in a choking voice how she had been forcibly pulled away from her two children, and how she had been not only prevented from following her kids but also beaten when she tried to run into the electric fence. She had been loaded onto the Skarżysko freight train, and her children, nine and six, were taken away by the guards. She knew nothing about them, nor of the fate of her husband, whom she last saw on a flaming Warsaw street.

My Education Continues

I began to wonder what could have happened to Dad, to my friends, to my relatives, to all those I had left in Warsaw. My hopes of finding them alive kept fading with each ghetto and camp story.

Again, life in our camp would "normalize." The KL girls started working at the plant. The missing men who had come with them on the train started showing up on the women's side of the camp wire—as Wanda had suspected, they were living on the other side of the fence. Among them were a couple of older guys, in their early thirties, Joziek and Leon. Whenever they could, they would cross into our side of the camp and tell us stories about the ghetto Uprising, about the work of the Resistance Movement; they described in detail how they themselves had jumped from a burning building into the arms of the German guards. Both were quite intelligent and very knowledgeable. They had been in the fighting brigades, and knew the whole Uprising story firsthand.

I liked both of them, but I had my eye on Joziek. I used to hang around him at every chance. I listened carefully to all his stories. Whenever I saw him coming over to the women's barracks, I was right by him. Once he even gave me a hug and a kiss right on the mouth. I thought that I'd die. I dreamed and fantasized that he had fallen in love with me.

My big love affair ended when he got friendly with a woman in her mid-twenties and began treating me like a child. He was still coming to visit our barracks and to talk about his ghetto experiences. He still kept up his friendly attitude, probably not even knowing how brokenhearted I was. Joziek, like most of the other KL men and women, was a welcome addition to camp life. They raised our nightly talks to more sophisticated levels. From them, we learned poems, songs, art, and Jewish culture. We talked with them about love and relationships—the same subjects we used to discuss with Wanda and Rachu, but from a completely different perspective.

On the nights whenever good kapos were on duty, we stayed outside in the yard past the curfew hours, joined by girls from other barracks and men who kept sneaking over to our section of the camp. We looked forward to these after-work meetings.

At one of these meetings, one of the KL girls asked me where I used to live and if I had any relatives in Warsaw on Nalewki Street.

"Yes," I answered. "Nalewki 35; Mom's Aunt Dora lived there with her family."

"Oh! That's where I know you from. I thought your face looked familiar. Do you know who I am?" I looked at her, searching my memory for clues, but I didn't know where to place her. I told her that I couldn't remember her.

"I was your cousin Sala's friend," she said. "I used to see you quite often at her house." Then looking at me carefully, she shook her head and added, "My! You look different.... I mean, you've matured since I last saw you—and your hair!"

Now I knew who she was. Her name was Sabina—Sabcia we called her. She, too, had changed a lot. I told her how I got out of the ghetto; about my stay in Sandomierz; about the hospital and how I lost my hair. I asked her if she knew anything about Sala and her family, or any of my other relatives. I told her that I knew about Cousin Moniek's and Aunt Dora's deaths. She said that my cousin Haim and his fiancée had joined the Uprising, and that she didn't know what had happened to them. She thought that Sala's youngest brother, Srulek, had fled to the Aryan side, but she wasn't sure; about Sala's sister, Zosia, she knew nothing. "All others I knew must have been deported or killed; there were

My Education Continues

hardly any older people or children left in the ghetto when they took me out."

Sabcia told me about my two cousins, Mina and Naomi, the two sisters who used to work with Aunt Naomi and whose father used to own the lumberyard on Dzika and Stawki Streets.

"They were with us in Majdanek," she said. "Mina almost came to Skarżysko with us. She was selected to work, but her sister Naomi...well, they didn't let Naomi through, because of a rash that she developed on her arms. The guard told Naomi to stay behind, that she'd have to go to the 'hospital.' Mina begged the guard to let her stay with her sick sister." Sabcia shook her head in disbelief. "You know, most guards never listened to pleas or cries, but this guard was 'nice'; he let Mina stay. They both remained in Majdanek."

Sabcia mentioned some other names of people that she thought I might know, but I didn't recognize any of them.

With the new people in camp, we had to adjust to different routines. The camp had become more crowded. The lines for soup had grown longer, the bread portions smaller. We were now sleeping cramped four to a bunk—two for the dayshift, two for the nightshift. But life had also become more interesting. Girls were making new friends, new "cousins." The guys with influence, those working in the camp police, in the soup kitchen, guys with "special jobs"—such as cleaning the plant premises, or digging potatoes—had the first choice of "cousins." Not all of these relations were "business" connections. There were actually some genuine love affairs in the camp: Boy meets girl and they fall in love. Only the part where they "live happily ever after" was missing from the end of the story. The "cousin" stories were interesting, and they gave us something to talk about. When we weren't gossiping about boys and girls, we were talking about political rumors that had been spreading at camp and at work.

The latest one circulating at work was about the War not going too well for the Germans. We heard that the city of Hamburg had been bombed, and that a lot of damage had been done to its port. That night in the barracks, we rejoiced, filled with new hope. "Hurray! Finally the Germans know what it feels like to have a war!" yelled a girl from a top bunk near the door. "I hope a lot of those sons-a-bitches got killed there!" shouted another one. "I hope a bomb hits the fuckin' painter!" added Wanda. "I hope a plague strikes all of Germany!" joined in another. Other voices added their wishes and insults.

Only Regina, "The Rabbi," as we called her, sat on her bunk, quietly. Her eyes were looking into nowhere, but she was listening to the talk. Her face saddened.

"Hey! What's wrong with you? Come on, holy virgin! Why aren't you talking?" asked Wanda, looking at her sorrowful face. "Did your mother just die?"[58] Regina didn't answer.

"Don't you feel well, Regina? I asked, climbing onto her bunk. "You haven't said a word all night."

"Don't you know," she finally said to me, quietly, "doesn't anyone here know that rejoicing at someone else's misfortunes isn't Jewish? I wish you all would leave me alone."

Yes, I knew that. I remember Grandpa telling me that; I must have been about eight or nine. I also remembered hearing it from one of the KL girls when she once recited an ancient Greek poem—maybe from the Odyssey.

Nevertheless, the tragic bombing of Hamburg made many of us feel well. All summer long, the news that was coming from the outside world suggested that the Germans were suffering defeats, that the Russian Front was moving westward, that English and

My Education Continues

American planes were bombing German cities. Again we weren't sure if any of these were rumors or actual reports. The papers never acknowledged defeats. It was understood, now, just as it had been during the German invasion of Poland in 1939, that one couldn't believe everything that was written in the papers or heard over the radio. However, this time there were obvious signs that indicated bad news for the Germans, other clues that called for our optimism: All essential supplies were being taken away from the civilian population and shipped to the Front. Almost everything was being driven out of Poland. Rations for the Polish population were being cut even more. Many Poles who had never done anything illegal now had to resort to smuggling and stealing. Even very patriotic Poles, and very religious ones, were feeling that patriotism and religion worked better on a full stomach.

Whatever was happening to the Poles, the situation was worse for the Jews. The Nazis blamed many of their misfortunes on the Allies, but most of their problems they blamed on the Jews. More Jews, we heard, were being driven from their homes; more were starving in the streets. Even the smaller towns—where conditions, until now, had been relatively tolerable—were suffering hunger and deportations. In our camp, the soup consisted of more water and less substance. Other rations were cut, too. Only soap and medical supplies were not cut in the camp—they had been nonexistent for quite some time.

What did increase were shipments of used clothing. Some of the garments that were coming in had been painted with red stripes, others not. These clothes were greatly appreciated, especially with another winter not too far away. There were blouses, dresses, and coats. Some of the items were quite old, others in fairly good condition. After a while, we became suspicious: The truck drivers who delivered them said that they were picking up the stuff from a city names Oświęcim. They were not sure how and where these cargoes were first loaded onto the trucks. They knew only that these trucks had already been loaded and driven into town by other drivers. Even more suspicions arose when recipients of the clothes began finding notes inside some of them. One note, found in a coat pocket, read, "We don't know what's going to happen to us." Notes found in other garments said, "Death to the murderers—avenge our fate," and "Don't forget what your enemy has done to you." This one was a translation from the Hebrew. We didn't know what these notes meant, but we did know that something was not right.

I had not received any news from Mom for quite some time, and I hoped someone would come from Sandomierz and let me know what was going on there. That little note that I found in the last package from Mom was the only thing that connected me with my home. I was still keeping it in the foot-wrapping.

All the people arriving to our camp were coming from other towns or from other camps. The next big shipment of workers came from Kraków, from a transit camp named Płaszów, where they had been toiling for the Germans. In contrast to the KL people, the Płaszów inmates only hoped that this camp would not be worse than the one from which they had just come. They told us that many Jews from small towns in southern Poland were being deported, that some were brought to the Płaszów camp, although the majority were shipped to some unknown places.

Slowly, another winter was upon us. Besides all the problems that were going on in the world, and at work and in the camp, I was encountering a few of my own. The dizzy spells that had bothered me since my illness were becoming more frequent and more

My Education Continues

aggravating. I had also developed frozen toes, and an abscessed tooth. There was little that I could do about the spells and the toes. The tooth was taken care of in the "Hospital Barracks" by a fellow whose knowledge of dentistry consisted of having at one time washed instruments in a dental lab. He performed the surgery with a pair of carpenter's pliers. The wound bled for days, and my face was swollen for weeks. Finally, the operation was declared a success.

Though my tooth was taken care of, nothing could be done about my other problems, or about the winter. Even during peaceful times, winters in this part of the world were feared: They were long and often severe. Since the War started, each winter seemed worse than the preceding one. During this winter, not even Wanda could get wood to heat our room. Icicles were hanging inside the barracks; the chamber bucket was frozen.

The latrine grounds and stools weren't any better. The long lines that would form around that wooden shed were not due to overeating or to the overcrowding, but rather to the diarrhea and dysentery that were infecting the camp. I missed out on both, but many others did not. Standing in the endless latrine lines, I watched the girls crossing their legs or trotting in place, cursing, while greenish liquid, often mixed with blood, soaked through their dresses or ran down their legs. Entering the inside of the latrine, we all slipped and slid on the frozen excretions; when we finally got to position ourselves over the open hole, we had to make it fast—not just because the uncovered parts of our bodies were freezing but because the girls outside kept shouting to us to hurry up.

It was a terrible winter. We lost many girls to selections and death.

With the coming of spring, many winter-related problems disappeared, but that didn't mean that we were left without difficulties: It would have been a disgrace had we been left trouble-free. As soon as the weather warmed up, the rats and swarming flies returned to the latrine, to the yard, and to our barracks. Rats as large as rabbits, fat with shiny hides, reminded me of the ghetto rats. Sometimes, during the night, they'd wake up from their gloomy sleep and run through the room or sit on our beds to keep us company. Wanda was the only one in our barracks who wasn't afraid of them. She'd get up in the middle of the night and chase them around, cursing, "Go to the shit-house, you damn son-of-a-bitch! You can eat yourselves to death out there!" Soon, these nightly adventures became part of our lives. Again, as in so many times before, we would redefine the word "normal" and learn to live with a situation.

The evenings we spent discussing, singing, or reciting poetry. The news now from the Front was that the Red Army was advancing westward. Russian planes were, supposedly, bombing German positions. Previously victorious Germans were being captured, many killed. This time the tales were supposed to be well-founded and not just unsubstantiated rumors. Even if they turned out to be rumors, such good news was always appreciated. Such talk kept us alive. We wanted to hear rumors, of the Allies' victories, about Nazi defeats, about...about anything that resembled good news. Polish workers were telling us that the Russian Front was nearing the Polish-Russian border, that many of their own friends and relatives were either seeing the fleeing German troops or hearing artillery shots. There were even reports that at night some people could see, far in the distance, fire coming from the Front. If we could only hold out a bit longer, we liked to believe, our liberators, the Russians, would be here.

Filled with new hopes, our nightly discussions turned to topics of the future: "What will we do when the War ends?" Since our respective homes were located in all different parts of the country, we started promising each other that we'd "keep in touch." We were full of optimism.

Our rejoicing, however, was short-lived. As the Front neared the Polish border, we started hearing rumors. New rumors. All kinds of rumors—the good and the bad. Now that the Germans were losing battle after battle, now that there was even the possibility that they might lose not only a battle but the whole war, the Germans needed some moral support, some joy in retaliation—something to keep up their morale. Not able to beat the enemy on the battlefield, they began taking all of their anger out on the Jews. They were going to finish off the Jews to complete the promise of the so-called "Final Solution."

Anyway, these were some of the rumors that we heard along with all the good news from the Front. Again, we didn't know what—if anything—to believe.

In our camp, the indication that something was changing was that random selections were becoming more frequent; there was also more work and more beatings. New transports of Jews were constantly coming in. No matter how many of us died, there were always new ones to replace us; there was no shortage of new workers. And no shortage of new rumors. The latest supposedly had come from camp authorities. It said that our camp was to be evacuated, that we'd probably be moved to another labor camp, which was, supposedly, located "somewhere" in Germany. Having heard so many evacuation and deportation stories, we were quite apprehensive about the place to which we were to be taken, this place that was "somewhere."

At the plant, the Polish workers, too, heard that the HASSAG munitions plant was to be shut down; no one knew when. From the information they had, the Polish workers were to be laid off, and all slave

Skarżysko

laborers were to be evacuated. There was no way to tell if this was another one of the rumors—a deliberate spread of disinformation by the Nazis to prevent panic and disturbances. Other rumors had it that we were to be shipped to a place named Oświęcim—better known by its German name, Auschwitz. This name sounded somewhat familiar: It was the place where our clothes were coming from. People were now saying that not far from Oświęcim were some camps, labor camps, a concentration camp, maybe even an extermination camp; no one knew for sure. It was being said that Jews, Gypsies, and other "undesirables" were being taken there for "some reason."

Even though it was impossible to believe all the rumors that we heard about this place (knowing by now the Nazis and their mastery of brutality), it was hard to completely disregard these rumors or to think of them as being just "crazy tales." We didn't know too much about this place, Oświęcim, but we were sure that we didn't want to go there. We were getting very nervous about the whole thing. The closer the time came for our alleged evacuation, the less we chose to believe that what had happened by now to many people could happen to us.

Many Poles in our plant were nervous. But their nervousness was founded on different reasons. Those Poles who had fought the Germans, those whose sons and daughters were in the guerrilla movement in the forests, were getting nervous from the happiness and anticipation of good times to come, from knowing that their struggle would soon be over. For often in their struggle they had hardly believed that their luck would hold out until the end. Also nervous were those Poles who had cooperated with the Nazis, for their luck was now running out. And nervous were all the Poles at our plant, for they were losing their jobs and their security. Nervousness was also getting to our Pan

My Education Continues

Wieczorkowsky, who was beating the Jews. He was calming his nervousness by drinking even more than usual.

One morning, like so many times before, he came to work drunk and in a terrible mood. In his vicious temper, he beat up two of the three Jewish men who worked for him in the boiler room. He broke the nose and jaw of one of them and kicked the other man in the groin; the latter fainted. The third man managed to escape into the hall. Before he ran away he yelled at the top of his voice, "Just wait, you old bastard! It won't be long till we get even!" Whether this warning got to his head, or his conscience began to bother him, I don't know; but the next morning the old man came to work sober, his mood having swung the other way.

The following day when Wieczorkowsky came to work, he brought with him what he called "a great plan"—a plan to help the Jews he worked with. He said that he made up this plan in his head during the night. He told us that he, too, had heard the rumors about Oświęcim, and suggested that if we were to be evacuated, we should defy the orders of the Nazis and try to escape. We should hide in nearby fields and forests. He had drawn a map of the best places to hide in the vicinity of the camp. "The guards can't shoot all of you. There aren't enough of those sons-of-bitches around here. Try to run in different directions. Those of you who manage to escape, I and some of my friends—I mean friends we all can trust—will help you hide." He then gave us a detailed plan of how he and a group of his friends would patrol the area; how they'd bring unmarked clothes for us to change into; how they would pick us up and hide us until we were liberated.

It was hard for us to tell what his real motives were; if he meant what he was saying, or just wanted to set up a trap. Maybe his conscience was bothering him; after all, he was a good Catholic; maybe he was just trying to make up for his previously committed sins. We thanked him for his good intentions and his consideration, and we told him that we'd think about his offer when and if the time came.

Actually, the escaping itself was never our biggest problem; that was true even before the latest plans. As difficult as escaping was, it was not an impossible act. The major reasons that prevented most of us from even thinking about escaping were two. One was the punishment that awaited those left in camp. We knew the torture that they would have to suffer. No one wanted to have other people's lives on her conscience. The second was that there was no place for us to go once we did escape. This second problem was a sad fact of life. The majority of the Polish population was not only unwilling to shelter or help Jews (which, under the circumstances, was quite understandable), but many of them were often willing, even eager, to turn Jews over to the Germans—sometimes for a reward, often without any.

Therefore, when the old man offered to help, we were very skeptical. We were even surprised that he was talking about the subject at all. Nevertheless, many of us did not dismiss his offer completely. After all, escaping was a deed of last resort.

Some time had passed since Old Wieczorkowsky's proposal, and more people at work were talking about the closing of our plant, and about the possibility of an evacuation of all slave labor. As a matter of fact, some people were even talking about the possibility of sending the Polish workers to Germany as so-called "voluntary labor." As for the Jews, no one said anything concretely. The belief was, deep inside people, Jews and Gentiles alike, that the Jews would be sent to some kind of a concentration camp.

My Education Continues

Anyway, the Russian front was getting closer to the Polish-Russian border, and the possibility of evacuation was drawing nearer. The decision whether to take a chance on escaping or take a chance that we were going to another labor camp somewhere in Leipzig, Germany, became more serious. From the stories that the KL girls had told us, and from those that we had heard from the others, we had reason to worry about being shipped to a concentration camp, maybe to be tortured or outright killed. If we could only trust the Poles to keep quiet and not turn us in, we were sure that we could survive in a forest until the Russians came. We heard that Polish partisans who were wholeheartedly fighting the Germans were at the same time killing Jews who were trying to help them in their struggle with the enemy. Chances of not being shot by the guards during an escape, and of not being turned in to the Germans by one of the Poles, were about as good as having a snowless winter in Siberia. The question to consider was whether the risk of being deported to an "unknown destination" was greater than that of surviving an escape in Poland. This crucial decision had to be made by and for oneself.

Some people were saying that the whole rumor of the Jewish evacuation was a hoax, that all railroads and cars were being taken up by military personnel and supplies, and that there was no way that the Germans would be using the badly needed trains for transporting Jews to faraway places.

One evening, as on many other evenings before, a group of us girls from different barracks gathered in the yard. It was way past curfew, but no one was patrolling the grounds. We stood talking and listening to distant rumbling that sounded like distant thunder. Far out at the eastern horizon, the sky was lit up. It looked like lightning, but the fire would last longer; it didn't disappear. I heard a voice in our group saying, "I wouldn't doubt if the fire is coming from the Front." Another voice said, "Those German bastards will never have time to get us out of here. The Russians are only about twenty or thirty kilometers from here." Other voices kept coming in. One male voice yelled, "Those stinkin' Ukrainian collaborators better start running before we catch them and beat the hell out of 'em. We'll get even."

As conversation was going on all around the yard, the pounding on the horizon continued. We talked about the Russians, about how they would behave, what they would do to us, and with us. We knew from previous stories that the Russians were no angels, and that soldiers on frontlines don't behave like knights, or like gentlemen. But now the Russians would be our liberators, and we could hardly wait to greet them.

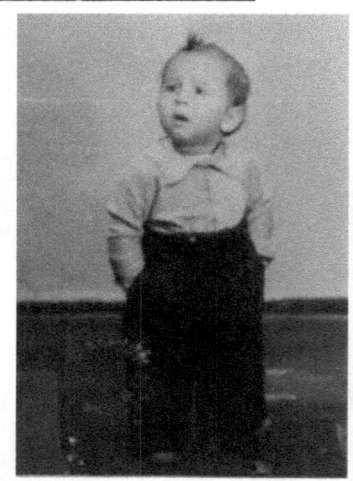

Students hear memories of Holocaust

Chapter 4. To Leipzig

We were still discussing our approaching freedom when, all of a sudden, and from all sides of the field, we saw Ukrainian guards, with rifles pointed, encircling the camp. Then we heard *Kapo* Gnat yell through a bullhorn, "Everybody out of the barracks! Run to the gate and get into formation! *Schnell!*" From across the field we heard another *kapo* echoing Gnat's order: "You have five minutes to get out of the barracks! Assemble at the gate in front of the trucks! Run! Run! Faster! Faster!"

A panic struck everyone in the camp. The rumors of evacuation suddenly became reality. We now knew that we were going to be deported. The question was, Where to? Are they taking us to a work camp in Germany, or to the furnaces of an extermination camp? Before we could grasp what was going on, Jewish police with their whips and clubs, Ukrainian guards with their rifles pointed, and German gendarmes with their dogs, began rounding up the inmates.

While the scheme of escaping mixed with the plans of celebrating freedom still swirled in our minds, the self-preservation switch turned on a warning light: "Be aware of the danger! Don't run!" Another voice from inside cautioned, "Avoid the whips! the clubs! the

To Leipzig

rifles! Try to keep your bones from being broken, you body from being crushed, your head from being shot off!"

My faculties became numb. Most of us became stupefied and obedient. We did as we were told. We lined up in front of the gate and were counted and then loaded into waiting trucks. In the darkness of the night, I heard someone asking a guard what he knew about the destination of our journey. But the bastard didn't answer; he only laughed. Other guards laughed, too. They seemed to be enjoying their superior position over the panic-stricken people. But one of the German gendarmes was heard to say, "Bestimmungsort: Leipzig, Deutschland"—"Destination: Leipzig, Germany."

No one said a word; we hoped and prayed that he was right. We believed that what he had said was true—not because we trusted him, but because we wanted it to be the truth. "Onto the trucks! Up! Mach' schnell!" the guards yelled. We did as we were told. A few guards stepped up to the outside platform and onto the running boards. The truck caravan proceeded forward.

I, like most of the other girls on our truck, was not sure why I had obeyed the order, why I and the others hadn't reacted differently. Why hadn't we run, resisted, or even jumped the armed guards? After hearing the horrible stories of Auschwitz and Majdanek, we had often discussed how we'd react if we were ever put into such a situation, if we were ever ordered for deportation. We had talked about it hundreds of times. Sometimes we even criticized people who, we'd heard, would go into the freight trains without resisting.

One time, two of my friends talked to me about escaping. We talked about it when the Russian Front was getting closer to the Polish border. But none of the three—Hanka, Irka, or I—came up with a workable

My Education Continues

plan. We had no money, no connections, and no place to go. None of us knew the roads around Skarżysko. Besides, we also had to think of the other prisoners, those still in German hands, who would have to pay the price. If one of us escaped, the German bastards would shoot ten, twenty—whatever number of prisoners they chose—in reprisal. They said many times that they'd kill ten for each one who escaped. We had reason to believe them. We knew, for a fact, that in the case of killing prisoners, they always kept their promises.

Nevertheless, the idea of running away was always with us. Under abnormal conditions, reasonable, "normal" thinking and reacting do not apply. Horrifying and confusing situations produce frightful weariness in which all logical thinking dies. Only the immediate preservation of one's life becomes important.

Our trucks drove through dark roads lined on both sides with thick brush and tall trees. I heard girls whispering to one another. One of them said that if we were ordered on a train, then, no matter what the consequences, she would escape; she'd never go on a train; she'd rather run under the wheels of a train than get on it.

By now, it was no longer a secret that the Nazis were using railroad cars designed for cattle and freight to ship their subjects to slave labor camps, and to death camps.[59] So whenever someone talked about committing suicide before entering a train, it was no surprise. A life wasn't such a big deal. As a matter of fact, there were a few girls on our truck talking about jumping under its wheels. (Talk of suicide was not new; for quite some time it had been going on. There had already been a few suicides committed by people who couldn't take the hunger, the dirt, the loss of loved ones, the humiliation. But to most people, life was too precious even to consider such an absurd act.) Most girls on our truck belonged to those who had never before thought of either suicide or escape. Now, being taken to an "unknown destination," they reasoned that they'd rather jump off the trucks—and take a chance on the dangerous road—than be burned in a crematorium. By now, everything that had previously sounded absurd and crazy became believable, even probable. I sat in a corner of the truck listening to the girls talk, the truck rumbling over a gravel road, the noises of its running engine. The truck hit a couple of bumps in the road, turned a corner, then stopped.

A silhouette of a freight train car appeared in the darkness. Far on the eastern horizon, fire was lighting the sky. We could hear the distant pounding of artillery. By the short distance ridden, we knew that we were not very far from our camp. It was almost obvious now that we were only a few kilometers from the Russian front.

Amid the pounding of artillery, we could hear the creaking sounds of boxcar doors opening. A few of us held hands and stared at one another helplessly. Some girls flung their arms around one another. Others sobbed. A few prayed.

Our truck stopped in front of an open cattle-car door. One of the guards unlocked the back gate of the truck and ordered us to jump off. We were commanded to climb into the train car.

The first few girls did as directed. But the next few running away from the train. In the darkness, I could only see their silhouettes disappearing into the forest. An array of bullets followed them. The girls kept running and the guards kept shooting. The stillness of the night vanished in rifle fire. How many girls escaped into hiding and how many escaped the torrent of bullets, no one could tell. I only know that the sound

My Education Continues

of the guns firing had prevented me and a few of my friends from escaping. I knew that instead of following the runaway girls, we had climbed obediently into the freight car. It was about three-quarters full when I got in, then it filled up to capacity.

One guard climbed onto the wagon roof; another pulled the sliding door shut. Then we could hear the door being bolted from the outside. Without food or water, we were locked in, and ready for shipment to somewhere. We all stood quietly. Not even a whisper could be heard. It seemed as though no one knew what to say.

After some time—seemingly hours—we heard remote sounds of colliding booms, felt a jerky motion (one that would have made us fall to the floor had we not been so tightly packed), and then sensed the movement of the train pulling away.

We knew that only a miracle could save us now. But most of us were past the stage of believing in miracles. Yet we were not ready to give up. Slowly, one by one, we tried to arrange some sitting space in a place in which there was hardly room to turn around. When we were almost settled, we realized, from the stench, that we would have to cuddle even closer together in order to leave a corner for an "outhouse."

Finally, with a lot of manipulation of body parts, with arms and legs overlapping and tangled around one another, most of us found a resting place on the straw-covered floor. Many girls fell asleep to the sound of the iron wheels gliding over the rails and to the swaying rhythm of the moving train.

At dawn we greeted the first rays of the sun that penetrated the tiny barred windows located above our heads, high in the boxcar's walls, close to the ceiling. We looked around the car, then at each other, assessing the extent of our situation. We realized that

To Leipzig

if this trip was not over soon, we would either starve or suffocate.

Our train kept moving forward as it had for most of the night. We were curious about our whereabouts, what existed beyond the boxcar walls. From our positions we could see through a few slits in the floor the boards between the tracks as they passed quickly by. With the strength that we still had, we established a human pyramid and put at the top a "seeing-eye" girl who could look out the window and report her findings.

We kept the pyramid and our hawk-eyed girl on a rotating basis. From the first spotter we learned that the outside world had not changed. There were fields and trees and roads. Some people were walking down the farm roads paying no attention to the passing train. Later in the day, one girl managed to pull away a splinter that was loose in the door. Climbing over one another, we took turns looking through that one-centimeter crack.

As the day dragged on, we started talking about our fate, about the possible destination of this trip, and we began speculating on the outcome of the War, giving one another courage in this hopeless situation. But by the evening, and into the next day, most of us were too exhausted to worry about such trivial things as the War, the world, or our whereabouts. We were more concerned about water and our weakening bodies. Our conversations became shorter and quieter until they almost ceased. Anyway, there was nothing good to talk about, nothing to be said. Eventually, we not only quit talking but gradually stopped using our limbs and our brains. Conversations, like body movements and thinking, used up too much energy. Energy had to be preserved.

"Stop all nonessential activities; save your energy for survival," warns that little voice of self-preservation

My Education Continues

inside us. "Sit in one place, keep the mouth shut, and the mind blank."

The following evening the train pulled into some kind of large railroad intersection and stopped. That night, and the next whole day, we stayed in this one place. Our hawk-eyed girl reported seeing a few unattached locomotives moving back and forth on different parts of the rails. Our locomotiveless train was stopped on a siding. At night, all of a sudden, we heard the familiar sound of colliding booms, a jerk, and then a forward movement, indicating that the train was once again on its way to "somewhere." Again we heard the clicking of the wheels on the rails.

During the following days on the train, we had the despairing feelings of exhaustion, suffocation, and abandonment. A couple of unconscious but slightly revived bodies were lying in one corner of the car, reminding us of our helplessness. Then came another night, and again we stood stranded for hours on some lonely track. By now it hardly mattered. Most of us were no longer interested in where we were or where we were going. Indifference and a feeling of "let's get it over with" set in. Occasionally a hand would touch mine and I would touch it back. It felt like a sign of temporary reassurance and affirmation: "Don't give up, sister. Not yet."

We expected to stay there for hours, but this time something unexpected happened. We heard someone banging on the freight-car door. Through our secret crack, one of the girls saw an armed, uniformed guard doing something at the door lock. We heard a jingle of chains, and the door rolled open.

It was a sunny but chilly morning. The bright light and the fresh air that entered the reeking car made me dizzy. I touched my head. It was still in the same place, but everything around me was whirling and turning. It

To Leipzig

felt like that day when I left Skarżysko Hospital. I thought that I was falling, but I had no place to fall since I was lying on the floor with my legs under the people around me. It took some maneuvering to pull out my arm and find a leg that would match my body. Finally, I managed to untangle all of my parts. I moved to the door to seize a breath of the fresh air. I looked out, but had absolutely no idea where I was or where the train had stopped. Nor did anyone else in our car.

From the position of our car, no city name was visible. We could see only a gray one-story building with two signs on it, one saying "Für Männer" and the other "Für Damen." The platform in front of the train, together with the surrounding area, indicated a part of a train station. The place was remarkably clean. It was almost abandoned. The Ukrainian guards who boarded our train in Skarżysko must have undergone a metamorphosis, for the ones who opened the wagon door were not Ukrainian but rather German soldiers, dressed in Feldgrau.[60] Standing next to them were two SS guards, in black uniforms bearing skull insignias on their hats, carrying rifles pointed at us. Lined up against the gray building stood, at attention, a dozen boys ranging in ages from about eleven to thirteen. They were staring curiously at the freight train and its unusual cargo. They were proudly displaying red and black swastika bands over their Hitlerjugend uniforms. The boys looked immaculate; the sun rays shone from their polished shoes like cold fire. Their faces, sober and dignified, and their uniformly short blond hair, their posture and behavior, all reflected strict discipline and obedience.

The boys looked as mystified as we did. As though on a specific command, all the boys turned around, marched into the building, and, after a couple of minutes, came out carrying tin cans. Walking over to the nearby water pump, they filled the cans, then very politely started handing this precious substance to the girls in our boxcar and the others on the train. As soon as they handed out all the cans, they turned around and lined up against the building as they had been previously.

Sharing a few sips of water without spilling it was an art because we got only ten cans per car. One went to revive the two girls lying almost dead in the corner. They were in such poor condition that they had trouble swallowing the water. While we were preoccupied with these two, the door to our car was rolled shut and locked. We heard the puffing of the engine; and black smoke hid the sun outside. A few soot flakes blew in through the tiny windows. The train started moving.

It kept moving, and stopping, sometimes halting for hours. Opinions varied about the duration of this journey: Some thought that we had been on the train for five days; others insisted that it had been longer, even as long as a week; all of us, however, were agreed that it seemed like a month.

One dark night, the train halted. I was closing my eyes, preparing for a long uneventful stay, when the wagon door pulled open and putrid air rushed out as a breath of fresh air blew into the car. Outside, it was dark. No moon, or stars or lights were visible. It might have been cloudy; it felt as if it had been raining. We heard a voice outside saying, "Raus! Alle raus! Mach' schnell!" Frightened and confused, we started untangling our limbs, then stumbling over each other as we began jumping off the train. "Line up for counting! Line up by fives! Mach' schnell!"

By the time I was ready to leave the boxcar, my eyes had adjusted to the darkness. I could see silhouettes of dogs and soldiers with rifles pointed surrounding the train. There were many rows of people in front of me, and there were quite a few behind me. In the row right behind me was one of the two girls

To Leipzig

who had been lying in the corner of the car. She was unable to walk. Two girls holding her under her armpits were dragging her along. A few rows to the front of me, guards with flashlights and notebooks in their hands were walking on both sides of the formation, counting the rows and recording their findings. Guards with dogs and rifles were walking beside them, watching us carefully—making sure, doubtless, that we were well protected. After all, who knows what might happen to girls during such a dark night? The dogs, we figured, were for added protection.

"Forward, march!"

The column started moving. I remember creeping along a paved road, my mind blank, my body completely exhausted. I didn't worry about the destination, or about my fate; not even about the danger. I walked in my row following the girl in front of me, just moving my legs, one in front of the other. In the distance, I remember seeing reflected lights illuminating the road. As we approached the light, I could see a couple of watchtowers, a barbed-wire fence stretching behind them into the darkness, and a large open gate with check booths on both sides.

At the gate we were counted: "Funf. Funf. Funf," I heard the guards on both sides of the column saying as I passed through the gate. The formation changed into a single line, and, one by one, we were led through a door into a red brick building.

By the time I came in, the large assembly hall inside the building was almost filled with women. All were sitting quietly on the floor, waiting for further instructions. A tall blond woman dressed in a white blouse under her black SS uniform, and armed with a whip, stood in the corner of the room, observing each girl as she walked through the door and directing her to a place on the floor by mechanically pointing her weapon toward the still available places. There were

My Education Continues

other SS women placed throughout the well-lit hall. A short husky one in a feldgrau uniform was standing only a couple of meters from me. When the room filled up, the door was locked.

"Ich bin Lagerkommandantin," the woman with the whip said in German, through an interpreter—"I am the camp commander. Everyone here: Undress! Leave all your belongings on the spot where you've been sitting. Line up at this door when you're called." She pointed her whip to a closed door on the opposite side from the entrance. "The shower rooms are ready. If you cooperate, you'll be processed in no time."

"It's a good translator," said the girl next to me, who spoke some German. A few of the girls used to live on the Polish-German border, where German was taught in school, and where some of the population was of German descent and knew the language quite well.

Everyone had listened to the speech, but no one was moving. I looked around and saw in the crowd many unfamiliar faces. A group of girls with yellow hair, skin, and fingernails was sitting in one corner of the hall. Another group, in KL-marked clothes, were sitting nearby. Not far from them were several girls from our boxcar, holding the tin water cans that they had brought back from the train.

I asked one of the girls near me where she came from and found out that they had been on our train, traveling in different cars. They had also worked for HASSAG in Skarżysko, but on different sites. The girls with the yellow faces had worked at Werk C—the finishing plant where their work consisted of filling grenade shells with yellow "Pikrina" powder. (Many slave workers died from this poisonous substance.)

"Everybody undress! I mean business!" yelled the Kommandantin. For emphasis, she cracked her whip in the air: "Macht schnell!"

To Leipzig

"Do it fast!" the interpreter echoed.

We didn't know where we were, and had no idea what kind of showers Frau Kommandantin was talking about. Among the many rumors that we had heard was one about Zyklon-B and cyanide showers, the showers rumored to be in Treblinka and Auschwitz—a rumor that we had previously disregarded, but which now came immediately to our minds.[61]

Cold weakness crept into our bones. Girls started crying, pulling their hair, cracking their knuckles; some just froze and turned numb. It became obvious now that the rumors circulating in Skarżysko had been real. Our time on earth was over.

The few girls by the shower door, who had started screaming at the initial announcement of the showers, stopped their hysterical outbursts and sat speechless and motionless.

Whether it was the fear of the Kommandantin's whip that kept them quiet, or the realization that their screams were useless and it was too late to react or worry, I don't know. I only saw how they slowly and hesitantly began taking off their clothes. We all followed.

I took off my shoes. From one of them, I took out a small piece of squashed, blackened paper. I straightened it out as much as possible. I looked at the few, barely recognizable, words: "G-ad--'re -K.— care...." I was going to throw this note into the foot wrappings so that no one would be able to find it; but I decided to save this last reminder—Mom's last note. I just held the note in my hand, not knowing what to do with it. I saw Frau Kommandantin standing by, quietly watching us undress. Whether she was aware of our thoughts, or of the "other kind of showers," no one really knew. From the look on her face and the manner of her behavior, she might have been puzzled over our reaction to the undressing. After all, one would think

My Education Continues

that after such a trip people would be eager to take a shower. She might have been listening to the whispering that was going on among us. I saw her talking to the interpreter and shaking her head.

The few whispers that I heard from the girls around me sounded like confessions, final farewells; like making one's final peace with God. Girls told one another of their sinful love affairs, and the lovers that they were leaving behind; and about treif food that they had eaten even when kosher was available. They talked about the lies that they had told their parents and friends. They were telling these personal secrets, not realizing—or perhaps because they were realizing—that talkers and listeners were destined for the same fate. Some girls sounded as though they were trying to vindicate God, to justify His deeds, and in this way to explain to themselves why they really did deserve to die at such a young age. One girl was saying to her friend that she wanted only to live long enough to see the end of the War. None of my close friends was sitting near me, and I didn't feel like talking to strangers. I just sat there looking at my note and listening to them talk. I think that I was just glad to be alone, having no one to worry about, not having anybody to feel sorry for, or anyone who would pity me.

Frau Kommandantin's whip snapped. My thoughts were interrupted. She cleared her throat and cried out, "Aren't you Schweinehunde ready yet?" Her whip went on the backs of two girls sitting next to her, as if to show us that she really meant business.

Undressing speeded up. The door to the shower room opened. Through it we could see a smaller room, and in it a few SS women seated around a right-angled table.

The first group of fifteen girls entered the room; the door closed behind them. Breathlessly, we waited to see what would happen. Maybe they would all come

To Leipzig

out all clean...after all, they had to come back and pick up the clothes that they had left on the floor.

Time dragged on, each minute seeming an hour. The longer the girls were gone, the longer seemed each waiting minute. An eternity passed. There was no sign of the girls.

Frau Kommandantin's whip snapped again. She stamped her foot. A second group of fifteen girls was taken behind the shower door. The first group still had not returned. We sat quietly waiting our turn. There was no way out of here now, nothing that could be done. We could only think about all the missed opportunities, about things that should have or could have been done: "We should have jumped off the train.... Maybe we should have hidden in Skarżysko and taken a chance." It didn't really matter any more. It was too late. Now, even thinking was in vain. Could we really have hidden in a forest after running away from the train? Where could we have gone from there? It had been so dark, pitch black and cloudy....

A third group of fifteen girls was called into the shower room. There was still no sight of any of the girls previously taken away.

"Fifteen: March!" yelled a voice next to me. The room was dead quiet. An SS woman counted: "Eins, zwei, drei....Fünfzehn! Schnell, macht schnell!"

The door opened. My group walked in. Inside that adjacent room there was still no sign of the other girls. An SS woman at the table looked at my face. She eyed my nude body from head to toe. "Name," she said in a peremptory voice. She checked a long list of names and numbers.

"Eleven-Ninety-One. Remember!" she said.

It was to be my new name for now. After registration, we went through other induction procedures. As in Skarżysko, we kept moving from one processing station to the next. At each of the stations

My Education Continues

stood SS women equipped with clubs, magnifying glasses, scissors, razors, and flashlights, all waiting for us to pass their inspection.

I watched the girls ahead of me being checked for lice. It took only one tiny nit, and click, click, went the scissors: The hair was gone. My hair had not yet grown back, and only a stubble was covering my bald head. The inspector left it alone. All underarm and pubic hair was automatically shaved off.

At the next station the checkers had an even more dignified assignment: Their job was to look into all body cavities—nostrils, ears, mouths, vaginas, rectums, searching for secret documents and hidden treasures.

Oh my! My piece of paper! It was still in my hand. I had taken it with me. A hot flash went through my body. I put the paper into my mouth, dissolved it into my saliva—one swallow, and it was gone. I closed my eyes thinking, What was coming next? I saw Mom's face; I thought of my sister, and how she must have grown by now; images of friends and relatives I left in Warsaw marched in front of me.

I heard, "Forward, march!" and followed the girls ahead of me, desperately trying to take my thoughts off of the upcoming shower. Our group had finished going through all the processing stations, and we were now being checked over for the shower. "If you want to survive," I kept telling myself, "You must believe that this is not happening."

The shower room door opened. The girls who had gone in before us were still nowhere to be seen. Reluctantly we dragged our feet into the shower room, trying to avoid a last-minute whipping. The door was shut behind us. We stood shaking, just waiting for whatever was to come out of the showerheads. Fifteen naked girls, waiting, shaking, cursing, praying.

A rumble in the pipes interrupted our worry. Then,

To Leipzig

to our amazement, and relief, the showerheads started spraying streams of warm, precious water. Real water. Clean, warm water. No gas.

I think that we still didn't believe it. I think that we were still waiting for the gas. "Water!" we finally screamed, almost simultaneously. "Water!" We embraced, we laughed, we clapped hands, we danced like little children playing in a fountain. Someone in the group must not have been so trusting, for I heard one girl's voice say, "Hey, girls! We still don't know where the other girls are."

But hardly anyone paid attention to this voice. We rejoiced as the refreshing water spurted on our dirty and stinking—but still young and firm, beautiful bodies. We could hardly believe that this was truly happening. We even got soap! Each girl received a piece of grey, harshly textured soap.

Years had passed since I had taken a shower. Even at home, in Warsaw, taking a shower had not been a daily occurrence. Most people used to wash in tubs. For showers, many joined others in public bath houses, or at school or athletic clubs. I had not seen a shower in either Sandomierz or Skarżysko.

After a few minutes of this great treat, the water was turned off. The opposite door opened. A voice yelled, "Raus! Alle raus!" We were thinking of getting back to the filthy, rancid clothing that we had left behind, and how we would put them on over our freshly washed bodies, when one of the SS women ordered us into a room that smelled of disinfecting powder, filled with shelves of nicely folded garments.

There, to our great amazement and joy, we found our "lost girls." They greeted us with tired but relaxed faces. We breathed a sigh of relief, not only because we were alive, but because we finally knew that the "shower stories" were vicious lies spread by Jew-haters.

My Education Continues

What an incredible sight! Our eyes filled with tears, which rolled down our cheeks and faces, down onto our naked breasts. With relief, we watched our friends put on their new wardrobes, which consisted of four items: an undershirt, a pair of underpants, a dress—all made of coarse material conspicuous for its broad prison stripes—and a pair of clogs. The attire came in two sizes: large and larger.

Before we got to join the girls on the benches, we were sprayed with disinfecting powder. After we got dressed, we were counted, given number patches to put on our newly acquired clothes, and led into a large hall full of three-tiered bunk beds. Before we were assigned sleeping places, we lined up for tea and bread. On the lid of the tea caldron, I read, hassag-leipzig. So, for the first time since we arrived at this place, I knew where I was.

The Leipzig camp was quite different from Skarżysko. Here was absolute German Law and Order. The SS made the Law; we obeyed the Orders. Unlike Skarżysko, where all inmates were Jewish, Leipzig was an international, all-female camp. When we arrived, there were already Czechoslovakian, French, Greek, Hungarian, Polish, and Russian women. We were the first and only Jews to arrive in the camp. Most of the inmates were women arrested for various, so-called "anti-German activities." Some were here for being in underground movements, some for political activities, some for smuggling, and some for hiding German enemies, among other forbidden acts. There were even German women accused of being anti-Nazi, or for alleged communist connections. Most of the Russian women were POWs taken from the Russian Front. Our crime was that we were born to Jewish parents. We were imprisoned, so to speak, "by the right of birth."

The block-long brick building where we were housed was enclosed by three rows of barbed-wire fences, of which two were electrified with enough power to kill on touch. We were grouped by nationality, each staying in its own area, or "block," as we called it. We were assigned to Block 20.

The well-constructed five-story building was equipped with hot and cold running water, flush toilets, electric lights, even central heating. It had been previously occupied by the German military, housing soldiers who, by now, were probably somewhere fighting on one of the fronts. Food here was not gourmet fare, nor was there an abundance of it, but we would not starve. Like Skarżysko, Leipzig was a labor camp. Outside of a small number of prison women who were assigned to kitchen duties, camp cleaning, or field jobs, all the rest of us worked in a munitions plant preparing killing supplies for the War.

I worked on an assembly-line making small parts for "something." The hall in which I worked was clean, warm, and well lit. My job was putting tiny pivot needles into small, rounded metal bowls that were laid out on trays and moved by me on a slowly moving conveyor belt. Of the approximately one-hundred-fifty people working in this hall, about three-fourths were prison women, the rest German employees—almost all women. The German males who worked in this plant were mostly old or disabled men, unfit for frontline duties. Among them were a few draft- dodgers. Other men and women who worked in this plant were forced laborers brought in from the German-occupied territories. They were called "free" workers, maybe due to the amount of pay that they were receiving for their work. Or maybe because they were free as compared to us prisoners. Many of them were actually "volunteers" who, forced by starvation, signed up for work in Germany because they had had no other means of

My Education Continues

support in the German-occupied territories. Some of them had been taken during roundups.

In any case, they did not live in the camps but on the city outskirts, or on farms in specially prepared housing. These foreign workers did not work on assembly-lines; they were assigned to more prestigious jobs, such as moving heavy loads, shoveling snow, hauling trash, or cleaning the yards. German male and female workers who intermingled with the prisoners and the foreigners were trustworthy employees, and inspectors of the killing gear. They guarded against any sabotage attempts since among the foreigners, there was always the temptation to sabotage some of the armaments.

Besides the civilian Germans, there were also SS women guards stationed throughout the work hall. They were guarding the prisoners lest there be any misbehavior or escape attempts, or any communication between the German workers and the foreigners.

At the beginning, the situation at work and in the camp was very tense. There was a lot of prejudice, resentment, mistrust, and often pure hate, between different groups of inmates and other plant workers. Each nationality tried to stick with its own kind. And, of course, there were language and cultural barriers. But the biggest barriers were mistrust and ignorance. Later, many unfortunate circumstances would force us to communicate with one another. By doing so, we accidentally found out how much alike we really were.

And so here in the Leipzig camp, my education continued. Here in Leipzig, as before in Skarżysko, I learned enough to fill a book. I had to keep all this information in my memory, hoping, one day, to add it to my diary.

To Leipzig

We worked six days a week; but on the seventh we did not rest. On Sundays, our day would start with a somewhat delayed Appell—there was only one Appell on Sundays, compared with two on other days—and then the remainder of our "day of rest" we spent washing clothes, checking for lice, standing in lines for food, and cleaning the premises; and, of course, collecting and spreading rumors. During these activities, we were usually getting acquainted with women from other blocks and those who worked in other sections of the plant.

Our Blockelste—block supervisor—was a Polish prisoner named Nunia. She despised Germans and Jews alike. She was a woman in her thirties, tall, husky, and broad-boned. She had blonde straight hair, cut very short. She lived in Block 6, with other Polish women, and was assigned to supervise our Block 20, which housed three-hundred Jewish girls.

I never had an argument with Nunia, but many girls did. I always tried to avoid "authority figures" if I could. The less I knew them, and the less they knew me, the better. Many arguments and fights went on between Nunia and the prisoners who were fighting over reduced food rations, unreasonable sleeping arrangements, and unfair chore assignments. Nunia, here in Leipzig, was not like Wanda in Skarżysko. Nunia was moody, unjust, often vicious. She didn't mind turning in girls to the SS just to show who was boss, even knowing full well that those she turned in would be put into solitary confinement, and could be beaten and starved for days. She expected her subordinates to give her respect, and to share with her parts of their rations in exchange for good treatment or special favors. She, then, would often exchange the extra food for cigarettes—a very complicated process that involved outside workers and smuggling talents.

My Education Continues

Luckily, we had a nice supervisor at work. Analese, our German Aufseherin—overseer—was an SS woman, but the total opposite of Nunia. She loved most of us girls, and paid special attention to two of us: a French girl from Lille and a girl from our block who was from Kraków. Both girls were personable, had soft dark hair, clear white skin, and very beautiful bodies. Most of the time, Analese was pleasant, fair, and helpful to everybody. She was especially nice to us whenever the other guards were not around. It was then that she would pay little attention to rules and be quite lenient towards us. With her on duty, we could use toilets without supervision, talk with each other, and with other workers, even with the German employees. As a treat, she'd occasionally order from the kitchen an additional caldron of soup for us. Analese was husky and rather short for an SS woman. Her rough features did not reveal her lovely disposition.

Besides Nunia and Analese, we met many new girls at work and on the "campus," as we called our living quarters inside the wires. Here we got to know girls from many nations, and of many nationalities. Some were from the other Skarżysko camps.

In Leipzig, as in Skarżysko, we spent many evenings talking. We shared stories, shed tears, confessed sins, learned from one another, and spread rumors. We heard that only a small part of the Skarżysko girls had come with us to Leipzig; all others had been taken to other places. The men, supposedly, had also been divided up, and transferred to a few different destinations. No one knew for sure where.

From the French girls we learned songs and stories of the German invasion of France. Basia, a Polish college girl who spoke French, became our translator. The French that I'd learned in the ghetto helped a little with some of the songs, but it proved almost useless when the girls started talking about the German invasion and about the atrocities committed by the Germans against French Jews. They told us about confiscation of property, deportations, and trains that took many French, Belgian, and Dutch Jews to some "unknown destinations somewhere in the East."

We learned many things from other girls, too. We tried to communicate with all of them, even though, at times, we had to use body language, our hands, and some of the German that a few of the girls in each group knew, to get things going. With the Polish girls, we didn't have a x or any cultural misunderstandings, so of course our conversations were more frequent and more involved. We learned that almost all the Polish girls who had been arriving here lately had come from Warsaw. They had been rounded up during the May 1944 Uprising, and charged with participating in a revolutionary movement. They told us that quite a number of young Jewish men who had managed to escape to the Aryan side during the 1943 Ghetto Uprising fought with the Poles in the 1944 Revolt, and that many of them got killed in the fighting; many others had been captured and sent away, or shot.[62]

In one of the discussions, the girls gave us a more detailed account of what had gone on: "The Germans arrested them just like they did us, not knowing that they were Jews. But when the Schwabs recognized a Jew in the crowd of detainees, they shot him or her right on the spot. Some gendarmes even beat the hell out of the Jews before they shot them to death. All that while we were watching." She covered her eyes for a moment, and was going to continue, when her friend interrupted: "Don't forget the Polish prisoners who were beaten and shot because they were mistaken for Jews." "Oh, yes," continued the first girl, "and don't you be surprised if you find some Jewish girls here among us.."

My Education Continues

All of this was new information. None of us, not even the KL girls knew what had happened after the Ghetto Uprising, when they were taken away to Majdanek.

Mostly we enjoyed the discussions with our compatriots. We were getting along fairly well with most of the girls. The Polish girls, like inmates of other nationalities, came from many walks of life. Among them were the poor and the rich, the college graduates and the barely literate; there was also a fair share of anti-Semites who could not, even in the camp, be cured of their prejudices.

So, along with the friendly and informative discussions, we had a few heated debates in which the KL girls reminded our compatriots that very little help came to the Jews from the Aryan side during the Ghetto Uprising. "We expected at least the Polish Resistance Movement to send us some help as we fought a common enemy," a KL girl commented. "We were disappointed."

Often the girls would praise those individual Poles who had had the conscience and the courage to provide food and ammunition to the ghetto fighters. The girl who spoke even commended those Poles who had sold the Jews necessities for large sums of money, because any help to the Jews was a risky business.

Our Leipzig news and rumors were of a somewhat higher standard than those in Skarżysko, where we had had only one source of information. Here, we had more channels, better reporters, and more underground sources. Occasionally, we managed to eavesdrop on German discussions, or on a radio program at work. We could find a newspaper article or a discarded letter somewhere in the trash. Many stories were also being picked up by foreign workers on clandestine radio stations. Some of those who were

To Leipzig

engineers by profession learned to intercept English and French radio transmissions and found translators to interpret the information.

We heard what the German media was not reporting. German propaganda was designed to keep citizens' morale up and keep them happy. Now, as before, we picked the part of the news that we chose to believe and called it "the truth." We liked to believe that the Americans were helping the other Allies on the Western Front, that the Russians were advancing to the German border, that there had been an assassination attempt on Hitler's life.[63] The rumors continued circulating, and they kept us going, and hoping, even though we knew in our hearts that many of them could have been only wishful thoughts.

Then, one day, something happened that confirmed some of the rumors. We knew then that the Germans were in trouble.

We were at work. It was about noon, just before lunchtime, that we heard the howling of sirens. We didn't pay too much attention to the noises, for testing air-raid sirens was a common occurrence. This time, however, we were told to stop work, vacate the building, and leave for the bomb-shelter, which was located on the plant premises.

The concrete shelter was about two stories underground. It was comprised of large and small rooms that were furnished with wooden benches, folded cots, and shelves filled with emergency supplies and equipment. When we came down, the German women who came with us said that we were here only for practice, that it was only a drill. Inside the shelter, they went to one of the smaller rooms, where a pot of coffee was brewing and the radio was playing "Rosamunde" (the famous "Beer Barrel Polka"). We prisoners went to one of the large rooms equipped with benches only. The only German in our room was

My Education Continues

Analese. She sat next to one of her favorite girls and smoked a cigarette.

After about an hour in that soundproof shelter, we were told to return to our workplaces. On the way up we could hear the sirens blowing the "all clear" signal. We finished our workday and then went "home."

Next morning at work, we heard that the practice drill the day before had not been a test but rather due to a real air-raid by American and British bombers. We knew now that at least some of the rumors that we had been hearing were true. And we were delighted.

No longer could the German people at work, or the SS guards at camp, disguise their concerns and worries. As the air-raids became more frequent, German faces and behavior told the true story. Many were crying over their destroyed homes and over wounded friends or relatives. Some were bringing to work letters that they had received from their men fighting on the fronts. Many women could not hold back their tears; they cried openly, mourning their fallen relatives.

Their newspapers and radios kept reporting successes on the battlefields and were still predicting victory, while the mail from their loved ones, even after being censored, was indicating problems, defeats, and misery. Yes, the people's disappointed faces were telling us a story.

In the evenings, while "on campus," we discussed these new developments. Even though we were under threat of bombings, and our food rations had been cut, we rejoiced at the raids on German cities, just as we had rejoiced at the bombing of Hamburg when we heard about it in Skarżysko.

As time went on, we spent more time in the shelter, less at work. We got to know more about the German women who worked with us. Our German-speaking girls started conversing with them more often. These conversations could best be carried on whenever Analese was on duty, when no suspicious people were watching; for no one ever knew who could be reporting such forbidden actions: Squealers could be found even among "nice" people. Most of the informers were actually very nice people who believed that they were simply doing a patriotic deed. They were the flag-waving Germans who loved their country and blindly obeyed all orders from their leader. We tried to be careful whenever we talked.

Since the bombing raids were becoming more frequent, the Germans at work started treating us with more dignity. And as they treated us better, we started feeling sorry for them whenever we saw them crying and praying for their men. We were in a terrible dilemma because most of us felt good about the bombings. We knew that the husbands and sons for whom these women were praying were the men who were killing our people, bombing our cities, and burning our villages. Yet knowing these women, and having worked with them for months, we couldn't help feeling sorry for them. Our morale went up and down like a yo-yo: We'd be delighted that the Germans were getting killed; then we'd feel sorry for them.

Meanwhile, our camp life continued in its normal routine. On Sundays, we cleaned the premises, and stood at Appell. Whenever the weather was nice we could see people strolling along the field behind the wires. We watched old people and young women, and small children, just out walking and enjoying the day. Many tower guards would pay no attention to them walking near the camp, but some guards would whistle and motion for them to get off the field. Some people would obey the guards' orders; others would ignore their whistling and just keep on walking near the wires.

My Education Continues

Whether those who walked by did it out of curiosity, or just for fun, was hard to tell. We saw children running and playing in the field, often stopping and pointing their small fingers in our direction, as though they were asking their mothers, What kind of animals are those in that huge cage? From afar, we must have looked like a herd of zebras.

The first Sunday I saw those people walking in the field, an electric shock went through my body. There were grandmothers and grandfathers and mothers with their children walking together in family units. I suddenly realized that for years I had not seen a child. Yet what surprised me more was that it hadn't occurred to me before. (I mentioned it to a girl who was standing next to me at Appell. She looked at me, astonished. "An interesting observation. I hadn't thought of it, either.") It was encouraging and at the same time depressing to see whole families. It was especially hard on the women who, by force, had been separated from their children. These sights brought about many sighs and tears. It seemed strange that somewhere, behind this barbed wire, lay a different world, a world where people had relatives and friends, where they were free to live and love. We often discussed these painful scenes in the evenings, comforting and reassuring the mothers who truthfully believed that they'd eventually be reunited with their offspring. It made us feel good, and it gave the mothers something to dream about, something to hope for.

Luba, a girl in her late twenties from Kelce, was the only one in our group who would become hysterical whenever the subject of children came up. Her behavior puzzled us even more because she was unmarried and had left no children behind. In Skarżysko, she had had a "cousin" named Itsek. She cried frantically when he was taken away to be transferred to another location. She also cried every

To Leipzig

time the subject of love or marriage came up in discussions. And this was one of our most popular, as well as touchiest, and heartbreaking, subjects. Those of us who had never loved or married, who had left behind no boyfriends, lovers, or husbands, had little to add to these conversations. Still, we had much to learn from the girls who did.

Having had teachers like pockmarked Wanda and "Rachu-the-Bitch" in Skarżysko, I was sure that my theoretical education in the field of love and sex was complete, or at least adequate. I was only sorry that I did not have the proper practical experience to complement the theory. Now, of course, it was too late; even those hopes had vanished. This all-female camp was so well guarded, we felt sure that every girl who came here a virgin would remain one.

Everything went by strict rules. No transgressions, no trespassing, no variety. Daily, uneventful routine: Appell; work; Appell; food line; sleep. For variety: rumors, air-raids, additional Appells. The frequent air-raids would give us time to reminisce. In the shelter, the Warsaw girls often recalled the 1939 bombing of our city. The bombings in Leipzig were as bad here now, but now we had no one to worry about, nowhere to run, nothing to think about, nothing to lose. We had learned, in our first camp lessons, that, here, you don't worry, you don't plan, you don't think. You do as you are told, follow the rules, don't ask questions. They tell you to go to the shelter—you go to the shelter. They yell, "Achtung! Appell!" and you stay at attention, stand for Appell. They bring the soup, you eat it; if they don't, tough luck; you never complain. In the shelter, such lessons have come in handy.

The bombs are falling; you hope that they'll miss you. You hope that the bombing will stop...well, maybe not; you have mixed feelings. Deep inside, you really want the bombing to continue. You really want German cities to be destroyed; you want the Schwabs to die—you just don't want to die with them.

Then you think again: Maybe you don't really want them to die; all you want is revenge, and you know that you cannot take revenge on dead people. So, what you really want is for them to live and then beg for your forgiveness and mercy. Well! You believe, you hope, that maybe you can be nice to them. You hope that you can.... All these voices are talking to you simultaneously. You really don't know what is going on. Will all this ever end, end for good? Are these only fantasies?

The door to the German room opens. The radio is playing patriotic music; we hear some kind of announcements. Then the music continues. Cheerful music...military marches. But the faces of the German women are dreary, sad.

Like other prisoners, I am here with strangers. I have no idea where any of my relatives are. Outside of Mom and Sis, all were in Warsaw. Most of the time I try not to think about them. It is just as well: I am spared the grief of seeing them suffer. I have no one to worry about. I hope to see them some day and tell them my stories of Sandomierz, Skarżysko, the train ride, Leipzig.

We hear new rumors: "The Russians have crossed the German border. Poland is now free. It won't be long now.... Families and friends will be reunited. Our relatives are waiting for us. Our dreams are coming true." German papers are still bragging about military successes and predicting a final victory. "We will save our beloved Vaterland!" yells the radio announcer. "We will fight to the last soldier!" He sounds like that announcer on Polish radio during the bombing of Warsaw, only this one speaks in German.

To Leipzig

We have been in the shelter for about two hours. We have had a nice discussion, about killing. Kind of philosophical: "According to the Bible, killing is a crime," said one of the girls in our group.

"Only if it's done on an individual basis," said another. "Haven't you read enough books to know that collective killing is called heroism or patriotism, or some other kind of ism?"

The radio in the German room is still on; the door is open. Eva, a girl from the Polish block, translates: "The announcer is talking about the heroic German soldiers performing miraculous victories on the front." Luckily, no one talks about the Jews. The Jewish issue is always a touchy one. We try to avoid it if we can. We talk about food. Foods eaten in different countries. The French girls in our shelter add their ideas of good cooking. We are getting very hungry.

The raid is over. We can leave the shelter. On the way up, we hear the siren's "All clear." On the stairs, we hear a German woman say, "It's not very heroic to drop bombs on defenseless people and fly away." Other German women agree with her.

Walking through the yard to the work hall, we see thick black smoke coming from the city. I think about the conversation in the shelter. Never before could I understand what was meant by "justified killing." Now I understand it even less.

Another winter was quickly approaching, and the prolonged curfew hours kept us inside the building during the long evenings. After the final Appell, only the tower guards and a skeleton crew were guarding the campsite. The SS women in charge were taking turns, alternating evenings, but Analese seemed to be on duty almost daily. She would roam the building, tiptoeing from room to room long after the inmates had gone to sleep. We paid little attention to her

My Education Continues

presence. If we needed something, she would treat us politely.

Other SS women on night-duty sat in their special room, drinking coffee, smoking cigarettes, listening to the radio, and talking to one another. They were feeling quite confident that Law and Order would be preserved. They could fully depend on their helpers, the Stubenältesten, and the informers; the slightest deviation would be immediately reported to them.

The long winter evenings we used to spend talking, singing, crying, as well as composing lyrics to familiar tunes and writing poems. On "organized" paper and with stolen pencils, we wrote about the camp and the War, and about home and freedom—the latter two we called "Fantasies." Our writings were happy and sad, and forbidden.

For Hanukkah, which we celebrated around Christmas time, we sang old traditional songs. No candles, no latkes—and no birthday for me.

We talked about longing for freedom, lost love, and home; and the fantasy of a new miracle, in which a small group of guerrillas defeats the mighty German Empire. Christmas writings and songs were, for the most part, about similar topics: a miracle child who grows up and saves the world. Christmas songs and writings came in many languages; every nationality had its own version—even the Russian non-believers would sing their versions of Christmas carols. There were also some "joint projects," composed and performed by girls of many nationalities. All of these compositions were written down, read, memorized, recited; then the papers were torn up and flushed down the toilets.

All of us, each group in its own way, celebrated the holidays by recalling the past and hoping for the future. Many trusted God's miracles; they believed that only God could save us. Others had long since given

To Leipzig

up the idea that God would intercede on our behalf, and called the stories of God's miracles necessary lies, or myths.

I wasn't sure who was right. I couldn't be angry with God, for after all, when I had wanted to see a real war, He granted me my wish—and I had to be thankful for it. Now I just wandered if it would be too much to ask for another favor.

I could hardly make the connection between a God of mercy and a God of misery. Somehow, Greek mythology, in which there are good gods and bad gods, started making sense to me.

On the issue of religion, I was all mixed up. Christian girls were insisting that salvation could only come to those who accepted Jesus as their personal savior. But they were unable to explain why God had allowed good, faithful Christians to be eaten by lions; nor could they justify their own suffering.

On the other hand, I was taught that Jews were God's "Chosen People," but I couldn't figure out what they had been chosen for. And how about Buddhists and Muslims and Hindus, and all the other religions: How about their God, or gods?

I envied people who could believe in God's justice and the coming of the Messiah. I tried. I did see the sun shining and the flowers growing; and I saw the flames burning, and the children starving and the people dying. I heard birds singing and women crying and rivers flowing and tears falling.

Sometimes I thought of my devout little sister. I wondered what she was saying in her daily prayers. We were taught never to question God; but occasionally I just wondered how He could watch all this misery—even watch the bombing of the Leipzig children—and do nothing about it. I began to believe that God, maybe, knows a lot about creation, about the heaven and the earth, about the stars, the sun,

My Education Continues

and the mighty universe—about big things like that; but I wasn't sure that He was knowledgeable about people. Maybe if God had worked on the seventh day, and rested on the eighth, we people would have been made better.

I saw many good Christians and Jews being beaten and kicked and spat on while they prayed.

An incident that happened on a freezing January morning, put even more questions into my mind:

It was a Sunday Appell. But this time the Appell was not routine: Somebody was missing at the count. We were counted and recounted, but the guards could not come up with the correct number. Frau Kommandantin was called out. With a few helpers, she herself conducted the counting. And, like the guards before, she could not come up with the right figure.

Frau Kommandantin called out for all her interpreters and through them announced: "All of you will remain here till that Schwein is found! Understand! Someone in this shitty bunch knows who that runaway bitch is!"

Assuming that her scare would produce quick results, she stood in front of us tapping her booted feet, waiting. No one came forward.

"Tell those foreign bastard spies," she yelled to the translators, "that I will have ten of them shot dead on the spot if that missing whore is not found within ten minutes!" She walked into the building to warm up.

The day was gloomy. It was about nine or ten in the morning when the Appell was called, and it was still quite dark. It had snowed the day before and all through the night. It stopped snowing just before we came out into the yard. After about an hour, the sun started coming out from behind the clouds. Behind the fence, far out in the field, children started throwing snowballs; playing and laughing. The tower guards chased them away.

To Leipzig

It must have been exactly ten minutes when Frau Kommandantin returned. She pointed to her watch. She was waiting for an answer. No one came up with the information about the missing girl.

Additional guards were called to help—even male wardens whose job it was to escort us to and from work and to tend the watchtowers, were summoned, so that the freezing guards who were watching us could go into the building to warm up and eat.

We kept standing outside. In the late afternoon, it started snowing again. Our feet were so frigid that they stopped aching. The three-quarter length striped prison jackets, which we had gotten for the winter, were covering up the icy stains of frozen urine that had by now soaked many dresses. We stood for hours. No one had yet been shot, even though Frau Kommandantin had twice repeated her threat.

After many hours, a part of the mystery was solved. Camp records revealed that the missing girl was Polish. They showed her prison number, her room number, her name, and workplace. But the girl was nowhere to be found.

Frau Kommandantin made a new announcement. "Everyone working or living with that stinking Polack better come forward with some information, or I'll beat the shit out of you!" She didn't mention the shooting with which she had threatened us before. Her new talk did not produce any more results than the previous one, either. She became furious. Many other guards, now cold and tired, and having wasted almost the whole Sunday watching the "rotten prisoners," were in no better mood than our Frau Kommandantin.

Time passed, and we kept standing. We remained at attention. Those who moved or fell were mercilessly beaten. Those who fainted were revived with a snow massage and put back into formation, or else pushed up against the fence.

My Education Continues

Finally, the Appell, which had started at nine or ten in the morning, ended, at nightfall. I am not sure why we were dismissed; if the guards were just too tired and had just had enough of it; or perhaps they knew that we had to get rested for the next day's work. Whatever the case might have been, we were allowed to go back into the warm, well-lit building.

As we entered our hall, we found, lined up in a orderly fashion, caldrons of hot soup and coffee waiting ready for distribution. Frozen and exhausted, we stormed the hot caldrons. Luckily, they did not overturn, but much of the hot liquid got spilled anyway. Many girls got injured, some suffering severe burns.

Next morning, everyone except Luba reported to Appell and then went to work. Even the girls with the burns showed up. Luba was the girl who used to get hysterical fits whenever we talked about children. When she didn't show up for Appell, many girls, including me, assumed that she was either frozen or too badly burned. Soon, however, the news spread that Luba had gotten very sick during the Appell, and had been taken to the hospital room on the top floor of the building.

Not until a few days later did word start getting around: Luba was with child. We had heard some time ago that there was a pregnant woman who came from a small town to Skarżysko. She was, supposedly, brought in shortly before our evacuation. She came to the camp pregnant; her husband had been sent to another destination. We didn't know who the woman was, but we knew about the situation. Almost everyone in our block knew Luba.

We were shocked and angry, frightened and sorry. We worried about Luba because here, like Skarżysko, people from the "hospital" were often taken away to unknown destinations. Here, as in Skarżysko, we had

To Leipzig

"selections," from which the sick and disabled were sent away, never to come back. But, unlike in Skarżysko, here the atrocities were better hidden, for here we had occasional visits from the International Red Cross or some other such organization. Anyway, we were worried about Luba and the fetus. We were surprised that she had been able to hide her secret for so long. We had noticed that she was getting "fat," but this was not as surprising as it might seem: Many of us were getting fat from not menstruating. Many were swollen and bulging; I was, too. But what Luba had done to conceal her growing abdomen was quite clever: She had traded clothes with girls who wore larger sizes. I'm not sure if they ever knew the reason for the trade.

The morning after that memorable Appell, we talked about Luba and about the missing girl. We talked about them in camp, to and from work, at work, and after. Because it was dark outside, the guards paid little attention to our chatting as long as no one was out of line. The German shepherds made sure that that didn't happen.

By the time we got back to camp, everybody knew, not just the story of Luba, but that of the missing girl, who was Krysia, from Block 6. We knew that she had been taken out in a trash barrel by a crew of foreign workers. The escape had been well planned. She was taken to her Polish boyfriend, who was working somewhere on a German farm, and who had arranged the whole escape scheme. A day later, the missing girl's best friend, Kasia, and a couple of her coworkers, were put into solitary confinement, a cold, windowless room in the basement, where they were interrogated. After a few days, the three girls were released. They had shaved heads and bruises on their faces and bodies. They talked very little.

Many of the girls who fell sick during that snowy Sunday Appell, and who were for a few days afterwards

My Education Continues

dragged along to work, were, like Luba, eventually taken to the hospital. It was sad to see so many friends sick. Only the constant bombing of Leipzig, and the hope that the end was getting nearer, kept us going. We could see the German defeats in the frightened and gloomy eyes of the German people at work. We could hear it now from their mouths. They were now telling us their problems, as though we were their equals. (Like most of the other girls, I got the German stories secondhand, through Bronia, the interpreter. She was from Oberschlesien; her parents were German Jews who had been deported to Poland.) Another indication that something was wrong in Germany came when a German woman who worked next to me, and who would never say a word to any of us, whispered something into Bronia's ear. I only saw the woman's ironic smile, but during lunch Bronia revealed the secret. "Frau Gleiwitz," Bronia said, "told me that she was afraid that the Russians might invade Leipzig at any time. She asked me if I would give her my dress so that she could escape when the time comes. Her husband is an officer. I'm sure she said it as a joke, but there might have been some truth in it." Bronia smiled.

Other Germans, too, were seeing the indisputable end coming. They only hoped that the Americans, the British, or the French—not the Russians—would take their city, because there was no longer a question of if Leipzig would fall, but only to whom it would surrender. "The Russians will surely kill us all," some women were now saying openly, thinking of all the devastation that the Germans had done to Russia. "We will be slaves, and you will be free," a German "coworker"—as she was now calling herself—said to one of the French girls. All of this sounded good to us, but still unreal. More funny than probable. We still did not believe that the end would come soon, but we

To Leipzig

began thinking that the War would end with a victory for the Allies.

"Analese is scared to death, too," Bronia told us one day.

Some girls asked, "What is Analese afraid of? She was always nice to us; no one will harm her." Bronia said nothing.

Another girl, who had been listening in, replied for her. "You girls must have come from another planet." She smiled. "Don't you think that 'Lisbijka' will have to answer for her love affairs?"

Many girls started laughing. I had no idea what was so funny about someone being "Lisabonian," and neither did a lot of other girls in the group. We had never heard this word before, so we figured that the funny part was that a woman from Lisbon, Portugal, had somehow gotten into the German SS.

It was a very educational lunch hour. The general information relating to the matter was explained to us by the more knowledgeable girls. The rest was refined in detail when we later got to camp that night. It seemed that many girls, including Nunia, our Stubenälteste, had known it all along. I wondered if Wanda and Rachu, whom until now I had considered the experts in the field, knew anything about lesbian activities. They never seemed to withhold any of their knowledge.

Slowly, Analese's mysterious behavior began to unravel: Why else would she have been hanging around our rooms late at night, or going with her two girls into separate little rooms reserved for the guards' naps? It also raised some questions: Did her girls go with her voluntarily? For food? Or by force? Would her lovers become her friends, or her enemies? Will they become lesbians? To these questions, no one had answers. I only knew that her girls always had extra food, special privileges, and private conversations with

My Education Continues

her. Through them we found out that Analese had been orphaned at an early age, and that she had been raised by an aunt who had made her join the Hitlerjugend, from which she had advanced to the SS.[64]

For inmates to get such information about guards was very unusual. We hardly knew their names. We used to call them by surnames that we had made up. Or we would name them according to their features or behavior: "The Fat One," "The Mean One," "The Pig." Analese was one of the very few who were called by name.

My education seemed to be a never-ending process. As the old saying goes, "You learn all your life and die a fool." Or, "The more you learn, the more you realize how little you know."

Winter finally came to an end and gave way to a sweet, sunny spring. Clouds cleared the sky and made room for Allied bombers. In the field outside the barbed wire, families were strolling again; boys were kicking soccer balls; girls were pushing their dolls in baby buggies. Children were running happily in the newly sprung blades of grass.

Inside the wire, little had changed. We still had our daily Appells, and still stood in soup lines (and for smaller portions). We were still going to work daily, and we were still preparing songs and poems for the upcoming Passover and Easter holidays. We were still waiting for the parting of the Red Sea, and for the miracle of Resurrection. Now, though, we were beginning to feel that these miracles were within our reach.

We asked Bella, our fortuneteller, to glance into her crystal ball and let us know what was in store for us. Bella was a tall, large-framed girl from Warsaw who had left the big city when the bombing started and gone to live with her grandparents and a sister in a small Galician town. She was in her early twenties. Like most refugees in that small town, she had supported herself by working odd jobs, and by trading with farmers; but, instead of trading merchandise, she would go from farm to farm, and from house to house, telling fortunes from cards. Bella told us that she had gotten the idea from a Gypsy palm-reader who once predicted her voyage away from home.

Bella improved on this Gypsy technique, and was making a living by fortunetelling. People liked her service, and paid her with food. The secret of her trade she revealed to us once during an evening discussion.

"It was all observation and psychology, if you think about it," she said calmly, as though there was nothing to it. "I always tried to go inside the people's houses. There were a lot of clues about their way of life, about their families. I looked at pictures, souvenirs, icons. I put out my cards on the table, telling my clients what I knew about them. For instance: I looked at the memorabilia and said something like, 'In my cards I see a young lady, a beautiful young lady,' and then I would look at my client's face to see the expression. If I saw a head shake in approval at my remark, I knew I had impressed her—my clients were mostly women—with my knowledge. When she smiled, I knew I was on the right track. I then would proceed with my work. Often my clients provided me with information by making such remarks as, 'Oh, this girl you are talking about is my youngest daughter who never got married.' The clients kept giving me more clues. If their faces showed disappointment I changed to another topic. If they liked what I had to say, I'd proceed. 'I see in my cards a nice young man,' I'd say; but not to give them too much hope, I would add, 'but I see an obstacle...it looks as if he might come....' I knew nice young men were very hard to find, so I made sure not to put a time limit on the young man's arrival. I always predicted a

My Education Continues

bright future. Never told them bad news. My clients were happy, and I got a few potatoes or a slice of bread. I was happy, too. No harm done."

So we knew what Bella was doing, and how she conducted her business; nevertheless, we kept asking her what was in store for our future. She had no cards to work with—an obstacle in her trade—so she turned over a soup can, moved it half a turn one way, then half a turn the other; then, looking at her crystal ball, she answered our questions with the assurance of a professional fortuneteller: "In my crystal ball, I see fields, streets, and houses: I don't see wires. No wires, no fences. I see people, many people, and I see the sun shining."

It may sound foolish, but it really made us feel good. Even stranger was the fact that after a few weeks, her predictions came true—to a certain extent. As you'll see.

Chapter 5. Liberation

I don't remember the date, but I do remember that it was after Passover and Easter when our established way of life turned around.⁶⁵ It happened after dark, as we were about to settle in for the night, when an unscheduled *Appell* was called. We assembled in front of the building and were counted in a very precise manner. All the usual papers were signed. We were not dismissed. The guards seemed unusually nervous. We thought that someone was missing again—we could still recall that snowy January Sunday.

From far off, we heard the pounding of artillery and the already familiar sound of falling bombs. I covered my ears with both hands, but the fearful noise penetrated this shield. Two searchlights were sliding along the horizon, lighting up the sky.

"The Front must be moving closer," I heard someone remark. "Allied planes must be bombing the city. It must be German artillery returning the fire," another answered. "The Russians are not very far from here, either," remarked someone from the back.

I held hands with Eva and Regina, the two girls at my sides. Bronia and Sala were on the outside of my row. No one was able to figure out why an Appell had been called at such a late hour. Someone mentioned

My Education Continues

the similarity of it to the last night in Skarżysko. It wasn't long before we found out.

"Turn left! Forward, march!" we heard a guard's voice say, from the darkness. As we walked through the wide-open gate in rows of five, we were counted again. Guards at the gate looked at our prison numbers and checked off each one carefully. More papers were signed.

"They are probably taking us to the bomb-shelter at the plant," was the common opinion of the girls. "It's dangerous out here."

We marched on a dirt road leading to the main highway. An unusually high number of guards were with us—guards on motorcycles, on bicycles, with rifles and dogs surrounding the long column of marching prisoners. Passing the intersection where we would always turn on the way to the plant, we proceeded straight ahead.

It was then that we began to wonder what was going on: "We are going in the wrong direction. Where in the world are they taking us? Why?" we kept asking one another. No one had an answer. We kept on walking. The front row followed the leader, who was a motorcycle guard. Other rows marched behind, one after the other, in step. After a while, the shooting stopped; it was finally quiet. The night was cloudy, dark, and fairly warm for April.

We were past all the familiar roads, but we still kept walking. We turned onto a strange side road. "There surely will be no work for us tomorrow," I heard a girl whisper. Then a gruesome thought ran through my mind: "Maybe they are taking us to the train." I don't know why I said it aloud, but I did.

Right then I could feel the tension rise in the girls around me. "You might be right!" said Regina, pressing my hand. "If we were going to the train, where do you think they would take us?" a girl asked

Liberation

from the row behind me. She really didn't expect anyone to answer.

We didn't know if everybody had been taken out of the camp. During the Appell, we heard that the sick and disabled had been locked up in the hospital room and left in the building. We didn't know how many were left, but we did know that most were with us now, walking. From the that row I was in, no end of the column could be seen. We walked down the side road for a long time; then the column turned to what seemed like a highway, and we continued walking on pavement.

"I don't think we walked this far from the train when we came here from Skarżysko," said Eva, grabbing my other hand. I agreed, but I said nothing.

At dawn, the march came to a halt. I looked around. The column of prisoners was endless. We were instructed to sit on the ground on both sides of a narrow side road. We were divided into groups of twenty-five each, with guards surrounding the field around us. In the wide-open space we looked like herds of zebras that had gathered by drinking pools. The ground was wet from the morning dew; the cold moisture was penetrating our clothes.

"No moving around! No standing or walking!" yelled the guard from across the road when he saw some of the girls lifting themselves off the ground. He then walked over to his motorcycle and, from its trailer, pulled out a few large loaves of black bread. He cut the loaves into five- or six-centimeter slices, then gave one to each of the girls sitting next to him. Other guards did the same. They then pulled a few tin cans out of the motorcycle sidecar, filled them with water from a nearby well, and giving one can full to each row of girls, said, "Share it! Take a sip and pass it on."

To the question, "Where are you taking us?" the woman guard standing next to my row gave no

My Education Continues

answer, and neither did any of the other, more humane guards; we didn't even dare to question the malicious ones.

After about an hour's break, everyone was back in formation. We were scrupulously counted, papers were signed, and the procession continued down a side road. We tried to figure out where we were, but, strange, most of the road signs were gone. One of the girls said, "They must have been taken off to confuse the invading armies. That's the way we did it in Poland when the Germans were coming."

We had no idea of our whereabouts or our destination; only by the sun could we tell that we were heading eastward.

The next couple of days and nights we spent walking. During the infrequent stops, we were instructed to sit in fields and ditches while the guards ate, fed their dogs, and changed work-shifts. The only nourishment that we had had was the bread and water that we got that first morning. At least we had no problem with waste elimination.

After a few days of hunger, we resorted to eating blades of new grass and weeds, which we pulled from the fields, and buds that we picked from roadside bushes. We continued walking down clean, well-kept side roads and abandoned highways far away from towns and villages. Only on rare occasions did we walk through some hamlets. Whenever we did, the places were always deserted.

Days and nights, we heard artillery pounding from far in the east; some nights the horizon was on fire.

After a few more days of no food or water, the pace of our walking steadily started decreasing. Besides being exhausted, hungry, and thirsty, we felt abandoned and helpless. Adding to the problem were our aching feet. Many girls, including myself, had taken off the clogs that were protecting our soles

Liberation

because they were rubbing against the blisters that had developed on our heels and toes. Walking barefoot on concrete pavement created bloody wounds on our feet.

But soon pains were overshadowed by hallucinations. We didn't care where we were going or if we'd ever get there. The idea of freedom was forgotten. Our brains no longer responded to reason or logic. We just dragged along.

Then started the shooting of those lagging behind. The girls who could not keep pace with the column, or who fell or stepped out of line, were hit with bullets. There were still enough guards who thought that it was their patriotic duty to obey the Führer's orders. They had orders to shoot; they told us so. And although some guards overlooked the strict orders and transgressed on their patriotic duty, there were many others who seemed to shoot with pleasure, as though for the sheer lust of killing, who would not deny themselves the delight of showing off their superiority. Sometimes, as we slowed down, the sound of a shot would be heard from the back. Then silence. It had been a warning to continue walking.

As our column dragged down the roads, we saw girls who were unable to continue walking and were now sitting or lying on the sides of the road, looking like skeletons, some with shaved hair and bulging eyes. I hadn't seen anything quite like it since I left the Warsaw Ghetto. We just walked by and looked, but could not stop. Not even asking a question or offering a word of hope.

One day we passed a girl whose apathetic look would haunt me for days to come. Actually, I wasn't the one who first noticed her. It was Eva who had seen her lying on the ground with her dress pulled behind her waist, her legs bleeding from wounds, her eyes glazed, foam coming out of her mouth. Passing by her,

My Education Continues

Eva poked me in the side. "I feel like vomiting," she whispered.

"There's nothing in your stomach," Bronia replied, having overheard her.

"Keep going," came a voice from behind us. "Don't stop!"

Green watery stuff was coming out of Eva's mouth, running down her filthy dress. Her steps weakened, her knees buckled. "Don't stop," we begged her, grabbing her under her arms. "You'll make it to the next rest-stop." Only about an hour later, we came to a stop at a small pond. The water was covered with yellowish-green moss, the leaves of underground plants, and starfish-like creatures. Around it were crawling snails and jumping grasshoppers or some other kind of creatures, and croaking frogs. We looked at the water with amazement. After days without a drop to drink, the water looked like an oasis. Regina was the first one to jump out of line. "May God Almighty be blessed!" she said as she ran to the pond. Several girls followed her. Holding our breath, we waited for what might happen; we listened for shots. They didn't come. We looked at the guards. Two stood next to me looking at the girls running to the pond. One guard had her hands in her pocket; the other had his cigarette in his mouth. We looked at them wondering what they were planning to do.

Soon we had no more power to resist the sight of the refreshing water, and, little by little, almost the whole marching column ran to the pond. Scooping the slimy water into our soiled palms, we began to swallow it—insects, vegetation, moss, everything.

I don't remember anything ever tasting better. I took one scoop after another, and was still reaching for more. A shot. We started running away from the pond. One guard without a word of warning started shooting. We saw him shooting into the air, amusing himself as

Liberation

he watched us running into formation, still licking the slime from our lips. Regina again blessed the Lord for giving us water. We blessed our "humane" guards who held in their power the future of our lives, and who had let us live another day.

After the nourishing break, our column moved mechanically forward, always keeping in mind that the angel of death was never far away.

Actually, at times, we weren't even afraid of dying. "You die because you have to die," was the general understanding. No problem. The brain no longer could perceive fear of danger. I couldn't even feel the pain that must have been present in my bare, raw, scab-covered feet, nor the bugs and lice that were helping themselves to the juices of my body.

Yet during all that resignation, there was always the spark that kept saying, "Don't give up! Not yet! Not now! Try a little longer. It's close to the end! So near the goal!" Artillery pounding usually brought new courage: "It won't be long...."

During all the days of marching we never stopped in towns or villages; only in open fields or in shallow ditches by the roadside. Whenever we had to pass a village, the inhabitants were ordered to stay home. The streets were deserted, though they were nice and clean and the houses neatly painted, with flowers on the balconies. Peace and tranquility seemed to dwell about. Walking on the outskirts of a village, we could sometimes see women, old men, and foreign workers in their marked clothes, working in the fields. But they were all kept away from us, away from the roads. Once, after a few more days of walking, a startling incident took place. It came about from an oversight of the guards:

Our road led us through a village, and since we usually slowed down in such case, we could see women and children curiously peeking through their

My Education Continues

nicely draped windows, surely wondering what kind of creatures were hiking through their town. While the guards were busy watching us, an old woman carrying a large heavy basket in her arms ran out of a roadside house and, very unexpectedly, started throwing raw, cut-up carrots into the column of starving, exhausted women. The marchers slowed down. The column came almost to a halt when the girls started trampling one another trying to grab a piece of that life-saving commodity.

I was lucky. I had been walking only a few rows from the house when the old lady walked out. But the girls from the end of the column, who saw what was going on, were running out of line to take part in the action, paying no attention to the guards who, at this moment, were arguing with the old lady (who was refusing to get back into her house).

My row was passing almost in front of the lady when Bronia heard her yelling; she translated for us: "You guys leave me alone! I hope someone would give food to my son who might now be walking somewhere in Siberia. God only knows where the Ruskies have taken him!"

The old woman was still yelling when our row moved on. We kept on walking with pieces of carrot in our hands, biting off bits, and sharing with those less fortunate, who had had no chance to get some of their own. We passed right by her, and didn't even have a chance to thank the gracious lady for her generosity.

As our row proceeded down the road, the girls walking further back saw the guards stepping on some carrots and—two of them—pushing the old lady into her house.

Before she went inside, she threw the rest of the carrots into the marching column.

Liberation

We kept on walking. Occasionally we heard shots, and we kept on walking. One time I passed by the body of a girl who had been shot. A female guard was scrupulously taking the girl's prison number off her dress to enter it into the roster. Everybody had to be accounted for, dead or alive. The corpse was then piled by other prisoners on top of corpses that were already on the motorcycle trailer.

The next evening, or perhaps one after that, we halted for one of our rests. The rain, which had been coming down all day, subsided. The raincoat-covered guards, mounted on their vehicles, herded us into a fenced-in field where we were to stay overnight. Only about half of the original number of girls were there. The others had been rerouted to another highway the day before, when we passed through an intersection. We were instructed to lie on the ground and not to move.

The eastern sky was being lit by artillery fire. In the west and the north the pounding had been going on for hours. Then the shooting stopped.

We were allowed to get up, but had to remain in the pen. Those of us who were still able to move got off the soaked ground. I stood up. The water that had penetrated my dress made my body shudder; but my blistered feet feel much better.

Soon word got around that someone had spotted piles of red and sugar beets stacked in the field outside the pen. Maybe for planting? Needless to say, whoever could move stormed through the wires and, disregarding the consequences, started running for the beets. We were expecting someone to stop us, or for the shooting to start; but neither happened. To our amazement, we found some guards asleep on the ground, wrapped in their sleeping bags and blankets. Those who were on duty seemed to be paying no attention to our looting spree.

My Education Continues

"They won't dare shoot now," said a girl's voice from the dark. "They'd disclose our whereabouts to the enemy if they did." This statement made a lot of sense, yet we still did not believe that these guards would let us get by with stealing the beets. Well, they were paying no attention. We sat on the soaked ground, devouring our prey and sharing some of it with those who had been unable to get up and take beets for themselves.

Chewing the beets, I thought of Sandomierz and of the farm where I had pulled beets from the frozen ground; how proudly I used to carry the earned commodity home. It had been a long time since I thought of anything about home, or about anybody. Like most of us girls here, I had a one-track mind that was preoccupied only with food and survival. But that night I did think of Mother and Sis and the city of Sandomierz. "It won't be long, and I'll see them. They must be back in Warsaw by now. As far as I know, the Germans are out of there."

For a moment I even thought of freedom. This would be a great time to escape. I even talked about it with some girls. The road was empty, wet, and dark. Even the dogs were away. No one could see us; the tracks would be washed away. We had talked about this possibility once before, forgetting completely our striped uniforms and the cruel fact that there was no place to go. And how about the language barrier? The little German that most of us knew consisted of words like "Schweinehund" and "verfluchte Schwein" and "verfluchte Jude," and other such vulgar expressions. Of course, we could always claim to be foreign laborers—if it weren't for our clothes. This marching without destination or purpose was too much to bear.

The rest of that night we nibbled on beets and conversed. It was something that we hadn't done since leaving Leipzig. "Where in the world are these idiots taking us? What for? Is there still a possibility that they'll shoot us all?" Logically, there was no reason for them to shoot us now. We could be used as a shield, or as prisoner exchange pawns. Maybe they are keeping us as hostages for some reason? Of course, no one had an answer, but at least after all that marching we could talk to one another again, just like in "the good old times." The talk was only senseless, stupid speculation. The truth of the matter was that we did not know where we were going or what awaited us at the end of this journey. We just didn't want to believe that anything bad would happen. From talks with a few of the humane guards, it seemed that they didn't know any more than we did. We only knew that we were running in circles: one day east; next day, north or south, maybe even west. We would watch the sun for directions.

The lesson that I had learned that first night in Skarżysko was becoming more vivid daily: "You think no thoughts; you ask no questions; you do as you're told." If you didn't learn it quickly enough from watching the beatings and kicking of those who had disobeyed, you'd surely learn it from the first few kicks that you got, with hobnailed boots, over your own body.

About midnight, most of us, filled now with beets and rainwater, fell asleep. If I dreamed anything, I don't remember. Other girls talked about their dreams in the morning.

The next day, we didn't walk. It seemed that the guards weren't quite sure what to do with us. They waited for orders that did not come. The law-abiding, faithful guards were getting confused, irritated, and more dangerous. They beat us with clubs, and rifle butts. They kicked us with their spiked boots, and they were screaming constantly. We sat in that soaked pen all day, finishing what was left of the beets. We even

My Education Continues

pulled some newly sprouted weeds and ate them for dessert. The long rest made us feel more relaxed. I tried to put on the clogs which I had taken off because of my blisters, but the soles of my feet were full of cuts, bruises, and scabs. I just put the shoes aside, using them as storage containers for leaves, grass, and other nourishment.

By the end of the day, shots and artillery were heard again. We could see planes circling in the sky; but it was hard to tell whose planes they were. We were ordered to lie flat on the ground. All the following night the eastern sky was lit by fire. The pounding continued until daybreak. At dawn we were ordered to get into formation. We assembled, but were not counted. We were ordered to move forward at high speed. Our column had lost any resemblance of discipline. What used to be strict orderly rows of five had now become rows of twos, threes, sixes. We dragged ourselves as fast as we could. Some girls gave up walking altogether; they just left the column and set themselves on the side of the road.

The guards seemed tired and depressed, and spoke very little. Some even stopped yelling at us. From time to time, we saw the guards on their motorcycles and bicycles going up and down the disarranged column—just doing their jobs. That day they didn't even bother the girls who dropped out of the lines. It seemed to me that there were fewer guards than ever before; many girls agreed with my observation. We even tried to recall which ones were missing. Many dogs were gone, too.

Those of us who still could walk did so, only because we didn't know what else to do, or what to expect from the guards or the local population. The road in front of us became lined with Frauen and children pulling their belongings in handcarts—repeating the same pathetic scene of a few years before, when the Polish refugees were fleeing from towns, cities, and villages, away from the German invaders. The German "Master Race" were now looking more like the Untermenschen whom they so much despised.

As we were passing, the guards made them clear the way for us. The intersections were blocked by motorcycles. The civilian population was told to wait until we had passed; after all, we had priority; that made us feel very important.

The guards were dirty, unshaven, tired. Those who walked were dragging their feet the way we were. As the night was falling, there were still long lines of German civilians lining the roads behind us, and in the fields around.

Looking ahead, far into the distance, we could recognize a silhouette that might have been a bridge. As we approached more closely, we knew that it was unmistakably a large bridge, stretching into a sightless horizon. "Over this bridge," we heard one guard say to another as they were passing on their bikes.

"Yes, over this bridge, and we got it made!" replied the other.

After all those days and nights of walking in circles, we finally found out that our aim was in fact to cross this bridge—the bridge that divided the Russian troops from those of the other Allies: the French and the English and the Americans.

"Macht schnell!" the two guards yelled simultaneously. "Make it faster! Faster!" they continued to yell, not realizing that the road in front of us was crowded with soldiers, vehicles, and civilians; in fact, it was completely impassable.

The sun was setting by the time the few remaining loyal guards led us to the riverbanks. We were to sit on the ground where the sandy beach met the paved street at the top of the bank, away from the German

My Education Continues

public, and wait for our turn to cross the bridge. The long column of prison girls had been split into smaller groups as we passed the fleeing crowds of German civilians and military. I was in a group of about one hundred. Farther down the road, we could see other groups of prisoners walking in our direction. The end of the German crowds was nowhere to be seen. From the place where we sat, we could view soldiers in their camouflaged uniforms and combat gear. We watched civilians, old men, women, and children, all heading for a bridge. The riverbank and the roads leading to it were crowded with fleeing Germans who by now had abandoned their vehicles and had dropped most of their possessions, so that they themselves could move faster and carry their children, as well as help the elderly and the sick.

Many soldiers, who had left their military vehicles in the fields, were now dropping their gear. Holding on to their rifles, they were running for the bridge. We saw quite a few soldiers change their uniforms for civilian clothing given to them by fleeing refugees. In their civilian clothes they tried to mingle with the civilian population, not realizing that the military police guarding the bridge and regulating traffic were giving priority in crossing to uniformed soldiers.

Farther into the distance, as far as the eye could see, we saw not individuals but a huge conglomerate moving in the direction of the sunset and joining the flood of people already assembled at the riverbank. The river was full of boats large and small, helping to get some of the people to the far side.

In the dimming daylight, we sat bewildered, curiously watching the ex-fearless heroes of the "Master Race" being caught between two enemy blocks and trying to choose not which of them was better, but which would be less evil. Like herds of scared antelope escaping a hungry lion, they were running for their precious lives. The courageous demigods were now being compelled to show their fearful faces in public. The pain, apprehension, and cowardice were revealing some more human qualities in the once "Superior Race," qualities that we never thought they possessed. How differently they looked from those powerful, decorated heroes who only a few years ago had proudly marched the streets of Warsaw in victory parades! Pushing through the crowds of German refugees, the officers were ripping off their hard-earned medals and decorations and dropping them to the ground, where they were trampled by thousands of feet.

What these former heroes thought about throwing away their awards was impossible to imagine: Maybe they were recalling the events for which they had been decorated; maybe they were looking back upon the things that they had had to do, or had willingly done, to be worthy of them; maybe some were even regretting the deeds that they had performed. Now, stripped of their power, wealth, and dignity, the poor souls were running to save their mere lives. From the bewildered looks in their eyes, it was obvious that they weren't sure of their choices, for they were running from one enemy into the hands of another.

They hated the Americans, the British, and the French, but they dreaded the Russians the most. The German soldiers knew in their hearts what they'd done to Russia and its people during the past four years. They feared reprisal. They feared that the Russian soldiers would now avenge the deaths of their families and the brutal horrors inflicted by the Germans; the burned homes, the devastated countryside. The Germans hoped that their other enemies, who were closing in on them from across the river, might be more merciful, that they might treat them with less vengeance than the Russians. That was why they all were running to the bridge.

My Education Continues

We could run, too. There were only a few guards left to watch us, and they really didn't care whether we stayed or ran. They must have been watching us out of sheer habit. We could have escaped easily. But there were some valid reasons why we didn't move. Truthfully, we still feared the Germans, who were very well armed and could, at will, shoot us if we got in the way of their escape route. Night was falling. The bridge was guarded. We could not run back because of the crowded roads and the terrible shooting coming from the east. Two more reasons for staying were that we were just too exhausted to move, and, again, that we had nowhere to go.

The dark eastern horizon was lit by fire; it looked as bright as day. Artillery pounding subsided for a while, but it was soon replaced by the roar of planes, which could not be seen but could be heard from the north and east. Most of us were lying down trying to rest. A cool wind blew from the river; it turned chilly. We moved closer together to keep warm. For a while the shooting would stop and there would be silence; then sounds of more explosions and shelling would come from the north and south; then silence again. I lay, tired enough to die, but forced myself not to fall asleep.

From out of nowhere, a ball of fire appeared in the sky. A thunder of guns and rockets broke the silence, followed by machinegun fire that started from very close by. I was afraid to move my head, not knowing whether the machinegun bullets were coming from the guards or from the soldiers, or in which direction they were flying. I lay quietly, with my arms wrapped around my ears.

The next thing I remember was somebody shaking my body. "Wake up!" I heard a voice yelling. I opened my eyes. It was dawn, but the nightly fog had not yet lifted. Sala was kneeling over my body, trying to wake

Liberation

me. I looked around me. Many girls who had been with me the night before were gone. Sala, Regina, Bella, Golda, and Hanka were still with me. There was another group of Leipzig girls next to us, but we didn't know any of them, even though they had been with us throughout the whole ordeal, and had stayed next to us since getting to the river. Three of the girls must have come to Leipzig from Skarżysko Werk C. We could tell it by their still yellow skin, nails, hair, and eyes. We welcomed the new girls, and decided to stick together.

The air around us was filling with smoke. Shelling could be heard nearby. "Up! Up!" the girls around me were screaming. I heard a male voice yelling something in a strange language. I looked in the direction of the voice and saw a young soldier with rifle pointed. He was not one of the guards; they were all gone. He wasn't even German. "Davai nazad!" he yelled at the top of his voice, pointing his rifle in the direction that he wanted us to go. "Stay back!"

"He's Russian," Sala said. "Get up, and let's run from this shooting!"

Other Russian soldiers soon arrived. They were screaming and shooting while they ran. All of a sudden, shells and bullets were coming from the direction of the river. All the Russian soldiers dropped to the ground. They started yelling at us in Russian, "Down to the ground! Down to the ground, you stupid bunch of women!" They yelled it again and again, pushing their bellies over the muddy soil.

An older lady, about thirty years old, who must have come with the new group of girls during the night, understood what the soldiers were saying. She remembered a few Russian words that her mother had taught her. She explained that the soldiers were telling us to drop to the ground. We did as we were told. When the shooting broke, and we saw the soldiers around us getting up, we followed suit. A few of the

My Education Continues

new girls who the night before had been too tired even to crawl, now, upon seeing the Russian uniforms in front of them and hearing the Russian language—even though they didn't understand a word of it—were so overjoyed that they started jumping and dancing around the young, confused soldiers.

The dirty, stinking, exhausted girls were grabbing the poor guys by their hands, hanging from their necks, kissing and hugging them, screaming and crying for joy, while the poor fighters with rifles pointed, who had expected enemies on the battlefield, did not know what to make of such an unexpected reception. They weren't sure whether to reciprocate, run, or to shoot. They seemed to like the warm greeting that they were receiving, and maybe would have wanted to return the favor, even remain with the girls; but they had no orders to do either. Soldiers obey orders.

Renewed cannon fire coming from the riverfront, and the hissing of bullets around us, made the decision for them easier. They started running and shooting and shouting, telling us to get down on our bellies, to drop to the ground again. It wasn't clear if they were running from our odor, the lice, or from the fire that was all around them. When the shooting subsided, we got up. By then, many Russian soldiers were around us. Like the first few, they seemed to have no idea who we were, what we were doing in the middle of the frontline, or what they were supposed to do with us, or to us. Some thought that we were Germans disguised in prison clothes. The older lady who spoke some Russian told them that we were Polish—Polish Jews.

One of the soldiers looked at us suspiciously and said, "German spies!" and ran down to the riverbank, following his comrades.

The scene around us had changed a lot from the night before. The bridge was still packed with people,

Liberation

but the crowds at the bank had dispersed. Sporadic shooting was coming from a few riverboats and from the riverbank. Our German guards were all gone. They must have escaped during the night, for we found their discarded uniforms on the ground. Russian boots were now trampling over the glorious swastikas engraved on the sleeves and collar points of the jackets.

"Keep on running to the back if you don't want to get killed here!" yelled one of the Russian officers. "Run as far from here as you can," yelled other Russians, as they chased away the fleeing Germans, all of them racing toward the bridge and the boats from where the shooting was coming. "Davai nazad!" was heard from all directions as the soldiers passed us by.

The side roads, which led from the riverbank to some towns as well as the fields farther down the road, were full of loaded carts, German tanks, combat gear, and military vehicles that had been abandoned during the night.

A few German women with children waving white handkerchiefs were running in the direction of the fields, away from the riverbank, away from the shooting. Assuming that the women knew the area, and the way to some safe place—like the nearest village, a shelter, or a trench—we followed them into the fields.

All around us the shooting continued. Planes roared low over our heads; German planes, Russian planes, all kinds of planes, chasing one another, diving, climbing.

The air was full of smoke and strange smells like acid, saltpeter, and blood. Corpses were scattered among the wounded. All through the fields, limbs separated from bodies were soaking in their own blood. German and Russian soldiers still alive but unable to move, covered the ground. Leaping over the dead and the wounded, we kept running away from the

My Education Continues

shooting. A woman's body lay partly uncovered amid the dead and wounded fighters. A soldier turned her over with his rifle barrel, exposing her bare breasts from under the torn dress. Whether she was dead or alive was impossible to tell; the soldier left her where he found her. We were going to stop, but he started yelling, "What the hell are you idiots doing here, amid all this shooting?" He didn't wait for an answer. He just ordered us to run.

Further down a side road, away from the soldiers, one of our girls suggested that we stop. We were starved, thirsty, tired; most of us had bleeding feet. "Let's halt here," she said, "and look in the abandoned carts. There might be some food in them, and maybe even some cloth to wrap up our feet with." But before she could finish talking, more shooting came our way, and we ran.

When the shelling stopped temporarily, trucks marked with red crosses drove into the field. Uniformed men and women with Red Cross armbands ran with stretchers to pick up the dead and the wounded. One soldier, who could not have been older than I, was groaning so loudly that we stopped to see if we could do anything for him. He was German. His left leg was almost disconnected from his body, and blood was streaming through his shattered pants. Two medics ran over to him and laid him on a stretcher that was set on the bloody ground. While one of them was cutting the young soldier's pants with a knife, the other ordered us to move on.

It was midday. By the sun, it was about two or three o'clock when we finally got out of the main area of shooting. But here, too, the roads were full of abandoned German refugee carts and deserted military vehicles. Supply wagons and Red Cross

Liberation

trucks were blocking the main roads. Russian guards and other combat personnel were keeping order.

Paying no attention to the Russians who were urging us to go on, we swarmed over the carts and started searching for food. We dismantled the first few carts, but we found nothing to eat. Someone must have looted these carts already, for everything in them was topsy-turvy. It could have been that the owners took all the food with them before they fled, or the Russians might have cleaned everything out before we got to it. Anyway, we persisted in searching the other carts. We were starving. Finally, in one of the carts, we found some bread, lard, and sugar. One of the new girls even found a cake and some cookies. We sat down under a tree and feasted. Then we rested for a while. We got acquainted with the girls who had joined us at the riverbank.

Our new group consisted of sixteen girls. It was comprised of my five friends, who had stayed together since Leipzig, six girls we had met at the river, three Hungarian girls we had met on the way here, and the older lady, Pani Konova, from Katowice, who would become our official Russian translator as well as the mother of our "pack." It was a union of girls who had gotten separated from their original groups on the long march, or, like my five friends and me, had just lost many of their long-time buddies. It was nice to be in a larger group, especially in strange territory. Aside from Pani Konova, the girls in our new group ranged in age from sixteen to twenty-one.

After the feast, those of us who didn't immediately get sick from gorging on the found food (hunger had caused us to misjudge the capacity of our shrunken stomachs) got back to the abandoned carts and started looting them anew, this time searching for clothes. Finding coverings for our bodies turned out to be easier than looking for food. We shed our zebra jackets

My Education Continues

and dresses—dumped them right there on the field—and got dressed in our new "civilized" attire. We actually talked about saving the striped dresses as souvenirs, but decided to leave them to the lice. Many of us, however, did rip off the numbers and save them. In Skarżysko, I had been Häftling 945, in Leipzig 1191. The dress that I found was light brown, made of a jersey-like fabric. It was embroidered with tiny pink-reddish flowers with pinhead-sized holes for pistils: It was quite elegant. The other girls, too, were dressed quite elegantly. It seemed that the refugees had put only their best clothes in these wagons. Dressed in fancy clothes, with hairless heads and bare feet, we stared at one another delighted and admired our new looks. Luckily, we had no mirrors.

The shoes that we pulled from the wagons we carried in our hands, for our cut, blistered feet were not yet ready for footwear. Hardly any of us took extra clothes, so that in case we had to run again, we wouldn't be bothered with carrying extra luggage, or have to suffer the painful feeling of having to part with the loot.

All dressed up, we proceeded farther up the battlefield. As we were looking back we saw some German women picking up our discarded striped dresses and walking off with them. We didn't follow them. Somehow, all of us were quite sure that we'd reach our destination without "guides," especially since we had no idea where we wanted to go. We only knew we had to move away from the danger zone, and go as far as we could since there was a lot of shooting still going on not too far from us. So we kept moving.

Down the road, where the Russian troops were regrouping, we had to get off the road and detour around the trucks and tanks and dead bodies that were lining the ground (where the medics were tending the wounded). As we were passing the rows of dead

Liberation

bodies, one of our new girls, Frida, ran over to where the corpses lay and, bending over one of them, she began doing something. We thought that she must have seen a body that was still moving, and wanted to help. So a few of us rushed to see if we, too, could render some assistance. But, as we got closer to her, we were absolutely stunned at what we saw. Here, in that godforsaken place, Frida was taking a ring off a corpse's finger. She seemed quite embarrassed when she turned around and saw us watching. She shyly apologized for her deed, and putting the ring on one of her own fingers, said, "Someone will take it if I don't. They don't bury soldiers with their rings on." We did not answer; we walked back to our group.

From a road behind the crossing, we saw a line of German war prisoners who, disarmed, distressed, and disappointed, and with hands over their heads, were following Russian tanks and trucks. They were being led by Russian soldiers who, with rifles and machineguns pointed, had surrounded the doomed losers. We watched the solemn, gloomy, unshaved faces of the once mighty "Master Race" dragging their bound-up legs, legs that not long ago had been marching in goosestep, that had seemed to have the whole world under their feet.[66] Like a flash of light, my father's old saying came to my mind: "Remember, nothing lasts forever." Surprisingly, I did not rejoice in their fate. I did not even think of revenge, of something that I had always secretly dreamed throughout the War.

Walking down the road, we talked about freedom, but we still did not really believe that we had actually been liberated from the Nazis. We were still on German soil, not knowing what to expect either from the remaining Germans or from the Russian liberators. The War was not yet over; shooting, shelling, and bombing were all around us, and there were still many

My Education Continues

pockets of German resistance scattered throughout the woods and villages. Our liberators were still fighting and themselves not sure of their fate.

Running in the direction of houses that were now visible a few kilometers up the road, we encountered remnants of a battle; more corpses. Some must have been killed not too long ago for the blood under them was still fresh and red. Not one of us could figure out how it happened that they had not yet been picked up, as this place was at the far end of the battlefield.

The mystery was solved when we saw a huge crater nearby. It must have been a bomb or a mine that killed them after the Front had already passed.

We kept running down the field, terrified by the sporadic shelling and the mines in the field, and by the running Germans, who were still armed, and the Russians, who were fighting and shooting and didn't know, and didn't care, who we were, or why we were there. Some of our liberators were even calling us "German collaborators" as they passed us by.

The sun was setting as we neared the village. Black smoke coming from that direction hindered much of our view. We would gladly have changed our destination if we could have thought of another place to go.

Next to the crater, and under a shattered tree, sat a group of Russian soldiers, guarded by a tank. We could only see a few of them, but we could hear them singing. The guards that were watching out for the enemy did not ask us any questions; they just commanded us to keep moving.

The closer we came to the village, the more apprehensive we became, for we had no idea whether the place was abandoned or still had some inhabitants; what awaited us if the German people were still here? Now that we were, supposedly, free, and the guards that had "protected us" were now gone,

369

we had to figure out, on our own, where to go and what to do, and who was our enemy and who was our friend.

Far out in the field, we saw other groups of girls, still in striped dresses, who were also heading for the village. It was almost dark, and getting colder, by the time we got to a farmhouse on the outskirts of the village. Just up the street we saw a skeleton of a house which the fire had already burned out. Smoke was still rising and darkening the air. We stopped at a farmhouse, but decided not to enter it for fear that it might be loaded with explosives, or that someone might start shooting. (It would have been ridiculous to be killed now by a defeated German.) We did find a place in a stable behind it. Through its open door, we could see that it was empty. We decided to stay there for the night.

The place was filled with loosely piled straw, but there were no horses inside. We stood for a while listening for suspicious sounds or movements, but the only noises that we could hear were those of the shellings and explosions that were coming from somewhere in the north. Exhausted and cold, half of us girls lay down on the straw, leaving the others on guard. We took turns sleeping.

When the sun rose, my friends and I were on duty. Many girls were still asleep on the manure-filled straw. One of the girls suggested, "Let's go to the house and see what we can find there." We went and knocked on the door. No one answered. We tried to open the door and two others, but they were all locked. We walked back to guard our sleeping companions.

A loud explosion shook the ground and awoke the girls in the stable. They started brushing the sticky straw from their clothes. We were just ready to move along when we discovered that two of our new girls were missing. Searching the stable, we found both of

My Education Continues

them still sleeping. One of them was Hayka's cousin, Masha. The other was Rosa, one of the Hungarian girls. They were sick and unable to get up. Most of us had recovered from the vomiting and stomach cramps that we had encountered after our meal; but these two were getting worse. We planned to move along and try to find some food and a place were we could wash and rest, but now we didn't know what to do about our sick friends. We had no idea how to go about such things. It was the first time in years that we had had to make decisions for ourselves; now no one was telling us what to do or how to do it. We understood that this was one of the prices that we had to pay for our freedom—and we had quickly realized that we weren't prepared for it.

We discussed our options and alternatives. We knew that our long-term plan was to get back home, back to Poland or to Hungary, but we had neither short-term plans nor any suggestions as to how to go about making any. We decided to do first things first: go around town and find some food and a resting place. We took from the farmyard a small, four-wheel, hand-pulled wagon, and after loading into it the two sick girls, we started wandering through town.

Roaming the streets, we found many burned-out houses; those still intact had been either taken over by Russian soldiers, occupied by German refugees, or filled by other freed prisoners. Walking through the town square, we came across the Russian temporary headquarters, which was set up in the city hall. Pani Konova and two of her friends walked inside the offices to ask if we could get any help from the Russian authorities. She found out that there was no assistance available: No one knew anything about the town, nor the people who lived there; the Russians themselves had been here for only a few days. They suggested that we go from house to house until we

Liberation

could find a vacant one. The rest of the day we spent "house-hunting." On the way, four of the girls who had joined us at the riverbank met a group of friends from whom they had been separated. They rejoined their old group.

Late in the day, on a side street near the end of town, we found a small, one-family house. A large white flag, made of a bed sheet, was flying over the entrance gate. The shed in the backyard was open, and in it we saw some shelves stocked with cans and bottles. We stopped and asked an old lady, who was looking out the door, if she'd let us in and give us some water to drink and to wash with. She looked scared. She said nothing. She moved away from the door, leaving it open. A few of us walked in, and the others followed.

The calendar on the wall showed "April 30, 1945." According to estimated dates, we must have left Leipzig about April eighteenth or nineteenth. Next to the calendar hung a few pictures of German military men. On the buffet stood two photos of soldiers, both ornamented with black bands; rosary beads lay nearby. When the old woman saw us looking at the photos, she pointed to the two with black bands and, with tears in her eyes and with a sigh, said, "I lost both of them in this ugly war. My husband, well, I don't know where he is." Then realizing that she was lamenting to the wrong people, she wiped her tears with her hands and left the room.

We spent almost two adventurous weeks in this house, sleeping on sofas, on the floors, in beds. The first few days we spent organizing food, soap, and fuel for the stove. And, of course, we rested.

Now that we had a stove, we started looking for things to cook, such as flour, cereals, vegetables, things that we had not had for quite some time. It was not an easy task. All chickens, ducks, and geese, we

My Education Continues

found out, had been already taken by the Russians. As soon as they came to town, they took care of everything that they could put their hands on. What we were able to find were only the leftovers.

One Friday morning, Dora, one of our new companions, went out on a food hunt and brought home a large fresh fish. "I saw a Russian soldier walking from the river carrying a bucket of fish. This large one was hanging over his shoulder. I just pulled it off and ran." She laughed, proudly displaying her catch. "Yes, he saw me, but said nothing." Pani Konova, who besides her other duties also had become our official cook, prepared the fish, and we all shared in the feast. We even lit a candle that we had found in the house.

Our lives began to become somewhat organized.

A few days later, I found some paper and a pencil. From that day on, I spent most of my time in the outside shed, writing notes. I thought that what I had written a few years ago in Warsaw might have, by now, been lost or destroyed. But I still expected to find the notes that I had left in Sandomierz. Nevertheless, I scribbled down everything about my life, and the lives of those I knew, hoping that soon I would be reading these notes to my family and friends. I started making entries of past and daily events. I had to start a new diary; I had no shortage of adventures about which I could write. Besides writing from my own memory, the girls I was with also kept suggesting important events that they thought should be included in the pages of my diary. It became a kind of joint project, even if no one ever volunteered to do the actual entries.

One evening, as we were sitting in the yard resting, three Russian soldiers came to the fence. "I saw the little German girl with my fish run into this house," one of them said in a broken German mixed with Russian. "I thought I'd come and visit, see how she's

Liberation

doing, and how she liked my fish. I brought my comrades to show them the place."

"We are not German," said Pani Konova in her broken Russian. And then she told the guys our story.

"Well," said the first soldier, "we just came to visit, not to get the fish back." The other one added, "Don't be afraid."

They talked with us for a while, then left.

Inside the house were Masha and Rosa, who were still too sick to join us outside. Masha would spit a dark yellow, greenish secretion mixed with blood, every time she tried to vomit. In the dress that she had found on a wagon, her skinny body was lost. We could only see her big brown eyes, which looked huge in her bony face. A dark brown mossy fuzz covered her otherwise bald head. Masha had been sick for some time. Roza had been feeling fine until she devoured the lard that she found on the wagon. She had eaten it on an empty stomach. Now she was vomiting, and had a terrible stomachache. We didn't know what to do with the two sick girls, or how to get them some help. When the soldiers were already back in the street, Masha's cousin, Hayka, ran out of the yard and caught up with them. She told them, as best she could, about the sick girls. "Okay," one of them said. "Let's see what we can do."

The next morning, a group of five Russian soldiers came to our house. Two of them we recognized from the day before. Among the three new ones was a fellow from the tank division who could speak Yiddish and who also knew some Polish words, which he had learned during the year his regiment had spent in Poland. His name was Boris. He was from the Ukraine. He told us how he had seen his father and little brother shot by the Nazis. Boris himself had escaped the shooting and, at the age of eighteen, joined the Russian military.

My Education Continues

We embraced him and thanked him for coming. We were thrilled, not only to see a Jew, but to know that some of them were in uniform, fighting the Nazis. Boris had come prepared to help us. He was going to take the sick girls to a Russian field hospital that was on the other side of the forest. He had a leave permit that was valid until five o'clock that day, and an old bicycle.

Roza, who was feeling somewhat better this day, said that she didn't want to go. But Masha's condition had worsened. There was nothing we could do but take her to that hospital. Our "landlady" gave us a blanket. We put it on the frame of the bike, put Masha on it, and, accompanied by her cousin Hayka, Marisia, and me, Boris started pushing the vehicle through the forest.

During the three-hour-long walk, Boris told us of how all Jews in the German-occupied territories had been killed, and how the Russian armed forces had fought the Germans all the way from Stalingrad through Poland, and how the Allies were now closing in from all sides of the Elbe River, and how the War would be over soon. He also told us proudly of how the Russian armed forces had liberated the Auschwitz death camp, and of the horrors that he had seen there, and the shocking stories that he had heard from a survivor. He asked us how we had survived the War, and was surprised to hear that some Jews had remained alive in labor camps. After all the things he saw and heard, he did not believe that there were any Jews left.

Masha didn't feel well. We had to stop frequently to let her rest. She didn't talk much, either, but at one of the rest stops, she told Boris that her older brother and a cousin had left for Russia when the Germans invaded her town, and that the last she ever heard from them was in 1942, when her aunt received a coded postcard saying that both were doing fine and that they had joined the Russian military.

Liberation

Sporadic shots were heard throughout the forest. We were scared that the Germans might be hiding behind the trees or in the trenches. Boris told us that he had to go back to the Front, "to finish off the bastards," and that he was only on a few days' leave.

As we neared the hospital, we saw Russian military trucks full of wounded soldiers. We stopped at the fence, where Boris showed his documents and explained our problem to the Russian guards. They let us through the gate.

After we finished filling out all the bureaucratic papers required by the authorities, the army nurse assessed Masha's condition. She suggested that we leave her in the hospital until one of the doctors was able to check her over. "They are all very busy with the severely wounded; I'll see to it that someone sees her as soon as possible." We had Masha and her cousin Hayka sign some papers. We were then told to leave the premises.

On the way home we asked Boris if he would visit us again; he said that he would be glad to come if he didn't have to go back to the Front in the next few days. "The two soldiers who visited you girls yesterday went this morning. That's why they didn't come with us to see you," he said, looking at the trees and the birds in the forest. Next day, Boris did have to report for duty. Of course, he didn't come to see us, but from that day on, we started having visitors every day. Russian soldiers would drop in at will, "to see how the Polish girls were doing." At the beginning, we really enjoyed these visits by our liberators, even if we did not speak the same language. The boys were young and full of pep. They laughed and sang and talked. Besides, it had been quite a while since any of us had seen a young man.

Soon, however, these visits began to be a nuisance. Some soldiers would come over drunk, and searching

My Education Continues

for more drinks. They would drink perfume, cologne, rubbing alcohol, whatever would pass their scientific test: They would set a match to the liquid, and if it lit up, it was good for drinking. Luckily, gasoline was rationed, and hard to find. We were getting scared of these frequent visitors, and so was our landlady, who until now had felt quite secure having former Nazi prisoners in her house. We had developed a kind of symbiotic relation with her: She took care of our needs, and we protected her from being thrown out of her house. But the problem with the Russian soldiers was altogether another matter. Soon we found out from other Leipzig girls who were staying in this village that they, too, were having problems with the Russian soldiers. Their problems were even more serious than ours: One of their girls had actually been raped. The other girls who lived with her had had to take her to the hospital. Thank God, she was checked and released.

The situation had gotten out of hand. Eventually some of the drunken soldiers, or "drunken sailors" as we called them, started looking for more than just drinks. Some of them thought that we girls owed them favors for having liberated us from the Nazi Devils, a claim that we did not deny; we simply didn't agree with the type of prize. When we refused even to consider their method of payment, some of them became frustrated with us and called us "Nazi collaborators who fucked around with the Germans."

Pani Konova understood the problem better than any of us younger girls. She explained to us the possibility of rape, venereal diseases, and pregnancies; and, she warned us, by all means, avoid contact with soldiers. She begged the guys to leave us alone; told them how wrong they were for having such dirty thoughts about us. She asked them to behave like gentlemen.

Liberation

Actually, there were many military men who did not have to be told. They were nice guys who would drop in just for conversation; they liked to tell us about their experiences in Poland, the problems they'd encountered with the language, how courageously they'd fought until they finally made it to Germany. Occasionally, they would talk about their families, or listen to our stories. But the drunkards and the vulgar ones made it bad for everyone. They didn't care for talking; they didn't even hear what Pani Konova had to say. They figured, "We are going to the Front. Tomorrow we may be dead. Yet these 'holy virgins' are trying to save their little pussies." We did feel sorry for these poor men; we understood their feelings. A few of us even suggested, and in real earnest, that we'd be glad to join their army and, if at all possible, help them to fight the common enemy. But they wouldn't listen.

We finally had to resort to a measure that we had wanted to avoid. Without identifying the offenders, a few of us, including Pani Konova, went to City Hall and reported our problem to the Russian authorities. Komrad Kommandant wrote down our complaints and our correct address, then politely told us not to worry; he'd take care of it. He apologized for the soldiers' improper behavior, explaining how military personnel were prohibited from entering private homes and that the boys were violating the rules. He promised that no soldier would bother us again.

We restated to Komrad Kommandant the offer that we made to the soldiers, that some of us would be glad to join the fighters and help out in the war effort; we knew that there were many women in the Russian armed forces. But this idea didn't appeal to him, either. His answer was, "Nyet! Let me see what can be done." He smiled.

My Education Continues

Well, Komrad Kommandant kept his first promise. For the next couple of nights, not one soldier came to our house.

The third night, however, as we were getting ready for supper, Komrad Kommandant, accompanied by two higher ranking officers, appeared at the door. The three were much older than the soldiers who would visit before. But they were also more polite. Komrad Kommandant asked if we had had anymore problems with the soldiers. We said "no," and we thanked him and his companions for prompt and helpful action. Komrad Kommandant then asked if he and his companions could come in, and we said "yes."

In their classy uniforms, with epaulets and medal-hung chests, the officers looked so handsome, so dignified, that it had been difficult to say "no." All three entered. They refused to eat with us, even though we offered them some of our food. They just sat and talked about the battles being fought not far from the village. They assured us that the War could not last much longer, saying that the remnants of the German armed forces were surrounded. The officers also expressed their sorrow for the young Allied men who were still being killed on the Front. They were also concerned about the upcoming casualties that they were expecting from the next battle. After a nice little talk, they left.

But they didn't stay away for very long. After that first encounter, our nice Komrad Kommandant returned with a few more friends, then started visiting us almost every day. Like the soldiers before them, they, too, were coming for conversation, and for all the same reasons that the others had come for. Those distinguished officers enjoyed talking about their great achievements on the battlefield, and about girls. They tried to avoid conversations about their families or love affairs. Such subjects were too painful, too emotional,

Liberation

for even these "macho" guys; good, strong men did not show their vulnerability. Such behavior might be expected from weak little ladies; it would not befit heroes.

Yet such embarrassing incidents actually happened more than once. I remember one time, when our conversation turned from war and heroism to family ties. Colonel Youra started talking about his wife and children, who were evacuated to Siberia during the German bombing of Kiev. "It has been about two years since I saw them. Even longer since I've seen my parents." He took out a family picture from his wallet. "I was looking forward to seeing them; I was scheduled for a leave, but I got wounded and spent two weeks in the hospital." He pulled up his pant leg and showed us a small scar just below his left knee. "After my hospital stay came the big German offensive, and I was sent back to the Front."

Colonel Youra looked at the pictures of his children, and we saw tears running down his face. Our brave colonel turned his head and, embarrassed, wiped his eyes. When it became obvious to him that we were watching, he just wept openly, overcome by his emotions. He said that he had not heard from his family for a long time, but liked to believe that it was the fault of the mail delivery. "There were times," he admitted, rather shamefaced, "when I had not even thought of them. About a year ago I didn't believe I'd make it. We were losing many battles and great numbers of our best soldiers." Then, after a short pause and a long, deep sigh, he continued: "With death chasing you day and night, your mind is not in working condition." His eyes got brighter, and with a faint smile, he added, "Now, for the first time since the War started, I really believe I'll survive."

"Of course you will," responded Komrad Kommandant. "Stop whining. I thought we came here

My Education Continues

to have a good time with the girls." Saying that, Komrad Kommandant grabbed one of our most beautiful, Tolla, who just happened to be standing next to him, and started hugging and kissing her. Then he threw her onto the bed. She begged him to leave her alone. We started yelling and pushing him away, but he threw himself on top of her and, holding her down, murmured something in Russian, either to her or to himself, something unintelligible. Before we could pull him off, he got up by himself, took a look at the crotch of his pants, and quickly sat down on a nearby chair, putting his hat over the spot on his crotch. He said to Tolla, who was still lying on the bed, shaking in disbelief, "I am sorry, my dear."

Colonel Youra and the other officer took him by his arms and pulled him off the chair. While walking him to the door, the Colonel said, "We all had one too many drinks." He didn't need to say it; we had smelled it when they first came in.

I went back to my corner in the shed, and by candlelight, I wrote down another entry in my diary. As the candle flickered above the bottle, I thought of the ghetto and how I used to do my homework by candlelight. I wondered if I'd ever get to go back to school; I thought about all the education that I'd been receiving these years, away from school. The diary that I was preparing now was to be read at home to my family and friends. I wanted to make sure not to forget any important events. Since I left the riverbank by the bridge, I had seen and learned much about life and human nature; I had learned things that I never thought possible. My education had become a never-ending process.

I saw long lines of military men of the "Master Race"—once powerful soldiers—walking disarmed, discouraged, disappointed, with their arms up, hands over heads, following instructions of a few young,

Liberation

armed Russian boys. I watched their frightened eyes and bearded faces, and I wondered what they were thinking of now. I saw mighty warriors overcome with affection, crying like babies. I saw weak old ladies gain unbelievable strength and self-reliance after their men were gone. I saw bloodshed, bravery, laughter and tears, love and hate, integrity and viciousness.

I was running out of paper trying to write it all down. I began to suffer from headaches as I struggled to sort out all of these things. I was still having the dizzy spells that had been with me since my typhus. The spells reminded me that things were not yet over.

For a couple of days after the incident with Komrad Kommandant, we had no visitors. Then about noon of the third day, our distinguished guests showed up in the yard, bringing a whole group of other Russian officers and soldiers with them.

We were surprised to see them at this unusual hour, and in such a festive mood: They were singing, laughing, cheering and jumping for joy. Those of us who were home, and who had seen them coming, were scared to death. We had never seen so many of them together, or behaving so strangely; not even in their drunken states.

Seeing our faces, one of the officers yelled, "Let's celebrate! Hurrah! Girls, be happy! Let's drink and be merry!" This talk scared us even more, but there was little we could do about it. "The War is over!" we finally heard them yell. "The Germans surrendered yesterday! This is the day we all have been waiting for!" our visitors screamed, almost simultaneously.

The wall calendar showed "May 9, 1945."

Six terrible years of indiscriminate killing, burning, shooting, bombing, shelling, starvation, epidemic, freezing, torture—all had finally come to an end.

We celebrated.

My Education Continues

Besides the drinks, the Russians had brought with them bread and crackers, sugar and jam, and dried herring and fresh fish. We ate, sang, kissed, and hugged. Two girls who had often told us about the love adventures that they had experienced before they were taken to camp, took advantage of this joyous occasion and, walking several of our visitors to the shed outside, celebrated the end of their celibacy. The third girl who was with them chickened out at the last minute and came running from the shed. She said, "I thought they were joking."

Actually, I thought that it would have been kind of nice to have my first experience with a heroic Russian officer. It was not on account of my moral persuasions, nor because of my religious beliefs, that I turned down a couple of good offers. I think that I was just scared. I also remembered Pani Konova's lecture; I got more frightened. I, too, had chickened out.

In the next couple of days, many of our visitors were transferred from our village and were replaced by officers and soldiers who were coming from the already disbanded front. It didn't take the new guys long to find our address.

We began to realize that our stay in this house must come to an end. Besides the problem with the visitors, we would soon be facing problems with food and housing. Food supplies in this village were running out. Everything from fish in the lake, to the reserves people had hidden away in their basements, sheds and barns, was looted out. Also, some German escapees had started returning to their homes, having no other place to run to.

One day, while I was in my shed writing, Hanka and Sala walked in and asked abruptly, "Why are you wasting your time with those silly papers? Pani Konova is thinking about leaving this place. It's time to plan our trip home."

Liberation

"Thinking" was a new word, a word that we had not heard for a long time. Thinking and decision-making had become an almost hideous process for us. For years we had been forced not to use our mental faculties for such a weird purpose. "Do as you're told! Don't reason! Don't ask questions! Obey our commandments!"

We decided to ask our Russian friends for advice. One of them suggested that we first get a travel permit from the Russian headquarters if we didn't want to be stopped on the way. We also found out that there was no public transportation any place close. All German vehicles had been either destroyed or confiscated; and military vehicles were prohibited from taking civilian passengers. But in the territories farther east (which had been freed some time ago) some railroad tracks had been restored. One guy even said that, with a little bit of luck, we might catch a freight train that was going east. We stayed a few more days before taking off.

Boris, who luckily returned unharmed (even though his tank had been hit by a shell), came back to see us. He told us about his last days on the battlefield, and even took Marisia and Hayka to see Masha in the hospital.

Masha was still very sick, but was glad to see her cousin and friend and Boris. The hospital would not release her; they weren't sure what was wrong with her, but they knew that she would never make it home in her condition. She asked the girls to tell her relatives at home that the Russians promised to drive her home to Kielce as soon as she could be released. When we knew that there was no chance of taking Masha with us, we had no choice but to go without her.

After checking all possibilities for transportation and finding none, we took off on foot. We took with us

My Education Continues

the wagon in which we had transported Masha and Roza. We had placed in it a few belongings that we picked up in the village, and whatever food we could find.

We took turns pulling the wagon. It was a few days' journey to the place where the train station used to be. During the days, we would hunt for food; nights, we would rest in abandoned houses, stables, or barns. Walking barefooted behind the wagon, I thought of the Gypsies whom I used to see as a kid walking the roads through Polish villages. I remembered how I had envied them so.

On the roads, Russian soldiers on trucks, motorcycles, and bicycles passed us by. They whistled and laughed, sometimes stopping and asking questions. Without our prison uniforms, we were often taken for German women.

One morning, a canvas-covered truck half-full of soldiers stopped in front of us. The driver asked us where we were going, and then offered us a ride. "All of you can climb on the truck," he said, "but you cannot take the wagon. With you girls, we should have no problem." He hopped off the driver's seat and was ready to open the back flap of the truck and let us into where the other soldiers were sitting, when Pani Konova asked him if it was against the law. He said that it was. "But, you know, rules are made to be broken, and for a bunch of young chicks like these here, who wouldn't break the law?"

As we were about to leave the wagon and get on the truck, Pani Konova changed her mind. "We'd better not go," she told us. "I don't think they plan to take us for free." We skipped the offer and continued walking.

A day later, however, we did accept a ride. The top of the truck was empty. The driver and his co-driver were sitting in the front. The two helped us with the wagon and took us to a place that was about thirty

Liberation

kilometers from the railroad tracks. There, they asked us to leave because they had to turn another way. We thanked them and hugged them and walked down the country road, pulling our wagon along. We walked and rested. And had a few more encounters with Russian soldiers before we got to the place that once had been a railroad station.

Hundreds, maybe even a thousand people, were lining the platform and the field around it. A Red Cross truck was parked at the bombed-out building. Some charity workers were giving out train information and hot coffee. We found out that we would have to wait here until a train came. "If it is not filled up, and if you're lucky, you may get on it."

Only freight trains could take us; all passenger trains were reserved for special passengers or military personnel. "Closer to the Polish border," the Red Cross worker told us, "the tracks are restored, and the trains run somewhat better. But they are usually off schedule."

Sitting on the ground, talking to other prospective passengers, we began to realize that getting away physically from war-torn places was only one problem; to get the War out of our systems was an entirely different matter. We were still full of uncertainties, mistrust, and fear. We didn't know what to expect at home. We had no idea what to do with the freedom that we now had. Inside, we were still slaves.

The people sitting around us were of many different nationalities and in Germany for many different reasons. There were Albanians, Bulgarians, Czechs, Greeks, Hungarians, Poles, Russians, Rumanians, and some Yugoslavians—all heading for their homes, all hoping to unite with their families so as to start new lives. All of these people had been kept in German camps, or had worked as forced laborers on farms; some had been taken into Germany as POWs.

My Education Continues

Some unfortunate souls were German collaborators who had been taken there as reward for their good work—and now would have to pay the price if found out by those whom they had betrayed.

After two days in this place, we saw the long-awaited train creep to a stop, its freight cars stretching far into the field. It was announced that the train was bound for Legnica; the previously German city Liegnitz was now Polish. It had changed its nationality and its name.

Everything east of the Oder River was now Polish territory.

Legnica was not the place that we wanted to go, but most of us were heading east, and that was the direction that the train was going. So we decided to get on as soon as the keepers of order would let us. We just wanted to make sure that our group stayed together. It was a nice, sunny day, and all the freight car doors were wide open. In one of them we saw a group of former male prisoners still dressed in their striped clothing. A few of us walked over to them to find out where they were coming from and where they were heading. We were almost shocked when among them we recognized a few men who had been with us in Skarżysko. Not all of the girls in our group knew them, but those of our original Skarżysko group did. We started inquiring about their experiences in Germany, and about some other men who had been taken away with them. They told us that the night we girls were evacuated to Leipzig, the men were taken to a camp at Schlieben, a subdivision of Buchenwald. Those who tried to jump the train in Skarżysko were shot. The men told us about their work, and the beatings, and about the long walk they, too, had experienced, and about the brutalities of some of their guards. They also told us that the Skarżysko inmates beat the "daylights" out of one of the

Liberation

"stinking kapos," as well as the evil camp policemen, once these former collaborators had been stripped of their rank and power. "Believe it or not, girls," came a voice from inside the car, "we really got even with them."

One skinny guy standing quietly in the corner didn't say a word. With his head bent forward and in his striped clothes, he looked like a candy cane. His ragged clothes hung on him as if on a hook. He was toothless, unshaven, and he looked like a man of seventy. We knew that he could not have been that old, because no one that age was kept in the camps, let alone allowed to survive one.

"Hi, girls," he finally said, in a weak, almost whispering voice. By his voice I recognized that he was Leo, the man from Warsaw who had come to Skarżysko from the Majdanek camp, who had told me all the stories about the ghetto uprising. One of the men told me that Leo had been beaten and his teeth knocked out when he failed to catch up with his column during the march. "He still can't sit, but he is lucky to be alive. He almost got shot," said a guy sitting next to him.

I tried to say something to Leo, but an announcement came over a bullhorn that all people heading for Legnica should be boarding the train. The ride was free of charge, but because room was limited, we would have to squeeze in as tightly as possible. Only one bag per person was allowed.

Leo and I said goodbye to one another. "Have a nice trip. We'll see each other in Legnica once the train unloads."

Just before we walked away, I yelled into the car, "Have any of you guys seen Itzek, you know, Luba's 'cousin' Itzek?"

One of the men yelled back, "Yes! He is somewhere on this train, probably in another car."

My Education Continues

"Thanks!" I said happily, and ran to the girls, who were waiting for me.

Then I remembered something else. I didn't even know what had happened to Luba, even if she was still alive. There was another Luba in our group whose name kept reminding me of our pregnant girl.

I told the girls about Itzek being somewhere on this train. We talked about Luba's and Itzek's fates later in the train car.

Of course the only thing that we could take on the train was one bundle per person. Mine consisted of the notes that I had written, a pencil, my brown dress, and a pair of shoes—all wrapped in a head scarf. I was wearing a blue skirt, a white sweater, and a pair of shoes two sizes too large—a looted outfit given to me by Pani Konova, who had said that it was too large for her. Pani Konova was skin and bone and nails. I looked, by comparison, like a stuffed pig with a swollen belly. She had given me that outfit because it fit me perfectly. Now I, like the other girls, looked stylish, ready for homecoming.

Our group had to split up before boarding the train because there wasn't enough room in any of the already filled cars for all of us together. I got onto a car with Regina, Sala, Hanka, and Bella, the fortuneteller. With the other girls from our group, we were to meet in Legnica once the train stopped. A girl named Halinka, from Warsaw, joined our group. She told us that she used to work on a German farm.

Our new companion was a nice looking, sweet girl from Poznańska Street. She told us about her experiences, and we listened attentively because they were different from ours. Halinka, who was nineteen, did not look Jewish, despite her brown curly hair and dark eyes. Her mother, she told us, was killed during the bombing of Warsaw. She herself and her older sister stayed with an aunt in the ghetto. When conditions in

Liberation

the ghetto had become unbearable, her bricklayer father arranged an escape for the two girls. One of her father's coworkers, a gentile man who was also a bricklayer, hid the girls in his mother's farmhouse. After a while, that place became too dangerous. The two girls took a chance and signed up to work for the Germans, who had advertised for help. Halinka was assigned a job in a military kitchen, somewhere near the Russian border, where she worked with other Polish girls. As long as no one knew her identity, she was safe. When the Germans pulled back they sent Halinka to Germany. There she worked on a farm. The work was hard, but she was treated fairly. She got used to the family, and even began to like them.

One day the family received news that their son had been killed in battle. His picture, Halinka told us, tears in her eyes, was put into a black frame and wrapped around with a black ribbon. The family grieved. They cried. Their relatives came to comfort them. "I couldn't believe that I would ever feel sorry for German people, but believe it or not, I found myself crying with them." After a short pause, she took a deep breath and added, "What a waste of young lives,' I thought, while looking at the picture of the young handsome soldier." Then, focusing her eyes on the car floor, she said, "I was ashamed of myself to think that way of a German soldier: He could have been the one who killed my mother."

In this car full of returning refugees, it didn't take long to engage in conversation with total strangers. "Where are you from? Where are you going to? What were you doing in Germany?" Any of these questions would start a nice chat. One man, however, caught our attention with the blackish-blue number tattooed on his left forearm.

"Where are you from?" was the first question, followed by, "What is that number on your arm?"

My Education Continues

He looked at us in disbelief. "Where in the world could you have been that you didn't hear about the hell of Auschwitz?" he asked the man who had asked him the questions. Then looking at us, he added, "Don't tell me that you girls didn't hear about it, either."

"We did hear some rumors about it," I said, "and we heard about Treblinka and about Majdanek, and a little about Buchenwald, but we didn't want to believe what we heard. It was better not to.... You see, sir, there was always the possibility that we might be sent there."

He started telling us, and the other people in the car who could understand his Yiddish or Polish, about his experience in Auschwitz, about how just a few days before the Russians were to liberate this death camp, the Germans had transported thousands of prisoners to the West. "Those German Schweine killed and starved many Auschwitz inmates, but especially the Jews and the Gypsies. Those two groups were not punished for anything they'd done, but only for being born into a 'wrong' people."

As the numbered man told everybody about his trip in locked-up freight cars, and about the long march he was taken on, all this sounded quite familiar to us, but not to all of the people in the car. He continued talking about all those who had frozen and died on the way.

To prove his statement he took off a shoe and the large bandage that was on his foot. He showed us his frostbitten, black-and-blue toes. "You see," he said, "they are all dead. My toes, soles, even the ankle. The toes have to come off—all of them, the doctor from the army hospital told me. If I am lucky, my foot can be saved. I didn't want to hear anymore; I just wanted to go home. So in that Russian hospital they put medicine on my foot, and then they let me go."

Liberation

The next two days—the time it took the train to crawl to Legnica—we heard more stories than we really wanted to. We also exchanged little notes with our names, cities of origin, and the people we were looking for—just in case we should, by chance, come across some of them. My writing supplies came in very handy. No one else in our car was carrying either pencil or paper.

This train ride marked the end of enslavement and the beginning of the aftermath. My education continued.

Book Three: The Aftermath

"Not all Germans were Nazis, and not all Nazis were German."

Chapter 1. Łódź and Jacob

Legnica had not been damaged very much by the War. Also, a few months had already passed since the fighting ceased. The area between the former Polish border and the Oder River, where Legnica was located, was now called by the Polish people *"Ziemie Odzyskane"* or "Recovered Territories"; the Germans called the same places *"Besetzte Gebiete"*—"Occupied Regions." Anyway, this territory, like Poland itself, and like East Germany, was now under Russian control. The once German city was now Polish.

By the time we arrived, law and order had been restored. Shops and markets were reopened. Russian soldiers were no longer drinking perfume and cologne since the bars were officially open and vodka available for purchase.

Red Cross representatives were helping thousands of returnees, who were clogging this transit city, to find some food and temporary shelter. The organization was also providing registration booths for those who were looking for friends or relatives; no more plundering food, no more sleeping in stables, no more guessing where or how to look for loved ones. We were now eating in soup kitchens and sleeping in almshouses, and we had our names instead of numbers registered in the big fat journals. Like all the other returnees, I signed up with the Red Cross. I looked through the book of previously registered people, but found no familiar name.

Our little Regina (as we called the girl from Łódź) found the name of an aunt who had survived the War in the Łódź ghetto and who was now living in that city. Regina got the aunt's address and suggested that we all go with her to Łódź, temporarily, and from there find our ways to our respective cities. All of us Warsaw girls decided to take up Regina's offer because we heard that our city had been destroyed, and that it was not advisable to go there. Besides, having no place to go, we knew of no one who would want us, or even who would let us in.

Our other girls—those who came with us on the train—were from other towns: Kielce, Częstochowa, Siedlce. They decided to go to their respective homes. Girls from territories now under Russian occupation—or as the Russians referred to them, "the Liberated Places"—had to wait for special permits.

Meanwhile, rumors were going around that in Russia all returnees, including the POWs, were being treated harshly; certainly not being welcomed home. The girls from the Russian-occupied places postponed their journey home until they could check the validity of the rumors.

We all stayed a few more days in Legnica, hoping to find a way to our cities. Łódź was still about two hundred kilometers away. Each day we stayed in Legnica, we would hear more shocking stories; and the more we listened, the more our hopes for finding our homes and relatives intact diminished. The Polish economy was in shambles, many cities in ruins. Reports about Jewish survivors were discouraging. There was little to expect. From moment to moment we began to realize that the dreadful tales that we had kept hearing all along were not rumors but actual accounts of what had happened to the Jews. Now, nothing seemed unbelievable anymore. Our dreams of a normal life after the War were fading. We knew that things had not turned out the way we had imagined. During our ordeal, we had been so preoccupied with the prospect of liberation that hardly anyone could think a step beyond. Now the magic moment was here, and instead of rejoicing, we were facing the bleak reality that the world we had hoped for was now going to be a disappointment. The sources of our strength, which had kept us going all those terrible years, were hope, a positive attitude, and our age and its naive belief in humanity and in the future. We had hoped that we'd return to our families and continue our jobs and our education; that we would "live in peace forever after." But now these dreams, even though not yet completely gone, were beginning to fade quickly. Each passing day we were ready to settle for less, and less: "If I won't find the home I lived in, maybe the yard will still be there. If Grandmother didn't make it through the War, Mother and Sister surely did. There will still be some cousins, aunts, uncles. After all, Regina has already found one of her aunts, and many of our people are still on their way home from concentration camps and labor camps and prisons. And there were those who fled to Russia."

Our trip to Łódź was on the open flatcar next to the locomotive, the only available place on the train that was going our way. By the time we descended, we looked like chimney sweeps. Nevertheless, we were glad to reach our destination uneventfully.

Łódź had not been damaged. Many sections, including the ghetto, had deteriorated, but only due to lack of maintenance rather than the destruction of war.

Here, as in Legnica, we were referred to an almshouse, where we registered, were fed, and received iron beds with straw mattresses and pillows and blankets. There were a faucet and basin and one toilet for thirty to fifty people, which was how many our shelter housed at one time. Every day people arrived and departed, some coming to visit, or to find friends or relatives. An initial conversation with any stranger might start something like: "Where are you from? Where did you survive? Have you seen or heard of such-and-such person?" Once in a while the answer to the last was, "Yes," but most of the time the answer was, "No."

After a few days in the shelter, Regina found her aunt and a cousin. The aunt had survived with one of her daughters. They were liberated quite a while ago, and now were living in a nice apartment which belonged to one of their richer cousins who had been killed. The aunt and daughter were financially well off. They recovered some hidden things that their relatives had left. The aunt invited Regina to stay with her.

Bella found a longtime friend. He, like Regina's aunt, offered Bella a place to stay. I don't remember this as being in one of Bella's predictions.

The rest of us stayed in the shelter.

Among our visitors were two men—barbers—in their late twenties or early thirties, who came one day looking for friends and relatives. After the initial questioning—where we came from, and so on—they introduced themselves. They told us that they had a large, two-room ground floor apartment not far from the shelter. The older of the two told us he had been married, but lost his wife in the War; the other one was a bachelor. They talked to us for a while, glancing at our outfits. We looked strange, some of us wearing oversized rags, some silk dresses and clogs; some of us were only skin and bone, others seemed fat from the swelling. These guys seemed not to mind our looks, for the older one said, "If any of you girls would like to wash off, or wash out any of your belongings, you are welcome to come over and use our facilities. We are at work most of the day, and the apartment stays empty."

We had forgotten the last time that we saw an apartment or got washed. The offer sounded too good to pass up. A few of us agreed to go. After scrubbing our bodies and washing our few pieces of clothing, Hanka, Halinka, and a new girl, Salka, went back to the shelter to make sure that our beds wouldn't be given away.

Sala asked me to stay with her and help her clean up. While I was washing the floor, Sala thought that it would be nice to cook a soup from potatoes and vegetables, which she had found in the house, and surprise the guys when they got home from work.

She was right. The guys were so happy that they didn't even let us go back to the shelter. After the meal, all four of us took a nice walk, talked for a while, then went back to the apartment, where we talked some more. It got late when Sala and I finally went to sleep. We slept on the sofa, with our clothes on. We declined the guys' generous offer to change rooms and take their beds.

The next day after the guys went to work, Sala and I got acquainted with a nice, forty-year-old Polish woman, *Pani* Basia, who lived next door. She was the building-manager and was very sympathetic to our plight. She told us about her life during the War, about how her father was killed in 1939, and about her son, who was now serving in the Polish army. She was very helpful and nice. We told her about our shelter and our plans to return to Warsaw. She suggested that we stay with the barbers a little longer. "They are nice people," she said.

But our arrangement with them lasted only three days. The fourth night, as Sala and I lay down to sleep, we had visitors: Both guys came over to our room. "We

My Education Continues

couldn't sleep," said the older one, "so we thought we'd come over and talk a little." The little talk lasted most of the night. At first all of us talked together. Sala told us about the boyfriend that she used to have, and about how he and she had taken advantage of the bombing by having sex in the bomb-shelter. Then Sala talked with the older man and I got stuck with the younger one, who kept telling me heroic tales of how he survived the War by cutting hair for the German soldiers. (There was always one German with a gun to his head just in case he tried to cut "incorrectly.") He talked about his family, about how out of five siblings, he had found only one brother alive. The brother survived in Russia. Then he abruptly changed the subject, telling me how much he loved me. If I would stay with him, he would marry me.

In the morning I told Sala that I was going back to the shelter. If she wanted to stay, I wouldn't hold it against her. We both went back to the shelter and, luckily, still found one unoccupied bed. We both shared it.

Whatever Sala had told her man that night must have been promising, for he started visiting her every day, bringing her presents. "My guy" got the message; he never showed up again. After a few days, Sala moved in with her friend. Within a few weeks, they invited all of us shelter girls to the wedding. It was a small Jewish ceremony: a *chuppah,* a cake, and a bottle of wine. A provisional rabbi said the prayer and declared them "husband and wife."

For us girls left in the shelter, things changed, too. The refugee organization found a one-room attic apartment for us. The stove in it would be for cooking as well as for heating. In the long hall connecting the other six rooms were a water faucet and a toilet. These facilities were shared by all six tenant families who lived on the floor. The apartment was furnished

Łódź and Jacob

with two iron beds placed on opposite walls of the room, equipped with straw mattresses, sawdust-stuffed pillows, and shredded blankets. We used them as beds, sofas, loveseats, and chairs. A three-legged table, supported by bricks, leaned against the wall that separated the two beds. The two windows on that wall looked out onto the courtyard's septic tank. Besides the beds and the table, our furniture included a wooden chair, all of whose spindles were broken out, and a stool on which we kept our tin washbowl. The refugee organization also helped us to find temporary jobs. I worked in a home workshop that made shoeboxes. The shop was owned by a young Jewish couple who had come back from Russia to Łódź right after Poland was liberated from the Germans.

As soon as I got settled into my new apartment and job, I went over to see *Pani* Basia, the manager of the barbers' building, to thank her for having been so nice to me when the two of us needed her help. I gave her my new address and asked her, please, to come and visit some time.

Hanka, Halinka, and Salka, my roommates, found jobs, too. One worked in a store, one in a restaurant kitchen, and one in a garment shop. We barely made enough to pay rent and eat, but at least it was a start.

Daily we were visiting the shelter and the Red Cross registration office to find out if anyone we were looking for had shown up. No one had.

Meanwhile, another girl from Warsaw came to live with us. Her name was Freda; we called her "Rooska." She was tall, twenty-eight years old, heavyset, and strong. She survived the War in Russia, where she had worked as a stoker on a train that transported soldiers and military equipment from the Polish border all the way to Russian Siberia. Halinka had met her on one of her trips to the shelter and brought her over to our

My Education Continues

house. Her contribution to the rent helped with our budget and savings.

Since all four of us were from Warsaw, the first thing on our agenda was to save up enough money for a trip to our hometown. Our free train rides had come to an end. We now had to pay a fare if we wanted to go somewhere. For that, we got to ride on passenger trains. Luckily, I didn't have to wait for money to accumulate. One day, *Pani* Basia came for a visit and offered to lend me money for a round-trip ticket to Warsaw. She knew that I truly wanted to go.

No matter how much I had heard, seen, and read about the Uprising, the revolt, and all the killings, I knew that I would find some friends and relatives once I got to Warsaw. I still hoped to find a few of my relatives alive on this trip, and I was sure that their names would be in the local registry—even though I knew that the city had been destroyed. Well, what I found was not what I expected. Warsaw was indeed completely in ruins. Trains were stopping in Praga, across from the Wisła River. I stayed in my customary accommodations—"The Praga Alms Hotel Chain"—and ate in the "Soup Kitchen Restaurant." I had no reservations for either of them. When I arrived at the quarters, all the beds were already taken. Like others who had arrived at the same time, I slept on an old newspaper laid out on the filthy floor. Posters on the walls gave the names and addresses of the nearest Missing Persons offices and other announcements (for example, that all men of draft age had to register with the Selective Service Office.)

I went over to the Missing Persons Office, signed up, and looked over all registration books. I found no familiar names. I met many people and talked with them, asking them the customary questions: "Where are you from? Where did you survive? Have you heard of such-and-such person?" To the first two questions, I was given the names of places; but the third answer was always "No." One young man, who was also looking for his relatives, said to me jokingly, after I told him that I was looking for my father, "Do you know, young lady, that before the War, whenever a father disappeared, there were three possibilities: He had moved with a girlfriend to another town, or he had left for America and gotten rich there. If these were not the case, his body would be found in a local mortuary. But now, my dear, I am afraid that neither of these apply to missing fathers." Then his face became more serious. "Sorry, young lady. Jokes aside, you may just be wasting your time."

I said that it was almost incomprehensible that everyone could have been killed, that I had many aunts and uncles and cousins and friends.... To which he replied, "Don't try to make sense out of it. Don't try to use logic. Standard reasoning doesn't apply in this case. What is rational and what is real are not the same. What happened here cannot be described or imagined in rational terms."

He told me that he had run away from the ghetto just before the Uprising. He lived on the Aryan side, took part in the Polish Uprising, got wounded, and married a Gentile woman; they now were living in the Grochów suburbs. He, too, came looking. Against his better judgment, and despite what he told me, he was still hoping that some of his relatives or friends would return from Russia, or from one of the camps. He recited a list of names of his lost people. I didn't know any of them. He then gave me some advice: "I hear that you plan to go to the ghetto side of town tomorrow. Remember, a walk through the ashes may be very emotional and depressing. Try not to go alone."

Others warned me not to expect miracles; that there was nothing left of the Jewish section of town, that the buildings that did remain in the Gentile part,

My Education Continues

even the occupied ones, were all damaged, burned, or had been shattered by shells. There was not one building that survived intact.

A day later, I went anyway. I was going to look for my home; or, rather, to see the heap of rubble that had once been my home. I took with me a girl whom I had met at the shelter. Mira, I think, was her name. She was originally from a small Galician town not far from Sandomierz. During most of the War she stayed in her town, but was later transported to Auschwitz. She was freed by the Russians in January, was reunited with one of her sisters, and was now looking for another sister who used to live in Warsaw. Mira had been through the Warsaw ruins once before, so she went only to keep me company. She said that she had never been in Warsaw before the War and had always wondered what this big city, which her sister used to write about, looked like.

For two days, I walked with Mira through the ruins and ashes of the once thriving city. It was hard to identify the streets. Krasińskich Park gave me a clue that I was on Świętojerska Street. Even the park looked strange. The iron railing once surrounding it was gone, and so were the swans on the lake; so were the wooden benches. The German soldiers, who used to strike fear into the souls of the people, well, they were gone, too. The small lake where I used to go ice skating in the winter was still there, and so were a few old trees. One of the signs that said "Don't walk on the grass" had survived the flames. Some grass and a few wild flowers were coming back to life. Otherwise, everything around was dead. We walked around, talking and looking. My shoes got torn on broken glass and nails, which were sticking out of scorched boards. We kept on walking. At night, we slept on a bench in a temporary police station. There, a police woman, who was working the desk, told us about the last days of

Łódź and Jacob

the Jewish struggle for survival in the ghetto, about the thousands of Jews who were deported to Majdanek and Treblinka camps.

She talked about the Poles who lost their lives in the 1944 Uprising, and other horror stories, some of which I had already heard but had chosen not to believe. She told us about the Jews who escaped the ghetto through the sewers—only to be killed during the 1944 Uprising—and about those who married Gentile women and were living now under assumed names, having assimilated into Polish Gentile religion and culture.

We asked her about the so-called "Resettlement Program" and what it had meant. She said that it had been a hoax. It was supposed to make people think that they had a way out of the ghetto. It promised opportunities, a new life away from the misery and hunger. Many Jews registered voluntarily to get the food that the Germans were offering to all who would sign up. Jews registered because they thought that nothing could be worse than what they were getting in the ghetto. We now were finding out what happened to all those who did.

The next day we spent walking. We returned to Świętojerska Street, stopping at Krasińskich Park, where we rested on the ground. Mira pulled up her blouse sleeve and showed me her tattoo. She talked about life in her small town, how she survived two months in the Auschwitz-Berkenau Camp. "The group of inmates I was with," she said, "was bound for the gas chamber. The crematorium ovens were filled to capacity. Our group was left in the barracks; we had to wait. Meanwhile, the Russians came and the Germans fled. We were saved."

I asked Mira if she knew what had happened to the Jews from her town and, maybe, those from Sandomierz. I said that my mother and sister were there. The only thing that she knew was that all the Jews had been deported. She had gone back to her town after her liberation and found the city *Judenrein*. The sister whom she found after the War had survived in one of the labor camps.

Occasionally, Mira and I passed other young men and women wandering through the destroyed Warsaw streets. We stopped, said "hi," exchanged information—"Where did you live? Who are you looking for?"—and then kept on going our respective ways, dragging ourselves through parts of the ghost town.

We were standing on the ashes and debris of my home. I didn't cry. Not even a tear came to my eyes. I just stood there, numb, looking at the skeleton that was left of our burned-out building. I didn't talk, and felt no grief, no pain. Mira asked me if this was the place where we used to live in the ghetto. I said that it was. But I was in no mood to talk about the ghetto; I didn't want to talk about misery, suffering, or horror. I didn't want to remember the fight against the omnipresent hunger, the food-snatchers, the dead and dying kids who had once lined the streets. I didn't want to think about their fate. So, as we walked the ravaged streets, I told Mira about all the good memories that I had of this city. I told her what the city had looked like before the devastation, before the ghetto, when I was a child, happy and carefree. I told her about my school, and about the streets and about the songs we sang. It took my mind off the disaster and the evil, off the idea, which was becoming constantly more probable, that I might be the only one who was left of my entire family. And so, for the rest of the way, I talked about all pleasant things. All stories about the big city were new to Mira; she listened curiously.

While walking through Rynek Starego Miasta—the now damaged fourteenth-century Market Square—I told her about my memories of this place. I told her the history of the narrow, brightly colored three-story buildings that surrounded the center square, and the winding iron steps that I used to race up with my friends, from basement to rooftop. I showed her the now partly destroyed bulwarks, bastions, and barbicans where we used to play hide-and-seek. We walked through the narrow street that led to the Saint John Cathedral, and the street stretching to Plac Zamkowy—the Castle Square—where "Kolumna Króla Zygmunta" was; a gigantic pedestal on which King Sigismund III stood holding a cross and saber. This forty-meter monument was built in the sixteenth century, when the capital was moved from Kraków to Warsaw. Then I showed her the severely damaged King's Palace, which overlooked the Wisła River. We walked down the famous Krakowskie Przedmieście, where all the foreign embassies used to be. I talked to her about all the other places that were located within walking distance from where I used to live. I told her how we kids used to play on the high wall that surrounded the Old City, how we liked to look down into the streets below, watching curious tourists admiring our city; how the photographers took their pictures.

Mira then told me about her life in the small town. We kept talking until we crossed the restored bridge and got back to our shelter in Praga.

A few days later, I returned to Łódź tired and disappointed, but glad that I had gone.

I took with me a list of names that my roommates had asked me to look up while in Warsaw. Every Jewish person whom I met was looking for somebody—friends, relatives, family members. The War had been over for a few months, yet the aftermath was just beginning. The full revelation of what had happened to

My Education Continues

the Jews of Europe was slowly coming into the open. Details of camp atrocities, gas chambers, and crematories had just begun to be made public. Even those of us who had seen most of it happen still could not believe the extent of the disaster. What we thought would be a recovery period became a shocking nightmare. Our physical pains and suffering were lessening; wounds were gradually healing. But the emotional, the psychological, suffering was rapidly increasing; our morale was deteriorating. During the worst of times, hope had kept us alive; hoping and dreaming and imagining. Jews had always lived with hope and faith in God. "It is better to depend on God," they would read from a *siddur*, "than to trust mortals, than to trust the powerful." Now, day by day, hope was diminishing. There was nothing to look forward to.

Despite all the information regarding the Nuremberg Laws and Hitler's threats, despite the knowledge of Jewish history dating as far back as the Pharaohs of Egypt, Persian Hamman, the Spanish Inquisition; despite all of this, the Jews of Europe still believed that such barbarism could never happen in "Modern Times" and in a "Civilized Nation."[67] Those of us who lived through the dreadful years, saw our homes consumed by fire and our loved ones starved, the corpses in the ditches, fields, and streets, the people being shot in front of our eyes—even we could not believe the extent of this horror. How would history report this catastrophe created by men? A new question haunted many of us now: Since manmade disasters happened in ancient times, and nowadays as well, what will stop them from happening again? What a dreadful thought. Now that belief in miracles had been practically eliminated, what was there to believe in?

All of the horror stories and nightmares, which we had hoped were rumors, were actually true. And we were finding out things that we didn't even hear about in those rumors. We were angry and heartbroken. We felt betrayed by our neighbors and our friends, and by the world. We had not expected the Polish or the Ukrainian or the Lithuanian people to risk their lives or to put their families in danger in order to save Jews; such sacrifices would have been too much to expect. (Besides, we had known that anti-Semitism flourished in these places. "Jews to Palestine" was not just a slogan; it was a message.) Yet, in spite of that, Jews had expected more humane treatment from their compatriots, the Poles, especially since they themselves were being mistreated and oppressed by a common enemy: the Germans; who had started two World Wars within twenty years. What we had expected from those "Pious Christians"—as some of these people were calling themselves—was that they would close their eyes and ears to Jewish hideouts instead of reporting them to the Nazis; and not to collaborate with their own enemy. It had been almost unbelievable, given the way that those occupied peoples themselves were suffering, that they would help the Nazis find and persecute their fellow citizens.

The Polish Jews who survived the War in Russia and who were now returning with most of their families intact—even with children born there—had their own stories to tell. They were prepared to tell us—who had remained in Poland—and their own families and friends of how they had suffered from hunger, disease, cold, and filth; how their children had gotten sick during freezing Siberian winters or under the scorching heat of Central Asia, where they had been evacuated to when the Germans, releasing their malicious venom on the population (especially on the Jews), invaded the European part of Russia. They wanted to tell us about their men who were wounded

My Education Continues

and killed fighting the Germans on the frontlines. They thought that their lives in Russia had been terrible—until they started finding out what ours had been like. The Jews in Russia had heard many talks about the atrocities committed by the Nazis in the occupied territories, about burning Jews inside synagogues, about Jews being tortured and murdered after being made to dig their own graves. Yet, like the rest of us, they had either completely disregarded the rumors or else thought the stories greatly exaggerated. Now, in seeing what had happened, and finding all their relatives dead, their towns destroyed, and their synagogues burned, they began to realize that, despite all of their problems and suffering, they had been the lucky ones. (Even we, the survivors of the ghettos, labor camps, and the death marches, didn't know how lucky we were to have missed Auschwitz, Majdanek, Treblinka, or Buchenwald—all of the "famous" death camps, with their torture routines, gas chambers, and ovens—until we started seeing the results of the genocide.) Among those who had come from Russia, we saw our first Jewish children in years. I had not seen a Jewish child, or an old Jewish person, since I left Sandomierz.

As time went on, we were told about Jewish uprisings in the Vilnius and Lublin ghettos, and about the guerrilla fighting in the forests. Most of us had, of course, already heard about the Warsaw Ghetto uprising, in which a few thousand Jews had fought the mighty Germans—and how no one came to their aid.

Now the world was being shocked by the horrors of the extermination camps and stunned by the reports of the carefully, coldly planned genocide. Even knowing all that, we, the survivors of the camps, were still not ready to accept the fact that all those whom we had left behind were really dead.

Łódź and Jacob

We were no longer rationally, but rather unconsciously, waiting for the miracle of finding someone alive.

Once in a great while, it did happen. Someone would meet a brother, or a sister would be found, or an uncle, or a cousin. One time I saw a woman at the market pressing a little girl to her breast. She was telling the peasant woman who was selling beets and turnips of how the child had been hidden by a Gentile family, how those righteous Poles had saved the little girl's life. But such a thing happened very seldom. They were exceptions to the rule; they just showed that it was possible, although not very likely.

There were reunion incidents; many with sorrowful endings, but some with good endings:

At the shelter, our Salka met a young man who had just arrived from Russia. He told her that due to his war injuries, he had been in an army hospital for some time, and had been released only a few weeks before from military service. He had come to the shelter to register and look for relatives. He had found his sister's name on the list of survivors. It had been a couple of weeks since he started looking for her, and he couldn't find her, nor the person who had written her name in the registry. After a long talk with that man, Salka found out that the man's sister had been in a German labor camp. Salka brought the man over to our apartment. He was limping, his right arm was bandaged up, and a few stitches were on the right side of his face. We told him about Boris, the Russian soldier who took one of our girls to a Russian hospital, because the description of his sister matched that of Masha. We told him that we had registered Masha's name in Legnica and here in Łódź. We also told him about his cousin Hayka, who had gone back to her hometown. We didn't have her address, nor any news from Masha. A few months later we learned that he

My Education Continues

had found Hayka, and together they had gone to the Russian hospital in Germany. Masha was still there, and still very sick.

Another good ending was when Itzek, the "cousin" who had left pregnant Luba, showed up in Łódź. We met him at the shelter, looking for people from Skarżysko camp. He was trying to find Luba; he had seen her name in the Kraków registration book and, through the Red Cross, had gotten in contact with her. In Leipzig, where he had first looked for her, he heard from some people, who had been freed with Luba, that she gave birth to a live baby but never saw it. She wasn't even told the sex of the child; had just heard it cry before it was taken out of the delivery room.

Luba herself was liberated by the Americans a couple of days after we were evacuated from the camp and sent on the march. Itzek claimed that he hadn't known that she was pregnant. He said that had he known, he probably would not have made it through the camp; the worries would have killed him. He said, "I suspected something was wrong with her when we parted." Then with tears of joy and sorrow in his eyes, he added, "When I found her name I immediately made plans to go to Kraków to find her, to see if she still wanted me." Before he left he gave me his picture. "As a token of remembrance," he wrote on the back of it. We all wished him well, and good luck to Luba. We knew that he had no one else to look for. He was raised in an orphanage, and the only relative whom he knew was his grandmother. We all knew that there weren't any grandmothers left. At least he did meet a couple of boys from his orphanage who survived in various camps.

I knew of a few more reunification cases; mostly people from small towns and from large families. Some of them met a brother, a sister, or some cousins. Two out of nine children survived in one family; in another one, two out of six; later, they also found a cousin, one out of seven, who survived in Russia.

As sad as the situation seemed, nothing could be done to change it. According to the law of nature, life does not stay still, nor does it go backward. As the old say has it: "Life must be lived forward, but it can only be understood backward."

People were getting married, or marrying again. Almost every week I was being invited to a wedding or two. Courtship periods are short. Boy meets girl; they date a day or two; they go steady for a week; a few days later, they marry. (Two months is considered a long love affair.) The wedding ceremony takes place in someone's apartment. It is unpretentious, attended by a few friends. It is performed by a rabbi, or someone claiming to be one, or a student of a rabbinical school, or one whose father was a rabbi (so he claims). Often the couple doesn't even get an official piece of paper. At most, the "clergyman" gives them a homemade *ketubah* and pronounces the couple "husband and wife" in the presence of a few witnesses and God. The couple is now considered married by all their friends.

I attended such a wedding when Bella the fortuneteller, after two months of courting and living together, got married to Yoshe. Since I had attended only two Jewish weddings before the War, I had little experience in such matters.

One was when Gucia, the woman who made candy in the Warsaw Ghetto, married a widower with a bunch of kids. Her wedding was in my aunt's house. It was attended by relatives only; my aunt's relatives, that is, for Gucia didn't have any. There was a *chuppah,* which was held up by four men. A rabbi with a long white beard performed the ceremony. Gucia, the bride, encircled the groom seven times, as expected by tradition. She was crying the whole time. The rabbi

My Education Continues

said some prayers, which the groom repeated. I didn't understand a word of them, for they were all in Hebrew. The rabbi gave Gucia a piece of rolled-up paper. There was a nice reception prepared by the relatives. Then Gucia and her new husband took a *droshka* to her husband's apartment.[68]

The other wedding that I attended before the War was that of my mother's cousin, Regina, the only daughter of Uncle Sruel and Aunt Hanna. Regina's wedding was very elaborate. It was on a Tuesday—a lucky day—and held in the late evening in a specially rented ballroom with a catered dinner, orchestra, a *badchen,* and a special coach to drive the bride and groom home afterward. My little sister and I were two of four flower girls. We wore blue dresses embroidered at the bottom, dresses especially made for this occasion; we also had blue ribbons in our hair. Freda and Rena and their two older sisters, Ida and Bluma, also took part in the wedding ceremony.

I was so impressed by this wedding that I told everyone in school about it; I even wrote about it for my "Most Memorable Day" assignment. I remember going to the bride's house the day of her wedding and watching her being dressed. Her hair-stylist came to her house and, with a hot curling iron, put waves in Regina's waist-long reddish-blonde hair. During the *chuppah* ceremony, the women cried. Later, the bride and groom were escorted into a small room, where they were then left alone. The door was closed. Two men, the *shomrim,* stayed at the door so that no one would open it. I asked Mother why I couldn't go in to see what they were doing. She said that they probably were eating some *challah* and drinking wine, since they both had been fasting all day. They might even kiss. Mom also explained how this Orthodox tradition had come about. She said that according to ancient law, marriages were arranged by the parents when the children were still little. (Rachel's had not been arranged.) After they grew up, and the rabbi married them, they were put into a little room where they could for the first time be alone and officially get acquainted, touch, and kiss. It was customary that the bride and groom not see each another until that time. Even during the wedding ceremony the bride's face was covered by a veil. I asked Mom if she had made such arrangements for me. She just laughed and patted my head. When Regina and her husband returned from the small room, we all had a big dinner: fish and meat, wines, and cakes. Then the guests separated; the men went into one part of the dancehall, the women into another. Traditional dances began. Everybody danced in a circle holding hands. After that, the *badchen*, dressed in a black tuxedo that was ornamented with a heavy gold pocket-watch chained across the vest, a white shirt, and a bowtie, sang traditional songs and told jokes. The people laughed, some cried, while he talked about the bride and groom. Then he announced all the major presents given to the young couple. The audience applauded. The final part of the party was a dance in which males and females danced in pairs. The bride and groom danced together to modern music. The live orchestra played waltzes, tangos, and foxtrots; quicksteps, polkas, and the newest, the "Lambeth Walk." (Some older folks still liked the Charleston best.) Photographers took pictures of everybody. They took one of my sister and me with the bride and the groom. (I cherished that picture for many years.) The wedding lasted until the early morning hours. Most of the stores were still shuttered up when we returned home. Here and there a milk stall was being opened, and a few delivery trucks were unloading goods to grocery stores. A young bakery man walked along the still lit street, artfully balancing a tray of freshly baked doughnuts on his head.

My Education Continues

Tzitzyot, the fringe from his ritual apron, hung down from under his flour-covered coat; a dog followed him down Fraciszkanska Street. It was the first time that I had ever been on the street at such an early morning hour.

In Łódź, the weddings did not resemble either of these. The people attending the wedding ceremonies were strangers or, at best, camp acquaintances. The bride and the groom would barely know one another.

Most of the problems created by the War were still unsolved. There was an acute housing shortage. Many Jewish apartments had been taken over by Gentile families, who had been told that the Jews were being relocated, never to return. (In most cases, they never did, either.) But occasionally, a son, a daughter, a niece or nephew, who did return, would try to claim the living quarters that used to belong to his or her relatives. The situation created fights, lawsuits, and very unpleasant feelings for both the Gentiles, who had no other place to go, and the Jews, who were in the same predicament.

For those of us who were strangers in this city, the situation was even worse. Besides the housing problem, very few of us had marketable skills, and even fewer had formal education past grade school. Survivors my age hadn't even finished primary school, which ran from first through seventh grade.

It was a long time since I had thought about school. My education had continued quite well without it. But now, in writing my diary, I remembered that I had initially started recording events so that I could read them to the kids in my class. Then I remembered writing so that I could read the accounts of my camp life to my relatives. Now I was going to keep my notes. I continued to write for whoever would return, for anyone who would want to read them—for myself, so that I could remember the special events and the people I had been with; also, to gather the important occurrences that had influenced my life.

Now that I was free to do as I pleased, and didn't have to report to any authorities (not even to parents); now that no one really cared what I was doing or why I wasn't doing anything at all; now instead of taking advantage of such an ideal situation to do things that were forbidden, or even those that were permitted, I did nothing. Somehow I couldn't figure out why I wasn't being more inventive in doing something exciting. Many of my friends found themselves mates: Matched or not, they were getting married. I was just sitting there, knitting, or writing in my stupid diary, reliving the suffering all over again.

Freda, the stoker from Russia, was going about and lying with a Russian soldier. Halinka was courting a thirty-year-old tinsmith. Salka was in love with Hersh, a guy twenty years her senior, who could kiss well and who had claimed that his wife was dead. Only Hanka and I were still single and unattached. We knew that there was an acute shortage of available men. Most men were sick or wounded; those who were in good shape knew their value. My reason for not going with the flow—to find myself a man and get married, or at least live with him—was not because I had no dating offers. Actually I had quite a few; but these "Let's get married quick" or "Let's try it out first" guys turned me off. Some soldiers, Russian or Polish, did excite me; men in uniform always appeal to young girls. But I was afraid to go out with them on single dates. I didn't like any of the guys whom I met in Łódź who had been with me in camp.

Joziek, the guy from Warsaw whom I kept my eye on in Skarżysko, never showed up in Łódź. He probably forgot, or didn't even know, about my secret

My Education Continues

admiration for him. Anyway, I wasn't ready for any commitments. Marriage was not one of my priorities. Besides, I needed time to digest all the information that was being brought in daily by those returning from all corners of Europe. It was very difficult to comprehend all that had happened and still be able to plan for a future. I kept remembering the words of the young man I had met in Warsaw, in the Praga registration office: "Don't try to make sense out of it. What happened here cannot be understood in rational terms." I registered for school; I would start on September first, six years late. School seemed much more appealing.

I tried to talk about some things with Regina. We used to see each other quite often in her aunt's house. Regina was financially well off. Her aunt helped her a lot, but Regina was having a problem finding a man her aunt would approve of. Surprisingly, Regina had not changed her views about miracles. She still believed that it was a miracle that we were saved; that all was due to God's will and to His mercy. I couldn't figure out to whom she attributed the fate of those who had perished. Anyway, I began saying to her what was on my mind. We'd been together for so many years; I felt that we could talk openly. She had attended the Beth Yaakov religious school for girls, and her brother at one time had wanted to become a rabbi. I tried to see it her way, but couldn't. What had happened to us could not be justified even on her own terms, for she claimed that the Holocaust must have been God's will. To reason as she did must have come from her upbringing, because it could not have been based on her experience. Most of those who believed in God's providence had lost all their belongings, families, friends, relatives, hope, and dignity. I could never understand the reasoning behind that Job story. Yet I never tried to persuade Regina (or anyone else) to change her beliefs; I only asked to be spared her puzzling views. I liked little Regina. She was a wonderful person. I only objected to her missionary work.

Once I told her about my religious little sister who had not yet showed up from any camp. "Sis tried to obey every law she knew," I told Regina, during one of our discussions. "Not only didn't she wash with soap on the Sabbath, but she hid the soap so that no one in our house could use it. She always waited the prescribed hours between eating dairy foods after eating meat, even though Mom and Dad tried to persuade her that children need not wait as long as adults. After Grandpa's death, Sis referred all her religious questions to an Orthodox uncle who had became her trusted advisor."

Regina didn't think that it was such a big deal. "That's the way all Jews should behave."

"Let me tell you something else. Maybe you can figure this out," I said to Regina. "One night, in Sandomierz, after talking to my sister, I dreamed I was with God. He appeared in the sky. I don't remember what He told me, or if He said anything at all, but I do remember His image. He was a white male, huge and old. He was sitting amidst grayish-white clouds. He wore a white *kittel*. His silver colored beard fell almost to His knees, blending with the color of the clouds and the sky."

"How did you know about a *kittel?*" Regina interrupted.

"I heard it from one of my uncles. He said that when a person dies, he leaves all his worldly possessions on this earth. This shroud is the only thing he can take with him to the 'other world.'"

"Well," she said, "you know more than I thought."

I told her that I was glad that she thought so, and continued: "I told this dream to my sister, just to see

My Education Continues

what she thought of it, but Sis didn't know what it meant. It made no sense to her that God would want to talk to me and not to her. I told her that He didn't talk to me either, just that I saw Him."

"Well," said Regina, again trying to persuade me that God freed us from the Nazis, "God probably meant for you to be saved. It was a miracle."

I was just about to ask her why such a miracle hadn't happened to my sister, why she had had to die at such a young age. But the word "die" would not come out of my mouth. She may still be alive somewhere, I heard a voice inside me say.

I knew that it was only wishful thinking.

Besides Regina and my other friends, I also had many acquaintances. Our home was always full of visitors. Each of my girlfriends, and each of their boyfriends, brought along their friends whenever they came to socialize. Outside of a few neighbors and Freda's Russian soldier and a few of his friends, all of our guests were Jewish survivors.

Almost all survivors had one thing in common: We were all looking for our lost families and friends, or just for a familiar face. Only a few tried to avoid familiar faces: They were former *kapos*, collaborators, or thieves who were hiding from those whom they had wronged. They hardly ever showed up in shelters or came to visit. By the time I came to Łódź, many of the collaborators had already been "taken care of" by their former victims, or by groups of vigilantes who were avenging their victims. Right after the collaborators lost their ranks and authority, they became vulnerable to attacks; they were beaten and robbed of food by their former subjects. Those whose cruel looks had once struck panic in people's hearts were now fearing reprisals. As time passed, former collaborators were no longer being arbitrarily punished but taken to mediators, like rabbis, lawyers, or groups of impartial citizens, who would devise the proper punishment.

We were never sure who our new unknown visitors were; we didn't know who were the "good guys" and who were the "bad guys." As for myself, I could not believe that through thousands of years, people had not learned anything besides better ways of killing one another. Now I knew that nothing had changed in human nature, and probably never would. I began to understand why our teachers would insist on reading the ancient classics: With all our Twentieth Century technology, our human minds were still operating on primitive levels. I could clearly see the similarity between ancient tyrants and the Nazis.

Even though I could hardly accept the behavior of the Nazis and their allies, what bothered me most was the behavior of the Jewish collaborators. It was not that they had behaved worse than all the others, but because they were *Jewish*. It might have been the way of my upbringing, or my later perception or misunderstanding of it, that, somehow, now, made me believe that Jews should behave differently from other people. Jews were more sensitive, more refined; they had traditional values. They had a sense of justice, and of fairness. They were gentler.... Weren't all of these reasons why we were Jewish? I didn't expect barbaric behavior from anyone. I believed that people were good. But cruelty perpetrated by one Jew on another downright sickened me. True, it was only a small percentage of the Jews who had participated in such outrages, but somehow their conduct had a greater impact on me. Maybe I was expecting too much from Jews—more than from others. I somehow had a need to believe—however naively—that no one who called himself a Jew would steal, or kill, or betray, even to save his own life. In the end, what

My Education Continues

scared me more than anything else was this thought: "How many of these so-called Jews would have joined the Nazis had they been acceptable?"

The War was over, and Hitler was gone. Anti-Semitism, although now illegal and punishable, was still alive and doing quite well in Poland. Jews who were returning from camps were being killed by Polish hooligans. Some Polish people who had taken Jewish homes and wealth were now afraid that they'd lose everything if and when the Jews returned; consequently, they were acting very harshly toward the Jews. Each day we learned of new anti-Semitic incidents. We worried about our lives. We also worried about housing, food, jobs, and the future. We had to make decisions, something that we hadn't done for years. We not only had current problems and worries about our future; we still had to deal with the sad reality of the past. The latest statistics were estimating the number of killed and murdered European Jews at around six million. This figure not only astounded us but made it clearer why no one we were looking for was showing up among the living.

To deal with this shocking news, many survivors again turned to God for an explanation. "The murdered Jews did not die in vain," some commented. "These people went on *Kidush HaShem*. They died to sanctify God's Holy Name." Others interpreted this catastrophe as punishment for the sins that Jews had committed by not obeying all of God's laws.

Neither of these statements made sense to me. They only reminded me of a nineteenth-century Jewish fairytale that I once read:

King Solomon was trying to persuade the Queen of Sheba that God, besides performing such miracles as creating the world in six days and parting the Red Sea, was also a matchmaker. To prove his statement, King

Solomon sent a virgin maiden to a secluded island and left her there, where no one could get to her. After a while, a ship sailing by, loaded with people, encountered a tempest. The winds tossed the ship, and everyone who was on it drowned in the sea, everyone, that is, except the captain's son, who managed to get to the secluded island and find the lonely maiden.

Of course, he married her; otherwise there would have been no story. The point is that this event was "proof" to the Queen of Sheba of the omnipotent power and wisdom of the Holy One, Blessed be His Name. After reading this story, I wondered why so many innocent passengers had had to die just to prove a point.

The explanation of the European catastrophe, as explained by the pious Jews, made to me just as much sense as the story of the "Maiden in the Tree." If there was any religious motive in either of these happenings, I must have missed it. It must have been beyond my comprehension. The "Maiden" fairytale, like the explanation of the latest catastrophe, satisfied many of my friends. I was really glad that it did, for at least they had found an answer. To me, though, the murdered Jews, like all the other murdered people, were victims of a vicious madness that had swept the world. I would not say that, among the murdered people, there were no martyrs who would have sacrificed their lives to "sanctify God's Name"; there probably were many. But we will never know, for no one was even given a choice, or a chance in this matter. No one was ever asked if he or she wanted to make such a sacrifice.

Throughout the ages, Jews have been pushed and beaten, tormented, and expelled. But most of the time they were given some choices: They could leave the country, be baptized, convert, serve the king, or die. True, these were not easy choices. Those who chose to

My Education Continues

leave the country often suffered in unknown places (if they didn't die on the way). Those who converted were mourned by their Jewish families as though they were dead. But at least they had been given a choice, which was more than the Jews were given during this war.

Life after liberation was difficult and depressing but, at the same time, interesting and full of curiosity.

I think that it was at the beginning of August that Salka married Hersh and then moved in with him. Freda's soldier was still coming over. He had been promoted, and was to be transferred to a base in Russia. (He got out of the transfer through a clever maneuver.) I was waiting for school to start. Now, in Communist Poland, even higher education was free of charge, if one could pass the exams.

Jewish holidays were coming up. A few of our male friends were planning to organize a prayer group. Moshe, one of our visitors, brought a *siddur*. He had to interpret some of the prayers, for the *siddur* that he had was written in Hebrew. The book talked about the "all-merciful God, Father of Abraham, Isaac and Jacob.... God who delivered the Jews from Egypt.... God exalted by justice and sanctified by righteousness.... God, who is like you, Master of Might.... You are our King and our Help, our Savior and our Shield...."

As always at that time of year, I recalled the holidays before the War, when I used to visit Grandma Ruth in the synagogue. She would be sitting in the bordered off women's section. Most of the women would be praying and wiping their tear-filled eyes as they prayed. I also remembered the holidays in the bomb-shelter, and how the women had cried and prayed and begged God Almighty to stop the bombing as the enemy planes flew over and around the city and the streets were corridors of flames.

Lódź and Jacob

Then I thought of a time long ago, when Dad took Sis and me to an Hasidic synagogue. It was *Simchat Torah,* the last of the eight-day *Sukkoth* festival, the holiday of Rejoicing in the Torah. By the time we arrived, most of the Hasidim were already half-drunk (it was one of the two Jewish holidays during which it was permissible to be drunk; the other was *Purim*). They were quavering, singing, and stamping their boots on the floor. The boys were hopping along with the men. There were no women among the dancers, nor were there any in the assigned women's section. The girls, who were not allowed to mix with the men and boys, were standing on the benches lined up against the walls. They were watching the boys having fun.

Sis and I stood with the girls as we waved small paper pennants, which were decorated with red apples, attached to the top of the thin pennant sticks. We were glad that we could participate in the "party," because the year before, when Dad took us to the festival, Sis and I were asked to leave the synagogue since we were speaking to each other in Polish; a "behavior that did not befit Jewish kids"! I never liked to go to synagogues because I didn't think girls were treated fairly.

From my reflections on the synagogues, my thoughts traveled even farther back, all the way to my maternal grandfather, who had taught Sis and me the Hebrew alphabet. (It must have been the *siddur* that Moshe had brought that reminded me of all the Jewish things from home, even though I had never read from a *siddur* or any other Jewish book.) Grandpa told us that if we didn't want to read Hebrew, we didn't have to. "God," Grandpa said, "understands all the world's languages," which sounded impressive for anyone to know. Then he said, "We can never know when our education might come in handy." It was from Grandpa that we learned that good Jews should be gentle and

My Education Continues

just and obey God's commandments. We loved Grandpa.

Now, being older, I saw him not only as our grandfather but as a human being. His life had not been easy. His ancestors came to Poland from England and Germany, probably originally from Spain. Grandpa had a sawmill, a lumber business just like Mom's uncles,' but his was in Grochów, a suburb of Warsaw. During World War I, his business was burned by raging armies crossing Poland. His wife, my blood grandmother, died, and he lost one of his daughters to typhus.

His second wife, Grandma Ruth, was a great help to him. They owned a small workshop at home that manufactured cotton and woolen socks. They employed two girls. During the mid-Thirties, Grandpa's only son, our Uncle Mendel, took his wife, Aunt Helena, and after traveling to China and India, made their home in Palestine. Some of Grandpa's relatives lived in Germany, some in Britain. Only two of his sisters, along with their respective families, lived in Warsaw.

I looked around me and then looked at Moshe, who was still sitting with the open *siddur*, reading a holiday prayer to Hanka and Halina. I told him not to bother me, that I didn't plan to go to the prayer house anyway. Freda was planning to attend the holiday services—she knew how to read a prayer book in Hebrew. She liked to go everywhere, everywhere she could meet people.

One day Freda came from work and told us that on the way home she had stopped at the shelter to see "what was known." There she met a man, who must have been in his twenties, who was looking for people from Warsaw. She told him that all of the girls who were living with her were originally from the destroyed

Łódź and Jacob

capital, and that she knew other ones, too. She told him that he was welcome to come over and meet the girls. "I gave him our address," Freda said apologetically. "I know we don't need any more visitors here. Had he not asked for people from Warsaw, I would not have invited him."

A few days later, in the early evening, a young man came to the door and asked for Freda. She wasn't home. He showed Hanka, who had opened the door to him, a piece of paper with the address Freda had written down for him, and asked if he was in the right place.

I was sitting on one of the beds, my legs tucked under me, using a set of five knitting needles and yarn that I had from an old unraveled sweater; I was manufacturing a pair of socks. I wasn't feeling well. I was menstruating for the first time in four years, and the cramps were killing me. I paid little attention to our new guest.

I heard the girls ask the young man where he was from. He claimed to be from Warsaw. I looked up from my knitting. He was of average height, slim, and polite. He had dark hair, but didn't look Jewish. He was tidily dressed, wearing a light-colored shirt and dark, neatly pressed slacks. A pen and some papers, or photos, were peeping out of his small shirt-pocket. His black shoes were nicely polished. Hanka pointed to the other bed and told him to sit down. He took out a folded newspaper that was sticking out of his hip pocket and sat down, putting the paper on his lap.

"I heard all of you girls are from Warsaw. Where did you live?" he asked, turning to Hanka. She told him that she lived on Elektoralna Street, but when she moved into the ghetto she used to live with an aunt on Nowolipki Street.

"That's where I went to school," he said, "Nowolipki Street 68. There was a Hebrew Academy for boys that was run by the Jewish Federation."

My Education Continues

"I was only eleven when the War started," said Hanka, "but my older brother, Heniek, knew many boys in that school. I have not found Heniek yet, nor the other two brothers who were in the ghetto."

While Hanka and the visitor were talking, Freda walked into the house. "I thought you lost the address, or decided not to come," she said in greeting the young man, "but I'm glad you did come."

The three of them talked about Warsaw and what it was like before the War. Freda, who was the oldest of us, remembered more places and events than did Hanka, Halina or I, so the young man talked mostly with her. Occasionally he mentioned some names of friends and relatives and asked us if we, by any chance, had heard of them. From his knowledge of places and events in Warsaw, it was quite obvious that he was no stranger to that city. Yet the way that he spoke—Polish as well as Yiddish—did not resemble that of the local Warsaw people. His Polish was mixed with a lot of foreign words; his Yiddish was even worse. With Freda he spoke in a Polish that was mixed with broken Russian and mispronounced Ukrainian words. He said that he knew some songs in English and some phrases in French—which was very strange for a guy from middle-class Warsaw.

Maybe he was Russian or Ukrainian? He didn't look Jewish at all. We thought to acquaint him with Freda's soldier; at least he wouldn't feel strange, then. I heard Freda ask him where he came from. He said, "A couple of weeks ago, I came from Belgium to Poland. The first place I went was Warsaw. I was very disappointed. The things I saw and heard there made me sick."

"Didn't you know about anything that had happened? Where in the world have you been?" Freda asked.

"I knew a lot; more than I wanted to know. I just didn't want to believe it. I saw enough with my own eyes."

"When did you come to Łódź?" Freda asked.

"Only a few days ago. I heard that many Jewish returnees were living here, and I was told about the shelter. I hoped to find some friends or relatives."

"By the way, what's your name?" Freda asked.

"Alexander," he said, "but you can call me 'Sasha' for short." His eyes were pointed at the ceiling, as though he was saying something wrong, or telling a lie.

"What kind of a Jewish name is this?" asked Freda, and, not waiting for the answer, went to open the door for her soldier, who had just knocked.

Since coming back to Poland, we had met so many strange characters, so one more didn't really matter. We just listened to what this new guy had to say and didn't think much of it. While he was talking, Salka and Hersh came in. A few of our daily visitors showed up, too. They all talked to one another and got acquainted with our new man.

I talked with Salka about her "marital adventure." She said that they were planning to leave the country; her husband had found a cousin who was involved with a Palestine movement, and who was going to help them get to Italy.

About midnight, the conversations ended, and all our visitors, besides Freda's soldier, went home.

A few days passed before Sasha appeared again. This time he brought with him a bag of groceries, which he put on the floor near the stove. "I am hungry," he said. "Would any of you girls like to fix something to eat?" In the bag we found bread, sausages, pickles, and some sweet rolls. He invited all of us to eat with him. Our next-door neighbor, a wounded war veteran, walked in and joined the party.

My Education Continues

Later that evening, more visitors dropped in. Seeing a new person started the usual conversation: "Where are you from? How did you survive? Did you see or hear such and such?"

Everyone, of course, was curious as to how Sasha had gotten to Belgium and, even more, what had made him decide to return to Poland (since hardly anyone was coming back from the Western countries).

"I was in camp there," Sasha said. "I was freed by the Western Allies during the D-Day operation. I came back to look for my friends and relatives, of course." Then, as if to avoid any more questions, he began to inquire about each of us. He asked where we lived, how we survived, what our future goals were. As he talked, his eyes were never on the audience, only on the ceiling. As he listened, he was either picking his nose or tearing off small pieces of newspaper, folding them into tiny squares, putting them into his mouth, and chewing them like bubble gum. He wasn't sure what he wanted to do in the future, but he did know that Poland was not the place in which he wanted to spend the rest of his life.

After this day, Sasha started visiting us often. Each time he came, he would bring with him a bag of food. One evening he sang for us—in English—"It's a long way to Tipperary." Very impressive.

Another time, I found out that Sasha and I had lived not far from each other, and that his youngest sister, who was about my age, had gone to the same school that I had. I didn't know her, but I did know her teacher.

All of the things that he would tell us sounded interesting. It was nice to hear something different from the, by now, banal tales that we were hearing daily.

Here in Łódź, Sasha lived on the outskirts of town in a very impressive neighborhood. The house, which

Lódź and Jacob

had originally belonged to a high-ranking Polish lawyer, *Pan* Meccenas, was first taken over by the Germans, then by the Russians; and now the lawyer, with his family, as well as a few Polish Jews who survived in Russia, were living in it. Among those survivors was Sasha's best friend's sister, Irenka, who, with her boyfriend, took in Sasha.

One day Sasha showed up and asked me to go with him for a snack. I accepted. We had ice cream, cookies, and lemonade in a nearby coffee shop. He took me home. In the entrance hall he grabbed me, wrapped his arms around me, holding me tight to his body, and kissed me on the lips. I didn't sleep all that night from the excitement. Next day at work I daydreamed. I was looking forward to his next visit.

We started going out more often. I began to like him more than I wanted to. I wrote long entries into my diary about the weird feelings that I was having. I kept these papers wrapped up and under the bed so that no one would find them and read them. I wasn't sure what was wrong with me. I felt such terrible longings, I thought I would die. I stopped eating. The girls told me that I was in love. I denied it. I said, I thought love made people feel good. I was actually hurting inside, and crying a lot. I wanted him to be near, but I was scared of my feelings. I thought about him whenever he wasn't with me, but I didn't know how to behave or what to say whenever he was.

I used to take acacia leaf clusters and read my fortune by picking off one leaf at a time: "He loves me; he loves me not."[69] I would get very upset whenever the last leaf came up on one of the unfavorable predictions.

I knew very little about this strange man's life. He was very secretive about his home, his camps, his present, his future. I knew that he loved soccer and reading; he had told me so. I knew that he liked young

My Education Continues

girls who were somewhat plump and blonde: He was always turning his head whenever he saw one. Often I'd get jealous. I even talked about it to *Pani* Meccenasowa. She said, "Don't worry, child! When men stop looking, they are dead."

Since he never talked about his home life, I began to believe that he might be hiding something—maybe a wife in another city; or maybe he had been a *kapo* in some camp. Maybe he was ashamed of his childhood. Sometimes I had the feeling that he had a touch of paranoia when it came to talking about authority figures or Jewish persecution. He just seemed not to trust anyone. I wanted to ask Irenka about him, but decided not to. He was her friend, and I didn't think that she would betray him.

One day Irenka gave a nice party at her house. It was for a kind of unofficial engagement with Marrion (they weren't yet sure about marriage). I was invited, and I was excited about it. I exchanged clothes with Halinka so that I could have something new to wear.

At the party everyone was drinking Russian style—hundred-proof vodka out of water glasses. The women were treated gently: We were given only small glasses of the same stuff. I had never had a drink before in my life. I swallowed the first glass-full in a quaff, just as the guys would do. They were all drunk. One refilled my glass. This one I drank slowly, but after a few sips, my head started spinning. I remember everyone singing and laughing and eating and raising glasses to "good health." They drank to the country and to the people who survived, and to those who died, and to Stalin, who was credited with winning the War. They drank for and to everything that they could think of.

Then I remember crawling behind the sofa, lying on the floor, and crying. When I woke up, in my bed, next morning, Hanka told me that Teressa, one of the girls who lived with Irenka, and another girl who was at the party, had brought me home. They were the only two people who were sober that night.

I knew for sure that my big love affair with Sasha was over. I wished that I could have changed the situation, but it was too late. I couldn't explain my behavior.

To my surprise, Sasha did show up, on Saturday night. He apologized for having gotten drunk at the party. From his talk it seemed that he didn't even know what had happened to me that night. Teressa told me that he fell asleep on the sofa after I left. Sasha and I didn't talk about the event anymore. But from that day on, we would drink only soda.

One day, when the subject of names had come up, I asked him why Irenka never called him "Sasha," only "Jacob." "Jacob," he told me, "is my real name. Alexander, or 'Sasha,' as you call me, is my assumed name. The name 'Sasha' saved my life. 'Jacob' sounds so Jewish. I will have to get used to it again." After saying that, Jacob quickly changed the subject.

"Come over tomorrow, Sunday, at noon," he said. "We will go out for lunch and spend some time together."

Sunday, it was raining. I missed the streetcar, and arrived twenty minutes late. *Pani* Meccenasowa, who let me into the house, handed me a note that Jacob had left for me: "I forgot to tell you about my soccer game. I had to leave. Please come to the soccer field. I'll see you after the game." I couldn't believe that he would do something like that (even though I knew that he was one of the main players). I asked *Pani* Meccenasowa where the soccer field was. She named a street that I had never heard of before. She said that I needed to take the streetcar near her house, then transfer to another one. She added, "Are you sure you want to go there in weather like this?" She shook her

My Education Continues

head. "Foolish child; you will see him when he gets back."

I went home and promised myself never to see him again. I told myself that he wasn't worth the trouble. He hadn't even told me his real name! Yet, in reality, I was regretting that I didn't go to the soccer field as he told me to do. I thought that he'd be angry and would never come back.

But *Pani* Meccenasowa was right. After dark, Jacob showed up at our house. His clothes were soaking wet and his shoes full of mud. He must not have seen his own face, or he would have washed it with rain water before walking into the room. He was limping and holding his knee.

I made no effort to greet him. Halinka, however, warmed up some water, poured it into a wash bowl, and let him wash up. Then she put a cold water pack on his knee.

Halinka's man seemed not to be very worried about Jacob; he didn't seem to care whether Jacob was wet or dry, or hurt; he only wanted to know who had won the soccer game, what the score was, and how much money they had taken in to donate to the relief organization.

After Jacob finished washing up, the girls prepared some tea, which they then served with cube sugar and lemon. They talked about the soccer game for many hours. Jacob bragged about his heroic performance, about how he had saved the game by shooting a last-minute goal.

We didn't see each other for a few days. Then, one day while standing with Freda in front of our house, we saw Jacob walking with a friend. He put his hands on my shoulders, kissed me on my forehead, and asked me how I was doing—as though nothing had happened. We went over to the apartment where Hanka and our veteran-neighbor were having tea. We

Łódź and Jacob

talked until late into the night. The boys missed the last streetcar (intentionally or not) and had to stay overnight. The veteran-neighbor took the other man to his room, while Jacob slept on a blanket, which we had spread out on the floor. Freda's soldier had his own corner in our room.

From that day on, it seemed as though Jacob had become more serious about our relationship; yet still very touchy about his personal life. Little by little, I started unraveling parts of his life's mystery:

"I was the oldest child in our family," he told me one day. "I had two sisters and a brother. I am still looking for them, but slowly I am losing hope of finding any of them alive." He had two other brothers who died in infancy. One fell off a table while being bathed; the other one died at the age of two of some kind of childhood disease.

"Do you know, there were four of us kids, and very little money to feed us on. But my mother never stopped crying over the loss of her two baby sons. What would she be saying now?"

I knew then that he must have grown up under different conditions than I did. I told him that we were not rich; my dad had struggled to make a living. We were just average people. But to him, "average" meant something else than it did to me. He said that average Jews in Warsaw lived the way he did: nine to eleven people in a two-and-a-half-room apartment. Most families had a lot of kids. I knew that on my father's side of the family, we had some aunts, uncles, and cousins who lived like that, but most of the people I knew did not.

"Most of the years I was growing up, I was without a father," he commented once. Assuming that his father had died, I didn't pry into any more of his personal problems. By now, I figured, if he wanted me to know something, he would tell me.

My Education Continues

We talked about different subjects—about Warsaw, the War, relatives. Once, when I told him about my cousin Zygmunt getting beaten up at Warsaw University by Polish hooligans, and how his parents had had to scrape up some money to send him out of the country to finish his studies, and that Zygmunt was in Brussels when the War started, Jacob said, "In my family, we, too, had somebody out of the country. But the situation was somewhat different, and a few years earlier."

Some time later, he said: "My father was a tailor. A good, skilled tailor. The two-and-a-half room apartment we lived in was used as a tailor shop during the day; at night, we folded up the cutting tables, pushed the sewing machines aside, unfolded a couple of extra beds, and the tailor shop turned into our home. In the kitchen we cooked and bathed, ate, and did our laundry. And we kids did our homework."

"I thought your father was dead," I said.

"I didn't say he was dead. I only said I grew up without him."

More information about his family came one day after we had seen a movie, *I Want to Return Home.* It was an old Jewish movie, with Polish subtitles. It portrayed Polish Jews who had gone to America and, having encountered a rough time, now wanted to return to their homes in Poland; but they had no money for the trip or to pay off their bills with. That was when Jacob told me the story of his father.

"I told you already that my father was a skilled tailor. He was very good at this profession. He made garments from scratch, even designing his own patterns. He belonged to a tailor association. Anyway, times were hard in Poland and in all of Europe. It was at the beginning of the Thirties, during the economic crises. Competition was fierce. Dad worked days and nights to make ends meet."

Lódź and Jacob

I interrupted his sad story, saying something that I immediately realized was out of place: "Some nights your dad must have been doing something besides working on his tailoring. After all, you said he had six children in eight years, and you told me your father was only nineteen when you were born."

"You're right," Jacob said, smiling. "I just meant to say that he worked many long hours. Every year a group of tailors from the society got together and pitched in to send one or two of their members to Paris to study the latest fashions and buy new patterns. They took turns going on these trips. One time, when Dad came home from his trip to Paris, he brought home a new idea besides new patterns. 'I am going to Argentina,' he announced to Mother. 'They are looking for tailors in Buenos Aires. Tailors, I heard, make a lot of money there. In a few years I can send for all of you. Maybe that will get us out of this dead-end situation.' Well, there was little that Mom could do.

"Within a two-year period, Dad together with his brother, Haynoch, and two other tailors, and left on their venture. Dad's brother and one of the men who were bachelors got visas to the United States. The other one, who like my father was leaving behind a wife and children, went to Buenos Aires. Actually, they had wanted to go right after my father returned from Paris, but it took them two years to get their visas and to put together enough money for the ship fare. Finally, we sold some things from home, pawned a few things, including one of our sewing machines, and Father got the money for the trip."

Now Jacob was getting into a very painful period of his life. He stopped talking, then resumed, but changing the subject. We started talking about the movie, and instead of talking about his father in Argentina, we talked about the problems that Polish and Russian Jews had encountered when they arrived

My Education Continues

in the United States at the beginning of the century—the topic of the movie we had just seen.

Another time we talked about other members of his family. I found out that after his father left, Esther, one of his father's sisters, came to help them with the tailor shop. Another one of his father's sisters, Dobba, who owned a produce business, helped with fruits and vegetables. His widowed maternal grandmother, Bobbe Tova, moved in with them to help with the children. Later, two of his mother's sisters, Meriam and Khava, both single, also came to work in the tailor shop, which his mother was now operating. "Nevertheless, after my father left, the tailor shop was not the same. Mother hired a skilled tailor, but he had to be paid, and my aunts needed money to live on, too. We were no longer making garments from scratch; we were working for a company that was giving us precut fabrics to assemble and finish. Kind of like subcontracting.

"Conditions in our home became so difficult that we had to board out the hall—the 'half-room,' we called it—in order to feed nine people and pay the rent. And, as you may remember, due to the housing shortage, rent in Warsaw was very high. Even the smallest living space required large sums of money. Many small-town people ventured to the big city seeking new opportunities and adventures, creating an even greater housing problem. My father and mother, too, had come to Warsaw from small towns. They were still very young, trying to make it in the big city."

Jacob's father's relatives, I learned, lived in Radzyń, and most of his mother's relatives, besides his grandmother and her three daughters, lived in Parczew and Międzyrzec, which, like Radzyń, were small towns in Eastern Poland.

The young couple who rented the hall in Jacob's apartment, like those before them, had come from a small town to look for work and a new life in Warsaw. The "room" that they rented was furnished with an iron bed, a small table, and a kerosene lamp. A suitcase under the bed served as the wardrobe.

"With toilet facilities," Jacob jokingly explained, "there was no problem. Everyone in our household, as well as the other sixty tenants in our apartment building, used the five-stool latrine located in the courtyard. We were accustomed to standing in lines and waiting our turn—even in winter. For the younger children, we had small chamber pots that we kept in the pantry located in the staircase next to our house door."

"That sounds like the conditions in the ghetto," I said.

"Don't say that!" he said. "It wasn't really that bad. We were a happy family. Of course, we missed our father, but we kids were always busy and having fun. Most of the day, we kids were in school; after school, each of us had his or her own interests. I belonged to a social club and a sports club, and I played in the street with boys my age. I spent a lot of time playing soccer in parks and sports arenas. I had many friends and, outside of a few, they all were living in similar conditions. Oh! I forgot. I also had a lot of homework and twice weekly choir practice—I sang in the synagogue choir."

Another time we met, Jacob told me about his school. When he was nine, he was transferred from a public school and his afternoon *chaider* to the Hebrew Academy, a private school for boys, which located in another section of town. The only way that he could afford to go there was through the full scholarship that he had won; so his tuition was free. But his books and bus fare for the new private school added another burden to their already tight budget. Often, to save carfare, Jacob would take the bus one way and walk

My Education Continues

about six kilometers on his way home. Only in very bad weather did he spend the extra money for a ride back.

Jacob and I had now been "going steady" for about two months, which, under the prevailing conditions, was a very long time. I knew that his name had been Alexander, and that he had assumed the name at some time during the War, but he wouldn't tell me where he had learned his broken Russian, or why there were Ukrainian words mixed in with his Polish, or how he had forgotten his Yiddish mother-tongue.

"It's a long, complicated story," he once said when I asked. "I will tell it to you some day."

I asked no more.

Often he slept over in our apartment, on the floor. By then, I was very much in love with him; yet it was not out of love but rather my terrible curiosity, that once, when no one was home, I invited him into my bed. I was afraid that if something bad happened, and he didn't come back, I would have missed a great opportunity. I wasn't about to start any new relationship with a guy. I'd already found out how painful such love affairs could be. I, of course, did not tell him anything about my curiosity. I just let it happen.

Once, while we were waiting in a restaurant to be served, Jacob asked, "Remember when I told you about my father? Well, it was a long time before we heard from him. In his first letter, he said he was working very hard in a Buenos Aires garment factory, and that he was trying to set up his own tailor shop while working all day on the job. Father occasionally sent us money, explaining that he couldn't send any more because he had to pay back, with interest, the money he had borrowed for his new shop. As soon as his tailoring business became successful, which he hoped would be soon because the potential was good, he would be able to send us more money and eventually visas to join him there. For a few years we got letters and money. We were getting used to the lifestyle. We kids were growing, and started helping Mom around the house and with her work. My oldest sister was only a year and a half younger than I, and my brother barely two years her junior. There was eight years' difference between my baby sister and me. (She was born after the two infant brothers died.) Besides our baby sister, each person in our house had an assigned duty, even Grandma. She took an outside job cooking for students in a nearby Yeshiva school; she also helped at home with the children, washing and cooking while Mom was doing the tailoring.

"My jobs were to pull the tacks out of garments and to blow the charcoal that heated the iron. When I was thirteen or fourteen, I picked up some extra pocket money by working in a mental hospital across the street."

Jacob stopped talking for a while, ordered more tea, then asked me if I was bored with his childhood stories. Would I rather hear about his German trip? I told him to continue about his childhood.

"You have already heard about the St. John Hospital. It was the largest and best psychiatric center in the nation. To make extra money, I ran errands for the staff and for the families of the patients who had come from out of town and were strangers in the city. When I wasn't doing that, I did odd jobs—helping in a bakery, selling newspapers, cleaning stores. My oldest sister was a tailor apprentice at a union-run tailor shop, a job she did after school.

"As I've already said, we had been getting letters and money from my father, but all of a sudden he stopped writing. We had not heard from him for a long

My Education Continues

time. We thought that he was very busy. Then we thought maybe he had gotten rich, or had found himself a rich wife—not a very unusual occurrence at this time and under those circumstances. By then, he had been gone from home for about four years. Then one day, a telegram arrived from Argentina saying, 'I am coming home. I will be in Warsaw in two months.' A letter followed explaining that Father was sick.

"He had terrible asthma, some kind of lung ailment, and all kinds of allergies. On his doctor's advice, he was returning home."

Jacob wiped the perspiration from his forehead. He was always very emotional whenever he talked about his father. But since he was already talking now, he continued his story:

"I remember the day my father came home. He was wearing a light-colored suit and a straw hat. He was slim and pale. He brought presents for all of us kids, and was astonished at how much we had grown.

"He also brought some jewelry for Mother, and a gold watch for himself. He had some money with him, too, and a few gold pieces." Jacob's face grew sadder. "This happiness didn't last long. Dad's illness got progressively worse. He developed lung problems, and was too weak to work. He was in and out of the hospital. Finally, he had to leave Warsaw and go to a treatment center in Otwock."

I told Jacob that I knew about Otwock: My dad used to sing there in his rabbi's choir, and my maternal grandmother was buried there. I also told him how after escaping from the ghetto, we stopped in Otwock, and then took a boat from there. By now Jacob knew most of my stories, but not how we had escaped the ghetto. He listened attentively before continuing with his own story.

"We started pawning all the things Father had brought from Argentina in order to pay his doctors' bills and his medications. A year and a half before the War, Father died."

After that, we didn't talk about Jacob's childhood for quite some time. It was painful. We were still looking for our relatives, hoping someday that someone would show up.

The only people Jacob had met so far were Irenka and a girl named Riva, a friend of his from Warsaw, who told him that she had worked with his big sister in the ghetto, in a German-run workshop. This gave Jacob new hope that his sister might still be alive. Riva also told Jacob about a couple of their common friends who, she thought, might be alive and living in one of the transit camps in Germany. Many Jews were living temporarily in these camps while they waited for countries to give them a permanent home. There was still no room for Jews in Poland: They were not welcome.

Meanwhile, we were still in Łódź, and with no specific plans. Jacob was going to a lot of soccer games. He played on a Jewish team that the boys had organized. If they weren't playing, they were training. I didn't want to spend my time on muddy fields watching guys kick a ball. I didn't understand much about the game, and I didn't care to learn. I couldn't care less whether the ball got into the goal net or next to it, or who had kicked it in.

I had a few other guys who wanted to go out with me; some offers even came from Jacob's own "friends." But I wasn't interested. There were a couple of guys I might have been interested in, but these never asked me.

Once, Jacob told me that he wanted to go out of the country, for there was no future in Poland for Jewish men. He might even be drafted if he stayed. The draft age had been extended because so many young men had been killed or wounded; also, many

My Education Continues

soldiers had had to be released because they had already served too long. Anyway, Jacob asked me if I'd go with him if he could make the proper arrangements to go to Germany. I asked him what he planned to do there. He said that he wasn't sure. If he were to get a *Zuzug Erlaubnisschein,* an immigration permit, he might even find a job. But all of this had to be "arranged." It didn't sound like a very promising future. But I always had in me an *esprit d'aventure*: I needed to move around. No money, no clothes. But I still liked adventures. Again, it was more curiosity and anticipation of adventure than calculated logic, that made me say, "Yes."

"I'll go," I said, adding, half seriously, half jokingly, "but if you want us to stay together you'll have to choose between your stupid soccer and me."

We had a long argument. He couldn't see any connection between the two. "I can see myself choosing between soccer and basketball; you can also make me choose between you and another girl. But what in the world is the relationship between a soccer ball and you? How are these two connected?" For a while he tried to reason with me. Finally, and hesitantly, he said, "If you make me choose, I'll probably choose soccer."

I was very hurt that a stupid ball was more important to him than our relationship. He must have seen the disappointment in my face because he pressed me to his chest and said, "I am sorry, dear, but why did you have to put me in such a predicament? You know a ball is a ball, and a girl is an altogether different matter."

I didn't know whether he was right or wrong, but at least, I figured, he was being honest.

A few days after that, he started talking about his life in Belgium. He liked to talk about that.

Lódź and Jacob

"While the War was still raging in Europe, I was free and living in Brussels. I was with a group of Russians, Ukrainians, Czechoslovakians, Yugoslavians, and other foreign laborers and freed prisoners. We were young and free and having a ball. We were taking advantage of every minute; we celebrated our freedom day and night.

"Our liberators, the Americans, the British, and the French, provided us with housing, food, and clothing. As for the girls, we had to take care of that ourselves. Most of the guys were still sick and weak and poor, looking a lot like dug-up corpses. But our looks and financial status seemed not to matter a lot. As soon as we settled in a housing project, groups of girls—some local, others freed prisoners—started coming over and taking care of us." He smiled.

I had already learned about the law of supply and demand. It was this law that made the girls do it. The male-female ratio in our age bracket was, to say the least, lopsided; men not yet dead were either sick, crippled, wounded, or, at that time, still on the frontlines, or in German prisons. So I was not surprised to hear his adventure stories.

During another one of our discussions, Jacob told me that after recovering from hunger, sickness, and wounds, most of the former prisoners tried to join the Allied Forces that were then fighting on German territory. "We wanted to help bring this terrible war to an end—and maybe even take some revenge. Many people were still being killed. Dead and wounded were still being brought in from the front every day. We really felt bad about it. We felt like doing something. But, before any of us felt well enough to be trained, the War ended, without our help. I'll never forget that May day when the War was finally over. All of the Nazi victims, all of our liberators, and the whole local population, celebrated together that victory day, the

My Education Continues

day the Nazis were finally defeated." Jacob talked enthusiastically about that great day; he could hardly stop. "I remember that day as if it were yesterday. The streets were filled with people. The victorious soldiers were lifted and thrown into the air. There were sighs and songs, cheers and tears. Tears of sorrow and tears of joy. Everyone was cheering the end of the six-year war that had brought so much misery and death. People were celebrating the end of the miserable past and the hope for a better future. Even the German POWs were relieved that the War had ended, even though they had lost it. When the celebrations were over, people started thinking about the future. Most European countries were destroyed. Although the exact numbers of dead were not yet known, judging from the corpses and the events we had seen, we figured that the numbers must be staggering, that millions of people must have been killed. Everyone was curious about how many of his loved ones were among the casualties. But this day, we celebrated and were merry."

On a later day, Jacob told me: "After we were freed, and the celebrations ended, most of the people I knew were anxious to go to their hometowns. Hardly anyone thought of staying here in the West, even though some of us could have registered to go to the USA. Americans were quite generous with visas for those who could prove that they had no place to go, or that they had relatives there.

"For a while, I thought of taking this opportunity and maybe find my uncle who, according to letters we had been receiving before the War, was still living somewhere in New York with a wife and a son. But I had some doubts. I couldn't make myself just take off. I still remembered the painful feeling when my father left for Argentina. I wanted to go back to my home to see my family, relatives, and friends; to mourn those

Łódź and Jacob

who had died, and to celebrate the victory with those who survived."

One day he told me how he got from Belgium back to Poland.

"It was in June," he said, "that the Allies announced a registration day for the people from Eastern European countries. Some hesitated to sign up because of rumors that returning prisoners were being treated badly by the Soviets. But the Western Allies did not believe these weird rumors, and they encouraged all those who were still undecided (because they believed the rumors might be true), to return to their respective homelands.

"A few days later, a large group of men and women of multinational backgrounds boarded trucks and buses that then took us, loaded with our newly acquired goods, to the place where the Western Allies and the Soviets had a common border—the place where East and West met.

"Among the returnees were young men and women from every country east of the Elbe that had been occupied by the Germans. I was next to a group of Russians who had been with me in camp. I tried to stay with the people I knew.

"We all said 'goodbye' to Western soil and crossed the border. On the eastern side of the dividing line we were greeted by Russian border guards with the following words: 'You damn traitors, where the hell were you when we were fighting the German beasts? You stinking bastards, you were hiding and deserting. And you,' the guards said, turning to the girls. 'You young whores, what were you doing when we were fighting and dying?' The guards were especially mean to the group of Russians, many of whom told them that they had been POWs. Then the Russian guards looked over our luggage, took whatever looked good to them, and after the looting,

My Education Continues

pushed us all into a field, where we were to wait for further instructions.

"There we heard rumors—or maybe the truth, for by now we believed even the most bizarre tales—that the Russian returnees, on coming back home, were being sent to prisons, or even to Siberian hard-labor camps. As I've already said, we were not sure whether it was so or not, but it was too late for any of us to change our minds. I just stood there and listened to these tales. I didn't hear anything about Poland. Then, all of a sudden, I remembered that on my ID I was still 'Alexander,' a Ukrainian name. I don't know why I had not changed my name right after liberation. I still don't know why I didn't reveal my identity. Maybe in the excitement I just forgot? No, that wasn't it. It must have been that the fear of being Jewish had not yet left me. Or maybe I hadn't wanted to disappoint my camp friends. They all knew I was a Westerner; I couldn't even speak their language well, but they didn't know I was a Jew.

"Anyway, it took quick thinking on my part—a skill I learned during the years in camp—to figure out what to do. When the officials asked us to register, I went over to a Russian guard and told him, in Polish and through an interpreter, that I was here by mistake. Which I actually was. I said that I was Polish, and had lost my Polish group, and that I had no ID. The guard asked me in Russian where I had lived in Poland. I said I didn't understand the Russian language. After consulting one of his colleagues, he sent me over to a group of Polish returnees.

"On the train to Poland, most passengers were Poles returning to their homeland. But there were also a few who had already been in German-free Poland, and were now traveling through occupied Germany. From them I heard in more detail of what had happened to the Jews in the German-occupied

Łódź and Jacob

territories. I began to believe that all my suspicions about the Jewish tragedy had been realized. I heard some passengers making sarcastic, derogatory jokes about Jews. I began to realize that my decision to go back to Poland was just as wrong as that of the Russians who were returning to their homeland. On the other hand, I could not imagine myself not going home before venturing out into the world. I could hardly wait to see some of my friends and relatives and tell them all my stories—even though I knew that I was now hoping against all odds that they were still alive."

I knew that I really wanted to be close to Jacob, but I still had that dilemma—"to go or not to go" with him into the world. So, before making my final decision, I talked to *Pani* Meccenasowa. I told her that I was confused, that Jacob was planning to move from Łódź, and he wanted me to go with him. I only knew that I loved him, but I still wasn't sure if going away with him into strange places was a wise idea. To be truthful, I knew that it was wrong. I just wanted *Pani* Meccenasowa to tell me that it was right. I always knew whenever I was doing something wrong, and I wasn't consulting her now for her wisdom. I was waiting for her consent.

She said that it was very good of me to take such things under consideration, and not to make such important decisions at the spur of the moment. She also said how much she appreciated my trust in her, and my praising of her wisdom. But she told me that if I didn't want to be sorry, I needed to find out more about the strange guy and his past before I made any decision.

Her advice made a lot of sense. I really already knew what I should do. But I did want to go.

After a lot of thinking, I figured that I would go. If things didn't work out, I could always stay in one of

My Education Continues

the DP (displaced person) camps. If Jacob would only wait until the end of December so that I could finish my course and get my grade school certificate, I would go on that adventure trip with him. I knew that by going to Germany, I would have to start many things from the very beginning. I would have to learn a new language, new customs, find a job, save some money. I asked Jacob if he would wait. He said that it all depended on the circumstances. We would have to go whenever conditions were favorable, not when school was out.

I was almost sure that I was going to go with him, but his obsession with soccer and his yet unrevealed war experience were driving me crazy. I already knew what his stand on soccer was; all I needed to know now were details about his mysterious past. On the other hand, what I didn't know didn't hurt me: "What if he reveals that he has left a wife somewhere? Would I want to live with the constant worry of his wife's reappearance, especially after I have heard of just such a scenario?" It was puzzling to me, how after all these years of being alone, I was so scared to lose a guy that I hardly knew. I could have asked him directly about his past, but I was afraid of the answers. I was depending on him for love, for moral support, for companionship.

The girls who lived with me were becoming less dependent on one another. Even Hanka now had a boyfriend. I was getting so used to Jacob that I even started buying clothes, since he wanted me to be well-dressed. I saved up enough money to buy a jacket at the flea market. Jacob bought me my first pair of high-heel shoes. I had a whole new wardrobe. It was already more than I needed or wanted. I hated the shoes. For many years my feet had been used to wooden, or oversized, shoes. Jacob amused himself by watching me try to balance my body on the high heels.

Łódź and Jacob

For real entertainment, however, he used to take me to movies, and occasionally, to the theater. The only movies that I'd seen before I met Jacob were children's shows, matinees, Shirley Temple movies, Disney cartoons in translation, or educational shows to which we often went for school. I had also been to some musicals, and to some stage performances and plays that were very popular with us kids. I had seen only one real opera and one operetta, both Polish productions.

Jacob spent a lot of his spare time in movie theaters. When he wasn't in his club playing pool, cards, or soccer, he was at the movies. He had friends working as ushers, ticket checkers, and cashiers, who would often trade show tickets for other favors or material things. Sometimes they would give their friends special sale prices. In Łódź, tickets for theater performances and sports events were relatively cheap. The performing arts and sports were being subsidized by the socialist government. We could afford to go to plays and movies quite often, even though the choices of movies were not great. They were mostly old, pre-War movies—still all new to me—or foreign movies with subtitles. Almost all new ones were war movies.

Theater productions were usually very good. It really didn't matter how good or bad they were; we appreciated anything, especially during the cold weather, when the trees in the parks were bare. We were happy just to be together, out of the house.

It was at one of our theater evenings that Jacob started talking about camp life and his time in captivity. We had gone to see a very popular dance group performing Polish folkdances. During intermission we saw two young men walking in the hall. Jacob kept looking at one of them, thinking that he had spotted a familiar face. We stopped. Not being

My Education Continues

able to recall where he had seen this man before, Jacob walked over to him. The two looked at each other strangely, as though each were trying to figure out from where he knew the other. Then, without saying a word they fell in each other's arms.

"Jacob!" the man finally said, almost choking on his words. "Jacob! I can't believe it's you. I hardly recognized you; you're all dressed up and clean shaven!"

"Stephan!" said Jacob. "I didn't believe I'd ever see you again." Stephan was about Jacob's age, maybe a little older. He was tall, with straight, ash-blond hair, blue eyes, and a pointed nose. He wore a gray striped suit and a white shirt that was almost covered by a wide red and black tie. The two men were holding each other by the arms and looking into each other's face, tears filling both men's eyes. The lights in the hall started flickering, announcing the beginning of the final act.

Bolek, the man who was with Stephan, walked over to me and asked what was going on between the two guys. I said I didn't know. I heard Jacob say to Stephan, "See you after the show. Be right here!"

The usher showed us the way back to our seats. Before the lights went down, I saw Jacob wiping his eyes and the perspiration from his forehead.

"We were in camp together," said Jacob, still shaking from the incident.

After the show, all four of us went to a coffee shop. Stephan and Jacob talked about what happened to them after their liberation, after the last time they had seen each another.

"Stephan was a translator, a guy with special privileges. He spoke very good German, and a flawless Polish. He knew some Ukrainian and Russian as well. When the War broke out he was studying something; a very well educated guy. Lwów, in Galicia, was his hometown. In 1939, after the Germans and the Russians divided Poland, his city fell to the Russians.

"You see," Jacob told me, "tonight we officially told each other that we are Jewish. We had kind of suspected it all along, but we didn't dare say a word before. We were the only Jews in that camp of a few hundred prisoners. If there were any others among us, which could have been possible, but not very probable, we didn't know them.

"No one knew about us, either, but back then I suspected that he was Jewish. In the theater he told me that he had suspected I was, too. He knew I wasn't one of the crowd in the camp, surely not one of the Russians or Ukrainians. He said that he thought to ask me, but decided not to. It would have been too dangerous for both of us to carry such secrets, or to hang around close to each other."

Now that Jacob had told me that, I wanted to know how two Jewish boys had gotten into such a mess, how they could have survived with a group of such anti-Semites as the Russians, Ukrainians, and Poles.

"In 1939, before the War started, I was in Warsaw. My Selective Service number had not yet been called to active duty. I was expecting a draft notice at any time. In the meantime, the War broke out. I was assigned to the OPL. My duties were to take care of the bomb-shelters and the firefighting equipment, and to sound the fire alarm, to aid the old, sick, and the wounded, and to pick up the dead.

"When casualties began to mount during the bombing of Warsaw, I was assigned to help with the evacuation of the St. John Hospital—when the mentally ill were moved to the city of Pruszkov, to a hospital outside of town. St. John was to be used as a field hospital for wounded Polish soldiers.

"I was lucky: Our street did not suffer any severe damage from the bombing. The worst destruction was

My Education Continues

in the Jewish section, and we lived in a mixed neighborhood—Gentiles and Jews together.

"When the bombing subsided, I was busy, too. Besides taking care of my assignments, I was organizing food and fuel for our family. With my friends, we were running through the blazing streets to find some nourishment. When the pawnshop on Fraciszkanska Street caught on fire, I ran there to see if I could find some of our pawned valuables.

"Another time, after a bombing, a group of young boys looted the still smoldering grain elevators and rice warehouses in Praga, across the river. When the Germans occupied Warsaw, I did a lot of odd jobs to help the family. My brother and sister helped, too. Our tailor shop had to liquidate. The Yeshiva, where Grandma worked, closed up. Mom's sister, Meriam, who was married two years earlier and had moved out of our house, had to move back in with us. She had a baby girl. Her husband was drafted by the Poles and had been sent to the Russian Front. Day and night Aunt Meriam cried, and so did her baby.

"We kids had been helping to sustain the whole family. Among my odd jobs was substituting for Jews who were being assigned to forced labor by the Germans.

"Every day, the appointed Jewish council had to deliver a certain number of Jews to clear the streets of dirt and debris, and to make public buildings ready for German occupancy. The German guards who supervised the work tormented the workers, especially the older ones, who could not keep up with their demands. It made me sick to watch young soldiers punching old men with rifle butts, or making them crawl on the ground. Some guards made the Jews lick German boots, just to amuse themselves. After fulfilling these sadistic demands, the Jews were still beaten and kicked. I watched a few Jews be shot, two of them fatally.

"Often we, the other workers, couldn't even look away, for the executioners made a show of it, and they made us look. This was done to civilians, to old, unarmed people, who hadn't even opposed the orders of their supervisors. Those who were called to these jobs, especially the older ones—there was no age discrimination when it came to hard labor for the Jews—were scared. Those who could afford to pay, hired substitutes. It was hard work under dangerous conditions, but I was making good money. After a while the situation worsened. There were many roundups in which people were taken off the streets and transported to forced labor brigades."

When Jacob finished talking, I said that I remembered these roundups quite well, because my father had been caught in one of them. I told him the story of my father.

A few days later, Jacob talked again about his life in the Warsaw Ghetto.

"One day, I was caught in a roundup, and taken to work at Zamek Królewski. There I was beaten; my nose was broken with a club. After a whole day's work, I was released. I went home still bleeding, with my face swollen. I started avoiding the German occupiers. To substitute for other people wasn't worth the money; the job had become too dangerous. I had to quit. Just walking in the streets was putting me into jeopardy. To top that, Jews were now being required to wear identification armbands, and they had to move out of various outlying neighborhoods. Many people, especially young men, started fleeing the city. I, too, thought of running away, since many of my friends were doing so. But I kept reconsidering because of my family. We wanted to be together, and I knew they depended on me for help. So I stayed.

"A few months passed, and the condition in Warsaw became almost intolerable. The family began

My Education Continues

to worry. Young men were being rounded up in the streets and sent away to hard labor out of town, their whereabouts unknown for days or weeks.

"My Aunt Meriam hadn't heard from her husband, Shmuel, since he was drafted. He wasn't on the list of fallen soldiers, nor was he listed as a prisoner. She heard from some people who came back from the East that he was seen near his hometown, Ludmo, which was located in the Polish territories now occupied by the Russians.

"Around the same time, a couple of my friends were leaving for Russia, and when they asked me to join them, I started thinking about it seriously. I still had that dilemma: I felt that nothing good could come out of my staying with the Germans, but I could not get myself to leave the family and go away.

"We held a family meeting, and we decided that it would be a good idea for me to go with my friends. First of all, I needed to get away from the Germans; then, if I could go through Ludmo, I might find out the whereabouts of Uncle Shmuel. Maybe I could contact some of his relatives. If I went through Ludmo, I might even get some useful tips and help from the people in his town.

"One nice day I stuffed all my material possessions into one small suitcase. Mother sewed some money into my outer garment. With Shlomo and Aron, I took off on the journey."

Now I began to understand many of the things that I had not been able to figure out before: I never knew why Jacob was always interested in people who lived in Warsaw during the ghetto uprising, or in what had gone on during the 1944 revolt; or in the crossing points through which people had smuggled food. Or in ghetto politics. His whole family was there when he left, and thus far he had not found any of them. His conscience was bothering him. He thought that he should have stayed with them after all.

I tried to explain that he could not have done anything to save them even if he had stayed. The only thing that would have happened: he would have perished together with them. I also told him that I was the wrong person to ask about ghetto politics since I understood very little of it; I was only familiar with some very general information. But I did answer his other questions. About the ghetto uprising and its liquidation, I said that I knew nothing firsthand. What I knew about the ghetto liquidation, I had heard from the KL people at Skarżysko; and what I knew about the 1944 revolt, I had heard from the girls in Leipzig.

Jacob said that, by now, he had heard more than he really wanted to know about the fates of our people and of his own family and relatives. He still refused to believe that no one in his family had survived—not his brother, not his sister, not even one of his cousins.

"When I returned to Poland from Belgium a few months ago," he said one day as we were walking through a park, "like most other returnees, I first looked through the registry. Then I went looking for my former home. I walked in the middle of the street because there was still the danger of chunks of debris crashing down on my head. The house I used to live in was right on the border of the Aryan section, where the ghetto wall ended. Surprisingly, the house was still there. It was pockmarked from shells, the plaster was cracked and falling; part of the building was completely ruined; but the few apartments that were still holding up were occupied.

"It was already long after the 1944 Warsaw revolt, but the smell of fire, dead bodies, and carbonized house rats still hung over the city.

My Education Continues

"I knocked on the door of our caretaker's apartment. His wife, a woman in her mid-forties, opened the door. She had aged ten years since I last saw her, four and a half years before. She looked at my face and froze in place as though she wasn't sure whether to scream or shut the door. For a moment I thought she was going to faint—that's how white her face got. Then, with her body still trembling from the shock, and her voice shaking as though she had seen a ghost, she whispered, 'Mr. Jacob! You are still alive?'

"I could have choked her the minute she said it, but I held myself back. I let her come to, and when she sat down on the chair near the door, I calmly asked her what she remembered about the Jews who used to live in our building.

"'All the Jews from this building,' she said, 'were still living here when the ghetto was being established, but they moved out before it was closed up. I haven't seen any of them come back yet, Holy Mary!' She then screamed out, 'How have you survived this hell?'

"She then told me how one day, Jewish police, supervised by German gendarmes, came to clear the building of Jews. Our street was one of the last ones to be evacuated since it had not been confirmed at that point whether it would be inside or outside the ghetto. Taking a deep breath, she said, 'Had the street been in the ghetto, I would have been the one who would have had to move.'

"She remembered that the police and Ukrainian guards had stormed Jewish apartments. They grabbed the old and disabled, dragged them out of their homes, and threw them down flights of stairs. 'I think it was because they couldn't run fast enough,' the caretaker woman said. She also said that all old people, including my grandma, were treated the same way. She told me how the other Jews, young and old alike, and the children, were hurried out of the building.

Łódź and Jacob

"I have no idea what happened to them after that. You know, Mr. Jacob, we had our own troubles.'

"I asked her if she knew anything about my sister and my brother. She said that the only thing she remembered was all the Jews running in a panic.

"I went back to my shelter in Praga. There was no one I knew on either side of the Wisła River."

Jacob stopped talking for a while. Then:

"Before I left Warsaw to set out on my journey, I had family, relatives, and friends totaling over two hundred people—people I knew by name. People I visited, played with, celebrated with, and cried with. Now no one was left. Outside of my dad, who died of natural causes, and two uncles who left Poland way before the War started—one to the USA, the other to Palestine—all were killed, deliberately."

It was hard to avoid such discussions. The streets were full of crippled soldiers and civilians. There were people on crutches, in wheel-chairs, with eye-patches or white canes, mutilated faces, tattooed forearms—branded by the Nazis—and many with missing limbs. And, of course, there were those with the invisible scars and pains.

Every public event—a play, a ballgame, a lecture, a movie—would start with a minute of silence or a prayer for the war dead. There was hardly a family in all of Poland—perhaps in all of Europe—that had not lost at least one member to this hideous war. With Jews, there were very few families in which someone had survived. I knew about Jacob's paternal relatives. They had owned a bakery and a house in Radzyń. Jacob liked to talk about the trip that he once took with his father to see his grandfather, aunts, uncles, and cousins. It was shortly before Jacob's father left for Argentina that he bade farewell to them. Jacob still remembered his Radzyń relatives, and talked about them with great respect. Besides those in Radzyń,

My Education Continues

Jacob also had relatives in Międzyrzec, Parczew, and in Warsaw.

What happened to Jacob on his trip to Ludmo, I found out while he and his recently found prison-mate, Stephan, reminisced about their camp experiences.

Stephan spent over three years with Jacob in German camps. His city, Lwów, was taken over by the Soviets in the 1939 division of Poland. Shortages of all necessities, as well as the influx of refugees from German-occupied territories, made life in that city miserable. To ease overcrowding, the Soviet government started offering "special opportunities"—food and money—for those who would voluntarily sign up for work in central Russia (where the labor shortage was most acute). Stephan was among the thousands of people who registered. As promised, all of them received food, some rubles, and, in addition, a copy of Marx's *Communist Manifesto,* as well as the "Communist Constitution." Then Stephan, with a trainload of other "volunteers," was shipped to a remote village in central Siberia, a place where only one train would pass each week, on a single track.

When they arrived at the place, they found—surprisingly—that other Polish Jews were already living there. It was so cold that spit would freeze in the air before it hit the ground. Local kids played a game called "spit and catch." In this remote hamlet, Stephan and many other refugee men were put to work with local lumberjacks cutting down trees and hauling them to the frozen river to float once the thaw came. In spring, accompanied by some friends, and armed with the "Communist Constitution," which guaranteed all citizens "freedom of movement," he left the village and headed south. After traveling for days on crowded trains, through forests and mountains and strange cities, they arrived in the Ukraine. There, Stephan lived in a boarding house and worked at odd jobs.

Lódź and Jacob

Meanwhile, the German front was progressing deeper into Russia. Stephan was drafted, sent to the Front, and then, along with thousands of other soldiers, was taken prisoner. For days the POWs were kept in deep ditches without food or water or facilities. Those who survived the ordeal were taken to a field circled with barbed wire, where they were kept with thousands of other POWs and captured civilians from German-occupied territories.

When Stephan described that field, Jacob knew that it was the same place where he, too, had been kept.

Jacob's adventures began once he and his two friends departed Warsaw. They were headed east for the Bug River, where in 1939, after the division of Poland, the Germans and the Russians established their common border. When the three travelers started out, they found that all main roads leading eastward were full of German troops, military vehicles, and tanks. For days, the men wandered through side roads and fields until they finally stopped in a village near Włodawa, a few kilometers from the river. There they were going to make arrangements with the local boatmen for an illegal border crossing. During the time it took them to wait for their turn to cross, they met a few people who, after a disappointing trip to the Russian side, were going back to their homes in the West, mostly to Poland.

They depicted the territory occupied by the Russians in the same bleak way that the Blind Man had once described it in Warsaw long ago. They said that besides the poor physical conditions that they found there, they were also very disappointed by the "New Progressive System," in which everything was the exact opposite of what they had imagined. What they found was a shattered economy, poverty, and a lack of basic human rights.

My Education Continues

Jacob and his friends were sure that no matter how bad conditions were in Russian territories, they could not be worse than those under German occupation. In any case, neither Jacob nor his friends considered returning home, or even remaining in German territory. "After all," they reasoned, "we are not running to the Russians; we are running from the Germans. At least in Russia, Jews are not referred to as *Untermenschen*, nor are they treated differently from all others. If there is anti-Semitism or ethnic discrimination, it is not being officially promoted by the government."

So, full of anticipation and curiosity, Jacob and his friends waited their turn to cross the river. It was to take a few more days.

But things did not work out according to their plan.

On a nice summer day at dawn, while everyone was still asleep, German troops entered the village. With tanks and gear, and at full speed, they were heading for the Russian border. Before the sun rose on the horizon, roaring planes were flying overhead. German soldiers roamed the city, rounding up all able-bodied males—including refugees, natives, and boatmen, Jews and Poles alike—and ordering them to assemble in the town square. From there all those assembled were, without personal belongings or farewells, taken away by the troops, who kept moving in the eastward direction.

During all the commotion, Jacob got separated from Shlomo and Aron. The thirty-odd men who were abducted from the village were later combined with men from other places, thereby comprising a group of a couple of hundred captives, who were then forced to follow the German troops. From that day forward, and until his liberation, Jacob was a prisoner.

The Germans, who would round up young males wherever their troops passed, dragged their captives along, force them to repair roads and railroad tracks, take care of vehicles, unload freight trains, and do other miscellaneous jobs. Most of the work was hard, but some of it was dangerous. Once, being forced to weld rods without protective goggles, Jacob was blinded. For three days, he couldn't even see daylight. He was lucky that he wasn't shot for not doing his work. At night, for "safekeeping," the Germans kept their captives in strictly guarded fields, ravines, ditches, and trenches.

"It was in one of those trenches that I learned to eat paper," Jacob said. "For a few days I nourished myself on pieces of paper that I found in my pocket. I never knew how valuable paper could be. But after a few days in that trench without food or water, not only did the paper taste good and ease my hunger pangs, but the chewing calmed my nerves. I even shared some of the paper with a couple of guys who were next to me.

"After a few days came a new work assignment. We were taken from the trench, given some food, and taken by trucks to the work location. The following night we were put out to sleep in a large fenced-in field."

Jacob was sure that it was the same field that Stephan had been talking about.

"It was already dark when our group arrived in this large field," Jacob said. "It wasn't until dawn that I saw the endless stretch of barbed wire, and the hundreds, maybe thousands, of people asleep on the ground.

"When the sun came out, all were awakened, organized into groups, and counted. Our group assembled for counting farther down the field. From my corner I noticed that some of the captives were wearing military clothes, suggesting they might have been POWs.

My Education Continues

"Usually, after the count, our group was 'sorted'— all able-bodied men were taken out to work; the sick and weak were left behind. This was our daily routine, no matter where we worked, or where we stayed for the night.

"But this one morning, after the count, we were told to remain standing. All other captives assembled in that field received the same instructions.

"Then, through Czech, Polish, Russian, and Ukrainian interpreters, the German *Kommandant* announced that he was going to make this field *Judenrein*, and he ordered all Jews to come forward and assemble at the right. I was trying to get through to the Jewish side, but the mass of prisoners held me back. When I pushed my way a little farther to the front, I saw Jewish men who had obeyed the order being beaten with rifle butts, struck with whips, and kicked with spiked boots.

"I wasn't sure what to do. I remembered the German gangsters from Warsaw. I had seen them torturing Jews. I knew it would be bad for me to go forward, but I figured it might be worse if I didn't. What if they catch me? I was confused.

"I decided to go.

"By the time I got to the front of the crowd, I saw a scene that made me change my decision.

"'You stinking *Schweine*! You dirty Jews! Why don't you follow orders!' I heard a German guard yell at confused Armenians and Georgians. One black-haired Pole from my group, who had no idea what was going on, was taken by his neck, knocked to the ground, and clubbed until he bled.

"My heart stopped. I made up my mind that I was not going. I was not a Jew. I pushed my way to the back of the crowd. When the final call for Jews came, I didn't answer.

"The next call was directed to the group of POWs. The Germans were still asking for Jews, then for all high-ranking officers, then for all Communist party members, to come forward."

Jacob said that after all the "undesirables" were taken out of the field and driven away in trucks, German officers started processing the remaining prisoners. Eventually, the POWs and civilian captives were divided into smaller groups, and then sent out to different camps throughout Germany and the occupied lands.

"While my group was being processed for departure," Jacob said, "I told them that my name was 'Alexander'—a name I had heard a few minutes before. I thought that it would be easier to remember. To the prisoners around me, I said, 'You can call me "Sasha"' (which is a diminutive of 'Alexander')."

His group was loaded into freight trains and sent to Germany. They were then taken to a camp that was a subdivision of the Buchenwald concentration camp. There the captives were processed and put into barracks. A few days later, representatives from the railroad and roadway industries, and the nearby plants and farms, came into the camp looking for workers. They were looking for interpreters, electricians, car mechanics, and railroad and farm workers. Jacob was none of these, but he applied as a railroad worker anyway, figuring that the few skills he had learned in captivity might help him. He, like all the other prisoners, was trying to get out of the main camp, in which conditions were gruesome.

Jacob was among those who were chosen. The group that was picked was divided into so-called *Arbeitskommandos*, or work brigades, and put to work in plants and on farms, railroads, road construction, and other miscellaneous jobs. These *Arbeitskommandos* were not run by the same people who owned and

My Education Continues

operated the worksites. The prisoners were handled by the German SS, the Gestapo, and the *Wehrmacht*, the same agencies that were running the camps. But the working prisoners had it a little better than those left in camp. Having a chance to leave the camp premises, even temporarily, could often make the difference between life and death.

Eisenbahn Baukommando, Jacob's work brigade, had been assigned to road jobs. They were to keep the railroad tracks and track-beds in working condition. Sometimes they worked on bridges, other times on roads, or on cleanup jobs behind construction crews. It was almost the same work that Jacob had been doing when he was first caught by the Germans in the village by the river.

"Before we left camp on our first assignment," he said, "the *Arbeitskommandant*, a Gestapo officer, assembled all of us in front of the gate and held a short but memorable lecture on the rules and regulations of the brigade. He said that we were very lucky guys because we would be working outside the main camp, which meant that we would be getting more food. But, he emphasized, if any of us ever got the idea of running away, we should keep in mind that for each escapee, five of the remaining prisoners, taken at random, would be shot dead on the spot. We'd better watch one another very closely if we didn't want to pay the price.

"At first, our brigade worked in the vicinity of Buchenwald and Schlieben. Then the work took us to other parts of Germany and to German-occupied lands. When the Allied bombing intensified, a lot of railroad track was ruined, and more repairs were needed. Our work took us to Greece, Yugoslavia, France, and Belgium—unfortunately, with no sightseeing tours."

Jacob credited his survival to a forty-five-year-old *Volksdeutsch* named Herr Waldowsky, who spoke both

Lódź and Jacob

German and Polish.[70] He gave Jacob what would be called a "lucky break." Herr Waldowsky was a *Wehrmacht* officer in charge of the "portable" auto garage; among other duties, he took care of the *Kommandant's* car. He would often take Jacob and a few other prisoners to work with him in the auto repair shop.

"I think the reason Herr Waldowsky chose me," Jacob said, "was that he could communicate with me in Polish, and because I once said that I worked on cars. It was not a complete lie. Among all the odd jobs I did for the Germans was washing cars.

"Anyway, my job was to keep the *Kommandant's* car clean, the tires pumped up, the oil changed, and the tank filled with gas—skills I learned from other prisoners.

"The work in the garage was very rewarding. It helped me obtain a few life-supporting items, such as bread crumbs, cigarette butts, and sometimes even a newspaper page that I would use for reading and then for chewing. These precious commodities were not given to me. They were part of the trash that I used to find in the cars that would come to the garage for cleaning.

"The bread bits brought me nutrition, the cigarettes made me friends, the papers gave me a connection with the outside world. Even the censored news in the German language gave me, as well as the other prisoners who illegally helped me read it, some idea of world affairs.

"Conditions on these work assignments changed from location to location, and from day to day. Often I worked on the railroad, sometimes in the auto garage. Sometimes we were fed better, sometimes worse; but never enough. The only things we could almost always depend on were beets and turnips. We had boiled turnips, turnips with greens, turnips with potatoes,

My Education Continues

turnips with bread, turnip peelings. Occasionally, we were given some cheese, sausage, or marmalade. This was our food on good days. On bad days, we often rummaged through garbage cans around the German kitchen. It was a life-threatening undertaking. One could have easily gotten shot by a guard, or trampled down by competitors.

"We slept in fields, in temporary shelters, in tents, in army barracks—it all depended on location, on circumstances, on availability.

"Health, food, enslavement, and shelter were the common problems encountered by all prisoners. I, however, had an additional burden to carry, which, of course, was my Jewish identity. I knew that if I were ever identified by my captors, or even by some anti-Semitic prison-mates, that would be the end of me.

"I knew that not all, but I was sure that some, guards would be more than happy to administer the 'proper punishment' for such a crime. To be truthful, I wasn't so much afraid of being shot, hanged or gassed, as I feared suffering before death. Punishments by the Nazis, for any crime, were not only 'cruel and unusual' but outright malicious. Sadistic. And the worst of all crimes was being Jewish.

"The instinct for self-preservation kept telling me that I was not Jewish. I had been telling it to myself so often that I started believing it. I not only stopped speaking Yiddish, but I even stopped thinking in Yiddish. I didn't even want to think about Jews or Jewish subjects. Nights on end I didn't close my eyes for fear of saying something in my sleep. I didn't sleep at night or during the day until I learned to be one of the crowd—that is, to live, behave, and even to think and to curse like the rest of my so-called coworkers and roommates. I didn't sleep until I persuaded myself that I wasn't Jewish.

Lódź and Jacob

"This tactic worked quite well till the word 'Jew' came up, as it did in an incident near a forest. One afternoon, as our brigade was repairing some bombed-out tracks, we saw a group of Jews marked with yellow stars. They were being unloaded from freight train cars and led into the woods. On returning to our barracks, all my campmates were talking about was 'the Jews.'

"At such a time I could hardly hide my identity: I was afraid it would show in my face, in my emotions. I knew that my life was hanging on a string, which could break any minute."

Stephan, too, had had many such moments. Whenever Jacob and Stephan got together, they would spend part of their time talking about some especially memorable incidents from their camp. I always listened and scribbled down some of the more eventful ones.

One time, Jacob described how he and a few of his prison colleagues went beet hunting in the garbage cans by the German kitchen, and how they were mercilessly beaten on their return to the camp. It all happened, he said, when a recruit guard found some of the beets in the prisoners' pockets. Jacob's nose, which had never really healed from the ghetto beating, was crushed again.

Another memorable incident that Jacob talked about occurred during a selection. This one was more emotional because Stephan, too, was involved in it, and remembered it well. It happened, Jacob said, when a group of "selectors" came to their *Arbeitskommando* and started pulling out the sick and the weak and those unable to work for transfer to the main camp where all "non-productive" prisoners were being held.

"Stephan was with a group of 'selectors,' translating for them," Jacob said, looking at Stephan,

My Education Continues

who was sitting there with tearful eyes. "I was standing in formation with the other prisoners when the selectors stopped in front of me, looked at my arms, which had broken out in a rash—most likely caused by the machine oil at the garage—and said something to one another, then something to Stephan.

"Stephan, who seemed to obey orders, came over to me and told me to leave the row and join the group that was ready for transport. Having no other choice, I obeyed the order.

"I was so scared," Jacob said, "that I just stood there watching the selectors walking down the rows of prisoners, picking more victims. I wasn't able to concentrate on or pay attention to what else was going on around me.

"Then, all of a sudden, I felt a tap on my shoulder. 'What are you doing here?' a voice behind me said. I looked around. It was Herr Waldowsky. 'They picked me to go to the main camp,' I said in a fearful voice. I don't know what Herr Waldowsky said to the group of selectors, but one of them walked over to me and, pointing his finger, directed me back into the row."

Recalling this incident, Stephan told us that Waldowsky had said that he needed Jacob for work in the auto garage.

"It was a very close call," Jacob said. "Besides Waldowsky, who was especially nice to us, there were a few other good guards at the *Arbeitskommando*, who while doing their jobs behaved quite humanely to the prisoners. I remember the one older man who, during his hours on duty while we worked near a dump yard, let us go through the trash. We promised not to disturb the order of the refuse, and to be back in a few minutes. And we kept our word. I don't know if someone blew the whistle on us, or if someone found some strange items in the barracks; I just remember that the next morning, during *Appell*, our

Kommandant took the older guard and, in front of all of us, had him do pack-drills, a kind of pushup exercise in full gear. The worst part of it was that we all had to stand there watching, unable to help the poor old man who now had to suffer for being kind. I could have jumped out and killed, or choked, that bastard who made our best guard do these maneuvers, but I knew it could only make matters worse. *Herr Kommandant* and his helpers stood there with loaded rifles pointed at us."

Jacob was angry just talking about it.

"I can imagine how you felt about the old man," I said to Jacob. "We, too, had a few good guards. I wish I could find them now and thank them. You were lucky, Jacob, just as I was, to have at least a few humane guards. Had they all been as cruel as most of them were, we would not be sitting here now talking to each other."

Jacob said that I was right. He said that in his camp, the young, inexperienced guards were more brutal than the older ones, who had already lived through a war. "You see, it was my good luck that later in the War, all able-bodied men were taken to the frontlines, and almost all of our guards were older men who themselves were getting tired of the War. Due to people like Waldowsky and other such guards, I didn't lose hope. I was living day to day, dreaming of the hour I would reunite with my family. You must always think about something in the future, something positive; otherwise you won't survive."

He told me about the final episode of his camp life:

"Our *Arbeitskommando* was eventually assigned to repair rails in France. But a call came from somewhere in Belgium asking for coalminers, and that was were I was sent. Believe it or not, it was the safest place I had been since the War started. No Germans ever came down the shaft. No one bothered us in the mine. We

My Education Continues

did our work and got our soup and bread. We had Belgian supervisors who treated us the same way they did all the other coalminers who were working there."

Then Jacob again bragged about the good time that he had had after his liberation, how well the former prisoners had been treated by the Allied military, and by the local population. He talked about his trip to France, and how they all had celebrated the Great Victory Day; and about the nightclubs, and the girls. And he again repeated the pain of his disappointing homecoming. Yet he never forgot to mention those who had helped him. We talked a lot about all the righteous people, about the Christian Christians, who had made the difference between our living and dying, who during the worst of times had shown the best of the human spirit; who in their behavior not only had proven themselves to be heroes, but who had also defended the dignity and honor of the human race. And we talked about the Allies who, with their sacrifices, had saved us from sure annihilation.

According to me, none of Jacob's or my camps could compare to the Warsaw Ghetto. In the camps—at least in mine—we either went to work or to the gas chambers: When we worked, we were fed; when we didn't, we were dead. Those who couldn't perform to the Germans' expectations, or who misbehaved, were shot dead on the spot: one, two, three—it was all over. Again, there was Law, and there was Order.

But in the ghetto, these bastards wouldn't even waste their bullets. They would just let us slowly pass away; physically and mentally disintegrate. On top of it all, we had to watch our loved ones suffer—and couldn't help them. Little children died in their mothers' arms; all the mothers could do was watch.

Lódź and Jacob

Even though Jacob had a lot of experience of the ghetto, he couldn't understand what I was saying, and why I thought so.

"Well," I said, "as far as I'm concerned, there were actually three reasons. For one, in the camps, I could count on my daily soup, or maybe even a slice of bread. I didn't have to worry: There was nothing I could do about the situation, or against it. The second reason was that, outside of a few special situations, like the hospital and the march, the dead and the dying were kept away from the working prisoners. The sick and the weak were taken out and sent away to some 'unknown destination' before they had a chance to die in front of us. In case of death 'on campus,' the corpses were cleared out quickly. No fuss, no delays.

"Even though we were quite sure about the shootings that were going on in nearby forests, and, later, about the gassing in crematories, we did not, except for a few shootings or occasional hangings, see masses of dying people. It is like comparing ground-fighting—and watching the blood flow—to bombing cities from the air.

"Finally, being away from my family, I wanted to hope that they would be okay when I returned. And, of course, in the camps, I didn't have to watch little children lying helplessly in the street, frozen, abandoned, starving. In camp I only worried, or didn't worry, about myself, constantly hoping that 'over there,' on the other side of the fence, things were better."

While talking about children, we realized how long it had been since either of us had seen Jewish children. The few that we did see had come with their parents from Russia (and there was usually only one to a family). As a matter of fact, there weren't even many Gentile children born during the War. "You see," mentioned Jacob one day during such a discussion,

My Education Continues

"that's why almost every young woman we see now is pregnant—trying to make up for lost time." We both laughed.

Here in Łódź, while we were discussing the past, and elaborating on the future, more people who had spent the War in Russia were now returning to Poland. They were reporting that the shortages of the most essential items were being blamed on the War. The population didn't complain; the people were sympathetic. The returnees also were saying that while the Russian people were celebrating the victory over Germany, glorifying communism, and idolizing their great Generalissimo Stalin—for that was what he was called after defeating the Germans—many human-rights abuses were also taking place. The most disturbing one by far was the mistreatment of the Russians who were coming home from German camps as former forced laborers, concentration-camp detainees, or POWs.

This made no sense to me, but it did explain why Stephan was staying in Łódź: His hometown was now in Russian hands.

In Poland, where during the German occupation, almost everyone had felt a prisoner, those returning from camps and forced labor were being treated with respect. But there *were* problems: Everyone was having difficulties adjusting to the new "socialist" Poland. The men of draft age were being taken into military service. Also, Jews were still facing anti-Semitism. Even though ethnic discrimination was forbidden, individual Poles and groups of the ENDEK were beating up and killing returning Jewish survivors who had returned in order to claim their properties, or even those who had come to reward the Righteous Gentiles.

We were in Łódź, trying to decide what to do. Jacob's idea was to get us out of Poland and, if possible, out of Europe. Meanwhile, I was working part-time and, formally, finishing my grade school education; Jacob was trying to make a living selling some things that he had brought from his German trip. He also was spending a lot of his time playing soccer, looking for survivors, and, with other survivors, analyzing the past and debating the future. (They just couldn't believe that even the terrible suffering hadn't cured Polish anti-Semites of their prejudices.) The survivors also analyzed the Nazi rise to power, and the subsequent tragedy.

Now, almost everyone interested in discussing the subject was an expert on what had gone wrong and why, at least in retrospect. Over long hours, Jacob and his male friends would trace the "what ifs": What would have been different, or could have been done, *if* Hitler's threats had been taken more seriously? *If* at the beginning Jews had been more united? *If* the world had responded to Hitler's invasion of Czechoslovakia? If.... If.... The irony of it all was that this catastrophe had happened in a supposedly "civilized" world and executed by an allegedly "superior people." When Germany invaded Czechoslovakia, Poland didn't help the Czechs but instead took another part of that now fractured country and annexed it. I even remembered the victory parades and celebrations when, in 1938, Poland "reclaimed" *Śląsk Zaolziański*.[71]

While these debates were going on about the past, our present and future were still uncertain. Among some Hasidic Jews, debates were still going on about whether the Messiah would come now or later. In the meantime, problems were developing between the Jews who wanted to go to Palestine and the Arabs who didn't want them there. (And the British, who had mandated the land, wouldn't let the Jews in.) For us, the War was not yet over. Germany had surrendered to the Allies in May, yet by December neither Jacob nor I

My Education Continues

had found any of our friends or relatives. We had no permanent place to live, no work, no country that wanted us, no prospects.

Many of our acquaintances—other survivors—were getting married and leaving Poland. After breaking up with Irenka, Marrion married a girl named Blanka. He invited us to his wedding. He said that they planned to remain in Poland because Blanka's brother, who had a Gentile wife, wanted them to be together. Most of our other friends were getting out.

In mid-December, the preparations that we needed to make for our trip out of Poland were completed. Jacob and I affirmed our vows. We signed up as husband and wife. We packed up Jacob's suitcase, into which I put my few belongings. We were ready to leave.

We bade farewell to Teressa, whose goal was to emigrate to Canada, where her new husband's aunt lived, and to all our friends who, for the time being, had chosen to—or simply had to—remain in Poland. We said goodbye to *Pani* Meccenasowa, who wished us well but felt sorry that we could find no future in Poland. We said goodbye to *Pani* Basia, the lady who had loaned me money for my trip to Warsaw; she was sorry to see us go, too. We also went over to the two barbers who still had their barbershop on Pomorska Street. Both were now married and had pregnant wives. Of all the girls who lived with me, only Hanka was still in the apartment; she was living there with her new husband.

Jacob and I took a train to Szczecin, an old German port city on the Baltic that was now part of Poland, part of what I called "liberated-occupied" territory.

We were on our way to new adventures, and more education.

Chapter 2. Berlin

On the train to Szczecin, Jacob and I discussed the issues that we expected to face on this trip, and beyond. Our destination in Germany was Berlin, the divided city that housed all four occupying powers—American, British, French, and Russian. We wondered how we were going to cross the border that divided Poland from East Germany, how life would be for us in this strange city with a foreign language and people whom we knew as "those who had brought about all our troubles." What would we do, if anything, when we met Nazis? How would we know who was a Nazi and who was not? For not all Germans were Nazis, and not all Nazis were German. Would we be able to forgive them, or would we try to take revenge? We knew, at least, that we wouldn't forget what they had done.

In Szczecin, everything for our trip was prearranged. We were met by a man who led us into a room in a boardinghouse where we would stay for a few days before continuing on our journey. As we entered this room, it seemed as though all our worries about the future disappeared. My heart pounded from joy and fear when, for the first time, I found myself with Jacob in a room to which no one else had a key, and into which no one could walk at will. Here for the first time, we felt that we belonged to each other. We

My Education Continues

didn't even care whether we'd stay like that forever or only for the time being; it really didn't matter; we were happy together. We felt as though the whole world belonged to us.

For the next few days, we toured the once German city, to which now more Poles were moving daily. A few nights later we boarded a covered truck and, along with other Jews, Poles, and Germans, were driven through a forest and over the border crossing. It was a freezing December night when the driver let us out at the railroad station where he had arranged for our train tickets to Berlin.

On the train to Berlin, I began to realize that I was now completely dependent on Jacob, that I knew nothing and no one. I had no money; my belongings consisted of a couple of garments, an extra pair of shoes, and my diary notes—all in his suitcase. I was quite confident that at his advanced age of twenty-six, and after his exciting adventures, he must know everything there was to know for our survival.

From the train, we transferred to the Berlin subway. We arrived at the Badstraße station and went to our prearranged living quarters, which consisted of a bed in a German family's apartment.

Germany was a divided country: East Germany was Russian; and West Germany was subdivided into three parts: American, British, French, with open borders between these three zones. Berlin, too, was divided. All four Allied powers were now ruling the former German capital.

Since the end of the War, Berlin had been transformed. It was no longer the capital city of hate and destruction. We now, jokingly, called it the city of "international love."

Berlin itself lay in ruins; half its buildings had been destroyed. Its people, who a few months ago had enthusiastically "Heiled" Hitler, and who had believed in the purity and superiority of the Aryan race, were now welcoming, with love and cheer, people of all creeds, races, and colors. The city that was to be forever Judenrein, had now become Judenvoll, "full of Jews." Some of those who were returning were German Jews who were there to look for survivors and former belongings. Many transit Jews, remnants of a once-thriving European Jewry and now homeless and destitute, were traveling to Berlin, too, bound for Western countries or Palestine. Many of them were staying in private homes, or in former Nazi's apartments, from which the inhabitants had once fled. Others were being placed in new, specially provided UNRA-supported DP camps in the Schlachtensee and Reinickendorf suburbs of Berlin.[72]

It was a time of resurrection not only in Berlin but in all of Europe. Hatred and destruction were now out of style, replaced by love and reconstruction. Enemies had become friends. "Brotherhood of People" was the new motto, replacing "Pure Race." Fewer people were dying, and hardly any were getting killed. More babies were being born; murders had ceased. For most people, life was becoming fun again.

Many young people—men especially—would become almost wild with emotion, not knowing what to do with this newly acquired freedom. They were getting drunk, running the streets, kissing and hugging girls (or anyone who might come their way). It was a time of great hope and expectation. The general feeling was, "We have learned the bitter lessons of war and hatred. Let us celebrate peace and love. No more wars! No more hate!"—the same messages that had been sent out for thousands of years, dating back to ancient times, in millions of books, fables, and stories. But now, the War was over, and at least for the moment, people of all creeds, races, and colors were to love one another and to live "happily ever after."

My Education Continues

That was the new "Public Opinion"—an opinion being handed down to the public by the leadership.

Although many European cities were still in ruins, and the smell of ashes still penetrated the nostrils, spiritual revival and physical reconstruction had begun. A new atmosphere of hope filled the air, even though most store shelves were still empty and bare necessities hard to come by without "special connections." It was a great time for speculation and underground business. The black market was booming. The once stable delivery of goods almost ceased. The once mighty Reichsmark had gone down in value; prices had gone in the opposite direction. It took a sack of German marks to buy a billfold of food on the black market. All other essential commodities were being rationed.

Despite the gloomy present, the mood of the people, especially the young, was still merry, full of optimism and dreams for the future. And while many Germans were still crying, and mourning the death of Hitler, others were trying to put the War behind them and adjust to the new Germany, to the happy-go-lucky bon ton that was sweeping the country. Many older people were reexamining the recently cured Hitler epidemic, as the younger generation, startled by the metamorphosis in their culture, were wondering what had happened to "Hitler-Religion" and to everything that they had been taught, to everything that they had once believed in. Hitler's bunker, his air-raid shelter, which had once been considered a holy shrine, was now a tourist attraction. For this was the place where the Russians had allegedly found Hitler's body after he had, supposedly, committed suicide.

The young German men who had survived the Front and the POW camps, were returning home. Many of them had never known anything but fighting. Very few had occupations except that of killing; hardly any had skills that could be applied to the peacetime economy.

Now the years of hostilities and malice were over. Like a raging tornado, the years had come and destroyed everything in their path—then disappeared into the sky, leaving pain, sorrow, desolation. What war had destroyed, peace now had to reconstruct—even the hatred, mistrust, vengeance. There was much loving everywhere. People were kissing and hugging in the streets, in streetcars, in buses, in parks, and in beds. Bars were staying open day and night. There were foreign bars, German bars, lesbian and gay bars; all of them welcoming everyone.

Girls of the "Master Race," who only a short time ago had lawfully and honestly obeyed Hitler's "pure blood" doctrine, were now in love with everyone, especially anyone in uniform—American, British, French, Russian.[73] They didn't discriminate. And, of course, they didn't decline love to the German POWs who were slowly returning to their devastated Vaterland. Believe it or not, these girls were even in love with Jews.

Not only did the Germans love everybody, but the Americans loved the Russians and the French loved the British. All four Allies were riding in a single jeep, patrolling the streets of Berlin. Even without knowing one another's language (for only the Americans and British had a more-or-less common tongue), all four communicated and understood one another: What a sight of love and understanding. These jeeps drove through all four sectors of Berlin; the borders were not guarded.[74] If it had not been for the signs that marked the different sectors, no one would have known that they were crossing international borders.

During our first year in Berlin, we lived in four different places. Apartments there were allotted by

My Education Continues

special permits; we didn't have one. So we rented a room from Fräulein Scopy, an old maid who lived with her elderly brother in a luxurious apartment in Pankow, a section now located in the Russian sector.

After a short time, we moved to the French sector, where we rented a room from a forty-year-old woman, Frau Turf, who needed money to support herself and her two sons, twelve-year-old Günter and ten-year-old Helmut. Her husband, according to the information that she had, was still being held in a Russian POW camp.

We were expecting our first baby. Our landlady was very helpful. She told me a few old wives' tales about having babies, and she would also give me some encouragement as I was vomiting in the mornings: She knew of no woman who had ever died of morning sickness.

In September, when the Jewish holidays came, I went with Jacob to a recently reconstructed synagogue. It was the first time that I'd ever been to prayer services. All other times before the War, I went with my father for Simchat Torah services, or with Grandma, who would sit in the ladies' balcony of the old Warsaw synagogue, praying during the High Holidays.

Here, in the heart of Berlin, I now saw Jacob receive the honor of praying at the pulpit. He read from the Torah. He was himself surprised that he could still do it, that he, even before rehearsal, could remember things that he had learned in his childhood and his teen years, but had not used for so many years.

I sat in the back, reading through the Polish translation in one of the siddurim that had been found in an underground shelter. Many verses, I did not understand; the ones that I did, made no sense to me.

During the breaks and at the end of services, the Jews talked about their war experiences. There were hardly any old people or children among the worshippers. Many of those present were German Jews who had recently returned from hiding places and from camps, and a few who had spent the War in China in the British-controlled sections, which had allowed Jews in.[75] We got acquainted with many new people, among them one named Herr Meier, who invited us to his roomy apartment and told us about his life in Berlin before the War and about his years in Shanghai. I told him about my Uncle Harry and Tante Trude; I thought that he might know them; but he didn't.

We wanted Herr Meier to visit us in our room, but before he had time to come, we had to move out of the place because our boarding lady's husband had returned from the Russian camp and she needed more room. It was an emotional reunion. All relatives, neighbors, and friends celebrated his return. Days later, after the rejoicing had subsided, Herr Turf told his family, and us, about his life on the Front, about how terrible conditions in Russian camps had been.

His wife remarked that she had seen prisoners who returned from French and British POW camps, but they had not been treated that harshly. I still remember what Herr Turf replied:

"For what we have done to their people and their country, I often wonder why they even let us out alive."

It was exactly what Jacob and I were thinking as he spoke. Nevertheless, Herr Turf was back in his country with his family, while Jacob and I, and our unborn babe, had to find yet another place to live; and had no one to reunite with.

We finally got our Zuzug papers, which declared us legal residents, and found an apartment.

Moving was no big problem. We took with us the suitcase, my diary, our memories, and the baby that I was carrying inside me. Nothing that reminded us of

My Education Continues

our previous lives, not even a photograph of our relatives, had survived the War.

The place to which we moved was a two-room apartment in the French Sector. There was one multipurpose room and a kitchen. The toilet off the stairway we shared with our next-door neighbor, Frau Hömpler, and her family. Frau Hömpler was a fifty-year-old German woman who lived with her husband and a daughter. She was tall, heavyset, and had a light complexion and short gray hair. She seemed very friendly. Every time she saw me in the stairway hall, she would try to engage me in a conversation. She would ask me about my condition and how I was getting along, to which I would always answer, "Danke, gut!" trying to keep my limited German to a minimum. Once she stopped me and asked, "Is your mother coming to help when the baby comes?"

"Nein," I answered.

"Do you see a doctor?"

"Ja," I said.

"When is the baby due?"

"Any day."

"If I can be of any help," she said, "just knock on my door."

"Danke schön."

One morning she asked if she could do my turn of toilet cleaning; she'd be glad to do it for me until after my delivery. I took up her offer, but only on the condition that she accept some food in exchange. We were getting CARE packages from the Allies and some special ration cards, to which the Germans were not entitled. These parcels contained canned and powdered foods that we liked a lot and ate daily. The coffee that we didn't drink, and cigarettes that we didn't smoke, we traded for other goods.

Another day, Frau Hömpler called me over to her apartment and introduced me to her husband, Art, and her twenty-five-year-old daughter, Eva. Eva had her mother's features; also plump, but much shorter. She was limping because of a broken hip she had suffered in an accident. From the doorway I could see into the apartment. It was an exact copy of ours. A bundle of wood was piled by the stove in the kitchen.

"Guten Tag," Eva said to me, politely, when she saw me at the door. Then she said something to her mother that I could not understand; I could only make out that they were talking about a birth and a baby. I was sure that they were talking about me.

I knew little about babies. I knew more about death than I knew about life. I was scared of the delivery, even though the old Jewish doctor at the Jewish hospital, Dr. Helischkowsky, who had been kept there throughout the War to handle emergency cases (even after most of the Jewish doctors had been deported), gave me good prenatal care and assured me that everything would turn out fine. His assisting nurse, too, tried to give me confidence by explaining that millions of women throughout the world give birth every day to millions of children, and they do it without medical help. Her talk really didn't diminish my fears; it only made me aware that bringing a new life into the world was not as big an achievement as I had first thought. It was a thought that reminded me that medals were only rewarded for killing.

One freezing, snowy January night, something happened to me that I wasn't prepared for: My water broke.

It was about ten in the evening. Jacob was in the room, playing cards with a group of his friends. I wasn't about to announce to all these guys what had happened to me, especially when I didn't know what it was. The doctor had never discussed it with me, taking for granted that this was a matter of common knowledge. I walked down to the corner store, the one

My Education Continues

with the telephone. It was closed for the night. The phone booth on the corner was out of order. I walked back to the house. Frau Hömpler heard me walking in the hall and came out. It didn't take her long to spot that something was wrong. She insisted that we not wait until morning, which was what had I planned to do, but that Jacob take me to the hospital right away. I told her that I couldn't tell him my problem in front of all these guys. Without a word to me, Frau Hömpler walked right into our apartment and, interrupting the card game, announced my condition.

Luckily, we still made it for the last streetcar, which took us to the hospital. We only had to walk three blocks from the stop. Jacob had to leave me there, for no outsiders were allowed.

In the morning, Jacob, the proud father, named his son Simon ben Jacob: Simon, after his dead father, the son of Jacob, as was customary among European Jews. He then organized a big reception in the synagogue dining hall and invited all of his friends. The place was right across the street from the hospital, so I slipped out of my bed and, uninvited, attended the party.

After a few joyous days in the hospital, Jacob took our son and me home. He had ordered a taxi ahead of time.

I remember well our homecoming. The coal-burning oven in the room was glowing, and there were flowers on the table. The things that I had for the baby were the few gifts that we had received from our friends, a few diapers, which I had made from old sheets during my ten-day stay in the hospital, and a small crib that Jacob had bought with the coffee and cigarette money a day before our homecoming. Jacob, like most Eastern European Jews, did not believe in preparing things for a baby ahead of its birth—an old wives' tale that he thought was worth preserving.[76]

As soon as I walked into the room, I put the bundled-up baby on the bed, looked at the tiny eyes—which, occasionally open, seemed to look straight at me—and burst out in tears.

I couldn't explain what had come over me. Somehow, thousands of thoughts had come into my mind, thoughts that I had never dreamed of before. I knew that I had never tended to an infant. I realized that despite the lessons all of us new mothers had received at the hospital on diapering, nursing, and caring for babies, I wasn't ready for such a responsibility. Also, I had no one whom I could ask for help in an emergency. All of a sudden, I imagined myself doing the wrong things; the baby getting sick, or even worse: I imagined myself dying and leaving the baby with no one to care for it.[77] I just kept looking at the bundle on the bed, unable to stop the tears from flowing. Whether my thoughts were rational or not, didn't matter. I had not cried since I came out of the Leipzig shower room. Crying, for me, was such a rare occurrence that I could quite well remember scattered episodes. Why were the tears coming now, on such a happy occasion? Jacob asked me what was happening, and why I was so unhappy. I could not understand it myself, let alone explain. From then on, I would often cry, and we would often argue about it. Maybe they were the cooped-up tears that had been inside me for years, or tears of joy, or tears of fear. I had no idea. But poor Jacob could not understand it. I didn't mean to make him miserable. I just couldn't answer his questions.

One morning, while I was crying, he saw the baby lying unattended on the bed. He gave me a long, unfriendly lecture about leaving babies alone, reminding me of his infant brother, who had died falling off a table. After the lecture, Jacob left for a

My Education Continues

business appointment. I was left with the baby. We were both crying.

In the early evening, Frau Hömpler knocked at my door. I was sitting by candlelight (all utilities were still rationed to a few hours per day for each district), reading and crying. I wiped my tears, opened the door, and let her in. She said that she wanted to see the new baby. I took her over to the crib. The baby was asleep. She glanced at him with a kind of grandmotherly look in her eyes, then she smiled and said, "Ein hübscher Junge. Ich gratuliere"—"A handsome boy. I congratulate you."

From that day on, Frau Hömpler would constantly ask about the baby: "How is he doing? Does he cry at night? Is your apartment warm enough? What do you feed him?" Not wanting to enter into long conversations, I would always give short answers: "Thanks, he is fine! He wakes up when he is wet or hungry. Yes, our apartment is warm; we just got some coal. I breastfeed him."

One day, Frau Hömpler stopped me on the stairway. She sighed deeply and said, "Good day, young lady, I would like to talk to you for a few minutes, if I may." Her voice was shaking, and she had tears in her eyes. "I may need to ask a favor of you shortly."

I figured that something had happened, and I asked her to tell me what was bothering her, adding, "Please speak slowly; my German is not too good." I wasn't really sure that I wanted to know her troubles or do her any favors.

"I would never ask for favors if they were for myself," she said, her voice breaking as she spoke. "Your people [meaning the Jews] have seen enough troubles in the last few years.... I am sorry!" She wiped her eyes. "But I don't know where else to turn. You have already met Eva. You see, I have another daughter, a younger one, about your age. You have not met her yet. If things go right, we expect her here shortly." Frau Hömpler told me that her daughter, Inge, was coming from Vienna with a baby boy, who was born about a month before Simon. Inge was waiting for the weather to warm up a bit before undertaking the long journey. "Every day I pray that she comes home safely. There is still a lot of mistreatment of German women going on...even rapes." Then, sighing, she said, "In her last letter, Inge wrote that she had little food and hardly any clothes for the baby. The boy was sick. I hope you can help us when she comes."

I said, "I'll see what I can do. Let her get here first."

Frau Hömpler started crying openly. She grabbed my hand, squeezing it in both of her large palms, and said, "I am sorry to have bothered you, young lady, and I am ashamed, too."

That night, when Jacob came home, I told him about my encounter with Frau Hömpler.

"What did you tell her?" he asked.

"Well, I didn't know what to say. I was really confused. I finally told her that I'd see."

"That was a good answer," Jacob said. "Let's wait and see. I am not sure what I want to do. You know how much I like all of them."

Then Jacob told me about his day. He said that he had met with Herr Meier, the German Jew who spent the War in Shanghai. "Meier wants to reopen his delicatessen business. He is getting reparation money for the store that the Nazis took from him. He needs a partner, and asked me if I'd be willing to go in with him. He should have no problem getting the right papers. He is only looking for a good place."

"What did you tell him?" I asked.

"I said that I would think it over, and let him know in a couple of days."

My Education Continues

I was still feeling weak and down. Most days I was home alone, not able to go to places because of the freezing weather and the baby. After a while we hired a fourteen-year-old neighbor girl named Helga, who would come after school and help me with Simon. Helga was living with her widowed mother, Frau Walter, in the same building as we. Helga was the youngest of three children. Her married half-brother was living in town, having returned wounded from the War; her other half-brother was still in a French POW camp somewhere in Africa.

Two weeks after I talked with Frau Hömpler, Inge arrived from Vienna. Frau Hömpler called me into her apartment to meet her daughter and to see the baby. The room that I entered was the one that I had once seen through the open door. It had bare floors, two wooden beds against the wall, and a table in the center of the room surrounded by a few wooden chairs. A two-branch chandelier with a forty-watt light bulb was throwing a dim light over the embroidered tablecloth. In the kitchen, on a table next to the wood-burning stove, Inge was diapering the baby.

The little skeleton with a large head was screaming. Inge took a diaper that was hanging on a string over the stove and put it against her face to check out its dryness, then she wrapped it around the baby's bulging belly.

Inge was the opposite of her sister. She was a tall, slim, good-looking young woman. Her makeup-free face showed stress. Her features typically "Aryan": dark blonde hair, blue eyes, a straight, slightly pointed nose. She started her conversation by telling me that she had heard about me from her mother, and that she was glad to meet me. Then we both talked about our babies.

We had what I would call a friendly conversation. In my broken German, I told her that had it not been for her mother, I would not have made it to the hospital in time. She said that her delivery didn't go very smoothly, either; and that Michael was born on Christmas Eve in a Vienna hospital. Then she talked about her trip to Berlin.

When I later told Jacob about my meeting with Inge, I realized that I had actually had a personal conversation with a German woman, and it seemed that both of us had forgotten our ethnic differences: We had talked like one mother to another.

Inge and I started meeting. I didn't mind talking with her and listening to her stories. I asked her to speak slowly and to use synonyms for words and expressions that I could not understand. Most of our talks concentrated on common problems that young mothers face; and we talked a lot about our blond-haired, blue-eyed boys. After a while, Inge's mother started "grand-mothering" both boys. I was breastfeeding mine, and providing some CARE food for Inge's.

Jacob was gone a lot; he was trying to find something to do so that we wouldn't have to rely on CARE packages or other handouts. Meantime, he was preparing to enter the delicatessen business with Herr Meier. Many legal enterprises were reopening in the city even as the black markets flourished. There were many opportunities, in both legal and illegal business. People were buying, selling, and exchanging items. Americans were selling their cigarettes for British coffee, French wine, and Russian vodka. The British were trading their coffee for American cigarettes, French wine, and Russian vodka. The French were selling wine and buying cigarettes, coffee, and vodka. The Russians were buying cigarettes, coffee, and wine. Cigarettes, coffee, wine, and vodka were traded for movie and theater and sports tickets—as well as for

My Education Continues

beer, entertainment, and girls. The Germans were trading gold and jewelry (most of which was stolen merchandise, brought to Germany from once-occupied countries) for food, fuel, and other necessities. Russians were buying from the Germans anything that they could put their hands on, paying with bread, lard, and devalued rubles. Anybody who could match up buyers with sellers—that is, work as a sort of middleman—was rewarded with merchandise, or paid in foreign currency; the once almighty German Reichsmark was worthless.

Jacob was spending a lot of time roaming the exciting city. He was meeting many new people, among them Jews coming from Poland and Russia. He was helping many of them settle into the newly established DP camps. He was also busy with Herr Meier and the new business.

But what Jacob was doing was not "all work, no play." He had decided to organize a new soccer club, or more correctly, to resurrect the old Berliner Hakoah, a Jewish soccer club that had been thrown out of the German major league, then disbanded by the Nazis. Jacob was going to make sure that this club got back its pre-Nazi place in the major league. Sports in Europe were amateur, but there were three leagues, and in order to reinstate that club into the major league, he would need good players. There were hardly any former players from the Hakoah club. Those few who had survived the War were now too old to play.

The soccer club, like Jacob's helping with the civic clubs, was a volunteer activity.

Jacob was always busy. Most of the time he was gone. I was at home, spending a lot of time with Inge. We played with our boys and took them places. We talked about children and about the role of women. We both came from girls' families—she had an older sister. We knew very little about raising boys. We talked much about our boys and how we should discipline them. How much obedience must a child learn? How much freedom should a child have? On this subject, we would often disagree. Inge had come from a law-and-order, totalitarian background. I had had more freedom, even though as a child I hadn't thought so. I had had some right to question my "authorities"; at least, this had been true in regard to my mother and my maternal grandfather. I could even disagree with them.

Inge and I also talked about school and music and the books that we had read, which were in both Polish and German. We talked about our youth and about our grandparents; sometimes, we talked about politics and the War—a subject that, no matter how much we tried, we couldn't keep from coming up.

In post-War Germany, there was hardly any German person who would openly admit to having had knowledge of the Nazis: No one had belonged to "The Party," or had even heard of anyone who did. Anyway, no one would admit to such unpopular and often dangerous associations. Post-War Germans had never known about the crimes being committed by the Nazis in the name of Germany. One would have thought that the people would at least apologize, that they would be sorry, or feel remorse, for their actions. Instead, they all had learned to deny any knowledge of the destruction, the killings, the deliberate annihilation of the Jews.

"Such bizarre actions could not have happened," said most Germans, who had spent the War in their own homes; and they sincerely believed that "such atrocities could not have been committed by our people." Therefore, when the Allies occupied Germany, they required that Germans living in the vicinity of Nazi concentration camps tour the location of the former camps and look at the heaps of corpses and

My Education Continues

bones that were still on the ground, waiting for burial, and at the gas chambers and crematories that constituted the killing factories. The Germans living in locations away from such camps had to watch documentary movies before they could receive their ration cards. None of what they saw could account for the miseries, destruction, and pain that they had caused the world, for the only things seen in these films were the physical destruction. But even then, the people didn't want to believe—the stories that they were hearing were so gruesome, so shocking. Those Germans who had witnessed, or who had participated in, these crimes firsthand, either ran to foreign countries or else changed their identities and were now living under assumed names in places where they were unknown.

Only after the Nuremberg Trials, when the captured Nazi leaders admitted their crimes of war and their crimes against humanity, did the general population of Germany reluctantly, and with reservations, begin to accept the undisputed truth of the atrocities that had been committed in their name.[78] But individually, the Germans would deny any personal involvement with Hitler or the Nazis.

Little by little, Inge told me about her baby's father, and about her adventures during and after the War. She was the first person whom I met who told me that she had spent most of the Nazi years in a Hitlerjugend Lager.[79]

At first, she did not give me any details. She had only mentioned it in connection with Michael's father. She talked about the discipline and education that she had received in this organization. Later in our relationship, she told me that there had hardly been any German children, especially between the ages of fourteen and sixteen, who had not belonged to some

Nazi club: "If they didn't join through persuasion, they joined from peer pressure, or by governmental requirements."

Talking about her baby's father, Inge told me: "I met Fred in Schleswig, a northern German province by the North Sea. He was handsome and smart. I had known him for quite some time. Right after the War, his spirits were very low, just like most of ours, as a defeated people; only his case was worse than mine, for he had fallen from a high status.

"During the War he was a combat pilot with the German Air Force—quite a prestigious position for an Austrian-born boy. Our Hitlerjugend Lager for girls was located not far from his base, which the British troops are now occupying. After Germany surrendered, we girls went there to cheer them up. These guys were very depressed. That's how I got involved with him. We were both away from our families, far from our homes. We fell in love with each another.

"We planned to marry. He wanted to go with me to Berlin. But by law, he had to return to his home in Vienna. Meantime, I got pregnant. He promised to marry me as soon as he was able to get the necessary papers. I could join him in the Austrian capital."

Inge took a picture out of her purse and, showing it to me, said, "Look: He was handsome, I loved him dearly. Yet, my trip to Vienna was a disappointment, nothing that I expected it to be." She picked up little Michael, kissed his forehead, and looked at his little face. "He looks exactly like his father, only his hair is lighter, and his eyes are blue.

"Fred lived in Vienna with his widowed, Hungarian-born mother, who was from the old Emperor Franz-Joseph culture of World War I. In her mind, the world had not changed. She still believed in very defined lines between the working class and high-class society. Even now, when she is

My Education Continues

poor and brokenhearted, she has not modified her views. She knew nothing about Fred and me. For a long time, he didn't tell her. When she found out, she went into shock. She had expected Fred, her only child, to marry his former girlfriend, a well-to-do, well-educated 'lady' from a prestigious Austrian family. His mother wanted no part of me, or the baby that she called a 'bastard.' Anyway, before I got to Vienna, Fred married his fiancée, his mother's choice.

"When I showed up, he was stuck between the women (three of them), and between money and prestige and the soon-to-be-born baby. He was confused. I loved him, hated him, and felt sorry for him, all at the same time.

"Finally, he decided to take some paternal responsibility. He arranged for my hospital, and when I went into labor, he took me to the delivery ward, checked me in—under my name, of course—and left to join his wife and mother, who were preparing Christmas Eve supper.

"It was a Christmas Eve I will never forget. I was in a strange city, with strange people, with a new baby boy. I felt like Mary, the Mother of the Christ Child.

"Oh, yes!" Inge suddenly said, "a few days later, Fred did come to check me out of the hospital and arrange a place for me to stay. That's when he saw the baby. His mother never came. She never saw the boy." Inge showed me a letter that had come from Fred a few days before. "He wanted to know if we got to Berlin safely, and said not to write to his home, for he was living with his mother. But he did give me an address of his friend through whom I could contact him if I needed to."

Inge had finished her story. It was the first time that I had heard a mother-in-law story that wasn't funny.

Berlin

My German language skills were improving, too. I kept learning a German vocabulary that was fit for public consumption; the German that I had learned during the War consisted of curses, orders, and foul language. I started taking German lessons, and I hoped to go back to school, finally, and get some formal education. I could already understand the radio announcers, and I could read the newspaper; even my writing was improving. I began talking German to my baby, so that he would be able to communicate with people around him. I was becoming acquainted with more German people, with their customs and culture. My life skills at the University of Experience continued....

I often wondered if the Germans who occupied and destroyed my country, killed my people, and put me into camps, belonged to the same "race"—or even to the same species—as the Germans whom I was now meeting. Or if they were all merely Jekylls and Hydes.[80] I had already begun wondering about it while I was working with German people in Leipzig, for they all had looked and acted like any other human beings. Inge told me that she, too, had wondered if the Jews whom she was now meeting belonged to the same "race" that Hitler had talked about.

"Personally," she said, "I knew only a few Jewish people. There was a Jewish girl named Gerta in my class. When the girl stopped attending school, the teacher told us, 'Gerta moved out of town.'"

The other Jews Inge used to know were merchants, and she knew a doctor, but according to her story, she didn't have much contact with them. Since the Nazis came to power, she had heard that Jews were not the kind of people she should associate with. Inge could remember the tumult of Kristallnacht in Berlin, but, she claimed, she had not

My Education Continues

been allowed to go into the street during that time. She also had known from the signs on many gates and doors that Jews were not allowed into many public places. She couldn't tell just by looking as to who was a Jew and who was not.

Later, after Inge had met Fred, one of their conversations turned to the Jewish question. Fred told her a story about his mother. Here is the story, as Inge told it to me:

"When Hitler's troops invaded Austria, all German decrees against Jews were also adopted in that occupied country. Fred's Hungarian-born mother, who was a dark-eyed brunette and looked 'quite Jewish,' had often been harassed because of her mistaken identity. Once, when she entered a Vienna restaurant, she was pushed, cursed, and thrown out. She was asked if she couldn't read the sign on the entrance door that said, 'Juden Verboten.' She remembered that terrifying experience, and for many years to come she had tried to be careful not to fall victim to any mistaken identity again. 'It must be awful to be Jewish,' the old woman told her son."

Inge said that she really didn't understand how bad it was to be Jewish until she became a German in Russian-occupied Germany. I told her that there was not even the slightest comparison between the two, and that I hoped that neither she nor anyone else would ever know that feeling.

Talking to Inge and to other Germans, I often wondered if the stories that they were telling me were really all that they knew about the persecution and the War. I felt like asking them what part they had really played in the killing of twenty-plus million human beings. I never really asked because I knew I would never get a true answer. The post-War Germans claimed that everything they read or heard had been censored.

During the War, I often thought that after the Nazi reign of terror was over, I would be able to find the SS, the Gestapo, and all the other Nazis, and at least have a "nice talk" with them. What I found out was that it was preposterous to assume that the Nazi was a special kind of beast, that it was a monster with big horns and a long tail; an animal that could be spotted from a distance and identified. Well, I was mistaken. The Nazi, or "former Nazi," seemed so much like any other human being that it was almost frightening. The Germans whom I had been meeting were, for the most part, very ordinary people: good parents, conscientious Christians, patriotic citizens Yet, I was sure that some of them must have been associated with "The Party," even if no one was now admitting it. Those who would occasional talk to me about the Nazi era claimed that hunger and unemployment had been the main ingredients that brought the Nazis to power. Poor economic conditions and the Depression of the Twenties and Thirties were responsible for the political unrest and the fall of established order. Such conditions had also brought Communism to Russia, and Fascism to Spain.

During crises, desperate people are prone to choose extreme measures in order to find quick solutions to complicated problems, instead of trying out moderate measures towards sound, long-term answers. I learned that the two main components for quick, short-term solutions are: 1) find a scapegoat (person or group) on whom to blame one's misfortunes, and 2) develop instant heroes to whom people can look for gratification and inspiration. Both of these items are easy to achieve, for it is easier to get to the top by stepping on others. The trick is to keep the masses preoccupied with hatred rather than on the real issues—like politicians who have no solutions to the prevailing problems.

My Education Continues

The scapegoat is not a new, sophisticated idea; it just seems so to those who haven't seen it in action before. Throughout history, it has been done many times. Hitler's scapegoat was the Jew; the enemy was the Communist. Had there been no Jews to hate, nor Communists to despise, someone would have had to invent them. In fact, even with the Jews and Communists around, the world seemed to have no shortage of other objects of hatred: The Protestants hated the Catholics; the Chinese hated the Japanese; the Blacks hated the Whites; the Turks hated the Armenians; the Iraqis hated the Kurds. The hatred is mutual; the list is endless.

People can be persuaded to hate those they love, and to love those they hate. Politicians are specialists at inventing enemies, or turning friends into foes, and vice-versa. The difference with the Nazis was that they hated everybody, even non-pure-blooded German Aryans—even Aryans who were not devoted to Hitler's doctrine. When one runs out of "hatees," new hatees will be automatically developed. If all Aryans become Hitler-lovers, we might have to hate those with non-blue eyes, or those who are to short, or too tall. It really doesn't matter, so long as there is an enemy on whom to focus attention in order to take minds off real issues.

Once I asked Inge what made the Germans hate Jews with such animosity. She didn't know. She said that she didn't hate anybody, not even the uncle who had brought shame on the family for being a Communist, or the Polish cousin on her father's side of the family who had been among the "undesirables" for being a Slav.[81] Inge said, "I didn't hate them, even though I knew I was supposed to."

I asked her jokingly, "Haven't you learned anything during all your years in camp?"

Inge and I could see all these political manipulations clearly. We talked over things that we had learned about previous wars in our respective history classes. It was "funny" how differently these war accounts were presented in her books when compared to those in mine. We listened to each other's views, trying to learn from each another.

It was hard to believe how little we knew about each other's history, culture, and religion, and how much misinformation each of us had received concerning the other's way of life. We were shocked by how much our "facts" differed. What we found interesting was the wide variety of ways in which history books were written, and how they would change over time. We looked at the "new" history book that Simon's babysitter, Helga, was now using in her class. Hitler's name was casually mentioned a couple of times as the Nazi ruler during the recently ended World War.

The history book written only a few years earlier, during Inge's school years, however, was full of praise for Hitler and Nazi achievements. In it, the 1939 German invasion of Poland was described as "a necessary measure" by the German government to "liberate" poor, abused Volksdeutschen, who were being abused by the Poles, and to "reclaim" the once-German territories.

In Polish books, the same action had been called an "outright, unprovoked invasion meant to occupy Polish sovereign land, so that the Germans could create more Lebensraum [living space] for their citizens and enslave the Polish people."

Another example of varying interpretations concerned the signing of the famous 1939 Non-Aggression Pact between Hitler and Stalin. Some historians saw Stalin as evil and stupid. They saw him as "playing right into Hitler's hands." Other historians, especially Russian ones, portrayed Stalin's action as a courageous and wise decision because, according to their interpretation, Stalin had signed the treaty in order to "stall for time so that he could prepare his defenses."

In Inge's books, the Nazis were the "good guys," while we were the "bad ones." I could hardly believe what I was reading. Not only were the same territories alternately called "liberated" or "occupied," but the same person who was doing the same action could be called, by one side, a demigod or hero, while by the other side, a rabble-rouser, or villain. Even a rifle could be called a "defensive weapon" or an "offensive arm."

I found out that not only could history be interpreted in different ways; it could be deliberately, or "unintentionally," distorted. Once history had been written and adapted, it could be, according to need, changed at a later date: It could be rewritten under the auspices (or pretext) of a "New Revised Edition," which means that friendly neighbors have suddenly turned into aggressive enemies, an invasion into a liberation, an attack into a defense, or a surrender document into a peace treaty. As the Russians say, "Our past is unpredictable." The process of rewriting history is not new; it was only new and surprising to Inge and me because we hadn't know about it. We thought that whatever was "in the book," or in print, was right. It was "the truth." We found out that history was really my-story, your-story, her-story, and, as we liked to call it in interpretation, his-story.

Throughout history, people have been distorting accounts of events, or, as they call it, telling "necessary lies," as the "undisputed truth." We have been fed many contradictory messages. We're taught that killing is a sin as young men are sent out to kill. "The Good Book" teaches us to love our neighbor, but our politicians, and even quite often our clergy, teach us how and whom to hate. We know that sharing is a virtue, but it probably was meant to be "sharing what is not ours." It is often hard to tell whether what we see, read, or hear, is fact or fiction.

If there are many young people, and maybe even some older ones, who believe the way that I used to, then it's no wonder that our leaders have no trouble convincing us that their beliefs are right. Especially easy to persuade are the younger generation, the kids who have not yet lived during a war, who think that wars are glamorous and adventurous. I should know; I thought so, too. I also thought that history was fact, and that war and adventure were synonymous. Most young people also think that all war stories that they hear have been either minimized or exaggerated, that the old folks who tell them the story really know very little about "modern" warfare; that their experiences are outdated, old fashioned. A "new" modern war is "different."[82] Those who have not been through a war think that the excitement and glory of war can be achieved without suffering, without paying the price.

Inge and I wondered if more people could have been persuaded to change their thinking by being given better living conditions, rather than by having bombs dropped on them.

Since creation, people have solved their problems by fighting and killing. Since Cain killed Abel, people have not found other solutions to cure their differences. Pure common sense would dictate that there must be other ways to resolve conflicts. To our understanding, for example, it would have been much easier, and cheaper too, to fight Communism by giving the war money to the Communists in order to turn all of them into capitalists, rather than spend the money to kill them off.

Inge and I knew, by now, how stupid it was to dream of a utopia. We understood that in order to turn the world from centuries-old beliefs and practices, one would have to change people's fundamental natures and basic thinking. And we knew what chances there were for this to happen.

But we had fun talking about it, anyway. As far as Inge and I were concerned, there was no legitimate reason for wars; nor was there such a thing as a "civilized" war—a war played by rules and regulations, like a chess game. After World War I—"The war to end all wars"—the League of Nations adopted a resolution to ban the use of poisonous gas. Everyone agreed that this was not the way that we wanted to kill people, and that's why we good human beings had to develop the atom bomb. That's how we went from Stone Age Technology to Twentieth-Century Technology.

I once told Jacob about the conversations that I had been having with Inge. He said: "You are too young to understand anything. You are hopelessly naive, foolish, and stupid. What else can one expect from a couple of women?" I got upset and told him that men just like to fight. They fight during ballgames. They enjoy boxing, wrestling, hunting—all this killing and hurting others, which they call "fun." We had a quarrel.

For Inge and me, fighting, like politics, made no sense at all. We recalled some of the political speeches that we had heard from our respective politicians. To us, they all sounded alike; only the language was different. All the speeches of political candidates sounded something like:

"Our production is low, prices are high. We have unemployment, crime, a housing shortage, and hungry kids. We must solve the problems quickly. We need better medical care, better schools, more food."

After explaining the problems (which, of course, the people know anyway), a politician will hardly ever explain how they will be eliminated, or who will pay for the improvements. Will the payments be in money, or in blood? Will their proposed solutions have side-effects that may be worse than the problems? The answers are almost always omitted, or left open-ended.

When I was younger, I didn't know much about politics. I didn't realize that political speeches had to be interpreted, or be read "between the lines." Not one of the politicians ever said, "I have evil intentions." Politicians justify their deeds by "juggling words." Only very seldom would the public bother to ask such a "trivial" question as, "How do you plan to achieve these promises?" And if someone ever did, he would get no answer—or else such a vague one that its meaning could hardly be understood. But regardless of whether or not there is answer, the response of the masses at political rallies is almost always a unanimous "Hurrah!"—loud applause, screams of approval. People like to believe that an easy solution has been found to a complicated problem. Emotion, rather than reason.

With Inge I could talk about all those crazy "philosophies." And we didn't mind if much of this talk made no sense to the politicians or to the military people. We were two young women with many "old" experiences, and we had fun talking.

It was different whenever I talked to Jacob, though. We could hardly agree on anything but love. When it came to politics, he would tell me to stop discussing fantasies and face reality. He would suggest that I stay away from subjects that I knew nothing about. "No one," he would say, "is going to change the world. Wars were fought before, and they will continue to be fought."

Jacob was busy, now working two delicatessens with Herr Meier. They had hired sales girls and stock boys to work, but they had to do their own buying and selling and the rest of the work.

Jacob's soccer club was going great, even better than he expected. Berliner Hakoah had gotten back its

My Education Continues

place in the Major League, Class A. The team consisted of a few former Hakoah players who were experienced but getting older, and some younger players who, for the most part, were children of mixed marriages whose non-Jewish parent had managed to hide them during the Nazi years; who now needed a lot of training.

Jacob was team captain.

Besides the men's soccer team, the Hakoah club also added a girls' handball team, which I joined.

Life for us was normalizing. We had our friends, our work, our fun, and everyday we were learning new things. I had my education. And the more I learned about the world and its people, the more confused I became. There was a time in my life when things were crystal clear to me. When I was young, before the War, or even during it, I knew that there were "good guys" and "bad guys," friends and foes. Everything was either good or evil. It either had to be praised or condemned.

After Liberation, when I was in Łódź, and alone, I would often think about the six long years of war, and of the ghetto, and of the camps, and of the people who had perished; of those I still hoped would show up from somewhere, and of those I knew would never come back from the ashes. I wondered what kind of people were those who had been capable of committing all of those atrocities, and how I would deal with those criminals if they ever crossed my path. I thought of vengeance.

But since coming to Berlin, I was finding that things had become more complicated. Inge, like many other Germans I would meet, seemed to resemble more the Germans whom my father knew during the First World War, than those whom I remembered from the ghettos and the camps. I found out that hate does more harm to the hater than it does to the hated—and I wasn't going to hurt myself. Besides, "public opinion" was now tilting toward love, not hate. And even though I had little regard for "public opinion," I liked the idea of love better than hate. I personally had a problem with "public opinion," just as I did with the politicians. As far as I could figure out, the public has little or no opinion of its own, and it is not because the public is stupid, but rather because it has no impartial information. The public knows only what it is told by its leaders, which is what the leaders want the public to know. "Public opinion" is handed down.

To avoid talking with Inge about all these conflicting and complicated problems, we would instead talk about our childhood experiences, about the good times and about our not so good memories. After she heard my camp and ghetto stories, she never tried to compare her childhood experiences to mine; she only wanted to show me that her childhood was not as rosy as I thought; that she was a human, not a monster. One of her stories remains in my memory. I called it the "Teddy Bear Story." Years later, after we were separated by the Atlantic Ocean, I asked Inge to write it down for me. This is the story that she sent me in a letter:

"In 1930, my father lost his job and joined the ranks of the unemployed. Times were bad. We already lived in Soldiner Straße [where we first met], but we were living in the attic apartment right over our present one. We had one room, a kitchen, and a hall. We used the same toilet that we shared with you, but, then, there were three families to use it, instead of the two we have now. The hall in our apartment my parents rented out to a young man as sleeping quarters. [Reading this part of Inge's letter reminded me of Jacob's home conditions: Two identical incidents, one in a Jewish family in Warsaw, the other in a German family in Berlin.] "What was the young man's name? He was a potter and also a stove maker, and he did have a job. He really liked us kids a lot, and we liked him very much, too. Sorry, but his name escapes me. Anyway, he was quite a profitable asset to our family.

"Our mother used to go twice a week to a lady we called Tante Huba, to help with the housecleaning. For this she was paid five marks per week. My father had to go every week to a nearby suburb, where the employment office was located, to report on his status and to get his unemployment card stamped. Often he would take us girls with him. Streetcar fare was a luxury. It was too expensive for our budget, so we would walk. It took us an hour each way. There, we had to stand in line forever before my father got to the registry window. That wasn't a very pleasant task, especially during the cold season. Looking at photographs from this period, I can still see the long lines of unemployed people. It was really very bad. In addition to the five marks Mother got for her job, she also received a bag full of groceries. In those trying times, it was a great help. My fourth birthday is still fresh in my memory. In the hall where Max slept (Hurray! I just remembered the man's name!), there was a wicker table and two wicker chairs, and in one of the chairs sat my teddy bear. On the birthday table were flowers and some other nice things. But in my memory, only the teddy remained. Of all the things that kept me company during my life, I loved that teddy the most. Now, sitting in the sofa corner, old and shabby, if that teddy could only speak, he could tell a lot of stories."

I, too, was telling Inge some little stories from my childhood. One of them was about something that happened when I was about nine, maybe in the third grade:

Our teacher, Dora Braff, must have been the best teacher in our school, and the certainly most beloved. Anyway, she broke her leg, and was gone from school for quite some time. We had a substitute. One day, it must have been out of boredom, I wrote a secret poem-song describing our sick teacher. The ballad went something like this:

I am the Old Maid Miss Dora
I'm already forty, but not a bore-a,
When I walk in my room and students misbehave
It hurts my feelings, but I don't rave;
I leave the room, go into the hall
Till the kids are ready to stay on the ball...etc.

During recess, I shared these lyrics with a few girls in class, singing for them a couple of the lines to a familiar tune. On purpose, I had kept the boys out of this "confidential" song.

The boys seemed not to like our secrets, so as the girls were reading the lyrics and singing, one of the boys grabbed the paper out of one girl's hand and ran away. We chased him and begged him to return it to us, but he swore that he had torn the paper up. After a couple of weeks, we had all forgotten about the incident.

When Dora Braff returned to school, one of the boys handed her a sheet of paper. I knew right away what it was. I turned crimson red. The teacher glanced at it, smiled, and put it under the inkwell on her desk. I was sitting in my seat, shaking. Academically, I was a very good student, even though my behavior in class was not always to be commended. The teacher liked me, and I liked her. I didn't want to spoil my reputation. Besides, I was afraid that she might notify my parents.

What I didn't know was that the boys had no idea who had written that little ballad. They only knew that

My Education Continues

it was one of the girls in our class. Anyway, I started sobbing, and that's how I betrayed myself. Everyone's attention focused on me. Dora Braff never said a word. With a friendly smile, she took class attendance and started her lesson.

I told Inge other little events of my childhood, and I listened to her memories of growing-up years. I don't know why I did it; I was supposed to hate her, to seek revenge. But for one reason or another, I couldn't do it. Maybe it was due to my grandfather's influence. He would tell us kids that hate was bad for our health, and for our complexion. Besides, I felt that I had so much in common with Inge that I kept forgetting that we should be enemies. Moreover, I was trying to put the past on the "back burner," so to speak, and go on with my life. I felt that for me, there was no future with the past constantly lingering in my present. No, I did not forget what happened. I was still hoping to find those responsible for the crimes, and was even willing to help those who would be authorized to administer just punishment.

I had difficulties understanding whether or not those who had done nothing to prevent those vicious crimes from happening, should be seen as accomplices to the atrocities. For if that were the case, the guilt would have to go way beyond Germany. I felt that for the Germans who had not been directly involved in the vicious crimes, seeing the Allies occupying their land and "resurrected" Jews returning to Germany; and German hopes and dreams destroyed and the "Master Race" at the bottom of the human scale at the mercy of the Untermenschen; all of this would be, in itself, great punishment.

Inge and I were good friends, and so were our sons; and we were trying to keep it that way. I knew many things about her past, including her involvement with the Hitlerjugend program.

About her parents' guilt or innocence during the Nazi era, I wasn't quite sure, though. From the way they lived, it was clear that they couldn't have benefited much from the Nazi reign. Whether their low profile was due to their anti-Nazi persuasion, or to their inability to rise to higher ranks, was hard to tell. I knew that, due to his age and his World War I injuries, her father had not been drafted into military service in the more recent War.

Since Germany lost World War I, there were never any rewards, parades, or medals for those who had fought in it. Inge told me that at the beginning of Hitler's reign, her father was called to the military headquarters. He was scared to death, she said, because one of her uncles had been accused of being in the communist movement, and her father thought that, by association, he might be questioned about his brother-in-law's activities. Instead, her father came home with a medal, which, they told him, was "long overdue": It was a reward for his fighting in World War I. By the time the Second World War started, Herr Hömpler had a medal to be proud of and a job that made him happy. Frau Hömpler had to work only part time. Inge joined the Hitlerjugend. Her four-year-older sister joined another group, also a Nazi Pioneer organization. Things really started looking up for the Hömplers.

According to one neighbor, Inge's mother, Frau Hömpler, had once kind of participated in an SS raid on Jewish homes—that she was seen pointing out the apartment where a Jewish family was living as an SS officer questioned her. Whether or not the Hömplers were Nazi sympathizers, the neighbor didn't know.

I asked Inge about this incident. She said that she was not aware of it, that she was in no position to know what was going on in her home while she was away at camp. She said that she could not recall such

My Education Continues

an incident while she was home, either. Her parents, Inge said, were neither Jew-haters nor big Nazi sympathizers. So I decided to ask Frau Hömpler herself and find out what she knew of the alleged accusation by the neighbor woman. I did not reveal the woman's name; I only asked if the story was true. Frau Hömpler said that she remembered the SS looking for Jews. "A Jewish family lived in the building," she told me. "One day, SS officers came to look for them. I was in the yard hanging clothes on the line when they came. One of the officers stopped and asked me where the Jews lived. I pointed to that apartment. This is the truth. But the Jews were no longer there; they had moved away about a month earlier."

As for her involvement in Jewish persecution, she said that she had never taken part in any anti-Jewish activities. The Hömplers, like most average Germans after the War, said that, at first, when the Nazis came to power, the people didn't know the extent to which Jews were being persecuted; then, by the time things got worse, they didn't want to get involved. When they first heard rumors about some bizarre atrocities, they thought that the stories were fabricated lies, or at best, greatly exaggerated. While the Nazis were at the peak of their power, it was too late to say or do anything. "You could land up in a concentration camp just for opening your mouth. So we minded our own business. And, by the way," she added, "till the very end we had no idea how bad it really was. I still can't believe it. I am very sorry."

It still boggled the Hömplers' minds how the Holocaust was possible, but since it did happen, they felt that those non-Germans who had helped in the process of killing Jews should bear some of the responsibility. Inge said that she understood the anger that the world was feeling against the Germans. She only wondered how long they would be blamed for it.

She didn't mind, she said, if the guilty ones were punished, but the architects and executioners of the crimes were nowhere to be found; they had just disappeared. She again repeated the question, "How long will we be blamed?" and then later added another one that, she said, she had wanted to ask for a long time:

"I heard," she said, "that not long after Hitler came to power, many Jews wanted to emigrate; some actually boarded ships to go abroad. There were ships full of Jews cruising the seas, but no one let them in. 'Keiner wolte die Juden!' [No one wants the Jews!] Do you know anything about it?"

Inge told me that early on, there had been many things about the Nazi period that bothered her, and she had wanted to discuss them with someone, but had had no one to talk to who could tell her the story firsthand, and from another point of view. It had taken her a while before she got together enough courage to discuss it with me. She had hoped that I wouldn't be offended. She asked me if I knew that Germans, too, viewed themselves as victims of the Nazis and of the War.

Well, I wasn't offended. I was glad that she wanted to know. My problem was that I had no answers. So I said that I was going to check it out. In the meantime, I would have a "preliminary" discussion with her. I said that I could only give her my personal opinion, not a real answer. To the question, How long will the Germans be blamed for the War and the Holocaust, the best I could come up with was to use the "Jewish way of answering questions," that is, to answer a question with a question: "How long do you think the Jews will be blamed for things they as a people didn't commit?" I asked her. "Remember, millions of Jews have been murdered through the centuries—and six million recently—just through various accusations,

My Education Continues

under the pretense that some Jew, somewhere, sometime, somehow, did something that somebody didn't approve of."

"You know, Inge," I added, "people can be very cruel. How history will treat the German people depends a lot on the circumstances, and on the conditions of the non-Germans of the next generations. If the world finds another enemy soon, it might forgive the Germans. (I don't think anyone will soon forget.) Countries—which means governments—don't relate to each other the way people do. People have friends. Governments have interests. If such a time comes that peace with Germany would be in the best interest of other countries, the Germans might even be forgiven for starting two wars within twenty years of each other. Their hatred for Germans may then be gone.

"To your question, How long will it take, well, dear Inge, your guess is as good as mine. Good luck! From my experience, I can only tell you that people's natures have not changed a bit throughout the centuries."

To her question about the ships full of Jews cruising the ocean, I remember giving her a made-up answer. I said that I was quite sure, that I would assume, that had the countries in question known the extent of the danger Jews found themselves in, many leaders would surely have bent their immigration laws, at least temporarily, and opened their doors to the wandering Jews.

I had no way of knowing the validity of my statement; I had just made it up because I wanted to believe that it was true.

I also asked Inge many uncomfortable questions. Once I asked her how she felt about the Hitler movement, and if she had changed any of her thinking since the War ended and the movement, officially, had been killed. She explained to me how the organization looked from her point-of-view, which, of course, did not even resemble mine. She said that almost all young people not assigned to military duties were in some kind of Nazi Youth organization. During the Nazi years, many kids were assigned to special "national obligations," such as helping in cities or doing farm work in order to replace those who had been taken into the military. Going away to camps and helping on farms was a special privilege in which only kids who made good grades and excelled in sports could participate. This was a kind of award for good achievement in the last year of school.

"We worked in groups of eighty to a hundred. We lived in former resort homes and in old castles. We slept on straw mattresses. Like soldiers, we had to keep our things in immaculate order. For the housekeeping, we established a take-turns system. The work was done under strict supervision.

"At seven in the morning we used to leave our quarters and head on foot to the assigned farms. During the War, when many young men had been mobilized, there was a labor shortage. I will never forget this one potato harvest. For weeks we had to walk behind the diggers and collect potatoes in stormy, freezing weather. At noon the farm women would bring us food. By that time we were so starved, we didn't care what they might feed us.

"All the work we did was well organized," she continued. "The Hitlerjugend, besides being a political movement, also provided young people with summer camps, trips, excursions.... It taught the kids music, poetry, and most of all, discipline.

"We worked under the motto, 'One for all, and all for one.' We worked for free. Kind of volunteer work. We sweated quite a bit.

"As a byproduct, almost unconsciously, we learned a lot. We learned table manners, work accountability, and, again, discipline, in all forms. We learned to cook

My Education Continues

and to sew; and also about so badly needed comradeship. We were also taught ethics, morals. We were never left unattended."

I could hardly believe what I was hearing. "Nazi ethics and morals"! The only thing I could say was, "I am sorry I couldn't join the elite club."

Inge didn't laugh at my comment. She only kept adding more praise for the organization.

I said, "There must have been a lot of brainwashing going on."

"Naturally," she said. "There were political undertones, but this was to be expected from the prevailing authorities. You never get something for nothing. While we were there, the camp also instilled in us members the value of hard work, respect for elders, respect for the Party, and of course, reverence for law and order. Most of all, love for the Fatherland and for the Führer."

I told Inge that I had heard how the Hitlerjugend were taught; that the three most important words were Führer, Vaterland, Partei—Leader, Fatherland, Party. Inge said that this was not the way she had learned it, but she did admit that this must have been the general idea that the authorities were trying to get across.

"Of course," I said. "And they were trying to get across that Germans were superior to all other people, that they were a 'special race,' and were not to mix with anyone of 'inferior blood,' with the so-called Untermenschen, which included everybody not classified as the 'Master Race.'"

Inge said that I had it all wrong. That I was misrepresenting the reality. She knew, for a fact, that in every country the German troops entered, the population was glad to have them. The people liked the Germans and their law-and-order policy. "Our troops freed the people. Our soldiers were greeted by enthusiastic crowds, with flowers and outstretched arms." She said that she even had proof of it: She had seen pictures of it all in the papers and magazines, even in the newsreels at the movies.

I was sure that she believed that what she was telling me was true. I really hated to disappoint her. I had to tell her of how these movies and photos had come about: I had seen some of them being made in Warsaw. I told her about the bombing of Warsaw, about how, for four straight weeks, the city was without fuel, food, or medicine; about how, finally, when everything in the city was on fire and the water was cut off, Warsaw finally surrendered. I told her that the people whom she saw in the movies did not go to greet the German troops who were marching in to occupy the city; the starving and destitute people had been running from the fires and running to catch bread, which the soldiers were throwing from their army trucks.

"That," I said, "is when they had their arms stretched out. That was when the cameras were rolling and the pictures were taken."

I could see the disappointment in her face. Still, she insisted that people in many countries were happy to see the Germans come. I had to agree with her on some points, for there must have been some people in each of the occupied countries who were actually glad to see the Germans coming. But these were rather exceptions, and it was before they had gotten to know their occupiers. The largest majority was not only unhappy but outright miserable, and scared of losing their country, their independence, and their lives.

"Can you imagine anyone in his right mind being happy about losing his independence, especially to the Nazis, who treated everyone as a subordinate, like a slave? I bet there must have been a few people among you Germans who were glad to see the Russians coming to Berlin."

My Education Continues

We were going back and forth in our conversation, arguing between her "true facts" and my "real knowledge," my eyewitness accounts.

Finally, I brought to her attention a few of my many experiences with "Nazi ethics and morals." I told her what the goals of the Nazis had been as far as I knew them: The Third Reich was to reign over the world for at least a thousand years, and the "Master Race" was destined by God to rule over all Untermenschen. And we Jews weren't even counted among these "sub-humans." We were, more or less, in the category of rats or bugs. German kids were taught in schools and camps to report all anti-Nazi activities, even those of friends and relatives.

Inge sat with her mouth wide open, surprised at what she was hearing. She said, "I never heard anything that absurd in all my life. I never knew of such German ambitions, nor of such a German education."

By the time we finished this argument, Inge had heard again of how the Nazis used to behave toward their "subjects."

"In person," she said, "I had never seen any of it. Working in the fields, I came across some Polish and Russian laborers who lived on a nearby farm. As far as I could tell, they were treated nicely. Of course," she added, "they were not free to come and go as they pleased, but neither were we. We were stuck in our Lager. That whole year, we waited for Christmas to come so that we could visit our families. You think we were happy?"

What kept Inge and me together was, first of all, that our boys were growing to love each other; they were like brothers. They played and ate and fought together. Later, after Jacob and I moved to another apartment, and the Hömplers moved, too, Inge and I remained very close. Our boys were still together. They attended the same preschool, her son full time, mine only during the morning sessions.

Another reason for our togetherness was that we were honest with each other. She eventually learned what the Nazis had done to the Jews and to the rest of the world, once it became public knowledge. She realized that the "facts" that she had been given by "The Party" were not the same as the ones that the rest of the world knew; she understood that her opinion was based on the "facts" that she had been given. Inge was not the only one who had once thought so. Other Germans I would meet were also confident that their knowledge of war events was the absolute truth. Those who knew that it was not so, were either no longer around or simply not saying anything. At least Inge was honest about her feelings. She said that she had loved the Third Reich, and had thought that whatever it was doing was right. Now, after the War, and in retrospect, many Germans could see things differently; but there was nothing that could be changed. Besides, most of the people, especially the young, didn't want to dwell on the past.

Some German girls, who for some time had been dating Jewish guys, were now getting married to them—a disgrace to the "Master Race," as well as to the "Chosen People"; to the race with superiority, special rights, and privileges, and to the people selected for special responsibilities, obligations, and suffering. A few of Jacob's friends were engaged to German girls who kept assuring their future husbands that they had had no Nazi involvement. I knew them well. We were meeting them in coffeehouses, at dance parties, and at sporting events and other social affairs. Occasionally, we would visit one another in our homes.

One afternoon, Inge and I were listening to records. The boys were playing. Unexpectedly, the doorbell rang. It was Greta, the fiancée of Jacob's friend,

My Education Continues

Marjan. "I was just passing by, so I thought I'd stop and see your new apartment," she said, in a friendly way.

I knew Greta quite well. Her father, I had heard from other German people, was killed fighting the Poles, even though she claimed that he had died of pneumonia at the age of forty-two. Anyway, Greta lived with her widowed mother and Marjan, who had moved in with them.

I told Greta that one of my friends was visiting, and asked her, please, to come in and meet her. It was a startling sight when the two women saw each other. Greta almost fell to the ground when she saw Inge in my house. Her face turned red; she didn't know whether to leave the room or to stay.

After calming down a bit, she said politely, "My name is Gre...Greta...." Her voice was shaking.

Inge answered, "Guten Tag, gnädiges Fräulein! [Good day, madam!] I am quite sure I know you from somewhere."

Greta didn't know what to say. She looked at the floor, then watched the boys playing. Then she looked at me, saying nothing. Inge broke the silence: "Weren't we in the Hitlerjugend together?" she asked.

After Greta's initial shock, the two women had a long conversation. They recalled some events and asked about common friends and acquaintances. Throughout the whole conversation, Greta kept looking at me. She was sure that it was the first time that I had heard about Inge's involvement with the Hitlerjugend.

After they finished their talk, I turned to Greta and said, "Don't be so surprised, Fräulein Greta. I've known all along what Inge was doing during the Nazi period. It was you who were hiding your past. I hope you explained it to Marjan."

Greta was shocked. She couldn't conceive that I was knowingly being friendly with a former

Hitlerjugend. Her eyes looked at me in disbelief. That's when I made it clear to her: "You see, Greta, at least Inge has been honest about her past; that's what I like about her. I wonder what Marjan knows about you. As a matter of fact, I know now that almost all young people were members of some kind of Hitler organization: It was the thing to do during that era, but only a very few of those young people will talk about it."

Before Greta left, I told her not to worry, that I wasn't going to tell Marjan what I knew. But I did suggest that she tell him before he found out. I felt that people who kept secrets had something to hide, and that Jewish men who got intimately involved with German women without checking their past deserved whatever they might end up getting.

Greta complimented me on the beautiful apartment that she was seeing for the first time. I told her that we had paid a lot of money for it. We bought it fully furnished from a German engineer before he left for Belgium on a contract. He had taken a small fortune just for vacating it, and he had seen to it that we got our legal permit to live in it. We were very proud of the place, especially since we had paid for it.[83]

After Greta left, Inge and I took a walk with the kids. On the way, she asked me an interesting question. She was wondering why there was so much talk about the Jews, why the Jews were singled out as "special victims" of Fascism, when according to accounts now available, millions of other people, including many Germans, had been victimized by the Nazis.

I thought that everyone who had lived through this period already knew the answer. It seemed that many still did not. I said that even though those others had also been victims, there was a big difference between Jews and the others. It's true that many intellectuals

My Education Continues

were arrested, religious leaders of various denominations were persecuted, POWs were killed, and anyone whose opinion differed from that of the Nazis was stuck in a concentration camp, to be starved and tortured. But all these victims were charged with some kind of a crime, or whatever the Nazis called a crime. Only the Jews, and, I must say in all fairness, the Gypsies, were victimized for no other reason than for their birth.

Inge always would always shake her head in disbelief whenever I talked about the Holocaust. She still wanted to believe that some of my relatives would show up. I tried to believe it, too, and that's why Jacob and I kept going to the Red Cross and other relief organizations, looking to see if anyone had shown up, even someone who at least could give us a clue, some information, about what had happened to our families, our relatives, our friends.

One day Jacob came home from a visit to the Schlachtensee DP Camp. When he came through the door, I knew that something was wrong. I asked him what had happened. He didn't answer. Only after a few minutes, and after his anger had subsided a bit, did he say, "I just heard from the Jewish agency that in Kelce, some anti-Semites have arranged a pogrom for Jewish survivors who have been returning from Russia.[84] Over forty Jews were killed; many more wounded. No one is sure yet whether AK or the ENDEK organized the raid, but what is clear is that it was professionally organized.[85] Those Jews who escaped the slaughter were on their way to DP camps in Germany. We had to organize some room for them. The organizers asked me to help."

With horror in our eyes, we looked at each other, then we looked at the baby, who was sleeping peacefully in his crib.

We later found out that, without saying a word, we had been both thinking the same thing: We were sure that our decision to leave Poland had been the right one: This pogrom was unbelievable. The murderers hadn't even needed Hitler's approval. But bad news was coming not only from Poland but also from Palestine. As the world was celebrating a new era of peace, the War for the Jews was not yet over.

As a matter of fact, a new war was just beginning.

The British government, which mandated the territory, was prohibiting Jews from entering Palestine. Many Jewish families were stranded in German and Italian and other European DP camps, without a place to go. Those who were getting to Palestine by means of underground channels were having to fight their way in.

In addition to the Jewish problem, the three Western Allies were squabbling with the Russians; the honeymoon between the East and the West was over. While we were almost sure that we, the people, had learned something about peaceful coexistence, actually we had only learned new methods of killing and destroying one another. I was disappointed. I thought that the "love affair" between the Communist countries and the Democratic ones was going to last forever. It took only a short time for the "brotherhood of men" to fall apart. And my education continued.

One time, I talked with Inge about the behavior of different people during the Hitler era. "We couldn't have been the only ones," she observed. She was trying really hard to take some of the blame and guilt away from her people. Also, she was trying to persuade me that it had been just as savage of the Allies to bomb German cities as it had been of the Germans to bomb Warsaw.

"If they had been as good as they claimed to be, even much better than we were, why then did they do

My Education Continues

the same thing to us? I have seen all those 'humane' foreign soldiers with rifles pointed, tramping over corpses. I watched them running in and out of buildings like wild animals, chasing our women and children out of their own homes. Those foreign angels were just as bad as our troops allegedly were." I was sure that she herself actually believed what she was saying.

So I asked her if the occupied people should have let the Germans trample over them, or have given their land to the Germans as a gift and themselves over as the Germans' slaves.

"No," she said, "that's not what I had in mind. Those 'good, nice humane people' you are talking about should have pushed us back to our borders, then left us alone."

It was hard for me to imagine her reasoning. I knew that even with our friendship, there were still disagreements, and surely even quite a bit of mistrust.

And so my education continued.

I learned that as terribly dreadful as the War had been, not everybody saw it, and experienced it, in the same way, even now. For example, let's face it: There are many advantages to war. It gets rid of unemployment, unrest, and boredom. War unites people. They work and fight for a common cause against a common enemy. Nationalism flourishes. Who is not for "The Cause" is a traitor. War cures overpopulation. Moreover, war is exciting. Not a boring moment, no shortage of adventures. And the most important advantage of war: money. There is a lot of money to be made in a war. Those who know how to use chaos and other people's miseries to their own advantage get very rich. With a little bit of luck, a lot of cunning manipulation, and some betrayal, many people manage to profit from disasters. The same ones also usually manage to escape the fighting, often by leaving the battle zone—that is, by leaving the country at war. Or else they escape the fighting by buying their way out.

I heard talk about war and its mysteries while I was still a kid. I remembered how happy I was when I finally had the opportunity to see one. Once, I told Inge how much I had always wanted to see a war. To my surprise, she said that she, too, had been happy when she heard about an impending war.

Later, when we were apart, she wrote to me, as she had with the teddy bear story, a letter describing the beginning of the War from her viewpoint:

"When World War II started," she wrote, "I was in a hospital with a broken knee I suffered in a bike accident. I can still recall how worried I was that I might miss the War. I was twelve, then; and in my eyes, I imagined war as a happy adventure. The things I heard from my father about the First World War didn't mean a lot to me. I didn't even have a realistic vision of fear; and, of course, I didn't think about the terrible grief and misery a war can bring to people."

Inge sounded so much like any other twelve-year-old; she was just like me. Yet she was a twelve-year-old Hitlerjugend; she was my enemy. She, like me, believed what she was taught. She couldn't see anything wrong with being "patriotic," which in the minds of many people was and is synonymous with: "Everything my government tells me is true—everything it does is right."

I think that when a country is having a "patriotic spell," its citizens stop thinking rationally; they stop questioning their leaders. They don't dispute, they don't criticize—such behavior is "unpatriotic." Their government can do no wrong. I, too, had believed that way when I was a kid. I had my childish illusions about governments. I also believed that only evil people had the potential to become Nazis. On this, and on

My Education Continues

many other issues, I was mistaken. I could now see that millions of people would have joined the Nazi Party had they been accepted, had they met the "required qualifications." I am almost sure that if not out of persuasion, they would have joined the popular party just to enjoy the promotions, the pay, the prestige and honor such membership would have provided. People, for the most part, like to get ahead, to accomplish things that bring them recognition. If this means following a leader, or the Party rule, so be it. Swimming against the current is a difficult task that very few people are willing to undertake.

From what I have learned, people's political persuasions start in their stomachs. The majority of people are more interested in feeding their families than in figuring out how political systems work. Patriotism is a nice, noble feeling, but it has to agree with one's pocketbook and stomach.

So I thought that Poland was the best country in the world, and our government was the smartest. I thought Poland was the center of the universe. My first disappointment, I remember, came when I was in the fourth grade. It was in third-grade geography class that we had learned to read the map. Next to the blackboard, on the wall, was a map of Poland. It was almost twice as big as the blackboard. I thought of Poland as huge and mighty. We traveled over this map from city to city; from the Carpathian Mountains to the Baltic Sea, from the German border to the Russian Frontier. Nothing beyond Poland could be seen on this map. Later, in fourth grade, we studied Europe, and, of course, we had a different map. What a disappointment this was. Here my big, mighty Poland was only one of many other countries; and next to the Soviet Union, it looked like a small speck. This was very hard for me to accept. It was almost heartbreaking.

There are many things that I don't quite understand to this day.

I learned that in time of war, there are always some young and naive people who, even if not drafted, will willingly go off to fight for their leaders, for their country, for the "right cause," hoping to gain honor and fame without realizing that corpses need none of the above; that for a corpse. a six-foot hole in the ground (and maybe a cross) is sufficient reward.

I learned that young soldiers who dream of might and glory face the grim reality of horror and cruelty, which is known as "bravery." I learned that in war, human suffering does not count. Casualties are only numbers. Killing is valor. Killing is only a sin if it is done on individualized bases: "Wholesale killing," or killing for a "cause," or with a "purpose," is not included in the Fifth Commandment. In wholesale killing, we do not kill humans; we kill enemies. This kind of killing calls for rewards, not for punishments. So I learned to look at things from opposing sides. I learned to listen to opposing views, even if they made absolutely no sense to me—even if they contradicted my beliefs. I just liked to know how others thought, how they would come up with what seemed to me to be weird ideas. I learned that during stable economic times, we have many "friends"; during crises, our friends can be turned into enemies and, if need be, scapegoats.

Throughout centuries, Jews have been blamed for many things. They have been killed, murdered, made to convert by force; they have been accused of all misfortunes that might befall the local population. During the Middle Ages, Jews were accused of bringing the plague. Ukrainians in a time of drought used to say, "The rivers dried up because Jews drank all the water."

My Education Continues

In the Twentieth Century, Jews were accused of being Communists and Capitalists at the same time; they were poor and dirty and, at the same time, in control of all banks; Jews didn't even have a country, but their ambition was to take over the whole world.

Hitler invented a perfect enemy to blame for all the problems facing Germany. Instead of concentrating on the economic depression and finding jobs and food for the people, he gave them a new goal, a purpose for life: "Fight the enemy!—Fight the Jews!" In order to make the people be willing to pursue this ambition, he used the popular tactic (but by no means new with him) that turns friends into enemies and reduces human enemies to beasts and locusts. Then he asked his people to destroy the plague.

The trick did not quite work according to plan, so he, supposedly, committed suicide, and left his people to deal with the consequences.

Now the German people, the guilty, the not-so-guilty, even the innocent—those guilty only by association—were being made to pay the price.

While I was learning all these things and adjusting to life in Berlin, the state of Israel was being born in the Middle East. Many DP camp residents were immigrating to the not yet quite established Jewish country. Only the Jews who were living in the cities remained, at least for the time being, in Germany, where they were encountering no financial hardship, but where political conditions were nevertheless quickly changing.

The love affair between the four Allies who were occupying Berlin was coming to an end. The Russians resented having the Western Powers at the center of the East Zone. Berlin had become a sore spot for the Russians because it was kind of an "eye" into the East Zone (and for the East Berliners, an "eye" into Western living). The Russians hoped that by blockading the city, they could get rid of these unwanted "spies." So, in April, 1948, the Russians blockaded the three Western sectors of Berlin, in effect stopping all land transportation of supplies and people to and from the city. The Allies formed an air bridge and started airlifting all essential supplies to the city. I remember standing with Inge and the boys on an overpass by the Tempelhof Airport, watching American planes land, one every five minutes. They looked more like train cars hooked to one another than planes landing at an airport.

This air bridge was not only a way to get supplies into Berlin; it was also the only way to get out of the city. We were waiting for a place, and a way to go....

Those who could, tried to leave the city. The Jewish relief organization, Joint, was registering Displaced Persons for emigration out of Germany.[86] They sent us a letter asking if we would like to register for a US visa. Jacob hesitated. He wasn't yet ready to leave all his work and fun and travel into the unknown. After his father's experience, foreign countries did not sound as glamorous to him as they did to others, even though he knew that his father's brother, his Uncle Haynoch, was living somewhere in New York.

To me, on the other hand, going to America meant new adventures, and a continuing education.

We registered. The Jewish association, in conjunction with the UNRA, was taking care of the arrangements. The UNRA would help with the journey—transportation by plane, truck, and ship—and Joint would help with the resettlement.

Meanwhile, our life in Berlin was proceeding as normally as possible under the circumstances.

One day, Jacob came home all excited; he had some very unusual news to tell me. "You will never guess who I met today," he said. From the way he

My Education Continues

talked, I thought that his sister was resurrected, or that his American uncle had showed up. Then he told me.

"Eating lunch at Cafe Gesundbrun, I saw sitting at another table none other than Herr Waldowsky. Do you remember, I told you about him. He was one of my camp guards, the one who helped me so much, the one I credit with keeping me alive. I knew that after leaving Poland, he went to live somewhere in the vicinity of Berlin. I couldn't believe my eyes when I saw him sitting just a few feet from me.

"He looked quite different without his uniform and rifle, but I recognized his face. I walked over to his table. He gave me a funny look, as if to say, 'Have I seen this face somewhere before?'—just like Stephan at the theater that night. He was sure he knew me, but he could not place me. When I said, 'Guten Tag, Herr Waldowsky,' he almost fainted."

It took Jacob some time to recover from all his excitement. When he finally calmed down, he told me about the sensational reunion; that they would meet again in the same cafe a few days later.

To this next meeting, Jacob took me and one of his friends. Herr Waldowsky came with one of his brothers. We told the people in the cafe, of whom Jacob knew quite a few, who we were and why we were celebrating. Some suggested calling the press and honoring Herr Waldowsky, but neither Jacob nor Herr Waldowsky wanted the publicity.

Jacob treated everyone around us to a drink, and we all toasted Herr Waldowsky. He, to us, was a true hero; he was one of a kind. There weren't too many people who having power over others had behaved as humanely as he had. Yet, I was quite sure, and so was Herr Waldowsky, that there were some Germans in this restaurant who blamed him and others like him for having behaved humanely to the enemy.

No words can describe the pure sadism with which some guards treated their subjects. I am not even talking about those who did the tormenting on assignment, nor about those who tortured out of political or religious persuasions; fanatics are able to do many illogical senseless deeds for their "cause." I am not even including those pitiful executioners who did it in order to get recognition or a promotion. I am talking about those who did the torturing and killing as a fun activity, as a pastime, as entertainment—just out of sheer pleasure, out of sadistic joy, as if to say, "Look! I, Mr. Nobody, have power over you. I decide whether you should live or die, and I choose how much you should suffer. Maybe I won't even harm you a lot this time, but I want to make sure that you are scared of me, that I can put fear into your heart. I, Mr. Nobody, never dreamed of having such power. I can even kill you, and all you guys assembled here, if I so desire. And I won't even get punished for it. I can become famous for doing it, maybe even get an award."

And yet, amidst these sadistic creatures, were guards like Herr Waldowsky, here, who had given new home to the human race.

Long after the party at the restaurant was over, we remained in touch with Herr Waldowsky. We were sending him food parcels even after he moved out of town. We finally lost contact with him when he moved away without leaving a forwarding address.

I often wondered if Waldowsky's friends and peers thought of him as a weak person, or even a traitor.

While Jacob kept telling all his friends the story of Guard Waldowsky, the survivors and many others, as well as the international Jewish press, were pondering many as yet unanswered questions: "How could a 'civilized' people have created such a hell on earth? Why had there been so little resistance in such a desperate situation? Where had the world been?"

My Education Continues

I had absolutely no idea how to answer any of these questions. They were much too complicated for me; I was even too stupid to ask them. The answers required explanations and a lot of research which, at that time, had not yet become available. I only knew that there had been some organized resistance movements in France, Belgium, and Yugoslavia; the girls who were with me in Leipzig had talked about them. I heard that not one of these organizations was successful. I later learned that there were actually quite a few small, isolated revolts in many ghettos and in some camps, about which more was yet to be said. Then there were also many cases of individual resistance; and, of course, there was the Warsaw Ghetto Uprising. The reason why we didn't hear too much about any of them was because they were all unsuccessful.

Besides the revolts, there were also Jews who joined different guerrilla groups in the forests; there would have probably been a lot more had it not been for the local anti-Semites, who tormented even those Jews who were going to help them fight the Germans. And there were more questions concerning why Jews couldn't just organize and start fighting the German forces. The question "to fight or not to fight" had no simple yes or no answer.

When the Nuremberg Laws were first issued, and the decrees against the Jews were published, Jews knew that they were in trouble, that bad times were ahead. But even though through the centuries Jews had suffered many disasters, no one in his right mind could ever have imagined that such preplanned barbarism could take place among human beings, let alone during the Twentieth Century.

Then, of course, as it is by now clear, and as I have already mentioned, the Holocaust did not start with gas chambers and crematories. In most parts of the

German-occupied territories, this was a systematic, well-thought-out process that went through all the stages of degradation, humiliation, dehumanization, and expulsion. Then came isolation, starvation, disease, and torture. Finally, the people were made exhausted, hopeless, helpless, and depressed. Then they were condemned to die. Freedom, as precious as it is, has little meaning on an empty stomach and in a dying mind. I had the "privilege" of testing this on a few occasions.

Real resistance at such a stage was impossible. Resistance, at any stage was virtually inconceivable without outside help. And this outside world was un: first unaware and uncertain; then unprepared and unable (because it had underestimated the problem); then undecided and, maybe, unwilling. Then it was too late. The isolated Jews had no arms, no information, no support, no moral encouragement. Now, in retrospect, we can see that even if the Jews had fought every step of the way, the outcome would have been the same as it was at the end of the War.

The truth of the matter is that after it was all over, the question "to fight or not to fight" still remained unanswered. It only brought up another controversial point: Couldn't an armed resistance have given the Germans a "legitimate right" to kill, or perhaps have made the Germans look like the "innocent victims" of vicious Jewish aggression? Would it have looked as if the Germans were killing Jews in "self defense"? And would the Jews have been less dead? Another question: If there is not even the slightest chance of winning a battle, is it wise or stupid to take a chance on fighting—and killing oneself? Is such an action suicide? Even with all the miseries that the Jews had been subjected to, there was still a drop of hope. Fighting a losing battle, however, would have meant sure death, and death was hopeless, death was forever.

My Education Continues

The problem was that during the Nazi regime, all logical assumptions did not apply. Didn't all those who resisted, die just the same as those who didn't? I am not even trying to answer any of these questions; I have many more to ask: What is a civilized war? What are the "laws" of war? I can't figure out the different expressions used for dead people, namely, "dying with" or "dying for" honor, "dying in vain," or "dying for Kiddush HaShem." Such talk really bothers me because it seems as though many people pretend to understand how one corpse differs from another. But I don't get it. I can't even understand the story of Job.

Life in divided Berlin was exciting. The politicians were making sure that there was never a boring minute. Going from and to the Russian sector of the city was now allowed by special permits only. People were adapting to the new conditions.... But soon the blockade was lifted, and economic conditions improved greatly. Life for the Germans was slowly stabilizing—especially in the parts under Western occupation. It was improving in the East, too, but at a much slower pace. People were calling it the "Post-War Recovery Period." For us Jews, however, even though the shooting had stopped a few years before, the War was not yet over. We were still looking for relatives, for a place to call home, for some stability in our lives. We were still hoping, against all odds, that some of our relatives might be found among the survivors. Such cases did, of course, happen, but they were quite rare. However, these rare events kept telling all of us not to give up hope.

The following is about one such resurrected relative, who, for all practical purposes, was not expected to return. It happened to one of Jacob's friends.

We got to know Malvin when he first came to Berlin with his wife and small daughter. He survived the War in Russia; his wife survived in one of the camps. They met in Poland, got married, and came to Berlin; now they were waiting to emigrate to another country. One day, Jacob came home from work and said, "Malvin's first wife and eight-year-old son showed up in Berlin. She arrived yesterday, and is now in the DP camp. The meeting between him and his first wife should take place tomorrow. It should be exciting. Everyone who knows him is in shock and impatient to see what's going to happen. Wife Number Two says that she will kill the first wife if 'that bitch' thinks she can break up their marriage."

After some arguments between Malvin and the two wives, a few of his friends had formed a so-called "people's court," and were trying to resolve the scandal among the parties involved. No one was interested in bringing such a case to the German authorities and having it be publicized in the press. After a lot of excitement and talking, the first wife, who really didn't care about getting her husband back after what he had done, decided to take a sum of money, a kind of child support, and leave town. So much for the dead coming back to life.

We had many friends who were now replacing our lost families. We formed a kind of "support group." Jacob was involved in his soccer club with his friends, and he was volunteering in some refugee relief organizations; and was, of course, working at his business.

I was spending time with Inge and the boys and a few other friends. I was also playing handball in Jacob's club and playing tennis with my other friends, taking my baby and his babysitter with me whenever I could. I was also busy with German lessons. I had also

My Education Continues

started math, history, and science. I was still trying to get the long-past-due diploma. In addition, I started taking accordion lessons. Inge was helping me with my books because all the instructions were in German and I still needed some help with the language.

I was adding pages to my diary, mostly notes about the Holocaust, while continuing my education.

In Berlin, our lives were sometimes happy, often sad, but never dull. For example, ever since we had become neighbors with the Hömplers, we would celebrate the Christmas holidays with them. It developed into a kind of weird tradition. Before the holidays, Herr and Frau Hömpler, who, because of the boys, were now called Opa and Oma by both of them, used to prepare cookies and small gifts for both of their "grandsons." The "Weihnachtsmann," who was usually one of the Hömplers' cousins, would bring toys and candies for the boys. The boys, with tears in their eyes, would recite their rehearsed rhymes: "Lieber, guter Weihnachtsmann."[87] We would sing carols and light candles on the Christmas tree.

Christmas was a big holiday in Germany, just as it used to be in pre-War Poland. All work would stop at noon on Christmas Eve. Only emergency workers and vehicles would be on duty. Businesses were closed, and there was no public transportation. These new peaceful and happy Christmases in Germany would remind Jacob and me of the tension and stress that Jews used to experience during the Christmas holidays in pre-War Poland. Those days were more memorable to Jacob than to me because there were more Christians living in his area than in mine; and also a different class of people—mostly blue-collar workers.[88] He still recalled the fear that used to befall the Jewish population during all major Christian holidays like Christmas, Easter, and Pentecost, which were each celebrated for two days in Catholic Poland.

It was a time for the hooligans to abuse Jews: It was their holiday fun. A lot of drinking would go on, and drunken "Christian" hoodlums would roam the streets attacking Jews, beating, kicking, and even stabbing them. Often they would throw stones, breaking windows in Jewish homes and businesses. The police could hardly keep up with them; many law enforcers didn't even try. Jews who lived in mixed or Christian neighborhoods would try to stay off the streets during these major holidays. That's why it was awkward for us to take part in a Christmas celebration—and, of all places, in a German home.

Jewish holidays were another matter. Whereas in pre-War Poland, we celebrated all Jewish holidays, now, of all the Jewish festivals, we were observing only the High Holidays and Passover. Jewish Holidays to us were sad days now. It was a time of reminiscence, a heartbreaking time. In the synagogue, people were wailing, mourning their loved ones, and screaming with the pain of past memories. Many who had lost children fainted, overcome with emotion whenever the cantor chanted the Kaddish or the "El Moleh Rachamim"—prayers for the souls of the dead.

Passover was no better. We would observe it with our Jewish friends, and with other survivors. All of us had memories of our families. No sooner had we started the Seder than the conversations would turn to pre-War Passover celebrations, and to talk of the War. Then everyone at the table would have a story to tell about the last holiday spent with the family. The evening would usually end in tears. Instead of asking the traditional "Four Questions," some of us would ask, "What has happened to God's miracles when we needed them? Why, out of all His children, did God pick us to be His chosen people? Is there going to be a 'holiday' commemorating the Holocaust? If so, how is it going to be observed? Where do we go from here?" And so forth.

My Education Continues

Many of our Jewish friends were leaving Germany. Some were going to Israel, others to Argentina, Australia, Canada, the United States, or wherever else they could get in. The reason that so many had decided to leave at this particular time was that this was the last year of the UNRA relief agency and the Joint organizations; they were closing their offices in Germany. Anyone wanting to emigrate after that time would have to do it on his own, that is, without subsidies or help, and to go as an emigrant, not as a refugee. So many of the previously undecided, and those who had kept postponing their departures, chose to leave. Most of us who had stayed this long were making a nice living, but hardly anyone had enough money for such ventures like traveling and resettling in another country.

Among those who had left a year before were our good friends, Ike and Lola. They had a seven-year-old son and a baby daughter. They were also the godparents of our son. Two other families with whom we were friendly had also left the same year. The destination of all three families had been a place called Kansas City, located somewhere in the Midwestern United States. They had all promised to write.

A few months had passed, but we had not heard from any of them. Besides being interested in their well-being, we also wanted to know what this place Kansas City was like. The Joint organization had found two work contracts that we could choose from: One for Kansas City, the other for Seattle.

Truthfully, we were not very excited about either place. We had never heard of these places, and we didn't know if Jews lived there; or if they were Indian territories.

While we were waiting for some letters (that never came), a couple of our bachelor friends, who had left for the United States months before, returned to Berlin for a visit. Actually, they had come looking for wives. Their original contract was for Seattle or Portland—I don't remember—but they had moved to New York, where one of them had an aunt. They had thought to find "nice girls" there. What they found, so they claimed, was that American girls were spoiled, demanding, and had no use for foreign men who spoke no English, had no jobs, drove no cars, and had no money. The bachelor guys also confirmed what we knew from papers and magazines, namely, that jobs in the United States were very scarce. One of the guys, Pavel, told us, "They don't need us over there. Despite all those American troops in South Korea, there are, nevertheless, a few million unemployed workers looking for jobs."

Jacob interrupted him, and pointing to me and to himself, added jokingly, "When we get there, they will have a few million plus two."

We all laughed, even though it was not very amusing. Pavel said that immigrants were called "greenhorns"; that without a language or profession, newcomers, even if they did find jobs, would have to work for minimum wage or below, usually washing dishes in restaurants or doing janitorial work.

News from the other countries to which survivors were moving was about the same, or even worse: In Israel, there was even a war.

To remain in Germany also had many problems: We were not citizens. We were classified as "Staatenlosen"—"stateless persons." Living in Germany, as nice as it was, also held many painful memories. Rightly or wrongly, we could see no future for us, or for our children, there. We knew that to emigrate would mean years of new adjustments, new hardships; a new language, a new culture, new friends, new occupations. For me that meant only new experiences, a new education, new adventures. I was

My Education Continues

excited about all the prospects of the new undertaking. Jacob was worried. And a few months before the deadline, he was still undecided.

If we wanted to be helped by the DP organizations, we only had a few months to make up our minds.

In midsummer, we decided to go.

We were called to the American consulate, where we had to fill out stacks of forms and answer many questions. Among them, we were asked, "Have you ever belonged to the Communist Party? Have you ever had a venereal disease or tuberculosis? Have you ever been a prostitute? Have you ever been arrested or imprisoned?"

The last one was the hardest one to answer honestly. It needed a lot of explanation. Lawyers for the refugee organization had told us to say, "No," but this was not an honest answer. There were other formalities that we had to go through before getting a visa: We had to have an interview with the American consul, undergo a medical examination, and pass a CIA investigation.

We decided on the contract for Kansas City because of the three families we knew there. We had already received a card from Ike and Lola. From their short note, we presumed that they had nothing spectacular to report, but we decided on Kansas City, anyway, because we knew no one in Seattle, our second choice.

In the local library, we carefully studied a map of the United States to find the exact location of our future home, then we consulted the encyclopedia to look up whatever we could find on Kansas City.

What happened a few weeks later was a mere coincidence. One day, the newspapers reported a great flood in the Midwest of the United States. An evening later, during the newsreel at the movies, we got to see Kansas City. It was underwater. From the

Missouri River, all the way to the railroad station, about three or four miles away, everything was flooded. It was a horrible sight. We were actually a little apprehensive, but decided to go there, anyway, because, we thought, there might be work for us cleaning up the mess.

We still had many things to do before departure from Berlin, things that people living in the DP camps did not have to do. We had to dispose of our part of the business; which, luckily, went quickly. Herr Meier took it over. We had to sell our furniture and transfer our apartment to the new tenants. We needed police clearance papers, and we had to pay all outstanding taxes. While going through all these legal procedures, we found out that we were legally not married: The marriage papers that we had from Łódź, Poland, would not be recognized by the American government as legal documents. Jacob and I, and about thirty other couples with the identical problem, then arranged a "communal wedding" at the American Consulate.

Now, twice married, we were legally ready to go. We had beaten the deadline by a few weeks.

It was a cold, sunny November day when we took a taxi to Tempelhof Flughafen. Accompanying us was the whole Hömpler family, Helga and her mother, and a few other friends. It was a sad farewell. We took pictures, reminisced over our years together, then we hugged and promised to write. Little Michael was crying. Little Simon, distracted by the oncoming plane and the whirling of the propellers, paid no attention to what else was going on. When from the plane door we waved goodbye to our friends, we could see that Michael was still crying. All the others were waving their handkerchiefs.

The two-motor Pan American plane took us over the Russian Zone to Bremerhaven in northwest

My Education Continues

Germany. There we stayed for almost two weeks in an American army barracks, before the military ship, the USS General Harry Taylor, on its return voyage from Germany to the United States, took us to the Port of New Orleans.

The End

Accounting Page

Of the ninety-six (96) family members and relatives (not including friends) whose names I knew, and who were with me, in Warsaw at the beginning of the War, fourteen (14) are accounted for.

Seven died of "natural causes":

1) Grandma Ester (72) died after getting sick in the bomb-shelter.

2) Cousin Moniek (c. 30) died of typhus during the epidemic in the ghetto.

3) Aunt Dora (50s), Moniek's mother, died right after her son's funeral.

4) Cousin Abram (18-20) lost a leg during the bombing; he later died of complications.

5) Aunt Tova (40s), Abram's mother, died of depression after the death of one son and the unknown whereabouts of her other son, who had been taken away.

My Education Continues

6, 7) Uncle Yakov and Aunt Rachel died of starvation and other ghetto-related conditions.

8) Dad's Uncle Pinchus died after a long illness.

9) Cousin Balka's death: accident or suicide.

All of the above have graves and headstones or markers. Some are buried at the Okopowa Cemetery in Warsaw. Others are at the Brudno Cemetery in Praga.

Survivors:

10) Cousin Mordekhei left for Palestine before the War in the mid-30s. His most cherished possession is a picture of his sister's wedding, a photograph of his immediate family that was sent to him just before the War started.[89]

11, 12) Cousin Sruel and his wife, Mollie, survived in the USSR

13) Cousin Luba also survived in the USSR
(All three live in Israel.)

14) Oh, yes! I, too, survived....

All others, those who "volunteered" for work assignments and those who were shipped for "resettlement," were taken away to "unknown destinations," and never heard from again. No

Accounting Page

photographs survive. Their names are registered with the Holocaust Museum in Washington, DC, and in the Yad Vashem in Jerusalem. **To them (may they rest in peace) I attribute my respect for life and my lack of hatred, for they taught me the gift of love.**

Inge and I continue our friendship to this day. We keep in touch through writing, phone calls, and occasional visits.

I am also in contact with a few of my camp friends, and with Greta and Moshe, who are still married.

Timeline

Date	Location	Fela's Life	World
Jan. 1933			Hitler appointed Chancellor
Feb. 1933			Nazi's burn Reichstag building
May 1933			Book burning throughout Germany
Sep. 1935			Nuremberg Laws passed in Nazi Germany
Mar. 1936			Germany occupies the Rhineland
Aug. 1936			Olympic Games in Berlin
Mar. 1938			German annexation of Austria (*The Anschluss*)
Nov. 1938			*Kristallnacht*
Dec. 1938	Warsaw	Chanukah; Birthday (12)	
Mar. 1939	Warsaw		Germany occupies Czechoslovakia
May 1939	Warsaw		MS *St. Louis*, with 937 Jewish refuges is turned away from Cuba, USA
Aug. 1939	Warsaw	**Book narrative begins**	

Timeline

		Returns from "Germany Experience"	
Sep. 1939	Warsaw	Germany invades Poland; Warsaw bombed	**World War II starts**
Oct. 1939	Warsaw	Poland surrenders to Germany	
Nov. 1939	Warsaw	Jews in Poland required to wear Yellow Star	
Dec. 1939	Warsaw	Chanukah (1st during war); Birthday (13)	
Feb. 1940	Warsaw	Jews deported from Germany to Poland	
Apr. 1940	Warsaw	Passover (1st during War)	Construction of Auschwitz concentration camp in Poland; Germany occupies Denmark
May 1940	Warsaw		Germany occupies France; creation of Kraków Ghetto
Jun. 1940	Warsaw		Romania joins the Axis side
Sep. 1940	Warsaw		Signing of the Tripartite Pact (Germany, Italy, Japan),

My Education Continues

			creating the Axis Powers
Nov. 1940	Warsaw Ghetto	Warsaw Ghetto sealed off	
Dec. 1940	Warsaw Ghetto	Chanukah (2nd during war); Birthday (14)	
Mar. 1941	Warsaw Ghetto		Bulgaria joins the Axis side
Mar. 1941	Warsaw Ghetto		Bulgaria joins the Axis side
Apr. 1941	Warsaw Ghetto	Passover (2nd during War)	Germany invades Yugoslavia and Greece
Jun. 1941	Warsaw Ghetto		Germany invades Russia
Jul. 1941	Warsaw Ghetto	Escapes to Sandomierz with mother	Construction of Majdanek concentration camp in Poland; Göring sends letter to Heyrich regarding "Final Solution to Jewish Question"
Sep. 1941	Sandomierz		First large scale of *Zyklon B*-on prisoners (in Auschwitz);Babi Yar massacres
Dec. 1941	Sandomierz		Bombing of Pearl Harbor, marking the entrance of USA into the War

Timeline

Jan. 1942	Sandomierz	Chanukah (3rd during war); Birthday (15)	
Feb. 1942	Sandomierz	Sis and Aunt Naomi arrive in Sandomierz	Sinking of the SS *Struma*, killing 768 Jewish refuges traveling to Palestine
Mar. 1942	Sandomierz		Large scale gassing beings at Auschwitz
Apr. 1942	Sandomierz	Passover (3rd during War)	
May 1942	Sandomierz		*NY Times* reports over 100,000 Jews machine gunned in Eastern Europe
Jul. 1942	Sandomierz	Forced to relocate to Skarżysko	*NY Times*, *London Telegraph* report over 1,000,000 Jews killed by Nazis
Dec. 1942	Skarżysko	Chanukah (4th during war); Birthday (16)	Construction of Plaszów labor camp
Feb. 1943	Skarżysko		Germany loses the Battle of Stalingrad
Mar. 1943	Skarżysko		Conclusion of the liquidation of the Kraków Ghetto
Apr. 1943	Skarżysko	Passover (4th during War)	Waffen SS enters the Warsaw Ghetto; the Uprising begins

My Education Continues

May 1943	Skarżysko		Liquidation of Warsaw Ghetto
Dec. 1943	Skarżysko	Chanukah (5th during war) Birthday (17)	
Mar. 1944	Skarżysko	Forced to relocate to Leipzig	
Apr. 1944	Leipzig	Passover (5th during War)	
Jun. 1944	Leipzig		D-Day—Invasion of Normandy
Jul. 1944	Leipzig		Closing of Majdanek concentration camp; attempt on Hilter's life
Aug. 1944	Leipzig		Liquidation of Łódź Ghetto
Dec. 1944	Leipzig	Chanukah (5th during war); Birthday (18)	Liberation of France
Jan. 1945	Leipzig		Germany loses in the Battle of the Bulge; Capture of Warsaw by Russians; Liberation of Auschwitz and Plaszów by Russians
Feb. 1945	Leipzig		Yalta Conference
Mar. 1945	Leipzig		Death of Anne Frank in Bergen-Belsen concentration camp

Timeline

Apr. 1945	Leipzig	Passover (6th during War); Leipzig march	FDR dies; Mussolini is executed; Hilter commits suicide
May 1945	Leipzig	Liberation; bried period in Lignica	Unconditional surrender of Germany: end of war in Europe
Jun. 1945	Lignica	Moves to Łódź	United Nation Charter signed
Jul. 1945	Łódź	Jacob moves to Łódź	
Aug. 1945	Łódź		Atomic bombs dropped on Hiroshima and Nagasaki; Japan surrenders
Sep. 1945	Łódź		**World War II ends**; Berlin divided between allies
Nov. 1945	Łódź		Start of Nuremberg Trials
Dec. 1945	Łódź	Chanukah (1st after war); Birthday (19)	
Jan. 1946	Łódź	Moves to Berlin	
Oct. 1946	Berlin		End of Nuremberg Trials
Dec. 1946	Berlin	Chanukah (2nd after war); Birthday (20)	
Jan. 1947	Berlin	Son Simon born	

My Education Continues

May 1948	Berlin		State of Israel created
Jun. 1948	Berlin		Start of Berlin Blockade / Airlift
May 1949	Berlin		End of Berlin Blockade; Israel jcins the United Nations
Jul. 1951	Berlin		Kansas City, MO, flood
Dec. 1951	Berlin	Moves to Kansas City with Jacob and Simon	

Book narrative ends

Glossary

American Jewish Joint Distribution Committee (Joint. During the War, it was responsible for delivering food, medicine, and clothing to survivors of the Holocaust. It also administered a program for relocation to Western countries outside the former war zone. [editor]

Assassination attempt. There were numerous failed attempts on Hitler's life. Perhaps the one referred to here took place in Berlin on July 20, 1944. Hitler exacted terrible retribution on all of those implicated.

Bat-Mitzvah. A ceremony initiating a girl into adult responsibilities, usually performed at the age of twelve to thirteen (from the Hebrew for daughter + commandment; analogous to Bar [son] Mitzvah, performed at 13).

Black Market. In conditions of unreasonable restrictions, or in times of economic chaos, such as occurred in the Warsaw Ghetto, black markets always appear.

China. Roughly seventeen thousand German and Austrian Jews were able to reach China, specifically Shanghai, which at the time required no visas or passports.

My Education Continues

Corridor. A strip of Polish land leading to the Baltic Sea, located between Germany proper and German Prussia.

Death camps. While some Jews were sent to slave labor, many others were shipped to camps, the sole purpose of which was extermination. Auschwitz, Treblinka, Belsec, Sobibor and Chelmno, and Mauthausen, were large ones, but others existed near Riga, Vina, Minsk, Kaunas, and Lwow. Many Russians and other "undesirables" were also killed in these camps.

Droshka. A horse-drawn taxi.

Eastern Front. Germany had invaded the Soviet Union from the east. (The Western Front was the French border—and, in a sense, the English Channel.)

Eighth day. The reference is to ritual circumcision (bris), performed on Jewish males eight days after birth.

Exodus and Resurrection. Jewish and Christian miracles. Moses' leading of the "Children of Israel out of the Land of the Pharaoh" is one of the greatest events in Jewish history. Similarly, the raising of Jesus from the dead after the Crucifixion is the central event in Christianity.

Extended draft age. Owing to the tremendous losses of life in the War, particularly of young men, the age of draft eligibility was extended upwards.

Final Solution. From the German: *Endlösung.* The term refers to Hitler's policy for the extermination of

Glossary

all Jews. On January 20, 1942, Reinhard Heydrich, head of the SS security service, held a meeting in the Berlin suburb of Wannsee to plan the final extermination of all Jews in Europe.

Gestapo. Short for *Geheime Staatspolizei,* the feared "Secret State Police."
Goosestep. The formal, stiff-legged march step of the German army.

Gypsy. Gypsies, a nomadic people arriving in Europe from migrations from India in the fourteenth century would later become a target of Hitler's racial extermination policies.

Hanukkah. An eight-day festival commemorating the victory of the Maccabees over Antiochus Epiphanes and the rededication of the Temple at Jerusalem. Also called "Feast of Dedication" and "Feast of Lights," since the oil in the triumph of the Maccabees, which was to burn for one day, actually lasted for eight days.

Hasidic Jews. Members of an ultra-conservative Jewish sect founded in Eastern Europe in the eighteenth century.

Hanukkah Gelt. Usually coins or chocolate money given to children as Hanukkah candles or oil menorahs are lit.

HASSAG. Hugo Schneider Aktien Gesellschaft. A German industrial conglomerate that manufactured weapons.

Inquisition. Egyptian Pharaohs (c. 1300 BCE) held Jews as slaves. Persian Hamman (c. 500 BCE) in what is today Iran, was a governmental official who sought the destruction of Jews. During the Spanish Inquisition (late 15th c.), Jews were forced to convert to Christianity; those who didn't conform were expelled from the country. All three refer to major persecutions of Jews.

Jehovah's Witnesses. A religious denomination founded in the United States during the late nineteenth century. It argues against war and governmental authority. In its evangelism, it preaches for the imminent approach of the Second Coming of Jesus Christ.

Jekylls and Hydes. A reference to the Robert Louis Stevenson story of the same name about a man of two opposing natures, the kindly Dr. Jekyll and the sinister Mr. Hyde.

Job. The Book of Job in the Bible recounts the story of an agreement between the Lord and Satan allowing the latter to "test" the pious Job to see if misfortunes will cause him to turn against the Lord. The sufferings are great and numerous, but Job passes the test.

K'riya. To execute K'riya or "cut Kinim" is to perform a prescribed ritual of mourning, in which the mourners have small cuts made in their clothing to symbolize the "rending of garments" in anguish for the departed.

Kapo. Abbreviation for *Kameraden Polizei* (Comrade Police). Prisoners, Jewish and non-Jewish selected by German guards to oversee prisoners in labor camps.

Glossary

Kibbutz. A cooperative farming settlement in Israel in which all activities are done communally. Food, education, and childrearing are offered.

Kikes, Schwabs. Derogatory slang for Jews and Germans, respectively.

King's Palace. Former residence of Polish kings; now residence of the Polish President.

Kippah. A skull cap worn in accordance with the scriptural injunction to men to keep the head covered. *"Jude."* German: "Jew."

Kohen. By tradition, Kohen was the name of a priestly class, who, in addition to other rituals and practices, weren't to be in the presence of the dead. They had special religious privileges and responsibilities.

Kosher-keeping. Rules dealing with what foods may be eaten and how they must be prepared. The rigor of Jewish dietary laws varied with the orthodoxy of the practitioners. The basis for the laws is found in the Torah and centers around the separation of milk and meat in food preparation.

Kristallnacht. German: "Night of the Broken Glass." Destructive raids unleashed by the Nazis, November 9-10, 1938, in which numerous synagogues and other Jewish institutions were burned. Additionally, many Jewish-owned businesses were looted or destroyed.

Luftwaffe. The German air force.

Mezuzah. A piece of paper inscribed with a verse from the Torah placed into a small case, which is then put on the doorpost of a Jewish home. *Cantor.* The leader of sung prayers in a Jewish service.

Minyan. A minimum of ten Jews (or Jewish men only, in Orthodox belief) is required for a proper communal religious service.

Neutral zone. A strip of land between Poland and Germany belonging to neither.

Nuremberg Laws. Various laws passed by the Nazi regime that, among other things, banned marriage between Jews and non-Jews, stripped Jews of German citizen, and curtailed most employment opportunities once enjoyed by Jewish citizens.

Nuremberg Trials. The post-War trials of some major surviving Nazi officials. The Trials are noteworthy in legal history because they established that military and civilian officials couldn't use the defense that they "were just following orders" in committing genocide.

Palestine. Since 1948, the country of Israel. From early 1900 until 1948, it was a British protectorate. (It has also been known as Canaan, Land of the Hebrews, the Land of Milk and Honey, and The Holy Land.)

Pani. Polish: "Mrs." The male equivalent is *Pan.*

Passover. The most important holiday of the Jewish year, it is an eight-day observance that celebrates the Israelites' escape from Egyptian slavery (c. 1300-1200 BCE) *Kosher.* Foods conforming to the dietary laws enunciated in the sacred books of Moses (the Torah).

Glossary

Pogrom. A systematic attack against Jews. The term is also used to describe a similar persecution or slaughter of other minority groups.

Potassium Cyanide and Zyklon. Gases used to kill people in the gas chambers of the extermination camps.

POW. Prisoner of War.

Praga. The "sister city" of Warsaw, across the Wisla River.

Pure blood." Hitler (like some geneticists at the time) believed blood carried genetic/racial traits.

Rabbe Gelt. Literally, "money for the rabbi"; idiomatically, "the cost of learning a lesson."

Red Army, the Soviet Army. "Red" being associated with revolution and communism.

Red Sea. The parting of the Red Sea, allowing the Jews to escape the onrushing army of the Pharaoh, and the sea subsequently swallowing up the Egyptian army, is recounted in the Book of Exodus

Restoration money. Some of the Nazi-confiscated property was being returned to their owners. *Marshall Plan.* Popular name for the U.S.-sponsored European Recovery Program, which was designed to rehabilitate the economies of post-War European nations in order to create stable conditions in which free institutions could survive.

Revolt. The Jews held out until May 16, 1943, after which the ghetto was burned to the ground.

My Education Continues

Survivors of the Uprising met their deaths in the extermination camps. The 1944 Revolt was carried out by the Gentile population and was put down severely by the Nazis.

Sectors of Berlin. The four Allies divided Germany into four zones. The city of Berlin was in the center of the Soviet zone, but the city itself was divided into four sectors, which were occupied by troops from all four Allied countries.

Seder. The traditional feast commemorating the exodus of the Jews from Egypt. At the Seder, four traditional questions are asked by the youngest child (in Orthodox practice, by the youngest boy): Why is this night different? Why do we eat matzo? Etc. The father answers the questions according to Haggadah, the narrative of the Exodus.

"L'Shana Haba B'Yerushalaim"—"Next year in Jerusalem." Diaspora Jews had a wish (and a promise) to return to their homeland in Israel/Palestine.

Selection. The process whereby officials would choose who in a camp would live or die according to his or her medical condition. Usually determined by doctors.

Shtetl. Yiddish. A small market village in Eastern Europe or Russia with a substantial Jewish population.

Slav. A member of any group of people of Eastern or Central Europe (Czechs, Poles, Slovaks, etc.), considered by the Nazis to be *Untermenschen*, inferior people.

Glossary

Spanish Civil War. 1936-39. A complex conflict in which an army general, Francisco Franco, led an insurrection against the newly installed Republican government. A testing ground for weapons and tactics used later in World War II, Franco's forces triumphed, and he quickly established an authoritarian, fascist rule.

The St. Louis. A German ship that sailed for Havana in 1939 filled with Jewish refugees. On its arrival, the Cuban government denied its landing permits. Eventually, the ship returned to Europe, where its passengers were ditributed throughout England, Belgium, France, and the Netherlands.

Sukkoth. A Jewish holiday also known as "Feast of the Tabernacles" or "Harvest Holiday." A sukkah was a portable sanctuary carried by the Hebrews during their wandering. Jews, mostly men, eat in a specially constructed sukkah for the eight-day duration of the holiday. Children decorate the sukkahs, sing, and play.

Super Race. Nazi doctrines asserted that the Teutonic-German-Aryan "racial" group constituted a "super- or master-race," or, in German, *Übermenschen*. Of course, that idea meant that all others were *Untermenschen*, quite literally, sub-humans.

Tehillim. Prayers from the book of Psalms.

The Third Reich. The term given by Hitler to the projected thousand-year reign of the Nazi government. It lastedtwelve years and four months.

Volksdeutsch. An ethnic German living outside of Germany; here, a German living in Poland.

My Education Continues

Yellow stars. Jews of central Poland wore white armbands, with blue Stars of David. Yellow stars indicated Jews from outside central Poland.

Yiddish. The "common language" of European Jewry evolved from German in the Middle Ages and was spread by Jewish migrations.

Notes

[1] *Neutral zone.* A strip of land between Poland and Germany belonging to neither.

[2] *Palestine.* Since 1948, the country of Israel. From early 1900 until 1948, it was a British protectorate. (It has also been known as Canaan, Land of the Hebrews, the Land of Milk and Honey, and The Holy Land.)

[3] *Kosher.* Rules dealing with what foods may be eaten and how they must be prepared. The rigor of Jewish dietary laws varied with the orthodoxy of the practitioners. The basis for the laws is found in the Torah and centers around the separation of milk and meat in food preparation.

[4] *Hasidic Jews.* Members of an ultra-conservative Jewish sect founded in Eastern Europe in the eighteenth century.

[5] *Yiddish.* The "common language" of European Jewry evolved from German in the Middle Ages and was spread by Jewish migrations.

[6] *Nuremberg Laws.* Various laws passed by the Nazi regime that, among other things, banned marriage between Jews and non-Jews, stripped Jews of German citizen, and curtailed most

employment opportunities once enjoyed by Jewish citizens. *Kristallnacht.* German: "Night of the Broken Glass." Destructive raids unleashed by the Nazis, November 9-10, 1938, in which numerous synagogues and other Jewish institutions were burned. Additionally, many Jewish-owned businesses were looted or destroyed.

[7] *Corridor.* A strip of Polish land leading to the Baltic Sea, located between Germany proper and German Prussia.

[8] *"The insane painter."* A reference to Hitler, who in his youth aspired to be an artist. He was rejected by the Vienna Arts Academy.

[9] *Obrona Przeciwlotnicza*, the civil air defense league. [editor]

[10] *Spanish Civil War.* 1936-39. A complex conflict in which an army general, Francisco Franco, led an insurrection against the newly installed Republican government. A testing ground for weapons and tactics used later in World War II, Franco's forces triumphed, and he quickly established an authoritarian, fascist rule.

[11] *Luftwaffe.* The German air force.

[12] *Tehillim.* Prayers from the book of Psalms.

[13] *Cantor.* The leader of sung prayers in a Jewish service. *Mezuzah.* A piece of paper inscribed with a verse from the Torah placed into a small case, which is then put on the doorpost of a Jewish home.

[14] *"Oy Veh."* The humor here is that the expression is a common Yiddish/Jewish interjection for "Oh dear!" or "Oh me!" or even "Alas!" in order to register astonishment.

Notes

[15] *Passover*. The most important holiday of the Jewish year, it is an eight-day observance that celebrates the Israelites' escape from Egyptian slavery (c. 1300-1200 BCE). Cherry wine was one of two food items that many housewives would prepare for Passover. The other was rendered goose fat.

[16] *"...cholera!"* A traditional Polish curse, used even by those who didn't know about the disease.

[17] *Kippah*. A skull cap worn in accordance with the scriptural injunction to men to keep the head covered. *"Jude."* German: "Jew."

[18] *The Third Reich*. The term given by Hitler to the projected thousand-year reign of the Nazi government. It lasted twelve years and four months.

[19] *Black Market*. In conditions of unreasonable restrictions, or in times of economic chaos, such as occurred in the Warsaw Ghetto, black markets always appear.

[20] *Praga.* The "sister city" of Warsaw, across the Wisła River.

[21] *Gestapo*. Short for *Geheime Staatspolizei*, the feared "Secret State Police."

[22] *Yellow stars*. Jews of central Poland wore white armbands, with blue Stars of David. Yellow stars indicated Jews from outside central Poland.

[23] *Narodowa Demokracja,* or "National Democracy." [editor]

[24] *King's Palace*. Former residence of Polish kings; now residence of the Polish President.

My Education Continues

[25] *POW*. Prisoner of War.

[26] *Aryan looks*. Blond or light hair, light skin, and blue eyes were typically considered "Aryan" traits.

[27] *Bat-Mitzvah*. A ceremony initiating a girl into adult responsibilities, usually performed at the age of twelve to thirteen (from the Hebrew for daughter + commandment; analogous to Bar [son] Mitzvah, performed at 13).

[28] *Hanukkah*. An eight-day festival commemorating the victory of the Maccabees over Antiochus Epiphanes and the rededication of the Temple at Jerusalem. Also called "Feast of Dedication" and "Feast of Lights," since the oil in the triumph of the Maccabees, which was to burn for one day, actually lasted for eight days.

[29] *Hanukkah Gelt*. Usually coins or chocolate money given to children as Hanukkah candles or oil menorahs are lit.

[30] *Seder*. The traditional feast commemorating the exodus of the Jews from Egypt. At the Seder, four traditional questions are asked by the youngest child (in Orthodox practice, by the youngest boy): Why is this night different? Why do we eat matzo? Etc. The father answers the questions according to Haggadah, the narrative of the Exodus.

[31] *Red Sea*. The parting of the Red Sea, allowing the Jews to escape the onrushing army of the Pharaoh, and the sea subsequently swallowing up the Egyptian army, is recounted in the Book of Exodus.

Notes

[32] *"L'Shana Haba B'Yerushalaim"* Hebrew: "Next year in Jerusalem." Diaspora Jews had a wish (and a promise) to return to their homeland in Israel/Palestine.

[33] *Special identity*. Since it was easy to spot a member of the Hasidim by his or her traditional clothing and hair style, the compulsory wearing of the six-pointed Star of David was, at the least, redundant.

[34] *Eighth day*. The reference is to ritual circumcision (bris), performed on Jewish males eight days after birth.

[35] But, as I think back, perhaps they *did* serve a purpose: The bands must have been designed to give "equal rights" to women.

[36] *Gypsy*. Gypsies, a nomadic people arriving in Europe from migrations from India in the fourteenth century would later become a target of Hitler's racial extermination policies.

[37] *New social system*. Communism, which promised a classless society, state ownership of property, and full employment.

[38] *Godless society*. In the Soviet Union, formed by Lenin and the Communists following the Russian Revolution, atheism was the state policy in conformance to the idea of Marx that religion was the "opiate of the masses."

[39] *Sukkoth*. A Jewish holiday also known as "Feast of the Tabernacles" or "Harvest Holiday." A sukkah was a portable sanctuary carried by the Hebrews during their wandering. Jews, mostly men, eat in a specially constructed sukkah for the eight-day duration of the holiday. Children decorate the sukkah, sing, and play.

My Education Continues

⁴⁰ *Minyan.* A minimum of ten Jews (or Jewish men only, in Orthodox belief) is required for a proper communal religious service. *Jewish men.* In traditions of Judaism, men took the responsibility of praying. In Orthodox synagogues, women and men are still separated in services.

⁴¹ *Kohen.* By tradition, Kohen was the name of a priestly class, who, in addition to other rituals and practices, weren't to be in the presence of the dead. They had special religious privileges and responsibilities.

⁴² *Feminine features.* Orthodox Jewish men were forbidden to look at a "woman" (by definition, one who had passed through puberty).

⁴³ *Job.* The Book of Job in the Bible recounts the story of an agreement between the Lord and Satan allowing the latter to "test" the pious Job to see if misfortunes would cause him to turn against the Lord. The sufferings are great and numerous, but Job passes the test.

⁴⁴ *Hitler's funeral.* The implication of the sentence is that peace will come only with the deaths of the Axis leaders (Franco in Spain, Mussolini in Italy, and Hitler in Germany), of the communist leader of the USSR, Stalin, and of all other heads of totalitarian regimes.

⁴⁵ "Cut *kinim.*" A prescribed ritual of mourning, in which the mourners have small cuts made in their clothing to symbolize the "rending of garments" in anguish for the departed.

⁴⁶ *Rabbe Gelt.* Literally, "money for the rabbi"; idiomatically, "the cost of learning a lesson."

Notes

[47] *Super Race.* Nazi doctrines asserted that the Teutonic-German-Aryan "racial" group constituted a "super- or master-race," or, in German, *Übermenschen.* Of course, this meant that all others were *Untermenschen,* quite literally, sub-humans.

[48] *Eastern Front.* Germany had invaded the Soviet Union from the east. (The Western Front was the French border and, by extension, the English Channel.)

[49] *Kikes, Schwabs.* Derogatory slang for Jews and Germans, respectively.

[50] *Shtetlekh.* Yiddish. Small market villages in Eastern Europe or Russia with substantial Jewish populations.

[51] *Red Army, the Soviet Army.* "Red" being associated with revolution and communism.

[52] *Kheyder* is a primary school in which children learn to read the Hebrew Bible. *Palant* is a game similar to cricket, in which a player hits a ball with a bat and then runs to a "finish line" without being tagged by another player carrying the retrieved ball. *[editor]*

[53] *Shmurah matzah* is made from grain that has been harvested under careful supervision to ensure that it has not undergone fermentation. *[editor]*

[54] *HASSAG.* Hugo Schneider Aktien Gesellschaft. A German industrial conglomerate that manufactured weapons.

[55] *Kapo.* Abbreviation for *Kameraden Polizei* (Comrade Police). Prisoners, Jewish and non-Jewish selected by German guards to oversee prisoners in labor camps.

My Education Continues

⁵⁶ *Selection*. The process whereby officials would choose who in a camp would live or die according to his or her medical condition. Usually determined by doctors.

⁵⁷ *Final Solution*. From the German: *Endlösung*. The term refers to Hitler's policy for the extermination of all Jews. On January 20, 1942, Reinhard Heydrich, head of the SS security service, held a meeting in the Berlin suburb of Wannsee to plan the final extermination of all Jews in Europe.

⁵⁸ This Yiddish expression was quite common. It meant, "Are things really that bad? That tragic?"

⁵⁹ *Death camps*. While some Jews were sent to slave labor, many others were shipped to camps, the sole purpose of which was extermination. Auschwitz, Treblinka, Belsec, Sobibor and Chelmno, and Mauthausen, were large ones, but others existed near Riga, Vina, Minsk, Kaunas, and Lwów. Many Russians and other "undesirables" were also killed in these camps.

⁶⁰ *Feldgrau,* or "field gray," the color (gray-green) of the field uniform of the Germany Army from World War I to 1945. [editor]

⁶¹ *Zyklon-B*. Gas used to kill people in the gas chambers of the extermination camps.

⁶² *Revolt*. The Jews held out until May 16, 1943, after which the ghetto was burned to the ground. Survivors of the Uprising met their deaths in the extermination camps. The 1944 Revolt was carried out by the Gentile population and was put down severely by the Nazis.

⁶³ *Assassination attempt*. There were numerous failed attempts on Hitler's life. Perhaps the one referred to here took place in Berlin

on July 20, 1944. Hitler exacted terrible retribution on all of those implicated.

[64] Ironic in itself, for homosexuals were the first of the Nazi victims.

[65] I remember because we had already celebrated these holidays in our usual camp manner.

[66] *Goosestep.* The formal, stiff-legged march step of the German army.

[67] *Inquisition.* Egyptian Pharaohs (c. 1300 BCE) held Jews as slaves. Persian Hamman (c. 500 BCE) in what is today Iran, was a governmental official who sought the destruction of Jews. During the Spanish Inquisition (late 15th c.), Jews were forced to convert to Christianity; those who didn't conform were expelled from the country. All three refer to major persecutions of Jews.

[68] *Droshka.* A horse-drawn taxicab.

[69] The Polish version goes something like, "He loves me; he likes me; he respects me; he doesn't want me; he doesn't care; the whole affair is only a joke to him."

[70] *Volksdeutsch.* An ethnic German living outside of Germany; i.e., a member of the German diaspora.

[71] "Trans-Olza Silesia" or "Lands beyond the Olza River." An area disputed between Poland and what was then Czechoslovakia. [editor]

[72] United Nations Relief Association. [editor]

My Education Continues

[73] *"Pure blood."* Hitler (like some geneticists at the time) believed blood carried genetic/racial traits. By his analysis, only Aryan or German blood was free from the taint of inferiority.

[74] *Sectors of Berlin.* The four Allies divided Germany into four zones. The city of Berlin was in the center of the Soviet zone, but the city itself was divided into four sectors, which were occupied by troops from all four Allied countries.

[75] *China.* Roughly seventeen thousand German and Austrian Jews were able to reach China, specifically Shanghai, which at the time required no visas or passports.

[76] I was surprised that after all these years of not being Jewish, he would still stick to such customs.

[77] We did have a few good friends whom we had made since coming to Berlin, but due to the housing shortage, we all were living scattered throughout the city. The large majority of the transit Jews were living in the DP camps, located out of town. According to German law, all foreigners who lived in the city had to register every few months in order to renew their resident permits. The Jewish families that we did know in the city did not live very far from us. But even with public transportation, or with bikes, it was difficult to get to them, especially during the winter.

[78] *Nuremberg Trials.* The post-War trials of some major surviving Nazi officials. The Trials are noteworthy in legal history because they established that military and civilian officials couldn't use the defense that they "were just following orders" in committing genocide.

[79] German: "Hitler-Youth Camp."

Notes

[80] *Jekylls and Hydes*. A reference to the Robert Louis Stevenson story of the same name about a man of two opposing natures, the kindly Dr. Jekyll and the sinister Mr. Hyde.

[81] *Slav*. A member of any group of people of Eastern or Central Europe (Czechs, Poles, Slovaks, etc.), considered by the Nazis to be *Untermenschen*, inferior people.

[82] It reminds me of an old saying: "Don't tell Grandmother where children come from; she won't believe you."

[83] Many people who had been identified as *"Opfer des Faschismus"*—"victims of fascism"—could get homes formerly occupied by Nazis, left vacant when their occupants fled the oncoming Russians. I knew two families of Jewish survivors who were living in such homes. They justified their taking of Nazi places by claiming that these homes were taken over by the Nazis from Jews or other persecuted people, and that these places didn't belong to those *Schweins* in the first place. We wanted no part of that, though. The people who lived in these apartments had their viewpoint, to which they were entitled. Jacob and I, however, agreed that even if this were the case, "two wrongs don't make a right."

[84] *Pogrom*. A systematic attack against Jews. The term is also used to describe a similar persecution or slaughter of other minority groups.

[85] *Armia Krajowa*. The most important Polish Underground force during the War. The group was known for anti-Semitism within its membership. [editor]

[86] American Jewish Joint Distribution Committee. During the War, it was responsible for delivering food, medicine, and clothing to survivors of the Holocaust. It also administered a

My Education Continues

program for relocation to Western countries outside the former war zone.[editor]

[87] "Dear, good Santa Claus." [editor]

[88] Only two other times did I ever remember seeing a real Christmas Eve observance. Once, when I was about five or six, the farm girl who worked for us, Jozia, took me with her to the midnight mass at her church. The other time was when she took my sister and me to her aunt's house on Kamienne Schodki in Warsaw, where we watched as they lit real candles on a real pine tree.

[89] He died in Israel. [added between composition of "Accounting Page" and final publication. *Editor*]

www.ingramcontent.com/pod-product-compliance
Lightning Source LLC
Chambersburg PA
CBHW031609160426
43196CB00006B/73